A HISTORY OF DANISH CINEMA

A HISTORY OF DANISH CINEMA

Edited by
C. Claire Thomson, Isak Thorsen
and Pei-Sze Chow

EDINBURGH
University Press

Edinburgh University Press is one of the leading university presses in the UK. We publish academic books and journals in our selected subject areas across the humanities and social sciences, combining cutting-edge scholarship with high editorial and production values to produce academic works of lasting importance. For more information visit our website: edinburghuniversitypress.com

© editorial matter and organisation C. Claire Thomson, Isak Thorsen and Pei-Sze Chow, 2021, 2023
© the chapters their several authors, 2021, 2023

Edinburgh University Press Ltd
The Tun – Holyrood Road
12(2f) Jackson's Entry
Edinburgh EH8 8PJ

First published in hardback by Edinburgh University Press 2021

Typeset in 10/12.5 pt Sabon
by IDSUK (DataConnection) Ltd

A CIP record for this book is available from the British Library

ISBN 978 1 4744 6112 2 (hardback)
ISBN 978 1 4744 6113 9 (paperback)
ISBN 978 1 4744 6114 6 (webready PDF)
ISBN 978 1 4744 6115 3 (epub)

The right of C. Claire Thomson, Isak Thorsen and Pei-Sze Chow to be identified as the editors of this work has been asserted in accordance with the Copyright, Designs and Patents Act 1988, and the Copyright and Related Rights Regulations 2003 (SI No. 2498).

CONTENTS

List of Figures   viii
Acknowledgments   xi
Notes on Contributors   xii

Introduction   1
C. Claire Thomson, Isak Thorsen and Pei-Sze Chow

PART I: FROM THE FIRST 'GOLDEN AGE' TO THE OCCUPATION

1. Surviving a Crisis: Nordisk Films Kompagni as a World Player   21
 Isak Thorsen

2. Asta & Co.: The Politics of Early Danish Film Stardom   30
 Julie K. Allen

3. The European Principle: Art and Border-Crossings in Carl Theodor Dreyer's Career   41
 Casper Tybjerg

4. Derailed: Danish Film during the German Occupation   51
 Lars-Martin Sørensen

PART II: NATIONAL GENRES

5. The Art of the Popular: The *Folkekomedie* Tradition   65
 Niels Henrik Hartvigson

CONTENTS

6. Social Realism of the 1940s: Between Paternalistic Care and Dignifying Humanism 81
   Birger Langkjær

7. Imagining Denmark: *Danmarksfilm* as Documentary Portraits of a Nation 93
   Ib Bondebjerg

8. Rural Dreams: Landscape, Family, Sexuality and Queerness in Homeland Cinema 105
   Niels Henrik Hartvigson

9. The Olsen Gang in Denmark – And Abroad 118
   Stephan Michael Schröder

10. Making a Life of Your Own: Films for Children and Young People in the 1970s and 1980s 128
    Christa Lykke Christensen

11. Pornography and Censorship 140
    Isak Thorsen

PART III: AUTEURS AND INSTITUTIONS OF THE NEW GOLDEN AGE

12. Into the Dark Forest: The Cinema of Lars von Trier 151
    Peter Schepelern

13. 'I Am No Longer an Artist': Heritage Film, Dogme 95 and the New Danish Cinema 161
    C. Claire Thomson

14. Stories of Scandinavian Guilt and Privilege: Transnational Danish Directors 174
    Meryl Shriver-Rice

15. Danish Television Drama in the Twenty-First Century: New Synergies between Film and Television 189
    Eva Novrup Redvall

16. New Danish Screen and The Sketch: The Role of Imposed and Self-Imposed Constraints in Talent Development 200
    Mette Hjort

PART IV: DECENTRING AND DIVERSIFYING DANISH CINEMA

17. Danish Documentary Production: An All-Female Company 219
    Anne Jerslev

18. Welcome to Denmark: Immigrants and Their Descendants in
    Danish Cinema   230
    Eva Jørholt

19. Dirty Films: Grimy Materialism and Ecological Aesthetics   241
    Benjamin Bigelow

20. Regional Film Funds and Production   252
    Pei-Sze Chow

21. 'Finally, We're Beginning to Tell Our Own Stories':
    Filmmaking in Greenland   263
    Isak Thorsen and Emile Hertling Péronard

References   277
Index   303

FIGURES

1.1. An early Nordisk Films Kompagni logo put Copenhagen at the centre of the world, and the polar bear on top of it. Image: public domain.   29
2.1 Valdemar Psilander starring opposite Clara Wieth in the Nordisk hit *Ved Fængslets Port* (*Temptations of a Great City*, August Blom, 1911). Framegrab.   33
2.2. Asta Nielsen as Magda with her lover Rudolph (Poul Reumert) in the iconic Gaucho dance scene in *Afgrunden* (*The Abyss*, Urban Gad, 1910). Framegrab.   35
2.3 Olaf Fønss (right), playing Dr Kammacher in the big-budget *Atlantis* (August Blom, 1913), helps to man the lifeboat. Framegrab.   37
4.1 Illona Wieselmann in *Afsporet* (*Derailed*, Bodil Ipsen and Lau Lauritzen Jr, 1942). She later had to flee to Sweden after being reported to the German occupiers by producer Henning Karmark. Image: Danish Film Institute.   52
5.1 In *Provinsen kalder —!* (*The Provinces are Calling — !*, Lau Lauritzen Sr, 1935) sound technologies such as the telephone are ciphers for inter-generational and regional communication difficulties. Image: Danish Film Institute.   68
5.2 Danish girls at arms: uniforms and landscape lend national specificity to the characters and action in *Piger i trøjen* (*Girls at Arms*, Finn Henriksen, 1975). Framegrab.   75

FIGURES

6.1	A poster promoting the problem film *Det brændende Spørgsmål* (*The Burning Question*, Alice O'Fredericks, 1943) is indicative of the film's blend of drama and social enquiry. Image: Danish Film Institute.	85
6.2	Location shooting embeds fictional characters in the real-life streets of Copenhagen, in *Soldaten og Jenny* (*Jenny and the Soldier*, Johan Jacobsen, 1947). Framegrab from title sequence.	90
7.1	In Jørgen Leth's *Livet i Danmark* (*Life in Denmark*, 1972), the Denmark-film tradition is subverted, to observe Danes clinically against a black backdrop. Framegrabs.	100
8.1	Carl Alstrup in *Den kloge Mand* (*The Quack*, Arne Weel, 1937). Here we see a mythical and instantly relatable interconnection between landscape, human and animal. Image: Danish Film Institute.	112
8.2	The intersection between landscape, human and animal suggests a mythical connection in this framegrab from Anne-Grethe Bjarup Riis' biopic of the racehorse *Tarok* (*Catch the Dream*, 2013). Framegrab.	112
8.3	Sexualised innocence: working bodies on display. Poul Reichhardt in *De røde heste* (*The Red Horses*, Alice O'Fredericks and Jon Iversen, 1950). Image: Danish Film Institute.	115
9.1	In *Olsen-banden ser rødt* (*The Olsen Gang Sees Red*, Erik Balling, 1976), the gang members consult the score of Friedrich Kuhlau's *Elverhøj* overture to calibrate the noise from their safe-cracking with the music from the orchestra playing in the theatre above them. Framegrab.	122
10.1	Søren Kragh-Jacobsen's *Vil du se min smukke navle?* (*Wanna See My Beautiful Navel?*, 1978) follows the subjective experiences of a group of teenagers on a camping trip with a mosaic-like narrative strategy. Framegrab.	136
10.2	Nils Malmros' historical drama *Kundskabens træ* (*The Tree of Knowledge*, 1981) reconstructs school life in 1950s Aarhus. Its inclusion in the 2006 Danish Cultural Canon for Film speaks to Malmros' auteur status and to the status of films for children and young people in Denmark. Framegrab.	137
13.1	In *Babettes gæstebud* (*Babette's Feast*, Gabriel Axel, 1987), the pastor enlightens his guests from the head of the table with a revelation. Framegrab.	164
13.2	In *Festen* (*The Celebration*, Thomas Vinterberg, 1998), Christian looks down the table towards his father and prepares to make his own revelation. Framegrab.	164

FIGURES

14.1	Characters from *It's All About Love* (2004) sidestep another person who has died from loss of love. Framegrab.	186
14.2	The closing shot from Vinterberg's *It's All About Love* (2003). Ugandans are tethered to their houses during an unexplained loss of gravity. Framegrab.	187
15.1A–D	Four framegrabs from Lars von Trier's *Riget* (*The Kingdom*, 1994) produced by Zentropa for DR. The opening credit sequence illustrates the meeting between Lars von Trier's previous art cinema work and the inspiration from US crime series such as *NYPD Blue* (ABC, 1993–2005) and *Homicide* (NBC, 1993–1999).	192
15.2 A–D	Four framegrabs from the opening sequence of *Forbrydelsen* (*The Killing*, DR, 2007–12), illustrating its unsettling and ambitiously cinematic composition.	197
16.1	Bharan eyes Rie in the ambulance, following their underground struggle to breathe through a single shared device. Framegrab from *Cutterhead* (Rasmus Kloster Bro, 2019).	212
16.2	*Cutterhead* opens with a scene of the drill penetrating a thick wall. Framegrab.	213
17.1	A portrait of an ageing farmer in Phie Ambo's *Så meget godt i vente* (*Good Things Await*, 2014). Framegrab.	228
17.2	A very different ageing face in Pernille Rose Grønkjær's *The Monastery: Mr Vig and the Nun* (2006). Framegrab.	228
18.1	Ulaa Salim's *Danmarks sønner* (*Sons of Denmark*, 2019) offers a frightening and visually stunning vision of a future marred by extreme nationalism. Framegrab.	239
19.1	This tableau emphasises the brothers' materiality and transcorporeality, and references Sigurður Guðmundsson's work *Mountain* (1982). Framegrab from *Vinterbrødre* (*Winter Brothers*, Hlynur Pálmason, 2017).	244
19.2	A foetal Emil caked in chalk. Framegrab from *Winter Brothers*.	249

ACKNOWLEDGMENTS

When we sat drinking coffee in a sunny Copenhagen courtyard some four years ago and began to discuss this project, we could never have known that we would be putting the finishing touches to the book amid a global pandemic. But even without the delays and tribulations occasioned by this unexpected set of circumstances, we would owe our wonderful contributors a heartfelt vote of thanks for their hard work, patience and good humour. The same must be said for Richard Strachan, Sam Johnson, Fiona Conn and Gillian Leslie at Edinburgh University Press, whose friendliness, efficiency and support for the project have been unstinting. Our colleagues and friends at the Danish Film Institute have, as always, been helpful and supportive well beyond the call of duty.

Pei-Sze gratefully acknowledges support for her research from the European Union's Horizon 2020 research and innovation programme under the Marie Skłodowska-Curie Grant Agreement No. 753597. She would also like to thank Lee Cossell very much for his support.

Isak would like to thank his beloved wife and three beautiful and gifted daughters.

Claire would like to thank her parents and sister, Catherine, Robert and Lizzi Thomson, for always being there, even in lockdown. She would also like to thank students of Nordic Cinema at UCL and elsewhere over the years for inspiring and enlightening discussions; and Peter Graves, for entrusting her with his film seminars on Dreyer and Sjöström almost twenty years ago, sparking a life-long passion and teaching her how to teach.

Copenhagen, Aarhus and London, August 2021

NOTES ON CONTRIBUTORS

Julie K. Allen is Professor of Scandinavian Studies and Comparative Literature at Brigham Young University in Provo, Utah, USA. She is the author of *Icons of Danish Modernity: Georg Brandes & Asta Nielsen* (2012) and *Danish but Not Lutheran: The Impact of Mormonism on Danish Cultural Identity, 1850-1920* (2017), as well as numerous articles about fairy tales, Danish immigration, silent film and other topics related to Nordic cultural studies. Her newest book, *Transnational Silent Film Before and After the Rise of Hollywood* (2022), explores the extent and significance of the circulation of European (primarily French, Italian, Danish, German and Swedish) silent film in settler-colonial Australia and New Zealand before and after World War I.

Benjamin Bigelow is an Assistant Professor in the Department of German, Nordic, Slavic and Dutch at the University of Minnesota, where he teaches Scandinavian literature and cinema. He holds a PhD in Scandinavian Languages and Literatures from UC Berkeley. His research on cinema and literature has appeared in the *Journal of Scandinavian Cinema* and in *Scandinavian Studies*, and he has also published on migration in contemporary graphic novels.

Ib Bondebjerg is Professor Emeritus, Department of Communication, University of Copenhagen. He was director of the Centre for Modern European Studies (2008–11), chairman of The Danish Film Institute (1997–2000), co-director of the research project *Mediating Cultural Encounters Through European Screens* (2013–16), and co-editor of the book series *Palgrave European Film and Media*

Studies (2013–20). He has written numerous articles and books on Danish cinema, such as *Virkelighedsbilleder. Den moderne danske dokumentarfilm* (2012) and *Dansk film og kulturel globalisering* (2017, with Ulla Bondebjerg). His most recent books in English are *Engaging with Reality: Documentary and Globalization* (2014), *European Cinema and Television: Cultural Policy and Everyday Life* (co-editor, 2015), *Transnational European Television Drama: Production, Genres and Audiences* (co-author, 2017) and *Screening Twentieth Century Europe: Television, History, Memory* (2020).

Pei-Sze Chow is an Assistant Professor of Media and Culture at the University of Amsterdam. She was previously a Marie Skłodowska-Curie Fellow at the Department of Media Studies and Journalism, Aarhus University, where she researched the regional screen ecosystem in Aarhus and West Denmark. She is the author of *Transnational Screen Culture in Scandinavia: Mediating Regional Space and Identity in the Øresund Region* (Palgrave Macmillan, 2021). Her interdisciplinary work takes a spatial, media-geographic approach to film and media research, focusing on representations of space and place, the cinemas of small nations and cities and peripheries on film and television. She has published and co-edited work on Nordic noir and geopolitics, urban space and architecture, and more recently on artificial intelligence and film.

Christa Lykke Christensen is Associate Professor in Film and Media Studies at the Department of Communication at the University of Copenhagen. Her research interests include film and media for children and young people. She has published on Danish children's film in a historical perspective and on children's and youth television with a specific focus on the representation and perception of children and young people. She has published on the media usage of children and young people, and she is currently part of the research project *Reaching Young Audiences*, funded by the Independent Research Fund Denmark, 2019–23.

Niels Henrik Hartvigson has published widely in the fields of genre, history, gender, sexuality and popular culture. His doctoral dissertation explored the central role of comedy in the transition from silent to sound film in Danish cinema, while a post-doctoral project dealt with sexuality in Danish fiction films made between 1930 and 1965. Hartvigson is currently researching the genre and traditions of *folkekomedie* – folk comedies or folk fictions – within theatre, film, television and electronic media. Another research project investigates the Enlightenment comedies of Ludvig Holberg with a focus on homosexuality and queerness. An External Lecturer at the University of Copenhagen, Hartvigson teaches audio-visual aesthetics, film and media history, media sociology and cultural studies. He is currently teaching media history at the Danish Department and Danish film studies at the Saxo Institute.

NOTES ON CONTRIBUTORS

Mette Hjort is Chair Professor of Humanities and Dean of Arts at the Hong Kong Baptist University, Affiliate Professor of Scandinavian Studies at the University of Washington and Visiting Professor of Cultural Industries at the University of South Wales. Mette's monographs include *Small Nation, Global Cinema* (2005). Her interest in the politics of talent development, including 'twinning' projects on a North/South basis, is reflected in the two-volume *The Education of the Filmmaker* (editor, 2013) and *African Cinema and Human Rights* (co-editor, 2019). Mette holds an Honorary Doctorate in Transnational Cinema Studies from the University of Aalborg. Appointed by the Danish Minister of Culture, she has served on the Board of the Danish Film Institute. She has also served on the University Grants Committee, appointed by the Chief Executive of Hong Kong, which oversees and develops policies for the eight government-funded universities in Hong Kong.

Anne Jerslev is Professor in the Department of Communication at the University of Copenhagen. Her major publications include *Realism and Reality in Film and Media* (editor, 2002), *Performative Realism* (co-editor with Rune Gade, 2005), *Impure Cinema: Intermedial and Intercultural Approaches to Film* (co-editor with Lucia Nagib, 2014), and *Ældre mennesker i et mediesamfund* ('Elderly People in a Media Society', co-editor with Christa Lykke Christensen, 2017). She has published widely on matters of ageing, gender, intimacy, fandom and the real in film and media, and is engaged in a long-running project about David Lynch and his *gesamtkunstwerk*.

Eva Jørholt is Associate Professor in the Department of Communication, University of Copenhagen. She specialises in national and transnational film cultures, with a focus on (post-) migration and France, and she has participated in the research project *Art, Culture and Politics in the 'Postmigrant Condition'*, funded by the Danish Free Research Council. Eva previously edited the Danish Film Institute journal *Kosmorama* and is currently the editor-in-chief of *Studies in World Cinema*. From 2009 to 2017 she sat on the Feature Film Council at the Danish Film Institute. Her latest book is *African Cinema and Human Rights* (editor with Mette Hjort, 2019).

Birger Langkjær is Associate Professor in the Department of Communication at the University of Copenhagen. He specialises in cognitive film and media theory, including theories of ecological perception and affordances, emotion, metaphors and narration, as well as realism, genre and film sound. He has published monographs on film sound (*Filmlyd og filmmusik*, 1996, and *Den lyttende tilskuer*, 2000) and on realism in Danish cinema (*Realismen i dansk film*, 2012). From 2013 to 2016 he was head of the research network *Film, Experimental Designs and Quantitative Analysis*.

NOTES ON CONTRIBUTORS

Emile Hertling Péronard was born in Copenhagen, but grew up in Nuuk, Greenland, with his Greenlandic mother and Danish father. Owner of production companies in both Copenhagen and Nuuk (Ánorâk Film, co-owned with director Inuk Silis Høegh), Péronard aims to build bridges between Europe and the Arctic, producing authentic stories in a Greenlandic context for international audiences. Through his involvement in the Greenlandic filmmakers' organization, FILM.GL, he has been highly active in promoting Greenlandic film content internationally and setting up talent initiatives for Greenlandic filmmakers. Péronard has been a guest programmer at the imagineNATIVE Film + Media Arts Festival, Toronto, and an advisor to the 2017 Berlinale NATIVe Arctic programme.

Eva Novrup Redvall is Associate Professor at the University of Copenhagen where she is head of the Section for Film Studies and Creative Media Industries. Her research focuses on film and television screenwriting and production, particularly in Scandinavia. She has published widely in books and journals, such as the monograph *Writing and Producing Television Drama in Denmark: From* The Kingdom *to* The Killing. From 2019 to 2023 she serves as PI in the joint research project *Reaching Young Audiences: Serial Fiction and Cross-Media Storytelling for Children and Young Audiences* (supported by Independent Research Fund Denmark). Besides her scholarly work, she has been a film critic for the Danish newspaper *Information* since 1999 and is a board member of the Danish Film Institute, the Association of Danish Film Critics and Carl Th. Dreyers Mindefond.

Peter Schepelern is Associate Professor Emeritus at the University of Copenhagen. He has published a number of books in Danish, including *Lars von Triers film* (2000), *100 års dansk film* (editor, 2001), and *Filmleksikon* (editor, 2010). Publications in English include papers on Jørgen Leth, Andy Warhol, Postwar Scandinavian Cinema, Dogme 95 and Lars von Trier.

Stephan Michael Schröder is Professor of Nordic Philology/Scandinavian Studies in the Department of Scandinavian and Finnish Studies at the University of Cologne. His main research topics are the relationship between Danish literature and silent film, Scandinavian cultures and literatures from the sixteenth to the twentieth century, the cultural history of northernness and literature on war in Scandinavia. His most recent monograph is *Literatur als Bellographie: Der Krieg von 1864 in der dänischen Literatur* (2019; Literature as Bellography: The Second Schleswig War in Danish Literature) Schröder is currently the German member of the research project *A Common Film Culture? – Denmark and Germany in the Silent Film Era 1910–1930*, conducted in cooperation between the Danish Film Institute, the University of Copenhagen and the

University of Cologne. For more information and a complete bibliography, go to www.smschroeder.de.

Meryl Shriver-Rice is the Director of Environmental Media at the Abess Center for Ecosystem Science & Policy at the University of Miami. She is the author of *Inclusion in New Danish Cinema: Sexuality and Transnational Belonging* (2015) and co-editor (with Missy Molloy and Mimi Nielsen) of *ReFocus: The Films of Susanne Bier* (2018). Her articles and chapters on Danish cinema have appeared in the *Journal of Scandinavian Cinema*, *Film International*, and *Speaking the Unspeakable* (2013). She is co-chair of the Scandinavian Studies Scholarly Interest Group of the Society for Cinema and Media Studies (with Missy Molloy). As a media anthropologist and environmental archaeologist, she is the co-editor (with Hunter Vaughan) of the *Journal of Environmental Media*, and she developed and teaches for UM's interdisciplinary master's program in Environment, Culture and Media.

Lars-Martin Sørensen is Head of the Research Unit at the Danish Film Institute and Editor-in-chief of the Danish film journal Kosmorama.org. Sørensen has authored the monographs *Censorship of Japanese Films during the U.S. Occupation of Japan: The Cases of Yasujiro Ozu and Akira Kurosawa* (2009), *Dansk film under nazismen* ('Danish Film during the Nazi Era', 2014) and *Sidste nyt fra Berlin* ('Latest News from Berlin', 2019). His contribution to this volume is based on his book *Dansk film under nazismen*.

C. Claire Thomson is Professor of Cinema History at University College London (UCL), where she is the Director of Film Studies and teaches Nordic cinema and cultural history, as well as translation from the Scandinavian languages. Her previous publications include the monographs *Thomas Vinterberg's Festen* (2013) and *Short Films from a Small Nation: Danish Informational Cinema 1935–1965* (2018), the edited volume *Northern Constellations: New Readings in Nordic Cinema* (2006), and numerous articles on short films, film and public health, multisensory cinema and the work of Carl Th. Dreyer and Thomas Vinterberg. She is an editor of the journals *Scandinavica* and *Kosmorama*.

Isak Thorsen holds a doctorate in Film Studies from the University of Copenhagen with a dissertation titled 'Isbjørnens anatomi – Nordisk Films Kompagni som erhvervsvirksomhed i perioden 1906–1928'. A revised English-language version was published by John Libbey in 2017, as *Nordisk Films Kompagni 1906–1924: The Rise and Fall of the Polar Bear*. He is the editor and author of the Danish entries in the *Historical Dictionary of Scandinavian Cinema* (2012). Thorsen has contributed to the anthologies *100 Years of Nordisk Film* (2006),

International Western Films: Re-Locating the Frontier (2013), *Dansk-tyske krige – kulturliv og kulturkampe* (2020) and written for journals such as *Film History, Kintop, Scandinavian-Canadian Studies, 16:9, Journal of Scandinavian Cinema* and *Kosmorama*.

Casper Tybjerg is a scholar of film historiography and Danish and international silent film. He holds a Master's degree in Film Studies from the University of Copenhagen, where he wrote his thesis on Danish silent film. Tybjerg has served as Associate Professor at the University of Copenhagen since 2000. He has assisted in the DFI's efforts to restore Danish silent films and has co-organised several retrospectives, including at the Pordenone Silent Film Festival. He has written numerous articles on film history and recently completed a book on the theory and method of film historiography, focusing on the work of Carl Theodor Dreyer. He is part of the DFI research project *A Common Film Culture? Denmark and Germany in the Silent Film Era, 1910–1930*, where his work focuses on style and historiographical concepts.

INTRODUCTION

C. Claire Thomson, Isak Thorsen and Pei-Sze Chow

In 1947, the Scottish film pioneer Forsyth Hardy observed that Denmark 'has a thriving film movement today' and that its documentary production 'would not shame a country six times its size' (Hardy 1947). There have been other periods in Danish film history of which much the same could be said – the decade from 1906, for example, or the quarter-century from 1995 to the present day. While the average cinemagoer may be hard pressed to differentiate between the five Nordic nations on a map, Denmark's 'brand' as a 'film nation' that consistently punches above its weight in cinematic terms currently seems secure.

Ask that same average cinemagoer what he or she knows about Danish film, and the answers are likely to include the auteurs Lars von Trier, Carl Theodor Dreyer and perhaps a few others such as Susanne Bier or Thomas Vinterberg; the Dogme 95 movement; high-quality television drama; and perhaps the early film star Asta Nielsen, a literary adaptation or two, or some vintage 1970s porn. That cinemagoer would be quite correct; all of these elements of Danish film history are to be found in this book. But so too are many of the films, filmmakers, institutions and cultural practices that go some way to explaining why this small nation of 5.8 million people has been able to develop and sustain the kind of productivity, quality, diversity and innovation that prompted Forsyth Hardy's contemporary, the English documentarist Arthur Elton, to describe the Danes as 'a film-progressive country' (quoted in Thomson 2018a: 72).

Part of the explanation is that Denmark is not a successful film nation *despite* her size, but *because of* her size – as much recent scholarship has suggested

(Hjort 2005; Hjort and Petrie 2007). One way to begin to unpack this paradox is to examine a fairly recent moment when the Danishness of Danish cinema became a cultural flashpoint.

Canons and Culture Wars

In late 2004, the then Danish Minister of Culture, Brian Mikkelsen, announced that seven expert committees were to be established, with the aim of identifying a new Danish Cultural Canon. Spanning 108 works in the fields of architecture, visual art, design and crafts, literature, popular music, classical music, performing arts, children's culture and, of course, cinema, the resulting canon was published in January 2006 as a website and a coffee-table book. The declared aims of the project included: sparking 'a vibrant cultural debate', because the perceived quality of the works in the canon would be open to challenge and discussion; making art and culture accessible to citizens; commissioning expert opinion on 'what in our cultural heritage is both valuable, of good quality and worth preserving for future generations'; identifying what is 'special' about Danish culture in a globalising world; and thus strengthening the national community by highlighting 'common historical baggage' (Kulturministeriet n. d.).

Denmark's best-known contemporary filmmaker, Lars von Trier, responded to Mikkelsen's initiative with an open letter. The canon was a horrible idea, declared von Trier; he very much hoped that he would not be included in it, and that the works he cared about 'would escape the fate of being stamped as national' (Larsen 2006). At that time, von Trier's production company, Zentropa, had taken to flying the Danish flag upside down on its premises in Avedøre, south-west of Copenhagen. If he were to be included in the Canon, threatened von Trier, he would stage a flag-burning ceremony in the car park. In the end, von Trier – or, rather, his film *Idioterne* (*The Idiots*, 1998) – was selected for the canon by the film sub-committee. But rather than burning the flag, von Trier made a short film, *Kultivér nationen*, exhorting Brian Mikkelsen to 'cultivate the nation – don't nationalise culture'. In the short film, von Trier cuts the white cross out of the Danish flag – the *Dannebrog* – and hoists the now-red flag aloft to the strains of the Internationale.[1] In other words, von Trier was advocating a dynamic, inclusive, humanist conception of the nation – not a state-sponsored, static, exclusionary vision of Denmark.

This skirmish is emblematic of the 'Culture War' that has haunted Danish politics and society over the past two decades. In her book examining the cultural politics of nationalism in twenty-first-century Denmark, Camilla Møhring Reestorff sees the debate around the Cultural Canon as analogous to more globally mediatised controversies such as the 'cartoon crisis' of 2006, when illustrations of the Prophet Muhammad in the newspaper *Jyllands-Posten* caused widespread outrage and sparked a violent debate about freedom of expression, as well as the 'jewellery law' of 2016, when a clause in a new immigration bill mandated confiscation of valuables from asylum-seekers (Reestorff 2017: 4–8). These media events serve as 'moments of intensification of an ongoing culture war' that are 'intertwined with a number of political participants – from politicians to comedians, authors and illustrators – who in different ways utilize art and culture in their articulating of the relation between the nation state, its citizens and the national symbolic' (Reestorff 2017: 8). This is a culture war that is fought domestically: which symbols, artefacts and practices count as 'Danish', and how are the boundaries of Danishness determined and policed? But it is also a war fought in the global arena, as what Kazimierz Musiał has termed the 'autostereotypes' of national identity – narratives and symbols of identity generated domestically – shape, and are re-shaped by, the 'xenostereotypes' about Denmark that circulate internationally (Musiał 2002: 235).

Such moments of national reckoning are mediated and mediatised – and thus intensified and globalised – in particular socially and technologically inflected ways in the twenty-first century. However, a self-reflexive interest in the nature of Danish national identity has a much longer history. This is in evidence, for example, in the critical postnationalism that typified Danish historiography and literary history of the 1990s (Mørch 1996; Østergaard 2003; Hauge 2003); the mid-twentieth-century dissemination of informational films about Denmark via post-war exchange networks of documentary and educational film (Thomson 2018a); and, even further back, the cultural labour of re-imagining Denmark as a small nation in the wake of successive territorial losses to Prussia in 1848–52 and 1864 (Hedling 2015). Michael Billig would see those nineteenth-century processes as 'hot nationalism': 'the force which creates nation states or which threatens the stability of existing states' (Billig 1995: 43). The corollary is the 'banal nationalism', the everyday 'ideological habits', from consumption of food to consumption of media, which constitute the ongoing reproduction of community (6). Reestorff proposes the intermediate phenomenon of 'tepid nationalism' to describe the contemporary sociopolitical dynamics of national identity in Denmark, whereby the nature of Danishness is repeatedly articulated and interrogated *as a political strategy*: 'tepid nationalism regulates the national symbolic by strengthening the social and affective relations between individuals and the nation state' (Reestorff 2017: 89). The 2006 Cultural Canon was framed in terms of sparking debate about what films or literature or architecture ought to be included, but predicated on the notion that some 'cultural baggage' can be judged more 'valuable' and 'worth preserving' than others because it is quintessentially Danish (Kulturministeriet n. d.).

To edit a book titled *A History of Danish Cinema* is therefore to step gingerly onto the turf of a culture war. National film history, after all, is also a form of national historiography; the history of an art form that, like other art forms, is engaged in co-constituting and contesting the 'imagined community' (Anderson 1991) that is the nation. Although Reestorff does not explicitly include filmmakers (or film policymakers) in her list of art activists or 'artivists' who intervene in the ongoing re-negotiation of national identity, it is clear that cinema is a significant contributor to what she calls the 'visual imaginaries' of the nation (Reestorff 2017: 15). This is not just about the politics of representation, although the medium-specific qualities of film can intensify such issues: live-action footage of the national landscape, for example, or the sound of the Danish language can connect film indexically as well as symbolically to the national community. Crucially, cinema is a key mover in tepid nationalism precisely because filmmaking, as a relatively costly and complex creative endeavour, has been subject to state intervention throughout most of its history, whether through censorship, regulation of production or exhibition, state subvention, or the political economics of archiving, preservation and digitisation.

Looking more closely at the film section of the 2006 Danish Cultural Canon fleshes out how the dynamics of tepid nationalism work in the particular case of cinema. Led by its chair, director Susanne Bier, the canon project's Committee for Film recorded its criteria and deliberations in a preface, as did the other sub-committees (Committee for Film 2006). Several details from the discussion are worth singling out for what they reveal about how one particular body discursively conceptualised the relations between cinema and national identity, within the parameters of its designated cultural-political remit.

First, the committee was disappointed to have to restrict its corpus to feature-length fiction films, excluding Denmark's strong traditions of documentary and short films. It is unclear whether this criterion was imposed by the ministry or adopted as a necessary filter, but either way it is indicative of a prevailing tendency to conflate film art with feature films. A second and related point is that seven of the twelve films are based on literary or stage classics. This is not only representative of a strong tradition of adaptation in Scandinavian cinema, but also speaks to the populist logic of a national film canon borrowing legitimacy from the national literary canon.

Third, the preface emphasises the medium-specificity of film: it is 'bound up with physical reality by its very nature' and thus 'even the best films are of their time and age quickly'. This point is explicitly connected in the preface to the definition of Danishness adopted by the committee: that 'the films should specifically reflect a Danish reality, with Danish actors and references'. This is presented as a guarantee of the Danishness of the films, since '[i]t is only the Danes that would make the effort to reflect the Danish language [. . .] and the physical surroundings' (Committee for Film 2006). However, each film was discussed on its own merits; the panel admits that the inclusion of *Sult* (*Hunger*, Henning Carlsen, 1966), directed by a Dane but based on Norwegian novel and with a Swedish actor in the main role, was designed to provoke discussion.

Finally, the somewhat arbitrary cut-off point of 1998 was adopted; flagrantly chosen to allow for the inclusion of two Dogme 95 films, this was justified as a nod to the principle of allowing a 'necessary distance' and historical objectivity. As the Committee for Film admits, their choices were predicated on which films had stood the test of time and were best 'seen with contemporary eyes'; the film canon itself would soon be out-of-date (Committee for Film 2006). In sum, these parameters resulted in a film canon that offers something to satisfy almost all combatants in a culture war:

> *Du skal ære din Hustru* (*Master of the House*, Carl Th. Dreyer, 1925)
> *Vredens Dag* (*Day of Wrath*, Carl Th. Dreyer, 1943)
> *Ditte Menneskebarn* (*Ditte, Child of Man*, Bjarne Henning-Jensen and Astrid Henning-Jensen, 1946)
> *Soldaten og Jenny* (*Jenny and the Soldier*, Johan Jacobsen, 1947)
> *Sult* (*Hunger*, Henning Carlsen, 1966)
> *Bennys badekar* (*Benny's Bathtub*, Jannik Hastrup and Flemming Quist Møller, 1971)
> *Matador* (Erik Balling, 1978–82)
> *Kundskabens træ* (*The Tree of Knowledge*, Nils Malmros, 1981)
> *Babettes gæstebud* (*Babette's Feast*, Gabriel Axel, 1987)
> *Pelle erobreren* (*Pelle the Conqueror*, Bille August, 1987)
> *Festen* (*The Celebration*, Thomas Vinterberg, 1998)
> *Idioterne* (*The Idiots*, Lars von Trier, 1998)

While it is perhaps not surprising that all but one of these films occurred of their own accord in the chapters by the contributors to this volume, the canon itself has some striking omissions, most of which can be traced back to the very specific remit from which the list emerged, and to what it reveals about the intersections between film history and the cultural politics of tepid nationalism. In what follows, we engage with some of these omissions to try to fill in the gaps in the canon – as well as the gaps that are inevitable in a book like this one.

(Hi)Stories of Danish Cinema

Notwithstanding its broadly chronological organisation, what a canon does not do is tell a story: it is a list, not a narrative. An oddity of the Danish language is that the word *historie* means both 'history' and 'story'. That historiography and fiction depend on similar narrative structures was established by Hayden White and others in the 1970s (White 1973), but there is also a tradition in Danish history of framing the national narrative in terms of stories or tales. A classic work of popular history dating from 1882, for example, adopted the title and form of *Forty Tales of the History of the Fatherland* (Jørgensen

1998). This vernacular form was re-appropriated by historians and archaeologists a century later, with Søren Mørch's *Last History of Denmark* in fifty-seven tales (Mørch 1996) and Rikke Agnete Olsen's forty-one tales of *People in the Fatherland's History* (Olsen 2004). Concerned as they are with causality and agency, such historiographical experiments cannot eschew chronology entirely, but they tend to be organised around an array of artefacts, people or places, and they let (hi)stories unfold through time in overlapping ways.

In one sense, this is what this book tries to do; while organised chronologically in a loose sense, the film (hi)stories that are told in each chapter stretch backwards and forwards through time, looking for continuities of genre or style, for example, seeking out connections and cross-currents across national boundaries and picking up on peripheral and forgotten case-studies. Such an approach weaves a film culture together diachronically and synchronically in ways that a canonical list cannot achieve. At the same time, gaps in the narrative are inevitably introduced, because while the (hi)stories told in the book's chapters overlap here and there, one contributor does not necessarily pick up where the previous one left off. The richness of perspective that is gained from an anthology of critical voices also sacrifices the cohesiveness of a monograph. As its title emphasises, this book offers *a* – not *the* – history of Danish cinema; one possible version of it, a snapshot of the concerns and specialisms of the cross-section of film scholars represented here. Between the national pedagogy (Bhabha 1994) of the Canon for Film and the twenty-one tales in this book, what other historical narratives might paint a more complete picture of Danish cinema?

Early and Silent Cinema

The most startling gap in the Canon for Film is the absence of any work dating from before 1925. Carl Th. Dreyer's *Master of the House* from that year is the only silent film in the canon. While the term 'golden age' has been bandied around so much in connection with Danish cinema as to be almost meaningless, it is indisputable that Denmark was a world leader in film production during the first two decades of film history. As Isak Thorsen details in Chapter 1 of this volume, the production company Nordisk Films Kompagni, established in 1906, was pioneering and came to play an important role in shaping the cinematic landscape as we know it today. In Chapter 2, Julie K. Allen examines another aspect of Denmark's international influence during the silent era: the contributions to acting style and the beginnings of a star system via the engagement of Asta Nielsen, Clara Wieth Pontoppidan, Olaf Fønss and Valdemar Psilander.

Conspicuously absent from the Canon for Film are a number of watersheds in early and silent cinema history: Asta Nielsen's first star turn in the erotic melodrama *Afgrunden* (*The Abyss*, Urban Gad, 1910); the astonishing disaster and science fiction blockbusters of the 1910s, such as *Atlantis* (August Blom, 1913) or *Himmelskibet* (*A Trip to Mars*, Holger-Madsen, 1918); the renowned horror *Häxan* (*Häxan: Witchcraft Through the Ages*, Benjamin Christensen, Sweden, 1922); or even the earliest known Danish film *Kørsel med grønlandske hunde* (*Driving with Greenlandic Dogs*, Peter Elfelt, 1897). The canon's preface provides clues as to why such mainstays of film history are excluded: the selections are based on what has retained its appeal and its cinematic value from a contemporary perspective (Committee for Film 2006). It is logical, then, that any work pre-dating the crystallisation of film narrative and film language into a form recognisable to early-twenty-first-century audiences is not likely to make the cut. Films from cinema's first two decades are, of course, challenging to watch today: the unruliness of unadulterated spectacle overturns our assumptions about how narrative should unfold in time and space, as a vampiric Asta Nielsen gyrates on screen (*The Abyss*), or a mass of suspiciously Nordic-looking Martians swarm to greet a band of over-acting spacemen (*A Trip to Mars*). The physical deterioration of many early and silent films is also perhaps a hindrance to their inclusion in a popular national canon. While silent film aficionados might swoon over the near-obliterated images towards the end of *The Abyss*, the ravages of vinegar syndrome may be exclusionary by dint of being a visible reminder that the films have not stood the test of time in a physical sense, thus disturbing the viewing experience and rendering the film text less absorbing.

As a side note, in respect of the pre-classical form and the physical condition of older films, it is instructive to compare the sections of the 2006 canon that deal with other forms of Danish culture. The Canon for Architecture, for example, includes a twelfth-century village church; the Canon for Design starts with a Viking ship dating from 1042; the Canon for Visual Arts incorporates the mid-fourteenth-century 'sun chariot' depicting night and day. These are artefacts dating from periods that pre-date modern norms of design and art, but neither their alien forms nor their physical deterioration presented obstacles to inclusion; in comparison, the focus on the sound era of cinema is noteworthy.

This balance is being redressed, however, by the Danish Film Institute's growing web resources on silent cinema, stumfilm.dk. Between 2019 and 2023, more than 400 films will be digitised and made freely available online, along with their posters, programmes, screenplays and other paratexts: 'fascinating, mysterious, awesome, sexy and funny stories hiding in the archive' (Danish Silent Film 2019). An element of this work is to awaken public interest not just in the films themselves, but in the craft of archivists and restorers. The explanatory blurb for *The Abyss*, for example, highlights the material deterioration of the film and engagingly explains that the erotic 'gaucho dance' scene in the digitised version is relatively unscathed, because that part of the film had been removed and preserved by the Swedish censors in the 1910s and could be reinstated (Stumfilm 2019). This is an example of increasingly pro-active work by the Danish Film Institute to make the nation's film heritage available via digitisation and open-access mediation. At the same time, such work broadens the definition of 'national film heritage' in its openness to being led by the content of the archives (and the available funding) rather than by any sense of a canon. A precursor to the Danish Silent Film site was danmarkpaafilm.dk (Denmark on Film), an innovative online archive of early *actualités*, film fragments, orphan films, amateur films and so on, embedded in an interactive map of Denmark, and inviting user comments.

Auteurs and Other Voices

Especially in light of the increasingly diverse online mediation of Danish film heritage described above, it seems all the more retrograde that the Canon for Film is almost completely constituted of films directed by men. Indeed, a quarter of the films in the canon were directed by just two men, the two most renowned Danish auteurs: Carl Th. Dreyer (1889–1968) and Lars von Trier (1956–). Given their status at home and abroad (although, anecdotally, younger Danes tend not to be familiar with Dreyer's work), this is hardly surprising. Linda Haverty Rugg has astutely articulated how canonical filmmakers like Dreyer and von Trier tend to become ciphers for particular national traditions: 'The study of cinematic auteurism is also necessarily the study of globalization, for the auteur has been by definition a filmmaker of international stature who is understood paradoxically as representative of a national culture while at the same time transcending national boundaries' (Rugg 2005: 221). As evinced by the selections included in the Canon for Film, both Dreyer and von Trier have contributed to the cinematic mapping of Danish daily life that the canon prizes. But their inclusion in the canon probably has more to do with the emblematic status that Rugg describes, rather than a consistent engagement with unequivocally Danish topics and settings. The first half of Dreyer's career in particular was spent working internationally, as Casper Tybjerg details in Chapter 3 of this volume. Von Trier has long been making films in English with global stars, as Peter Schepelern's overview of his career in Chapter 12 shows, although von Trier has consistently contributed to developing Danish film culture in a number of ways (Hjort 2006, Schepelern 2000, Thomsen 2016 and 2018).

Auteurs such as Dreyer and von Trier pose two particular problems for a volume such as this one. On the one hand, so much has already been written and published on both of these directors that it is hard to commission any new research that is not also so esoteric as to be too abstruse to say something general about Danish cinema. On the other hand, not to include them in a volume such as this would be unthinkable. In the end, we invited the two Danish scholars who have worked most extensively and consistently on these filmmakers to write overviews of their oeuvres from a perspective of their choice. Casper Tybjerg considers the international connections that shaped Dreyer's life and work in Chapter 3, and Peter Schepelern, Lars von Trier's former tutor and biographer (Schepelern 2000), reflects on his erstwhile student's career in Chapter 12.

One set of voices that is rather well represented in the canon, not as directors but as viewers, is children and young people. That both Nils Malmros's historical drama *The Tree of Knowledge* and the classic animated film *Benny's Bathtub* are included sends a clear message about the centrality to Danish cinema of films for children and young people. This is a topic explored by Christa Lykke Christensen in Chapter 10 of this volume; she explains the contribution of such films to the renewal of Danish realism, as well as the regular crosscurrents between the fields of children's films and mainstream cinema.

Yet, the wave of films by filmmakers from immigrant backgrounds is not captured in the canon at all. Eva Jørholt's account in Chapter 18 of the recent emergence of a generation of Black and Minority Ethnic filmmakers goes some way towards remedying the dearth of information in English about this aspect of Danish film culture, and Mette Hjort's investigation (in Chapter 16) of talent development strategies and practices in the context of New Danish Screen and other schemes is suggestive of an ongoing process of nurturing a new and more diverse generation of film talent.

That Susanne Bier, the chair of the Committee for Film, is now an Oscar-winning auteur in her own right (awarded in 2011 for *Hævnen* [*In a Better World*], 2010) does not absolve the committee of its failure to recognise the contribution of women filmmakers in Denmark. By almost any measure, women filmmakers have historically been exceptionally well represented in the Danish film industry, relative to most other nations. Denmark was the first country to submit a film directed by a woman to the Academy Award for Best Foreign Language Film: Annelise Hovmand's *Ingen tid til kærtegn* (*Be Dear to Me*, 1957). Although Hovmand did not receive a nomination, Astrid Henning-Jensen did so for *Paw* in 1959. Henning-Jensen is the only woman to appear in the Canon for Film, credited as co-director with her husband Bjarne Henning-Jensen for *Ditte, Child of Man* (1946), although her official role was that of Assistant Director.

Such accolades are one thing; productivity is another measure of a significant career, and the Danish filmmaker with most film credits of all time was another woman, Alice O'Fredericks. She collaborated on seventy-two films in all as actor, screenwriter and/or director, and between 1934 and 1967 was sole director of twenty-three films (Petersen 2017). But O'Fredericks was a director of what she herself called *hyggefilm* or cosy films – 'popular' entertainment in both senses of the term – and thus liable to be excluded from the canon by virtue of the committee's declared focus on cinematic art rather than well-crafted films. Her less prolific contemporaries Annelise Reenberg and Bodil Ipsen moved into directing from cinematography and the stage, respectively, also focusing on popular genre films. In two chapters written for this volume, Niels Henrik Hartvigson explores two inter-related, distinctively Danish genres to which these and other women directors made key contributions: the *folkekomedie* or folk comedy (Chapter 5) and the *hjemstavnsfilm* or homeland film (Chapter 8). Birger Langkjær's chapter on 1940s realism (Chapter 6) is also part of this story.

The 1998 cut-off point for the canon may also be a contributing factor in its unrepresentative exclusion of women directors. The turn of the millennium saw the breakthroughs of several Danish women directors: Lone Scherfig, Annette K. Olesen and, not least, Susanne Bier, who by that time was established enough to chair the Committee for Film. Bier and Scherfig are given due attention in Meryl Shriver-Rice's account of the trajectories of selected auteurs in Chapter 14 of this volume. A decade later, a generation of women documentarists was breaking through, and their works (together with their innovative working practices) are discussed by Anne Jerslev in Chapter 17.

Communities and Border-Crossings

In line with the committee's declared criteria, the works in the Canon for Film all 'specifically reflect a Danish reality, with Danish actors and references' (Canon for Film 2006). They are all set in Denmark, apart from the exception noted by the committee – that is, *Hunger*, which is set in Oslo (or Christiania, as it was known at the time of the action). Interestingly, two films in the canon are adaptations which move the setting of the source text to Denmark: *Day of Wrath* is based on a play, *Anne Pedersdotter*, by Norwegian playwright Hans Wiers-Jenssen but relocated to a seventeenth-century Danish parsonage, while the Isak Dinesen novella adapted by Gabriel Axel as *Babette's Feast* also moves the action (and thus the scenery) from the north of Norway to the Jutland coast. This centripetal dynamic also obtains at plot level in several of the films: Pelle the Conqueror and his grandfather come to Denmark in search of work; Babette is fleeing the regime that had killed her family in Paris; and Christian in *Festen* returns from France to his father's house to face a reckoning. Overall, the films in the canon provide coverage of a broad sweep of Danish life, from the cities of Copenhagen and Aarhus to rural heathland, farmland and sea. In this sense, the Canon for Film fulfils the logic of a national canon: this is not just a matter of adopting the landscapes, cities, people and customs of the nation as setting, but more a matter of *national integration* of the kind that Hartvigson in this volume sees as a driving force in folk comedy and homeland cinema (Chapters 5 and 8). There are scores to settle, families to reconcile, debts to be paid, debates to be waged, but overall the dynamic is towards community formation within the material spaces of the nation. The Danish landscape is also crucial as the backdrop to the self-consciously national genre of the *Danmarksfilm* (Denmark-film), as Ib Bondebjerg explains in Chapter 7. The Greenlandic landscape is part of the national imagination, too, or perhaps, rather, a (post)colonialist imagination; Chapter 21 explores the history of Danish depictions of Greenland, as well as the burgeoning Indigenous film production. Meanwhile, against today's backdrop of climate change and environmental activism, filmmakers and critics are increasingly moving away from a deterministic or romantic idea of the connections between land and people, and towards a more relational, materialist portrayal of our entanglement with the world, as Benjamin Bigelow argues in Chapter 19.

There is also a more centrifugal dynamic to be found in Danish cinema. This is most obviously the case in the transnational border-crossings undertaken by successive generations of directors and actors. The filmmakers, stars and films of Danish silent cinema operated internationally, as the chapters by Isak Thorsen, Julie K. Allen and Casper Tybjerg in Part I examine. Running parallel with the development of mid-century genres for the domestic audience was a strong tradition of documentary and informational filmmaking that brought images of Denmark to the world, as Ib Bondebjerg discusses in Chapter 7. And even the most Danish of Danish genres, the Olsen Gang films, had a strong fan base in East Germany, as Stephan Michael Schröder explains in Chapter 9. Closer to the present day, the direction of travel has often been trans-Atlantic, and not uni-directional, as Meryl Shriver-Rice plots out in Chapter 14. In Chapter 19, Benjamin Bigelow's focus on *Vinterbrødre* (*Winter Brothers*, 2017), directed by Icelander Hlynur Pálmason, illustrates how the cohorts emerging from the National Film School of Denmark often include filmmakers from across the Nordic region. And as Chapters 13 (C. Claire Thomson) and 15 (Eva Novrup Redvall) show, the politics of representation and distribution of media are often entangled with economic interests, individual cultural entrepreneurship and bilateral cultural policy agreements.

This volume, then, tries to tell stories about Danish cinema's engagement with the wider world, as well as how it functions as national culture for a domestic audience. But a related question is: where are the boundaries of Denmark? Since the mid-nineteenth century, the Danish autostereotype has been of *et lille land* – a small country. But Denmark was once a very large state indeed, encompassing Norway, Iceland, the Faroes, Greenland and even some colonies in the West Indies, the Gold Coast and elsewhere. A recent wave of scholarship has done much to map out the legacy of this colonial history for literature and visual culture in the broader Nordic context (see, for example, Stenport and Lunde 2019; Körber and Volquardsen 2014; Mackenzie and Stenport 2014b; Körber, MacKenzie and Stenport 2017). Denmark's remaining self-governing territories, Greenland and the Faroe Islands, presented us with a dilemma: to what extent does it make ethical or logical sense to fold their respective cinematic output into a history of *Danish* cinema? Arguably, the islands having achieved home rule in 1948, Faroese cinema culture is established as a small-nation cinema in its own right, with its own national film institute (filmshusid.fo), film prize and Faroese-language filmmaking stretching back to the 1970s. In the end we opted for a compromise: Chapter 21 provides a snapshot of the emerging indigenous Greenlandic film industry in the form of a short essay and interview with filmmaker Emile Hertling Péronard, providing insight into the interplay between cultural identity and film institutions in a devolved polity.

The question of Denmark's southern border with Europe was also a fraught one for centuries; even well within the age of cinema, in 1920, the position of the Dano-German border in the Duchy of Slesvig (Schleswig in German) was decided by plebiscite. Today a model of bilingual and bicultural transnational cooperation, this border was once one of the bloodiest in Europe (see Rerup 1995). Indirectly, the southern border was the subject of some cultural blood-letting again as recently as 2014, when the television series *1864* was made to commemorate the 150th anniversary of the Battle of Dybbøl. The defeat to Prussia in 1864 and the consequent loss of a third of its territory (some of which was reinstated in 1920) had long festered in the Danish collective memory. That the series, directed by filmmaker Ole Bornedal, took a post-historical, semi-fictional approach ruffled feathers, not least among populist politicians. As Erik Hedling's work (2015) on the reception of the series shows, at stake was a particular fixture of the relationship between the government and film and television production: *armslængdeprincippet*, or the principle of arm's length. This is the system that ensures that state funding for film and television does not equate to state control of the content of that same production. Approval for state-funded programming, so thought Pia Kjærsgaard, former leader of the right-wing Danish People's Party (Dansk Folkeparti), particularly should be subject to checks on historical accuracy. This specific question – how visual culture, and by extension the identities and boundaries it articulates and shapes, is funded and governed in Denmark – leads us to one other (hi)story of Danish cinema that we want to outline here: its institutions.

Institutions

The 2006 canon itself was an expression of governmentality and became a site of contestation, as we have seen. While its sub-canon of films is a useful diagnostic tool, the Cultural Canon itself was fairly incidental to the development of Danish cinema. However, the works listed in it were all shaped, facilitated, regulated or funded to some degree by a range of state or semi-governmental film institutions in Denmark, which have developed markedly over the century of cinema.

Until 1910, the content of films was more or less unregulated, although permission had to be sought from the police to show films, and guidance documents circulated from 1907 onwards. At that time, cinema fell under the jurisdiction of the Ministry of Justice, which indicates its status as a form of entertainment to be policed, rather than a form of national culture to be nurtured. From 1911, an entertainment tax was levied on the price of film screening tickets. Statens Filmcensur, the state censorship office, was established in 1913. In 1922, a first

Film Law recommended that films screened should be morally beneficial to the public. To carry out their tasks the censors could either allow a film for everyone, prohibit it for children, ban it, or cut violent or erotic parts or scenes from the film before it was shown in cinemas (see Thorsen 2016b). In 1960, age limits of either twelve or sixteen years were introduced for children.

A series of Film Laws adopted at regular intervals throughout the twentieth century bear witness to an increasing willingness on the part of government to pro-actively support cinema as culture and even education, rather than simply reactively regulating it (Bondebjerg n. d.). The Film Law of 1933 began to work with the idea that the state could intervene to promote the more edifying aspects of cinema, redirecting intake from the entertainment tax to support the development of educational film. The semi-governmental agency Dansk Kulturfilm (Danish Culture Film, see Thomson 2018a) was established in connection with this law, to act as a clearing house for informational film projects commissioned by ministries and non-governmental organisations such as associations and charities.

This principle was further strengthened by the next Film Law of 1938, which Bondebjerg (n. d.) sees as the first articulation of a film policy recognisable as such. Limited support for film production was facilitated by two bodies, Filmsrådet and Filmsfonden (the Film Council and the Film Fund). Funding continued to be directed towards enlightening film, with the establishment of the distribution authority Statens Filmcentral (the State Film Centre) in 1938. From 1941 onwards, during the German Occupation of Denmark, this was further buttressed by the establishment of Ministeriernes Filmudvalg (the Government Film Committee), working in tandem with Dansk Kulturfilm to make shorts supporting the war effort and, later, promoting aspects of national culture to its own citizens and abroad (see Bondebjerg, Chapter 7 in this volume, and Thomson 2016 and 2018a). This Film Law also mandated the establishment of the Film Museum in 1941, the forerunner of the later Danish Film Institute and a concrete expression of the need to organise preservation of the national film heritage. The years of German occupation, then, from 1940 to 1945, were in fact a time when Danish cinema blossomed. This was due in part to a series of amoral compromises and questionable strategies adopted by major film companies, as Lars-Martin Sørensen details in Chapter 4. But more positively, as Sørensen's discussion suggests, the Second World War was also a time when the relations between state and film were buttressed, laying the groundwork for post-war cultural and film policy. Characteristic of the post-war years is an ongoing indirect shaping of mainstream cinema practice by state intervention, whether because educational film informed the particular brand of realism that grew up in the 1940s (Langkjær, Chapter 6), or because of an elite suspicion of popular genres (Hartvigson, Chapters 5 and 8; Schröder, Chapter 9; Christensen, Chapter 10; Thorsen, Chapter 11).

A further Film Law in 1964 responded to the existential threat posed by television. In particular, state support was now available on a more meaningful scale for quality feature films, as well as documentary and short films; a Film Workshop model facilitated experimentation and talent development, often in collaboration with DR (Danmarks Radio, the national public service broadcaster). The mid-1960s also saw the establishment of the Danish Film School, led by the documentarist Theodor Christensen (1914–67, who also contributed to the establishment of Cuba's Film School; see Thomson 2018a), to train new generations of directors, screenwriters and technicians. The lasting impact of the National Film School is crucial in nearly all the chapters in Parts III and IV of this book. These developments of the 1960s, as well as the development of Film Studies as a minor at the University of Copenhagen, testify to the growing acceptance of film as a medium and an artform.

While the new Film Law and institutions of the 1960s responded, at least in part, to the threat posed by television, it is interesting to note that things have come full circle; as Eva Novrup Redvall explains in Chapter 15, the synergies between the Danish film and television branches in recent years (and media convergence more generally) have strengthened both, nurturing a generation of screenwriters, directors and other professionals who move comfortably between the big screen and the small screen – and, increasingly, portable screens.

Indirectly, the laws of the 1960s also drew attention to Danish film internationally. When in 1969 Denmark, as the first country in the world, decriminalised picture pornography, the intention was to restrain images of sex, but quite the opposite happened: Denmark became synonymous with pornography in the early 1970s (see Thorsen, Chapter 11). Although different age limits were upheld until 1997 and replaced by age recommendations for children, there has been no censorship for adults since 1969.

A 1972 Film Law saw further consolidation of this proactive approach to shaping and supporting film culture in Denmark. The Danish Film Institute was founded by this law as a dedicated government agency for the organisation and implementation of film policy. A significant step was the introduction of *konsulentsystemet* (the consultant system) which brought the talents of a shifting corps of professionals and academics to bear on supporting specific film productions, rather than leaving decisions to committees. The provisions of the 1972 law were strengthened by increased funding in 1982, with a quarter of funds ring-fenced for films for children and young people, the impact of which is explored by Christa Lykke Christensen in Chapter 10 in this volume.

Before the new Film Law proper of 1997 came a number of significant revisions at the end of the 1980s. These are discussed in more depth by Thomson in Chapter 13 and Shriver-Rice in Chapter 14, but one key development was the disassociation of national language from the funding criteria: this made it possible for filmmakers wishing to work in English, not least Lars von Trier, to access funding. Another important development was a new system of financing which supplemented the consultant system, offering 50/50 match funding to projects commercial enough to raise a portion of production costs. This shifted the balance of state support away from arthouse-type projects and towards films with some degree of commercial viability. This scheme was later revised to a 60/40 arrangement. The Council of Europe's Eurimages fund was set up in 1989, and in 1990 the establishment of the Nordic Film and Television Fund under the aegis of the Nordic Council provided interesting new opportunities for support and collaboration with neighbouring Nordic film cultures (Nordisk Film & TV Fond 2020). These developments coincided with the energy unleashed in the sector by Denmark's two successive Academy Awards for Best Foreign Language Film in 1988 (Gabriel Axel's *Babette's Feast*) and 1989 (Bille August's *Pelle the Conqueror*).

The 1997 Film Law amalgamated the Danish Film Institute, the National Film Board and the Film Museum under one roof in a renovated building on Gothersgade, in central Copenhagen. Known as Filmhuset (Film House), the building welcomes the public to its cinematheque and film library, and it is also home to the institute's archives, as well as departments such as marketing, production, talent development, strategy, research, public engagement and a range of other functions which benefit from being housed in the same building. (The film preservation and restoration facilities are located to the west of the city, in Glostrup, where there is space for specialist cold storage.) In early 1998, under the newly-appointed CEO Henning Camre and the Chair of the Board, Ib Bondebjerg, the new DFI negotiated a 75 per cent increase in government funding for film (see Hjort and Bondebjerg 2001: 12).

Today, the DFI operates on the basis of the 1997 Film Law but re-negotiates its strategic plan and funding with the government at four-year intervals. The current agreement (2019–23) has been shaped by the fast-moving media landscape, and its aims include the following: to develop artistic and popular filmmaking; to encourage economically sustainable productions; to develop promotional channels and distribution mechanisms; to achieve a 29 per cent share of cinema box office sales in Denmark; and to ensure that at least ten Danish films a year are seen by at least a million Danes, via theatrical distribution, on demand streaming, or other means (including innovative film-related events and mediation). To sustain international exposure, ten to twelve Danish films a year must be shown at international film festivals (Danish Film Institute 2018c). A notable priority for the DFI is to harness new technologies – restoration and digitisation tools – to preserve the nation's film heritage and make it accessible to a wide audience. Recent projects include Danmarkpaafilm.dk (Denmark on Film, an interactive film map of orphan and documentary footage) and stumfilm.dk (Danish Silent Film, a major digitisation and mediation project focusing on the silent era).

Even within a small country it is important to note that there are peripheral, regional aspects of the notion of 'Danish cinema'. A small but no less significant facet of the 1997 Film Law included the legislative groundwork for supporting regional film culture across the various municipalities beyond Copenhagen and the Capital Region, as Pei-Sze Chow explains in Chapter 20 of this volume. Since then, the regionalisation of the Danish film landscape – as part of a broader push towards greater diversity – has become a focus area in national film policy, with increasing amounts of funding allocated to the two regional film funds, Den Vestdanske Filmpulje and Filmfyn. They have become important institutions that work to support and foster regional film culture across Jutland and Funen.

THE SHAPE OF THIS BOOK

The discussion above deliberately eschews a linear presentation of the organisation of this book, preferring to indicate points of connection, continuities and contrasts across different aspects of cinema culture and different eras. Nonetheless, a few words of explanation about the structure of the book may be in order.

The four parts of the volume are conceived roughly chronologically. Part I covers the period from the first 'golden age' of Danish cinema to the Occupation, paying particular attention to institutions such as the major film companies, not least Nordisk Films Kompagni, and to other institutions such as stars, key directors and modes of production and regulation, as well as the profoundly transnational nature of this period. Part II examines a range of popular genres which are fundamental to Danish film culture, but which have not received much attention in English-language scholarship: the *folkekomedie* or folk comedy; social realism; the *Danmarksfilm* or Denmark-film; homeland cinema, including the Morten Korch films; the Olsen Gang films; films for children and young people; and pornography. While this section is arranged in rough chronological order according to the emergence of the genre in question, it is striking that the chapters tend to demonstrate the persistence, dynamism and legacy of the genres.

Part III focuses on what has often been called a second 'golden age' of Danish cinema: from the late 1980s onwards. The international renaissance of Danish cinema is a story of individual movers and shakers as well as institutions, and this section looks at the international and trans-sector mobility of those people and films, as well as policy, praxis, strategy and talent development at home in Denmark. Section IV, 'Decentring and Diversifying Danish Cinema', points forward and outwards, looking at recent initiatives, trends and policies. Again, it is striking in this section that diversity in terms of voices is closely tied to effective institutions. Overall, then, the volume not only exploits the well-worn 'golden age' trope of Danish cinema history to give some order to the contributions, but also tries to complicate that grand narrative.

The essays in this volume necessarily refer to a great number of sources in Danish. Except where otherwise indicated, the translation of quotations into English has been undertaken by the author of the relevant chapter. English-language sources have been referred to where possible to facilitate further reading, but many sources are inevitably in Danish. Films are usually referred to by their Danish title first, followed by their official English title or a translation of the Danish title as appropriate.

Envoi

'This is the History of Danish Dreams, an account of what we have dreaded and dreamed of and hoped for and expected during this century' (Høeg 1996, loc 37–58). A canonical work of (post)modern Danish literature is Peter Høeg's novel *The History of Danish Dreams* (*Forestilling om det tyvende århundrede*, 1988). A magical realist account of twentieth-century Denmark, the novel is narrated by an amateur historian who knows – just as we do – from the very beginning that his ambition to construct a history that is as 'exhaustive' as it is 'simple' is doomed to failure. So many wonderful filmmakers and films have had to be left out of our narrative; what we can do is to provide some points of entry to the prodigious film culture of this self-declared 'little land'.

But Høeg's narrator has a trick: something akin to a cinematic close-up or freeze-frame. His preface to the novel goes on to explain: 'I believe that, encapsulated within any everyday event – and yes, possibly any event whatsoever – lies the essence of an entire century'. In this spirit, we offer an event close to the origin of cinema, a concentrated moment that suspends within it the potential of a century:

It is a late summer day in 1899, at Bernstorff Palace, to the north of Copenhagen. Gathered on the stone steps leading up to the palace entrance are several of the crowned heads of Europe; so tentacular are the genealogical connections of the Danish royal family that this gathering includes King Christian IX of Denmark, Dowager Tsarina Dagmar, Tsar Nicholas II of Russia, King George of Greece and various blue-blooded offspring dressed up in sailor suits. They are going to sit for group and individual portraits with the Photographer to the Danish Court, Peter Elfelt (1866–1931). About eighteen months earlier, Elfelt had been the first Dane to record moving images and project them at the Panorama entertainment venue run by his friend Vilhelm Pacht in the centre of town, using equipment modelled on the Lumière brothers' cinématographe (Ernst 1964: 156–57). With privileged access to the royal court, Elfelt was in a position to make films that showed the royals on horseback, on bicycles and the like, entertaining a public hungry for novelty and spectacle, while humanising the monarchy (see stumfilm.dk for more Elfelt films).

As a pioneer in still photography, Elfelt's early moving images often use the frame for comedic or dramatic effect (see Chapter 21 in this volume for an account of this technique in his earliest known film). But on this day, he positions the camera obliquely, filming the royals from a forty-five-degree angle as they arrange themselves into formation on the steps for a group portrait. The children bounce around; the ladies smooth their dresses and hair; the gentlemen smoke, chat and laugh. The camera captures all this, while the royals are waiting for another camera, the one to immortalise and freeze this gathering of monarchs past, present and future. But Elfelt is cranking his movie camera and films them as animated, lively beings, waiting for something that is about to happen, a frozen moment about to be captured. Usually, Elfelt plays with the frame, the space that is out of shot; here, he is playing with a moment in time that is out of shot.

Elfelt calls the film *De kongelige skal fotograferes*, a title that is almost impossible to translate accurately, because of the 's' on the verb 'at fotografere', to photograph. The 's' denotes a voice somewhere between passive and active in English, and here it is modified by the modal verb 'skal' to suggest that the royals are going to be photographed, shall be photographed . . . a point suspended endlessly in the future, imminently ahead of these moments of sheer vitality.

For one minute, Elfelt's camera whirrs, capturing an event in which can be glimpsed the potential of the new medium – the essence of the approaching century of Danish cinema.

Note

1. The film is still available at https://www.youtube.com/watch?v=K3Ujl3FEDdc

PART I

FROM THE FIRST 'GOLDEN AGE' TO THE OCCUPATION

1. SURVIVING A CRISIS: NORDISK FILMS KOMPAGNI AS A WORLD PLAYER

Isak Thorsen

In the history of Danish cinema, Nordisk Films Kompagni stands out as a constant. For more than a century the company's trademark with the polar bear standing on top of the globe has been familiar to Danish cinema-going audiences. Established in 1906 as the first film company in Scandinavia, Nordisk Film is known for being the world's oldest continuously active film company. On a national level Nordisk Film is the only survivor of the four major film companies which dominated the Danish film industry from the 1930s to the late 1960s, the other three being Palladium, ASA and Saga. Films from Nordisk Film guarantee well-crafted, but perhaps a bit traditional entertainment. Today Nordisk Film is by far the largest national company within production and distribution and runs the biggest chain of cinemas in Denmark.

In the silent era, Nordisk Film was not only the dominant company nationally, but it also counted among the major film studios on the world market and came to play an important role in shaping the cinematic landscape as we know it today. The Danish silent era is known as the 'golden age' (see, for example, Schepelern 2010), and in many ways developments in Danish film during this period are synonymous with the development of Nordisk Film. In general, one can trace two approaches to understanding the success of Nordisk Film in the early years: aesthetic and economic (see, for example, Ulrichsen 1956, Neergaard 1960, Engberg 1977, Christensen 1997, Thorsen 2017a). In the following the perspective will be economic – or organisational – paying special attention to the period around 1910 when Nordisk Film re-organised its production to accommodate multiple-reel films. This led to major changes in production, distribution and exhibition of film, not only in Denmark, but also around the world.

Success and Crisis

Central to the story of Nordisk Film is its founder Ole Olsen (1863–1943). Olsen came from a very poor rural background, and before entering the film industry he had earned his living with different odd jobs and as a showman on traveling fairs. In 1896, the council of the Swedish town Malmö asked him to establish a permanent fair similar to the Tivoli pleasure gardens in Copenhagen. Olsen successfully ran the fair and returned to Copenhagen in 1901, and with the money he had earned he opened the second cinema in Copenhagen, Biograf Theatret, in 1905. Olsen's move from the fairs to cinema corresponds with a general trend, in which many early entrepreneurs in the film industry had a background in variety shows and traveling fairs.

Olsen entered the film business at the right time, as cinemas were emerging in most metropolitan areas, often established in former shop fronts. Constantin Philipsen opened the first successful Danish cinema, Kosmorama, in 1904, and by 1908 there were sixteen cinemas in Copenhagen and about eighteen in the provinces. A visit to the cinema consisted of a programme of several shorter films, usually made up of non-fiction films of nature or about current events, comedies and more serious dramas.

Olsen's cinema was an attraction for the Copenhagen audience, but a major problem soon emerged with getting enough new films for his cinema, and so he started his own production. Besides the photographer Peter Elfelt, who had shot several films beginning with the first Danish film *Kørsel med grønlandske Hunde* (*Driving with Greenlandic Dogs*, 1897; see Chapter 21 in this volume) and numerous films of the royal family, almost no one in Denmark had experience with making films. Just to get hold of a camera was difficult; according to Olsen, he had to obtain one from France (Olsen 1941: 50). Originally, Olsen had hired the ventriloquist and impersonator Louis Halberstadt to direct the first fiction film. Halberstadt held a reading with the actors, but when it came to the actual shoot, he came up short in directing the actors. Instead, Viggo Larsen, who was a supervisor in Olsen's cinema, took over. Larsen was a former army sergeant and understood how to command people; he became the director of nearly all of Nordisk Film's fiction films from 1906 to 1909. Axel Graatkjær, who worked as a souvenir programme seller in the Biograf Theatret, turned out to have a steady hand cranking the camera and, thus, he became the cameraman. The story of the first shoot is a fine example of the entrepreneurial and pioneering attitude towards filmmaking in the early years; everything more or less had to be invented or made up from scratch. On average, from 1906 to 1909, the company made sixty fiction films every year, and Viggo Larsen directed nearly all of them in a great variety of genres. Of his part in the production Larsen later said: 'The best thing about the job was that in my quadruple capacity of scriptwriter, dramaturg, director and actor I was sovereign. My instructions were: make it fast, make it cheap, and never more than 165 meters' (Hending 1958: 644).

Officially Nordisk Film was established on 6 November 1906, and within the same month Olsen established the company's first sales office in Berlin, followed by offices in London, New York and Vienna. From the very beginning Nordisk Film was conceived as an international company. The company's copying laboratory, where the film stock was exposed, edited and copied, was situated in the free trade zone in the harbour of Copenhagen in order to avoid tax on the imported film stock as well as on the exported films.

In 1906, a majority of the company's films went to the export market; only 6.9 per cent of the films stayed in the domestic market; this percentage dropped to 4.5 per cent in the following year. Europe and the United States constituted the main markets. Not a lot of information about the economy of Nordisk Film in the early years has survived, but sources indicate that, in 1906, the takings were less than 200,000 kroner, and three years later they had risen to roughly 1.3 million kroner (Thorsen 2017a: 30–31). It seems as though producing film was a very lucrative business for Olsen.

Around 1908 the European film industry experienced a severe crisis. In the United States, the Motion Picture Patent Company formed a monopoly excluding most of the European film companies, and at the same time a second-hand market for film emerged. Instead of buying new film from the producers, cinema owners began to trade among themselves the films they had already shown. Even though the major European film producers held meetings to solve the situation, they were not able to find common ground. The management of Nordisk Film was in serious doubt about how to cope with this crisis.

Multiple-Reel Films

In 1910, the Aarhus-based company Fotorama released *Den hvide Slavehandel* (*The White Slave Trade*, Alfred Cohn, 1910). What was novel about the film was its length: 706 metres, or approximately thirty-five minutes. It became a great success in the Copenhagen cinemas, and Olsen sent his director August Blom to see the film and to note down every scene, so that less than four months later Nordisk Film could release their version of *The White Slave Trade*. Due to uneven copyright laws at the time Nordisk Film got away with the plagiarism.

Together with films like *Afgrunden* (*The Abyss*, Urban Gad, 1910), *The White Slave Trade* had shown a path out of the crisis in the international film industry: longer films, which could fill out an entire programme in the cinema. Nordisk Film was the first film company to re-organise its production to suit longer films. In 1910 only one long film was produced, but the following year the company made thirty-four; this was the same year that the dominant French companies Pathé Frères and Gaumont began their production of multiple-reel films.

The transition to long feature films was not entirely smooth. In September 1910, the German trade journal *Der Kinematograph* reported of the new Danish films that were playing to packed houses in Denmark: 'All these Danish films share the fault of being too long, 700–1000 metres' (Anonymous 1910). Two years later the magazine had changed its opinion:

> The Danish film art then brought the great atmospheric and lively drama like those we read in novels; the artistic films that win our hearts through calm pictures and tell a simple story which almost imperceptibly rises in suspense – things we had not thought films capable of. That is how *Afgrunden* works in Germany, and this is where Danish films are best received and best understood (Anonymous 1912).

In his 1914 book about the American film industry, Robert Grau states: 'It was the Great Northern Company [Nordisk Film] that first introduced the multiple-reel subjects in this country, and from this beginning sprang the feature of today with its still-growing possibilities for the future' (Grau 1914: 76). Similar testimonies about Nordisk Film's central role in the international film industry's transition to multi-reel film can be found from several countries (Thorsen 2017a: 95–96). Longer films meant that the entire culture of going to the movies changed. Unlike the early days of continuous screenings that allowed audiences to enter and leave the darkness of the cinema as they pleased, cinemas built for the purpose of showing film were erected. In the centre of Copenhagen, the cinema Palads Teatret was established in 1912 in the former central train station, with 2,500 seats and a live orchestra. Going to the cinema was now reminiscent of the theatre. In a few years film had gone from being an attraction at travelling fairs to becoming an established entertainment offer. As Gunnar Sandfeld states about this development: 'Now you could go to the movies and still be genteel' (Sandfeld 1966: 48). This can be seen as a general embourgeoisement of cinema, and a part of this was that film 'borrowed' from already established art forms like theatre and literature. In the early 1910s Nordisk Film initiated the short wave of 'Autoren'-films, films based on works by famous authors or collaborations with authors on the scripts. The most famous example is the prestigious 113-minute-long disaster movie *Atlantis* (August Blom, 1913), based on German Nobel laureate Gerhardt Hauptmann's novel by the same name.

With the advent of longer films, new distribution systems were introduced in Britain and Germany. In Britain, the first film to be distributed through the new exclusive system was Nordisk Film's *Den hvide Slavehandels sidste Offer* (*In the Hands of Imposters*, August Blom, 1911) (Low 1949: 46). The exclusive system, or 'Monopolfilm', as it was called in Germany, was a forerunner of the distribution system as we know it today. A distributor or cinema owner had exclusive (or monopoly) rights to a film in a certain area for a specified period of time, instead of having the same film competing against itself by being shown in several cinemas in the same town or area.

The competitive advantage that Nordisk Film gained from being a first mover in producing multiple-reel film led to some very advantageous distribution contracts. Distributors covering one or several countries agreed to buy a set number of films from the company each week in the years to come. In order to obtain the rights to the attractive long films the distributor agreed to buy a bulk of not yet produced films, including short comedies and non-fiction. This is reminiscent of what the American film industry would later call 'block booking' and 'blind selling'. Nordisk Film was hereby guaranteed to be able to sell its films years in advance; now it was just a matter of organising the actual film production to fulfil the contracts.

'Copenhagen Hollywood'

The transition to longer films meant a tremendous change for the company, and Nordisk Film was re-organised into a departmentalised mode of production, anticipating the mode adopted by Hollywood to great success in the late 1910s. Janet Staiger calls the classical Hollywood organisation of production the 'central producer mode' in which 'the modern manager of a well-organized mass production system was now necessary to produce the quality multiple-reel film' (Bordwell et al. 1985: 134). The organisation of film production was divided among various departments, each with their own task in the production, while the central producer managed and distributed the undertaking. Olsen was the central producer, but to oversee the many different aspects of the production he engaged managers. Whereas the large French film companies at the time decentralised their production, and as the production of multiple-reel films gained ground later in the United States than in Europe, Nordisk Film's centralised and industrialised production mode was unique for its time.

Re-organising production to make long films took larger investments and a smaller guarantee of recouping the investments. Olsen had been the sole owner of the company, but in 1911 Nordisk Film became a limited company, primarily with investors from *Fotorama*, and in 1912 the capital was doubled. This time it was two Copenhagen-based banks that were willing to risk investments in the new entertainment offer. Among other things, the capital was used to undertake an expansion of the company's studio lot in Valby and the construction of additional stages, finally reaching five in 1915.

With the films already sold, Nordisk Film could carefully plan the annual production, and in the spring of 1911 an actual script department was established. The department grew and consisted of five or six writers, who each specialised in different fields: comedies, crime films, adaptations and so on. The content of the film was controlled closely by the management, with a set of 'Guidelines for Scriptwriters' outlining what kind of films Nordisk Film would favour, as well as which elements and themes to avoid. 'The action has to take place in the present day and play out among the upper classes. Dramas that take place among people of humble means and farmers will not be accepted', read one instruction in the guidelines. National traits were downplayed because the films should cater to an international audience. One of Nordisk Film's characteristics was the production of 'count films', which took place among the upper classes. Another instruction in the guidelines told the writers: 'Nor is it allowed to write anything derogatory or unfavourable about royalty, persons of authority, priests or military officers. Nihilism, anarchism and suchlike may not be introduced' (Thorsen 2017a: 106). The emphasis on avoiding political subjects and offence to authorities in the films was due to the censorship rules on the export markets. Nordisk Film kept a close eye on the varied and ever-changing censorship rules at home and in different international markets, and even began to customise the films for different markets. The making of alternative endings, also known as 'Russian endings', is very visible evidence of this practice. Russian audiences preferred sad or tragic endings, and Nordisk Film was able to deliver alternative endings for the Russian market, even if the film was originally conceived with a happy ending. The practice spread, and the company also made happy endings for films with unhappy endings if they were wanted by the distributor (see Thorsen 2016b for a discussion of the relationship between censorship and self-regulation in the domestic and international markets).

Because of the necessity of strong sunlight, the actual film shooting season lasted from early spring to late autumn, and just as Nordisk Film employed a small ensemble of screenwriters, the company had a stock group of directors, cameramen, actors, craftsmen and so on hired for the season. Approximately 200 persons performed their daily work on the lot. The permanent directors specialised in making certain genres, and often worked in teams with the same cameraman and actors. In this way the efficiency of the actual shooting was enhanced, but it also secured a consistent standard across the films. Films from the company were recognised for their craftsmanship, and testimonies from audiences indicate that they were aware that a film was produced by the Danish company and considered of high quality. Another important part of the stock company were the film stars (see Allen, Chapter 2 in this volume). In order to increase the probability of recouping the investments in the more expensive longer films, it was important to brand them, and stars became essential to maintaining sales (Bakker 2008: 278). An often-quoted 1911 letter from Nordisk Film to the London office illustrates this shift from keeping the actors anonymous to using them as part of the marketing of the films:

> Add to [sic] the footnote on your letter we beg to say that we principally decline to state the names of our players. The name of the Gentleman in question is W. Psilander, but this information is only to [sic] your use and must not be given to someone other (Thorsen 2017b).

From being kept anonymous at first, Valdemar Psilander rose to be Nordisk Film's biggest and best-paid star. His name was used extensively in the marketing. Postcards of him were sent from Copenhagen to Nordisk Film's branches and agents by the tens of thousands, and he was promoted as 'the darling of the audiences' and 'a sure box-office success in difficult times' (Thorsen 2017a: 123).

The departmentalised mode of production led to a high degree of bureaucratisation. Nordisk Film's lot in Valby was called 'the film factory', and Olsen referred to the films as the 'company's film-fabricata, or consumer film-goods' (Thorsen 2017a: 75, 144). Like the clear directions about the content of the films, Nordisk Film's rules and directions propagated elaborate guides for fines if an employee was late for work and rules on how to shoot the film most efficiently. For instance, only 100 metres of film at a time were handed out to a director. If the director did not turn in anything useful on those one-hundred metres, he had to prepare a report about his failure before he was given the next hundred metres. The efficient production peaked in 1915, with a total of 174 films, of which ninety-six were long films, corresponding to about two feature films per week.

The 1910s indeed were a 'golden age' of Danish cinema. Films from the company were seen around most of the world, the largest export markets being Germany, Russia and South America. When Nordisk Film held its first general meeting in 1912, Olsen was honoured with shares worth 200,000 kroner, and the board decided to pay a further bonus of 1,000 kroner for each ordinary share, which amounts to a dividend of 100 per cent per share. The following year, a dividend of 60 per cent per share was paid and in 1914 a dividend of 33 per cent per share. Together with bonuses to trusted employees, a total of 2,803,811.10 kroner was paid from 1912 to 1914 all in all, which would equal around 171 million kroner (£20,000,000) in 2019. In 1913 Olsen claimed that Nordisk Film was the world's second-largest film company, only surpassed by the French Pathé Frères. Although it is difficult to estimate the size of the individual film companies at the time, Nordisk Film now belonged to the big players on the world market. In the wake of Nordisk Film's success, twenty-two other Danish film companies emerged between 1911 and 1914 (Thorsen 2017a: 146–48).

The End of a 'Golden Age'

On the surface the outbreak of the First World War could be seen as an obstacle to Nordisk Film, with closed borders limiting the export of film. On the contrary, this brought new possibilities for the company. Being from a neutral country, Nordisk Film could uphold its distribution to both sides of the belligerent nations, and the strong and efficient production mode was the basis for the expansion policy that Nordisk Film followed during the First World War. With an increase in the company's share capital, Nordisk Film began buying up film and distribution companies as well as cinemas mainly in Germany, Central Europe and Russia. The widely branching business network was seen as a threat in Germany, because cinema could play an important role in propaganda, and the foreign company Nordisk Film now controlled a large part of the German film industry. In early 1918, Nordisk Film's business network was taken over by the German State and became the backbone of the newly established Universum Film Aktiengesellschaft (Ufa). By the end of the war, Nordisk Film had lost most of its foreign investments, and the lucrative contracts according to which the films were pre-sold had expired; moreover, the company had gained a dubious reputation among the winning allies. With Olsen at the helm, Nordisk Film had plans to regain its former international position, this time as a film trading company. But failed investments, especially in American films, and a major economic loss due to the devaluation of the German mark brought the company to its knees, and in 1923 the share capital was reduced from nine to three million kroner. A new management and board of directors with strong connections to the Copenhagen stock exchange took charge in 1924, and despite efforts to get the company back on track, Nordisk Film went into liquidation in 1928, only to be re-established the following year.

Conclusion

The 1910s were golden years in Danish film history. Rarely has Danish cinema taken an important part in shaping film history, but by being the first of the European film companies to re-organise its production to multiple-reel films, Nordisk Film did so in the early 1910s. The longer films led to the feature film as we know it today and came to set a standard that influenced production and distribution as well as the exhibition of film and, just as importantly, the introduction of film stars (see also Allen, Chapter 2 in this volume).

Although Nordisk Film came to play an important role in the shaping of international film history, the golden age has been largely forgotten outside the closed circles of film scholars. As mentioned in the Introduction to this volume, only one silent film was included in the 2006 national film canon, probably because the early films are challenging to watch today. But another reason for the films' absence in the collective memory is their downplaying of the national. Nordisk Film produced films for the foreign markets, as the company customised the films to please the majority of the international audiences, especially after 1910. Yet, a trace of Nordisk Film's former international glory is still present: the polar bear on top of the globe still greets you with a roar when one watches a film from the company.

Figure 1.1   An early Nordisk Films Kompagni logo put Copenhagen at the centre of the world, and the polar bear on top of it. Image: public domain.

2. ASTA & CO.: THE POLITICS OF EARLY DANISH FILM STARDOM

Julie K. Allen

While Nordisk Films Kompagni was undeniably crucial to Denmark's film industry in the 1910s, early Danish film owed much of its global success to the actors who brought the films themselves to life and who were capable of bridging Danish and international cinema markets. In the era before the film industry became heavily director-centric, four of the most successful and prolific Danish film stars – Asta Nielsen (1881–1972), Olaf Fønss (1882–1949), Clara Wieth Pontoppidan (1883–1975) and Valdemar Psilander (1884–1917) – used their artistic gifts and their ability to negotiate the competing, sometimes conflicting demands of the early film industry to attain international stardom. Although Asta Nielsen's name is the most widely recognised today, all four of these actors, who knew each other well and worked together often, were among the most famous and beloved screen personalities of their time, both at home and as far afield as Australia, Brazil and Russia. Between them, they made more than 300 films in Denmark, Sweden and Germany, reaching audiences around the globe and earning Danish film international prestige. The stories of these four Danish stars, as told in their own memoirs and contemporaneous biographies, offer insights into the productive tensions that underpinned stardom in the early Danish film industry.[1]

BETWEEN STAGE AND SCREEN

All four benefitted from being in the right place at the right time, with the skills necessary to take advantage of the opportunities that Denmark's early prominence in the film industry offered and to capitalise on the transition to multi-reel feature films in the early 1910s (see Chapter 1 in this volume). Born in Denmark in successive years in the early 1880s – Nielsen was the oldest, born in 1881, and Psilander the youngest, born in 1884 – they all went into theatre at a young age and were in their mid-twenties when the Danish film industry took off. Clara Wieth (then Rasmussen, later Pontoppidan) had the earliest start in the Danish Royal Theatre's ballet school in 1890, at the age of seven. When she transferred to the Royal Theatre's drama school, she met Asta Nielsen, whose mentor, actor Peter Jerndorff, secured her a place at the school. Both Nielsen and Wieth came from fatherless working-class homes; the theatre offered them a way out of the poverty that their mothers endured. Wieth debuted at the Royal Theatre in 1901, Nielsen at the Dagmar Theatre in 1902. Olaf Fønss and Valdemar Psilander came from more middle-class, two-parent homes and were intended to go into the church or business, but instead chose to try their luck in the theatre. Fønss ran away to Copenhagen at age seventeen, where he began working alongside Nielsen at the Dagmar Theatre in 1903, while Psilander had his start in regional theatre at age sixteen, working his way through the provincial theatre circuit until making his official debut, at eighteen, at the Odense Theatre in 1902. A lack of professional satisfaction and financial compensation in live theatre led each of them to make the leap to the new medium of film – Nielsen, Wieth and Psilander in 1910, Fønss in 1912.

At the time, film was regarded as a poor substitute for live theatre, but it was a rapidly growing and increasingly profitable industry in Denmark, thanks largely to Nordisk Films Kompagni, which Ole Olsen had founded in 1906 (see Chapter 1 in this volume). Filming conditions were initially very primitive; legend has it that Olsen began making films with a Pathé projector in a rented garden plot on Mosedalvej with backdrops painted on a fence, while for five kroner a day Robert Storm-Petersen wrote the screenplays, painted the decorations and starred in the films, each of which had a maximum budget of 100 kroner. Nordisk rapidly professionalised, however, establishing a printing laboratory early on and training the former souvenir programme seller Axel Graatkjær as cameraman (Thorsen 2017a: 44). From 1906 to 1909, Viggo Larsen worked as director, scriptwriter, dramaturg and actor, supported by a motley crew of amateurs 'who needed to earn a few kroner a day' (Fønss 1930b: 18). Larsen himself later recalled: 'Of course, we were all bloody amateurs as well as technically illiterate' (Thorsen 2017a: 44). As Olsen's films became profitable, in the wake of *Løvejagten* (*Lion Hunting*, 1907), he hired professional actors, including Carl Alstrup, Oscar Stribolt, Laurits Olsen and Axel Breidahl. In 1910, Olsen hired Folketeater actor August Blom, who soon became one of Nordisk Film's most prolific and highly respected directors, alongside A. W. Sandberg, Hjalmar Davidsen and Lau Lauritzen Sr. Blom directed Nielsen, Fønss, Wieth and Psilander in at least one film each and, in the cases of the latter three, many more.

Growing domestic and international demand made Danish film lucrative and therefore competitive, particularly in terms of recruiting actors. By 1912, Olsen bragged that Nordisk alone had a larger budget than all of the private theatres in Copenhagen put together (Hending 1942: 43). Given the high social status but relatively low wages of the theatre versus the financial attractiveness and low social capital of the film industry, the decision to make films was a consequential one for Danish actors in this period, even after high-profile actors and directors like Martinius Nielsen led the way. Wieth recalls: 'People regarded film as a definitive step down, at least a few steps below the theatre, and there was a price to pay for that' (Pontoppidan 1968: 228). However, it paid well. Nordisk was the oldest and largest production company in Denmark, and it had no qualms about appropriating ideas and actors from live theatre or its competitors in the Danish film industry, including Skandinavisk-Russisk-Handelshus (Scandinavian-Russian Trading Company), Regia Kunstfilms and Fotorama.

The immediate benefit to the film industry of this competitive situation is evident in the fact that Wieth, Psilander and Nielsen all made their first feature films in 1910, although none of them started out with Nordisk. Wieth and Psilander were both motivated by momentary unemployment to make a few short films, in a shabby attic, with Regia Kunstfilms. Wieth went first, making her first film, the ten-minute short *Elskovsleg* (*Game of Love*, Unknown, 1910), which premiered in May 1910. She then co-starred with Psilander in *Dorian Grays Portræt* (*The Portrait of Dorian Gray*, 1910), but they continued to work in the theatre, notably in a production of *A Midsummer Night's Dream* at the open-air theatre in Dyrehaven gardens. Arnold Hending insists that Psilander's interest in film was purely economic at this point, explaining: 'By the time the last scene had been filmed, it had not increased Psilander's desire to occupy himself more frequently with the silent art. The whole thing had been a little "financial operation", nothing else – and the actor completely "forgot" the task he had, for his part, completed so masterfully in the only 475-metre-long film' (Hending 1942: 45).

Clara Wieth Pontoppidan and Valdemar Psilander

Their performances in this otherwise mediocre film brought Wieth and Psilander to the attention of Olsen and Nordisk, who promptly engaged both of them for leading roles in bigger-budget productions. Olsen offered Wieth the lead in *Den hvide Slavehandels sidste Offer* (*In the Hands of Imposters*, literally 'The White Slave Trade's Last Victim', 1911), the sequel to Nordisk's first blockbuster erotic melodrama, *Den hvide Slavehandel* (*The White Slave Trade*, 1910), which it had copied from the Aarhus-based company Fotorama's successful film released earlier that year. While an extra earned five kroner a day, Wieth's salary was 300 kroner. In her memoirs, Wieth recalls that Olsen earned at least 100,000 kroner on the film (Pontoppidan 1968: 213). One day not long after its premiere, he visited her at home and gave her a 100 kroner note, with the remark, 'Here's a gratuity for you, Fru [Mrs.] Wieth' (214). Wieth reflected later that 'the most important part of it for me personally was that, from then on, a film with Clara Wieth could sell, which at that time meant in the whole world, even before it had been made. Yes, I had found a sweet spot for myself out there in Valby' (Pontoppidan 1968: 214). Wieth then starred opposite Psilander in *Ved Fængslets Port* (*Temptations of a Great City*, 1911), which proved to be Nordisk's greatest success since *Løvejagten* in 1907, selling 246 prints, more than twice as many as *The White Slave Trade*. Wieth went on to co-star with Psilander in many more films, with her first husband, Carlo Wieth, in a few films, and to make several important films with notable directors, such as Benjamin Christensen's *Häxan* (*Häxan: Witchcraft Through the Ages*, Sweden, 1922), as well as two with Carl Theodor Dreyer: *Blade fra Satans Bog* (*Leaves from Satan's Book*, 1920) and *Der var engang* (*Once upon a Time*, 1922). Yet, although Wieth made more than fifty films during the silent era, she also continued performing regularly on stage and identified primarily as a theatre actor. Many years later, she devoted just one chapter of her multi-volume memoirs to her film career, focusing the bulk of her attention on her work on the live stage.

Figure 2.1   Valdemar Psilander starring opposite Clara Wieth in the Nordisk hit *Ved Fængslets Port* (*Temptations of a Great City*, August Blom, 1911). Framegrab.

Competing accounts of how Psilander, who came to be known as 'Verdens Valdemar' (the world's Valdemar) for his global fame, began to work for Nordisk showcase the tension between the public acclaim for live theatre and the tangible rewards of film. Wieth and Hending give conflicting accounts of how Psilander joined Nordisk, offering valuable insight into the social capital of theatre and how that could be parlayed into greater credibility for film. Wieth recalls seeing an unshaven, unkempt, unemployed Psilander begging Blom for a film role (Pontoppidan 1968: 227), while Hending, although he agrees that Psilander could not afford to shave, insists that Psilander 'did not for a single moment let his glance stray to the side where film offered the temptation of easily-won mammon' until Olsen 'sent one of his trusted directors to offer him [Psilander] a role in an art film. Psilander listened without immediate interest to the film man sitting in his parlour, and decided, when the conference had gone on for long enough, that he could not imagine wasting his time on an art form that didn't attract him in the least' (Hending 1942: 45). Wieth and Hending agree that Psilander, who had earned twenty-five kroner a day for *The Portrait of Dorian Gray*, demanded the unheard-of sum of fifty kroner per day, and received it. In Wieth's view, however, Psilander's boldness was born out of his desperation, while in Hending's case, it was disdain, for since 'film had come calling at his door, *ergo* film had to pay what it cost' (Hending 1942: 45). Psilander quickly became Nordisk's highest-paid actor, earning as much as 10,000 kroner per film. He made more than eighty films with Nordisk in less than a decade and had just founded his own production company, Dansk Film, when he suddenly died in February 1919, at the age of thirty-five.

Asta Nielsen

For her part, Nielsen's entry into film was also a side effect of the competition between stage and screen, which she hoped to leverage in order to receive better theatre roles. She attributed her motivation for accepting Urban Gad's invitation to star in his first film in June 1910 to her artistic frustration with a lack of opportunities on stage. She had struggled to find a niche in Danish theatre, a problem that Fønss attributed to 'her foreign appearance and her bold manner' (Fønss 1930a: 117); she was given few substantial roles. Frustrated with collecting a paltry monthly salary of fifty kroner for doing nothing, she and Gad decided to make *Afgrunden* (*The Abyss*, 1910), in order 'to show the theatre directors in Copenhagen what we two were capable of' (Nielsen 1966: 102), little dreaming of the way in which this film would change their lives and the cinema itself. Unable to interest Nordisk in their project, they secured 8,000 kroner from Hjalmar Davidsen, a friend of Gad's who owned the Kosmorama movie theatre on Østergade in Copenhagen. Nielsen's salary for the film was 200 kroner. Olsen also turned down a chance to acquire international distribution rights

Figure 2.2 Asta Nielsen as Magda with her lover Rudolph (Poul Reumert) in the iconic Gaucho dance scene in *Afgrunden* (*The Abyss*, Urban Gad, 1910). Framegrab.

to the film for 5,000 kroner; when the German distributor Ludwig Gottschalk earned 800,000 German marks on the film, Olsen defended his decision to his London branch with the following explanation: 'We don't find her [Nielsen] particularly good, but that is a matter of taste, after all' (Engberg 1977: 260).

Instead of better theatre roles, Nielsen and Gad's successful film debut led to offers from both the German company Deutsche Bioscop to make two films in Berlin and Nordisk's rival Fotorama to make the film *Den sorte Drøm* (*The Black Dream / The Circus Girl*, 1911) opposite Psilander. Nielsen's decision to pursue these opportunities grew out of both her positive initial experience with film and the ongoing lack of opportunities for her on the Danish stage. In her memoirs, she relates that, while pursuing contract negotiations with the Royal Theatre, she responded to director Dr Karl Mantzius's condescending comment that, 'if you prefer film to the Royal Theatre, there is nothing to be done about it' with the declaration: 'I prefer roles in film to none in the theatre, so the doctor is correct that there is nothing to be done about it' (Nielsen 1966: 115). Convinced that 'an artist ought not to divide her work between film and theatre, because one of them will always suffer', Nielsen decided 'to invest all of my strength in the artistic opportunities that

I had felt, during the making of my first film, lay dormant in it' (Nielsen 1966: 115, 111). Whether or not this rationale was retroactively adopted, Nielsen's decision resulted in some of early Danish and German film's most memorable productions. Film historian Marguerite Engberg argues, for example, that *The Black Dream*, of all of Nielsen's surviving films, is the one in which 'her unique beauty comes into its own', not least because this film offers the first close-up of Nielsen's face (Engberg 1977: 230). When Nordisk finally offered Nielsen a role, she accepted, starring opposite Psilander once more in the film *Balletdanserinden* (*The Ballet Dancer*, 1911), for a salary of 5,000 kroner (Malmkjær 2000: 89). But by the time the film was done, she had accepted an offer of 80,000 German marks a year to film in Berlin with Deutsche Bioscop. Nielsen went on to make all but four of her seventy-four films in Germany.

Olaf Fønss

Fønss was the last of the quartet to begin making films, in 1912, which he did with the aim of trying to elevate film to the status of theatre. He had had a very successful career at the Dagmar and Casino Theatres, playing ten to twelve leading roles every season from 1903 to 1912, appearing at least 150 nights a year on stage, for an annual salary of 10,000 to 12,000 kroner, but he craved more variety and more regular employment (Hending 1943: 30, 32). Biographer Carl Gandrup insisted in 1919, perhaps as a dig at Psilander's fashion consciousness, that Fønss 'did not enter the service of film in order to walk around with a monocle in his eye like a well-dressed advertisement for a menswear boutique', but in order to participate in 'leading film into the channel of *art*' (Gandrup 1919: 45–46). Fønss initially turned down Psilander's offer of a home at Nordisk, choosing instead to make his debut with Scandinavian-Russian Trading House, where he made two films before changing his mind and joining the team at Valby.

By the time Fønss made the leap to cinema, the field of Danish stars was getting rather crowded; actors had to claim their niche, which was initially, in his case, the depiction of hyper-masculine men. When his second film *Bryggerens datter* (*The Brewer's Daughter*, 1912), written by Carl Th. Dreyer and directed by Rasmus Ottesen, premiered in August 1912, it had to compete with Psilander's *Dødsspring fra Cirkuskuplen* (*The Great Circus Catastrophe*, 1912) at the Panoptikon Theatre, Asta Nielsen's *Der fremde Vogel* (*The Strange Bird*, 1911) at the Phoenix and Clara Wieth's *Et Hjerte af Guld* (*Faithful unto Death*, 1912) at Kosmorama (Hending 1943: 50). Critics praised Fønss for his depiction of a 'poised and manly' labourer, a theme that recurred a few months later in reviews of his 'beautiful and manly' performance in the film *Konfetti* (1912). After eight months with Scandinavian-Russian Trading Company, Fønss accepted an offer to play a bear-tamer in the independent film

Zigeunerorkesteret (*The Gypsy Orchestra*, 1912). Hending reports that Fønss took out a hefty accidental death and dismemberment insurance policy before filming began (1943: 56), which proved to be foresightful, given that he had to interpose himself between an angry bear and a venomous snake in one scene, and wrestle the bear to death in the ocean in another.

Fønss chafed against this typecasting, however, and moved to Nordisk in search of more artistic freedom. He appeared in eleven Nordisk films per year in 1913 and 1914, earning particular acclaim for his depiction of Dr Friedrich von Kammacher in an adaptation of German author Gerhard Hauptmann's novel *Atlantis* about a shipwreck, one of the most expensive films ever made at the time. Moving to Germany in October 1915, he persuaded Deutsche Bioscop, despite their concerns that he was too attractive for the part, to give him the title role as a synthetic human in the six-part series *Homunculus*, which became the most popular serial in Germany during the First World War. On Psilander's death, Fønss became artistic director of the former's newly founded company, which he renamed Dansk Astra Film in 1918. Although he made several more films in Germany and Denmark in the 1920s, Fønss concentrated on renewing his theatrical career, became a member of the Danish Actors' Guild

Figure 2.3   Olaf Fønss (right), playing Dr Kammacher in the big-budget *Atlantis* (August Blom, 1913), helps to man the lifeboat. Framegrab.

in 1927 and served as its foreman from 1933 to 1947. Keeping his hand in the film industry, however, he worked as a national film censor from 1932 to 1946. In 1946, he was granted a five-year cinema license for the World Cinema Theatre on Jernbanegade, joining the ranks of many other Danish film industry alumni – including Urban Gad and Benjamin Christensen, but not Asta Nielsen, despite her repeated applications – for whom lucrative state cinema licenses served as recognition for their contributions to Danish film.

Danish Stars at Home and Abroad

While each of these actors had their start in Danish film, their stardom rested on the international success of their films. All of them were besieged with fan mail from around the world, confirming both their individual appeal to fans and their representative role for Denmark's visibility in the world at large. In her memoirs, Wieth reflects that, although she remained physically in Denmark, her films allowed her to connect with people in many countries:

> Not just I, but every actor born in a small country, must dream of making a splash at some point in life. For me, it happened when film conquered the world. That is to say, I both went abroad and stayed home! . . . You could travel in your thoughts and still know that all over the world, Nordisk Film's polar bear was nodding in a friendly way to all of the foreign inhabitants, bringing greetings from our little land, while you yourself stood laughing or suffering in front of them on the screen, were totally absorbed in the role and yet present among them so clearly and intimately that it inspired them to send greetings back. Oh, what I didn't get in the way of exciting letters and billet-doux with praise for my blondness and Nordic expressiveness (Pontoppidan 1968: 210).

Aside from a few films made in Sweden with Victor Sjöström and Mauritz Stiller, Wieth spent her entire career in Denmark, but the global reach of her films brought her – and the prototypical Nordicness she embodied – out into the world. In contrast, Psilander's biographer Helge Wamberg emphasises the foreign exoticism that Psilander inherited from his Greek ancestors, explaining that he did not conquer the world on the strength of his 'Danish characteristics', but with the help of his exotic heritage and Mediterranean charm. Wamberg concludes that '[h]is temperament did not belong to our climes. There was something foreign, dominating in his being, which is not Danish. [. . .] He was born to impress and to charm. And it was with the help of these valuable treasures that he became the most talked-about film star in the world, the irresistible and unconquerable' (Wamberg 1917: 6). Both the stereotypical and the exotic served to promote Danish film abroad.

The extent to which global fame enhanced or inhibited these actors' status in Denmark seems to have been contingent on the success of Denmark's national film industry. Nielsen's arrival in Germany coincided with both the peak years of Danish cinema and the beginning of Germany's exclusive film distribution system, which neccessitated stars with enough prestige to sell entire series of films sight-unseen, often before they had even been made. As one of the first representatives of this star system, Nielsen's films, her image and her name were exported to the entire world, associated with all manner of branded wares. In the 1910s, when her films were shown to great acclaim across Denmark, many Danish critics were delighted about the prominence of a Danish actress in the global cinema market. Danish journalist Adolf Langsted, who wrote the first biography of Asta Nielsen in 1916, marvelled: 'I sat in Paris and saw film's star rise: with wonder I discovered that it was – *Danish*. The first film actress to attain world renown was *Asta Nielsen*' (Langsted 1918: 11). Yet, Danish coverage of Nielsen often employed a rather disdainful tone, particularly after Danish film lost its global prominence in the 1920s. Psilander's selection as most popular cinema actor in Ukraine and Siberia in 1913 and in Brazil in 1915 suggests that his world renown was quite as robust as Nielsen's, but since he remained firmly grounded in Danish studios, it aroused no national resentment.

Nielsen's stardom was international from the beginning, which may explain why other Danish critics and fans remained conflicted about how valid her stardom could be, given that she had not earned it in Denmark. Comparisons between Nielsen and the ugly duckling of Hans Christian Andersen's fairytale – such as Fønss's assessment that, with her move to Germany, 'the ugly duckling had become the proud swan, which raised itself up from the familiar duck pond and flew in the golden sun out into the wide world' (Fønss 1930a: 118) – seem to suggest that Denmark had been too confining for Nielsen, too narrow-minded to recognise her talent. In response, some Danes refused to be impressed by a woman who had failed to conquer the Danish stage or earn Ole Olsen's approbation; as an article in the *Maanedsmagasin* on 24 November 1912 noted: 'It came as somewhat of a surprise for Danish audiences a few years ago to suddenly learn that Miss Asta Nielsen was an actress who mattered because she enjoyed worldwide fame' ('Asta Nielsen' 1912). When the Danish film industry went into decline in the 1920s, this studied indifference became outright hostility towards Nielsen and her increasingly artistically innovative films; Danish censors blocked most of Nielsen's later German-made films from even being screened in Denmark. Long after Nielsen's return to Denmark in 1937, where she lived until her death in 1972, many of her Danish contemporaries regarded her with suspicion because of the years she had spent living and working in Germany. Biographer Ib Monty concludes: 'It was in Germany that she became world famous, and we in Denmark have never forgiven her for it' (Monty 1998: 7). Nielsen regarded the repeated rejection of her applications for a cinema license as evidence of this disapproval, although the fact that she had to give up her Danish citizenship when she married first a Swede and then a Russian offers a more bureaucratic explanation.

Gender expectations might also have played a role in Danish resentment of Nielsen's international success, since Fønss experienced none of the same disapproval for his many successful forays into German film, from the *Homunculus* films he made in 1915–16 to his starring role in Joe May's two-part film *Das indische Grabmal* (*The Indian Tomb*, 1921). After the German premiere of *Atlantis* in December 1913, Fønss was fêted at cinema houses around Germany, touring for more than a month from one adoring crowd to the next. A Viennese noblewoman even wrote to request his 'favour' for a week in order to conceive a child with the hero of *Atlantis*, promising that, if the child were a girl, she would name it Atlanta (Hending 1943: 87). Unlike Nielsen, however, Fønss seemed able to resist believing in his own myth. Biographer Carl Gandrup described Fønss as the 'most convincing example of an artist who has been able to preserve his talents fresh and intact from a popularity that knows nothing of geographic borders, but which has the entire world as its homeland' (Gandrup 1919: 33). What protected Fønss, in Hending's eyes, was his loyalty to Denmark: 'The lovely thing about a man like Olaf Fønss, he who became one of the most international Danish artists, is that he never forgot his hometown, where his first dreams came to life, or Copenhagen, where one dream or another most certainly went awry, but others, however, came true' (Hending 1943: 10–11).

Conclusion

As the intersecting but distinctly different career trajectories of Asta Nielsen, Olaf Fønss, Clara Wieth and Valdemar Psilander reveal, the pursuit of stardom in early Danish cinema was a high-stakes endeavour. Made possible by the unique historical conditions present at the birth of a new art form and commercial commodity, including Ole Olsen's audacity and Hollywood's belated rise, it required not only talent, but also ambition, resilience, stamina and courage. Film paid better than live theatre and allowed actors to reach a global audience, but the wealth and fame it promised could be both fickle and fleeting, and the price of success, as Psilander and Nielsen in particular learned, could be astronomical. Yet, in large part it is thanks to actors such as these four, who took the risk of dedicating themselves to an untried, disrespected medium and dared to defy conventional wisdom about gender, nationalism and aesthetics, that the golden age of Danish silent film left a lasting legacy for both Danish culture and global cinema.

Note

1. Some material in this chapter is presented with images and digitised films as part of the Danish Film Institute's Danish Silent Film web resource. See Allen 2019.

3. THE EUROPEAN PRINCIPLE: ART AND BORDER-CROSSINGS IN CARL THEODOR DREYER'S CAREER

Casper Tybjerg

Carl Th. Dreyer (1889–1968) is regarded by many as the greatest Danish filmmaker. His film *La Passion de Jeanne d'Arc* (1928) has appeared again and again on lists of the greatest films of all time, and his canonical stature seems secure. Several major books have been dedicated to his work; David Bordwell (1981) and Edvin Kau (1989, unfortunately not translated) both focus on Dreyer's style, while Drum and Drum (2000) provide a shorter, informative overview of his life and career. Dreyer is far better known to international cinephiles than any of his Danish contemporaries, and even the most famous modern directors such as Lars von Trier and Susanne Bier have not, in my estimation, attained the kind of unquestioned eminence in international film culture that he has long held. Since this chapter is part of a reader on Danish cinema, I will seek (through a brief outline of his career) to discuss the extent to which it makes sense to talk about Dreyer as the greatest *Danish* filmmaker, drawing on the theoretical concept of *entangled history*.

Entangled history challenges the tendency to look at a subject such as film art or the work of a film artist within the framework of a particular nation-state, insisting that international interconnections must not be ignored. It also asks historians to think about the significance of their own place within a scholarly infrastructure (such as universities or archives) that tends to be anchored in a particular national context. In the present case – a study of Dreyer by a Danish film historian in a book on Danish cinema – this is an especially apt approach.

Dreyer as International Director

Dreyer had an international career. During the silent era, he never – apart from his first two pictures – directed two films in a row in the same country. His most famous film, *La Passion de Jeanne d'Arc*, was French. While his later sound films were mostly Danish, he worked on a number of unrealised projects that would have been international in character and financed by American or British production companies. He was born in Copenhagen, but Dreyer was actually of Swedish parentage. His unmarried mother was a Swedish servant-girl; his father, possibly her employer, has never been conclusively identified. The pregnant young woman travelled to Copenhagen to give birth discreetly and gave the child up for adoption (Dreyer's biographer Maurice Drouzy uncovered the circumstances of his birth in the book *Carl Th. Dreyer né Nilsson*, 1982).

In his interviews and writings, Dreyer rarely brought up his nationality. He clearly believed that there was such a thing as national character: in a long newspaper essay from 1939 about the idea then being discussed of making a big Hans Christian Andersen biopic, Dreyer warned against letting such a film 'emerge as an international factory product', arguing instead that 'it will win greater interest the more we show our own face and the less we grovel for foreign taste' (Dreyer 1973a: 81–82). By 'we', Dreyer clearly meant 'we Danes'; 'our face' is the countenance of the Danish national character. Even here, however, Dreyer's main concern was not the nationality of filmmakers, but whether their artistic personalities were allowed to express themselves, or whether they were submerged by the impersonality of the commercial film industry and its desire to turn out a predictable, bland product.

In a 1931 interview, Dreyer identified this as the characteristic difference between filmmaking in Europe and in the United States. In Hollywood, he said, a film is not 'the work of an individual or a few individuals':

> A movie is created by the 'Organisation' through a kind of dough-kneading process [. . .] The director may give advice, but has no voice. He comes to the studio and performs his staging in strict accordance with the plan drawn up by the 'Organisation', which must be followed. Nothing is more important than this work plan. [. . .] In contrast to this organisation principle stood until the introduction of the sound film the European principle of production: the principle of individuality. Here, the director was the central driving force. [. . .] The demand was for quality above all. Making a movie took more time, but it came out better, and it had an individual character (Dreyer 1931).

Dreyer goes on to describe how famous European filmmakers after their arrival in Hollywood 'lost all character and individuality', like the Swede

Victor Sjöström, or became 'Americanised', like the German Ernst Lubitsch (Dreyer 1931).

Dreyer's hostility towards Hollywood, however, was based on artistic principles, not nationalistic ones. A decade earlier, he had lambasted the Danish cinema for similar reasons. In Denmark, so Dreyer wrote, 'films have always been manufactured' (Dreyer 1973b: 22). They were assembly-line products, made in factories. 'A doubtful odor' clung to Danish films, 'an odor so persistent that the public in our more fastidious neighboring countries still hold their noses at the sight of a poster for a Danish film' (Dreyer 1973b: 23). By contrast, Dreyer praises the Swedish cinema profusely, particularly the films of Sjöström. For Dreyer, the true source of a film's value was the director's genius and commitment to artistic excellence, and the worth of national film cultures depended on whether they helped or hindered filmmakers in their efforts to create true art.

The Concept of Entangled History

The international character of Dreyer's career makes it a promising subject for *entangled history*. Entangled history (*histoire croisée* in French) is a historiographical approach that seeks to evade what sociologists have termed 'methodological nationalism', a term introduced in the 1970s to describe approaches in which 'basic social data are always collected and evaluated in terms of large-scale entities called "nation-states"' (Smith 1983: 26; see also Chernilo 2006). Entangled history stresses interconnections; it questions whether not just nations, but all other kinds of historical phenomena and indeed historians themselves can be isolated from all those things with which they are interconnected. The approach takes as its starting point that 'there is no historical phenomenon that exists as an isolated unit and is not characterized by an encounter, an intertwinement' (Neunsinger 2010: 18). In the words of its leading champions, the French scholars Michael Werner and Bénédicte Zimmermann, *histoire croisée* is 'relational, interactive, and process-oriented' (Werner and Zimmermann 2006: 39).

Werner and Zimmermann stress the highly reflexive character of entangled history. Historians must historicise themselves; they proceed from a starting point that has its own entanglements, which affects how they can approach the object of their research: 'Basically, the construction of the object, which may be envisaged in a Weberian perspective as the adoption of one or more particular points of view on the object, is already the result of various acts of crossing' (Werner and Zimmermann 2006: 40). While this makes a lot of theoretical sense, from a more practical perspective this reflexivity may be the Achilles heel of entangled history, because its multiplying complications risk tripping up the inquiry: 'Taking into account the intertwinements in both the researcher's point of departure and in the object of investigation increases problematisation exponentially, which evidently causes problems for both practical analysis and for the presentation of the inquiry' (Neunsinger 2010: 18). The metaphor of 'entanglement' captures this: it suggests something messy, constraining, ensnaring – a dangerous liaison, as it were. We should not forget, however, that the French *croisée* is more orderly, less threatening and confusing: things braided together rather than trapping each other.

That being said, reflecting on one's own perspective is important for the historian. For me personally, being a Dane has been significant for my work on Dreyer, not just because a great many important primary sources are in Danish, but also because it helped me see more clearly that Dreyer's work – both at home and abroad – was carried out inside various European film industries, and that his achievements as a filmmaker could advantageously be seen in this context, rather than regarding him in isolation (as much Dreyer criticism has tended to do) as a lone giant brooding in austere solitude on the nature of love and the divine.

Furthermore, Danish state institutions concerned with preserving and promoting Danish cultural heritage regard Dreyer as their responsibility. After Dreyer's death, the Danish Film Institute (DFI) acquired his personal archive of scripts, letters and other papers, an invaluable resource for researchers; the DFI also maintains a substantial website dedicated to Dreyer (Danish Film Institute 2010–21). In Dreyer's lifetime (at least in the post-war era), the Danish Ministry of Foreign Affairs took a hand in supporting and promoting Dreyer as a Danish cultural figure of international stature and renown, sponsoring exhibitions, film screenings and so on. When *La Passion de Jeanne d'Arc* was revived at the Cinéma d'essai in Paris in February 1952, the Danish ambassador was the guest of honour on opening night (Tybjerg 2019a: 310–12).

My own ability to write about the Cinéma d'essai re-release was greatly facilitated by the large number of clippings from French newspapers in the Dreyer archive at the DFI, clippings that Dreyer possessed because the cultural attaché at the Danish embassy in Paris had collected and sent them to him. In potentially significant ways, my research is therefore entangled with the activities of Danish government institutions specifically charged with disseminating Danish culture, both past and present – the helpful cultural attaché in 1952, as well as the DFI preserving and allowing access to Dreyer's personal archive today. They made it practical to study the Cinéma d'essai re-release (arguably an event in the history of *French* film culture) without leaving Denmark; and this was probably what made it possible for *me* to write about it at all.

The entangled history approach has already found use among film historians. For instance, in studying the emergence of film culture in interwar Europe and examining the development of debates about film art and the film medium, Malte Hagener argues that 'we can map an entangled history of mutual influence as much as of misunderstanding and adaptation over the course of several decades, ranging across different countries and institutional regimes' (Hagener 2014: 5). In the course of these crossings-back-and-forth, both concepts and practices undergo a process of change. The dichotomy Dreyer sets up in his 1931 interview, for instance, between the assembly-line commercialism of Hollywood and the personal artistry of European films, has long been a commonplace in debates on cinema. Yet, it is worth noting that a decade earlier Dreyer took a much more approving view of American cinema, praising its realism, its mastery of editing and use of different shot scales, as well as its storytelling prowess (even if he felt that it lacked 'soul' in comparison to the Swedish films he so admired; Dreyer 1973b: 27). Nor was this admiration for American filmmaking confined to Dreyer's writings.

Dreyer's Career: Griffith and the Swedes as Models

David Bordwell has argued persuasively that Dreyer's first two films as a director, *Præsidenten* (*The President*, 1919) and *Blade af Satans Bog* (*Leaves from Satan's Book*, 1920) – both made for Nordisk Films Kompagni, the dominant Danish production company – were stylistically much more like American films than any of those made by other Danish directors at the same time (Bordwell 2010). *The President* (its title is better translated as 'The Chief Justice') is a courtroom drama of sorts, using a complex flashback structure to tell the story of powerful men who abandon the women they have impregnated, evading responsibility for the suffering they cause. Dreyer uses a large number of camera setups within individual scenes, cutting fluidly between closer and more distant views. Before receiving the opportunity to direct this film, Dreyer had worked for Nordisk for several years, as a title writer, editor and screenwriter. Three-quarters of his credited screenplays for Nordisk were adaptations, and half of those were based on non-Danish literary works, including *The President*, which was adapted from an Austrian novel (for more on Dreyer's screenwriting work, see Schröder 2010); there is no emphasis on Danishness here.

Dreyer's second feature was the epic and hugely ambitious *Leaves from Satan's Book*. Its four-part structure, showing Satan tempting mankind in four different historical epochs (Palestine in the days of Jesus, Spain during the Inquisition, France during the revolution and Finland during the 1918 civil war), has often been assumed to derive from D. W. Griffith's *Intolerance* (1916), but this is false: the original script by playwright Edgar Høyer had in fact been submitted as early as 1913, with the last part set during the Russo-Japanese War of 1904–5 (for details, see Tybjerg 1999). Dreyer did acknowledge, however, the great impact that Griffith's use of editing and close-ups had on the way in which he made this film.

The great ambitions that Dreyer had for *Leaves from Satan's Book* put him on a collision course with the management at Nordisk; even though he had been given a budget larger than that of almost any previous Scandinavian film, he wanted more, and when the management said no, Dreyer wrote a long letter condemning their tight-fisted philistinism (Thorsen and Redvall 2019).

Most of the remainder of Dreyer's silent films were made abroad. First, *Prästänkan* (*The Parson's Widow*, 1920) was a Swedish production, made on location in Norway. It is a beautifully shot comedy-drama about a seventeenth-century would-be parson and his fiancée; to take over the position, he is forced to marry his predecessor's widow while his fiancée pretends to be his sister. Shifting adeptly and movingly from comedy to tragedy, the film depicts a situation that fatally prevents love from flourishing, with the psychological acuity characteristic of the Swedish films Dreyer so admired. The film's convincing effect is deepened by Dreyer's decision to stage the film entirely in actual seventeenth-century buildings (see Sandberg 2006).

In between two films made in Germany (see below), Dreyer came back to Denmark to make *Der var engang* (*Once Upon a Time*, 1922), perhaps the most explicitly *Danish* film made during the whole of the silent period. Based on a highly nationalistic stage play by Holger Drachmann, which itself was based on a fairytale, it tells a *Taming of the Shrew*-type story of a haughty princess from Illyria who spurns the handsome Prince of Denmark but finds herself given away to a scruffy tinker instead. Fortunately, he turns out to be the prince in disguise. The only surviving print is incomplete – one-third of the film is missing – but judging from the extant material, Dreyer was largely able to rid the story of the overt sexism of Drachmann's play.

Here, Dreyer aimed at making a 'national film'. This term was widely used at the time, particularly in connection with the films regarded as emblematic of the so-called 'Golden Age' of Swedish cinema just before and after 1920 (see Florin 2010, 2012: 22–24). A movie such as Victor Sjöström's great two-part film *Ingmarssönerna* (*Sons of Ingmar*, 1919) was not just based on a celebrated Swedish literary work and shot with the beauty of the Swedish landscape as a backdrop; with its evocation of old customs and traditional costumes, it was felt by commentators to embody a particular *Swedishness* (see also Oscarson 2013). Around 1918, in imitation of the major Swedish production company, Nordisk had adopted a production policy of making high-cost, high-quality literary prestige pictures. Instead of adapting Danish material, however, Nordisk's flagship productions were adaptations of Charles Dickens. Dreyer's *Once Upon a Time* was thus the clearest attempt to make a 'national film' along Swedish lines (see Tybjerg 2001). There is of course something paradoxical about this 'national film' model being a foreign import, but it also illustrates how impossible it is to disentangle the 'national' from the 'foreign' in film history (Tybjerg 2015, 2016).

Dreyer's Career: European Art Films

Dreyer made two films in Germany, *Die Gezeichneten* (literally, 'The Stigmatised Ones' AKA *Love One Another*, 1922) and *Michael* (1924). The first is a powerful indictment of anti-Semitic prejudice; it shows the persecution of Jews in czarist Russia, culminating in a brutal and deadly pogrom. The second is set in a cosmopolitan milieu of artists and aristocrats; it describes how a famous and celebrated painter sinks into depression and dies when he is betrayed by his handsome young protégé. Both films are set in milieux that appear quite exotic from a Danish perspective but were actually based on books by Danish novelists (Aage Madelung and Herman Bang, respectively). Both writers were very successful in German translation. Dreyer also maintained a connection to Denmark in another way: in both films, he cast Danish actors in major roles (Johannes Meyer as the malevolent police spy in *Die Gezeichneten*, Benjamin Christensen as the master painter in *Michael*).

Michael, despite its large and opulent sets, is often described as a *Kammerspielfilm*, a German term for intimate film drama introduced to promote the film *Hintertreppe* (*Backstairs*, Leopold Jessner and Paul Leni, 1921) (Jacobsen et al. 1993: 54). Dreyer brought the idea of the *Kammerspielfilm* back to Denmark for his next picture, *Du skal ære din Hustru* (*Master of the House*, 1925), a serious comedy of a marriage in trouble that takes place almost entirely within the confines of a two-room flat. *Master of the House* was tremendously successful in France, and Dreyer was invited to Paris after shooting a Norwegian film, *Glomdalsbruden* (*The Bride of Glomdal*, 1926). This was a rural melodrama, a very popular genre in Norway that closely followed the conventions of the Swedish tradition. The film was beautifully shot by a Danish cinematographer, Einar Olsen.

In France, Dreyer began work on the screenplay for *La Passion de Jeanne d'Arc* in late 1926. Shooting began in the spring of 1927 and continued until the beginning of the new year, with some additional scenes being shot just weeks before the film's premiere in April 1928. A major and very expensive production, it was attacked by right-wing figures because the production was insufficiently 'French' – not just because the director was Dreyer, a Dane, but because of early rumours that the American actress Lillian Gish, star of many of D. W. Griffith's films, would play Joan of Arc (Drouzy 1988: 10).

Dreyer eventually cast Maria Falconetti, a French actress, but de-emphasised the heroic figure of Joan of Arc beloved by nationalists, the battlefield leader determined to liberate France. Dreyer's aesthetic inspirations were international and varied. The sequence of Jeanne fainting in the torture chamber, with its odd angles and rapid-fire editing, is reminiscent of the way in which French 'impressionist' filmmakers like Abel Gance and Jean Epstein used camerawork to convey states of mind. The austere sets are famously stylised in the manner of fifteenth-century book illustrations, and while it is somewhat misleading to call them 'expressionist', they arguably take from the German cinema a pictorialist understanding of set design, emphasising atmosphere over realism. And the scene of the people's uprising at the end of the film is evidently inspired by Soviet montage cinema; Dreyer spoke later of how he had 'learned something' from Eisenstein's *Battleship Potemkin* (1925) and Pudovkin's *Mother* (1926) ('Instruktørernes valg . . . ' 1963: 19). *La Passion de Jeanne d'Arc* was thus connected to and drew on the three most vibrant national movements in the art cinema of the time.

The transition to sound, however, de-internationalised cinema, forcing many filmmakers and actors with international careers back to their native countries. Dreyer stubbornly resisted this trend. With *Vampyr* (shot in 1930, released in 1932), he sought to overcome the limitations of spoken dialogue by keeping it to a minimum; he shot the film silent and had the actors mime their lines in three different languages. Unfortunately, the available post-synchronisation technology was not equal to what Dreyer wanted (Koerber 2008). The strange, dream-like film was a commercial failure and seemingly took Dreyer's career down with it (Drouzy 1993 provides biographical details). Dreyer had to move back to Denmark, his financial situation increasingly precarious. He continued to think in international terms and apparently did uncredited script work on the British GPO documentary *North Sea* (Harry Watt 1938; Tallents 1968: 65). He kept proposing projects to producers in various countries – although not in Germany. Unpublished letters in his archive show that Dreyer detested the Nazi dictatorship and wanted to make anti-racist films (an unfortunately lost script was called simply *Race Hatred*).

Dreyer's Career: The Later Years

It was only after the German occupation of Denmark in 1940 that Dreyer had the chance to revive his career. The Danish government invested in the production of state-sponsored documentary shorts, helping Danish film companies and counterbalancing the presence of German propaganda on Danish screens. The civil servant in charge of the programme, Mogens Skot-Hansen, was a film fan and lobbied the production companies to give Dreyer the chance to make a comeback (for more on Dreyer's state-sponsored documentary work, see Thomson 2016). The film company Palladium eventually produced *Vredens Dag* (*Day of Wrath*, 1943), a stark and brutal story of seventeenth-century witchcraft persecutions, showing the power of oppressive belief systems to warp minds and crush rebellious souls.

Dreyer's last two films, *Ordet* (*The Word*, 1955) and *Gertrud* (1964), were both made in Denmark, one based on a Danish play (by Kaj Munk), the other based on a Swedish one (by Hjalmar Söderberg). Although the stories are very different, both films are shot on sets that have a slightly abstract, austere feel. They also both rely on very long takes and minimal editing. There are very few close-ups. The actors speak their dialogue deliberately, and the lines are often framed by pauses, giving them weight but also producing a somewhat stylised, at times almost funereal effect. This austerity and overwhelming seriousness has been linked to the Lutheranism of the Scandinavian countries (Sémolué 2005), a link that seems all the more inviting given the specifically religious subject-matter of *Ordet*. In this film, faith is a central part of the characters' lives, theological issues are explicitly debated, and the story culminates in a miracle.

Seeing Dreyer's aesthetic as marked by Lutheranism is a way of emphasising his Danishness (or at least, Scandinavian-ness). However, if we take a somewhat broader view of Dreyer's activities during the last decades of his career, we find him engaged in a number of projects of a much more international character. He stayed in Sweden for the last two years of the Second World War, where he made the infrequently seen *Två människor* (*Two People*, 1945). A modern-day drama of marital infidelity and academic fraud, it has only two characters, and Dreyer was forced to use two actors whom he thought completely wrong for the parts, leading him to disown the film; but aesthetically, it is quite similar to his three Danish sound films. He then worked on a large-scale film about Mary, Queen of Scots, to be produced by J. Arthur Rank in the UK; while this film remained unrealised, Dreyer put almost twenty years of work into the project (see Thomson 2015).

Dreyer's greatest ambition was to make a film about Jesus. He wrote an English-language screenplay and sought American financing for an epic-scale project, requiring vast sets of first-century Jerusalem and location shooting in the Holy Land. His pursuit of Hollywood backing was oddly diffident, however; he relied on the help of an American go-between, the theatre producer Blevins Davis, sticking with him despite Davis 'never lifting a finger to do anything serious' about the project (Nannestad Jørgensen 1989: 7).

Dreyer's professed aim was to stress the Jewishness of Jesus and to firmly attach the blame for his death to the Romans occupying Palestine rather than the Jews whom long-standing Christian tradition stigmatised as 'Christ-Killers'. He was evidently far more concerned to craft a pro-Jewish vision of Jesus than one that matched any particular Christian doctrine. Interviews that Dreyer gave during and after the making of *Ordet* ascribe the miracle in that film to ESP-like psychic powers rather than divine intervention, showing Dreyer to be strikingly heterodox about the theological issues at the centre of Kaj Munk's play (Tybjerg 2003). In the last years of his life, he also worked on adaptations of Euripides' Greek tragedy *Medea* (his treatment was eventually used as the basis of Lars von Trier's 1988 made-for-television film *Medea*) and of William Faulkner's *Light in August*.

Conclusion

Throughout his career, Dreyer's work was deeply enmeshed with an international film culture. We have seen how he identified himself with a 'European principle' of giving control to the film director as artist. Dreyer knew that he was oversimplifying, that the 'manufacturing' of cookie-cutter entertainment movies was a big part of what the European film industries did; but it is clear that he believed to the very core of his being in the uncompromising pursuit of artistic truth and that he held commercial pandering in disdain. This belief tied him together with filmmakers in other countries and a wider European film culture. As we have seen, Dreyer would cross national borders repeatedly during his career as a filmmaker, and it would be impossible and deeply misleading to seek to disentangle his work from this international context; yet, Dreyer cannot be disentangled from a Danish context either. He kept returning to Denmark and almost always had Danish actors, crew members, or assistants working with him when he made films abroad.

To answer the question that I asked at the outset: it does make sense to talk about Dreyer as a Danish filmmaker, but his Danishness is not the most important thing about him. It does affect how he is studied, and who the researchers are who study his work. If Dreyer were generally considered a Swedish filmmaker, this chapter would probably not have been written, and it would have no place in this anthology. As scholars, we are tied into institutional structures that are in many ways organised according to national principles; historically, this is just how institutions of learning and preservation were typically set up, and we would probably be wise to regard this less as an impediment to our work and more as a condition of possibility for it. Nor, however, should we regard it as an all-determining framework; we should not let our national ties trip us up and prevent us from tracing other entanglements in pursuit of what we regard as historical truth.

4. DERAILED: DANISH FILM DURING THE GERMAN OCCUPATION

Lars-Martin Sørensen

This chapter focuses on the manoeuvres of the Danish film trade in the face of the German occupation from April 1940 to May 1945, as it played out in the executive offices and behind the cameras. I argue that, generally speaking, the Danish film bosses allowed business interests to overrule ideological concerns and that they did so with impunity. The chapter is based on extensive archival research in German and Danish archives and draws on my previously published book *Dansk film under nazismen* (Danish Film during Nazism, Sørensen 2014, untranslated).

The Danish feature that gathered the highest critical acclaim during the German occupation was *Afsporet* (*Derailed*, Bodil Ipsen and Lau Lauritzen Jr, 1942). The film, a *noiresque* drama of a young woman suffering from amnesia, who loses herself and her heart to a gangster in a seedy Copenhagen red light district, is highly indicative of the messy and conflicted situation which the Danish film trade navigated during the occupation years – not so much in terms of the film narrative itself, perhaps, as the properties of its cast and production history. *Derailed* had a female Jewish lead, Illona Wieselmann; it was filmed by a Danish cameraman, Alf Schnéevoigt, who had voluntarily joined the notorious Nazi-German elite corps, the SS; it had a male lead, Ebbe Rode, who would later escape German persecution to neutral Sweden, where the female lead, too, had fled. She had to escape because the producer of the film, Henning Karmark, had informed on her Jewish ancestry to the German occupiers in Denmark. Karmark, also the CEO of the producing company of the film, was eagerly trying to lubricate his business relations with German authorities. To this end, he not only informed on his own employees, but also joined the Danish Nazi Party. Moreover, despite its Jewish lead, *Derailed* was screened at the film festival in the world least likely to feature Jewish film stars at that point in European history – namely, at the Venice Film Festival in autumn 1942, at the zenith of Nazi-Fascist hegemony in Europe.

If the above seems somehow unsettling, then add to those facts that for Danish film as a whole, the occupation years were marked by expansion and progress in all aspects of film culture. By autumn 1940, the Germans had banned the screening of British films, and since the war at sea made imports of new American films all but impossible, competition eased considerably for Danish cinema. The popularity of domestic fare – including reruns of numerous pre-war films – increased. The number of features produced annually in Denmark more than doubled, from nine productions in 1939 to a zenith during the occupation years of nineteen films in 1942, and Danish studios ventured into genres where Hollywood had hitherto reigned supreme. Cases in point are dark crime dramas and screwball comedies such as the above-mentioned *Derailed* and *Mordets Melodi* (*Murder Melody*, 1944), also

Figure 4.1   Illona Wieselmann in *Afsporet* (*Derailed*, Bodil Ipsen and Lau Lauritzen Jr, 1942). She later had to flee to Sweden after being reported to the German occupiers by producer Henning Karmark. Image: Danish Film Institute.

directed by the prolific woman director Bodil Ipsen (1889–1964). Lighter fare was provided by the elegant comedy *En Herre i Kjole og Hvidt* (*A Gentleman in Top Hat and Tails*, Bodil Ipsen, 1942). Thus, the aesthetic quality and variety of Danish films improved, exports increased, more new cinemas opened, and box office sales grew from 28.2 million tickets in 1939 to 47 million in 1945 (Dinnesen and Kau 1983: 194). While the world outside was on fire, Danish film celebrated the business opportunities brought about by the German occupation. More specifically, the good times lasted from 1940 until late 1943. From then until liberation day in May 1945, conditions – in some, but not all respects – gradually deteriorated in tune with Germany's dwindling wartime fortunes.

Glorious Past – Present Opportunities?
The Inter-War Years in Danish Cinema

In the silent era, especially before the First World War, Danish film enjoyed a position among the most prolific European film nations. The films and stars of Nordisk Films Kompagni and Palladium were celebrated and in high demand throughout the world, not least in Germany, where silent film diva Asta Nielsen's stardom was unrivalled; Nordisk dominated the market and owned a lucrative chain of cinemas (Thorsen 2017a; see also Chapters 1 and 2 in this volume). The First World War put a stop to this golden age of international Danish film. After the war, competition with Hollywood grew fierce. With the advent of talkies and the great depression around 1930, the Danish film trade diminished and retreated to primarily producing for the domestic market. Among Danish film bosses, however, the hope that the golden days would someday be back had not dwindled.

By 1935, Nordisk adopted a new strategy to make international films. The company employed German dramaturg Adolf Kobitzsch with the stated purpose of returning to the international market. The initiative immediately paid off. *Fredløs* (*Outlaw*, George Schnéevoigt, 1935), a large-scale international production set in eighteenth-century Finland with an explicit anti-Russian inclination, became a hit in Nazi Germany.

Major distributors also showed a renewed interest in importing German films. Around 1935, the crass propagandistic content of Nazi-German films softened, and the stated purpose of Propaganda Minister Joseph Goebbels changed to inducing propagandistic content in 'homeopathic doses' – that is, downplaying militant and direct political messages to a more subtle level of politicisation. During the 1930s, the pattern of import of German films changed; in the early years of the decade, a handful of minor companies handled the distribution. By the end of the decade, distribution deals were held almost exclusively by the three majors: Nordisk Films Kompagni; the distribution branch of Palladium,

Filmcentralen Palladium; and the major distributor Teatrenes Films-Kontor (The Film Office of the Theatres).

Importing and screening films from Nazi Germany was by no means an uncontroversial issue in contemporary Denmark. In the early 1930s, there were already vocal protests against the screening of German features, and newsreels in Denmark were subject to hostile newspaper campaigns. Danish dailies reported on the racist *Gleichschaltung* – that is, the purging of Jews from the German film industry. The atrocities of the Kristallnacht in November 1938, the state-organised assault on German Jews, was met in the Danish dailies with almost unanimous condemnation (Sørensen 2019). Nevertheless, well aware that Germany was a ruthless tyranny, which had placed high-profile Nazi-party members on the boards of the strictly government-controlled German film companies, the executives of the Danish film trade placed their bets on trading with Nazi Germany (see also Sørenssen, Salmi, Kau and Olsen 2012). It is recognised by historians that the golden age of Danish silent cinema was, to some extent, based on the Danish film trade's ability to adapt to the demands and political preferences of foreign markets and film censors (Thorsen 2016b). With the rise of Nazism and the occupation of Denmark, this tradition was revived.

The Early Bird Catches the Worm

In January 1940, the German biopic by Hans Steinhoff *Robert Koch, der Bekämpfer des Todes* (*Robert Koch, The Fighter Against Death*, 1939) became a box office hit in Copenhagen, selling almost 200,000 tickets at more than 250 screenings between January and March. Nordisk imported the film, and the success prompted the head of Nordisk, Carl Bauder, to extend an invitation to the male lead, Emil Jannings. The visit had to be cancelled due to inclement weather, but the notion that German films could attract Danish crowds had been proven, and the interest in expanding cooperation with German film companies and the supervising Reich Film Chamber of the Propaganda Ministry grew. The paper trail of the Nordisk Archives held at the Danish Film Institute proves that, during the early spring of 1940, the months leading up to the German invasion of Denmark in April, correspondence and contacts intensified between the primary agent of German film in Denmark, Hans-Jürgen Maximilian von Hake, and the executives of Nordisk. And – perhaps contrary to what one might expect – the German invasion of Denmark spurred an even stronger interest in cutting deals with the Germans, especially on the part of the head of Nordisk, Carl Bauder, but also – to his misfortune – among his domestic competitors.

To put this issue of business cooperation into historical perspective, it is important to note that the situation in Denmark was somewhat special as compared to other German-occupied small nations. On the day of invasion,

Denmark entered a course of cooperation – or, if you like, collaboration – with Germany, based on a deal stipulating that the occupiers would not interfere with Danish internal affairs, provided that no Dane would hinder the German 'protection' of Denmark against the Allies (see, for example, Hong 2012). Danish authorities negotiated the fiction that Denmark was a sovereign nation, albeit occupied by Germany, until August 1943, when this so-called 'policy of cooperation' broke down in the face of rising unrest among the population and armed resistance and sabotage against German interests and facilities. Conducive to this change of heart by Danish authorities was of course the fact that at that point Germany's luck on the battlefields was drastically deteriorating. This policy of cooperation/collaboration also meant that the occupiers could not just regulate the Danish film trade by decree but had to enter a course of negotiations with the Danish Ministry of Foreign Affairs and representatives from the major companies and trade organisations. In the Netherlands and Norway, for instance, the German occupiers instated military rule and regulated the movie business much more harshly (for a comparative overview of conditions across the Nordic countries, see Sørenssen, Salmi, Kau and Olsson 2012). As a result of the Danish situation, Jewish actors were not officially banned from Danish films by the Germans but were nevertheless almost completely elbowed out on the initiative of the film bosses, who were eagerly trying to do business with the Germans. Also, film censorship was officially undertaken by a Danish censorship board throughout the occupation, although German officials took part in the actual censoring. Knowledge of the empirical outcomes of this practice is sparse since the archives of the censorship board went up in flames in a sabotage attack in 1944.

Three weeks after the 9 April German invasion of Denmark and Norway, on 30 April, at 10am, the head of Nordisk, Carl Bauder, attended a high-level meeting at the Reich Film Chamber in Berlin. Present at the meeting was the head of the foreign trade branch of the chamber, Günther Schwarz. On the agenda was a plan for the foundation of a Danish-German distribution company, a subsidiary of Nordisk, headed by Bauder's closest German contact in Denmark, Hans-Jürgen von Hake. According to the German minutes of the meeting, the Reich Film Chamber would control the company with 51 per cent of the shares, and Bauder and Nordisk would own the remainder. The initial plan was that the company would undertake distribution of all German films for the Danish market. But during the negotiations, Bauder proposed including all distribution to Swedish and Norwegian cinemas in the deal, too. This was an unexpected proposition to the Germans, and nothing final was decided, but the parties agreed that Bauder would draw up a preliminary contract upon his return to Copenhagen. The draft landed in Berlin a week later.

In the meantime, however, German enthusiasm for Bauder and Nordisk had cooled off. According to the files and correspondences of the Reich Film

Chamber, there were concerns over the risk of placing all German bets on one monopoly company; how this would sit with the Danish film trade in general. In addition, the investment by Nordisk in the proposed company was deemed too meagre. Bauder defended his proposition as merely a draft; it was only intended as a basis for further negotiations. In the end, Bauder and Schwarz agreed to continue negotiations face to face in Copenhagen at the beginning of June.

During the month of May, Bauder busied himself fortifying his position prior to the negotiations with the Reich Film Chamber. Nordisk hired a new manager for its lab, a German national named Heinz Graff, whose only qualifications for the job were apparently that he was German and a member of the German Nazi party. He had no experience in the film trade whatsoever, and his appointment probably triggered either astonishment or direct criticism, judging from the fact that Nordisk took the unusual measure of explaining in public exactly why Graff had been hired. Critical readers of the Danish daily *Ekstra Bladet* on 21 June 1940 may have caught a whiff of the idea that Nordisk had other motives for hiring Graff than the publicly stated one: that he – as a manufacturer of cosmetics – had valuable skills in management. Having a member of the German Nazi party on board soon proved useful for Nordisk. Graff accompanied Bauder on his business trips to Berlin and was singled out to become a board member of the planned distribution monopoly. Nordisk also signed up another prominent German Nazi in Denmark, namely captain Ernst Schäfer, leader of the Danish branch of the German Nazi party. According to internal memos from the German Reich Film Chamber, Schäfer would exert supervising influence in the new company.

By the first week of June 1940, Nordisk had everything prepared for the concluding negotiations with Günter Schwarz in Copenhagen. Bauder welcomed Schwarz by inviting him for dinner at his private mansion, but on the way to Copenhagen a local informer reported to Schwarz that Bauder had opened a second avenue of negotiations with the German embassy in Copenhagen, without conferring with the Reich Film Chamber. The two agencies fell under the German Ministry of Propaganda and the Ministry of Foreign Affairs, respectively, and were engaged in constant turf wars, not just in Germany but in the occupied territories, too. Therefore, this was an unwelcome move by Bauder. Moreover, Schwarz had consulted Danish allies in Copenhagen to inquire about potential alternative partners in the Danish film trade. Of the three major distributors previously mentioned, only Teatrenes Films-Kontor had earned a recommendation as a suitable prospect for distributing German films in Denmark in case Schwarz were to decide against Nordisk. The merits of the third major, Palladium, which held the rights to distribute films from the two German majors, Terra and Ufa, apparently had not impressed the Reich Film Chamber, and consequently Palladium was left out of consideration.

Upon his arrival at Nordisk, Schwarz declined Bauder's dinner invitation; he preferred to keep the negotiations strictly business. After just a few hours of initial negotiations, the German delegation headed for a meeting with the head of Teatrenes Films-Kontor, John Olsen. The minutes from the meetings show that Olsen managed to snatch a considerable slice of the distribution rights from Bauder, who had his eyes firmly set on a monopoly. Olsen expressed a keen interest in distributing not only German features but also in promoting the screening of the controversial German newsreels in Denmark (for more on wartime newsreels in Scandinavia, see Sørensen, Helseth and Jönsson 2012, and Sørensen 2018). At the end of the day, Olsen had netted a contract to distribute the films of the German major Tobis; Bauder, to his consternation, was offered 80 per cent of the total distribution volume. Having bargained for a monopoly, Bauder rejected the offer and placed his bets on using his contacts at the German embassy in his favour – a move which due to the above-mentioned rivalry between the Reich Film Chamber of the Ministry of Propaganda and the Ministry of Foreign Affairs complicated matters rather than paving the way for a signed contract.

The negotiations dragged on fruitlessly throughout summer 1940; in August, the Germans decided to open a subsidiary of Ufa in Copenhagen, which would be responsible for the distribution of all German films in Denmark, except for Tobis' films, which were in John Olsen's hands. Hans-Jürgen von Hake, who had been close to the negotiations of the monopoly distribution company with Nordisk, became head of the new Ufa office.

A Gateway to European Occupied Cinemas

Only a week after the opening of the Ufa branch in Copenhagen, the CEO of the Danish major production company ASA, Henning Karmark, made his first move to become the preferred partner of the occupying Germans. He joined the ranks of the Danish Nazi party. At this point, the business opportunities had narrowed somewhat. The Germans were distributing their own films in Denmark, while Nordisk had netted contracts on carrying out the technical work of subtitling and copying German films for the Danish market. However, what was still up for grabs was the prospect of exporting Danish films to German-occupied Europe and distributing foreign films from occupied European nations in Denmark. In the autumn of 1940, however, the Germans were more bent on ridding Denmark of British films and trying to elbow their own features and newsreels into Danish cinemas rather than cutting deals for import and export.

In early summer 1941, a window of opportunity opened for Karmark and ASA, when the German Ministry of Propaganda convened the International Film Chamber in Berlin. First established in 1935, the Chamber was resuscitated in 1941 as a means for organising and placing the film trade in German-occupied

Europe under the firm control of the Propaganda Ministry of Joseph Goebbels (Martin 2007). The paper trail documents that, during the conference, Karmark not only managed to become head of the Danish IFC committee responsible for foreign trade, but he apparently also impressed the head of Ufa Copenhagen, Hans-Jürgen von Hake, with his eagerness to cooperate with the Germans in Denmark. Back home again, the two met on several occasions during the summer, and von Hake reported to Berlin that, in his view, Karmark clearly had realised the usefulness of cooperating with Germany while attending the IFC conference. The correspondence also shows that von Hake's recommendation was based on the fact that Karmark informed on prominent officials in the Danish film trade; he named those harbouring anti-German sentiment and alleged 'social democrats'. Additionally, he promised von Hake to obstruct the ongoing Danish effort to have state-subsidised short films substitute for German newsreels in Danish cinemas and revealed that the hidden agenda behind the production of domestic short films was, in fact, to obstruct the spread of Nazi newsreels in Denmark. Finally, he promised von Hake to work out an estimate of the supply of film stock in store by Danish production companies – useful information for the Germans, who repeatedly threatened to cut off the supplies of film stock if Danish companies and officials did not play along with German ambitions to pressure their films onto Danish screens. In short, Karmark used just about every dirty trick in the book to ingratiate himself with German film's most powerful executive in Denmark.

During autumn 1941, German methods of making the Danish film trade toe the line swung from stick to carrot. A representative of the German company in charge of all film distribution throughout occupied Europe, Transit Film, visited Denmark, and in January 1942 von Hake drew up a list of titles suitable for European export. The list included five titles from Nordisk Films Kompagni, none from ASA and none from Palladium. After being snubbed by Transit, Henning Karmark, alongside the boss of Palladium, Tage Nielsen, complained to von Hake at Ufa, who, in turn, sent a complaint to the Ufa Headquarters in Berlin that Transit was making his cooperation with his Danish counterparts difficult by exclusively favouring Nordisk Films Kompagni. According to the letter, Karmark and Nielsen had 'especially bemoaned' that, while they made every effort to rid their films of non-Aryans in order to do business with Germany, Transit had bought a film from Nordisk in which the female lead was of non-Aryan ancestry (Sørensen 2014: 208). The actress in question was explicitly named and thus put at risk of German persecution, which, at this point in time, had not yet taken a dangerous turn in occupied Denmark. Nevertheless, the production companies had followed a somewhat haphazard and inconsistent course of 'pre-emptive anti-Semitism' from the early days of the occupation. The assumption was that employing Jewish cast and crew would not improve business relations with the Germans, even if the latter did not directly demand an ethnic cleansing of Danish film along the lines of the purge that had been carried out in Germany in the early 1930s.

After this meeting, Henning Karmark appeared to place all his bets on a German business adventure. He founded a new distribution company and netted a deal with von Hake and Ufa Berlin to distribute films from German-occupied or German-allied European countries in Denmark. He signed a strictly confidential agreement with von Hake that no screening of those films would take place in Denmark unless accompanied by a Nazi newsreel. The paper trail also reveals that Karmark bemoaned having had to employ a 'non-Aryan' actress as the lead of his great success, *Derailed*, and assures von Hake that no such thing would happen again, now that he had entered such close cooperation with Ufa. Preserved letters also show that Karmark flagged his membership of the Danish Nazi party when contacting German business partners outside Denmark and saluted them with a 'Heil Hitler'.

A Turn of the Tide

Initially, Karmark's efforts paid off. Foreign films from Italy and Hungary started trickling into Danish cinemas, and in spring 1942 Karmark's closest partners at the ASA studios were invited to, or attempted to, launch careers in Germany. His co-manager, Lau Lauritzen Jr, who was in charge of artistic repertoire, was invited to make a test film in Germany by Fritz Hippler, who directed the notoriously antisemitic propaganda film *Der ewige Jude* (*The Eternal Jew*, 1940). Whether or not Lauritzen accepted the invitation is unclear, but he did receive an offer to direct a film for the Germans in summer 1942. At the same time, a leading director at ASA, Alice O'Fredericks (see also Hartvigson, Chapter 8 in this volume), approached von Hake in order to have him bestow on her an invitation into German film circles. In August, Lauritzen and Karmark attended the screening of *Derailed* at the Venice Festival.

By early summer 1942, however, the Danish press started to report on Karmark's German business adventure, and he insisted publicly – and untruthfully – in a press release that his recently established distribution company, Merkur Film, was purely Danish and completely unrelated to Ufa. The ever-growing illegal press in Denmark then picked up the story and denounced Karmark as a Nazi and traitor in several articles. John Olsen, who won the distribution rights to German films immediately after the German invasion, was also smeared as a Nazi in the illegal press.

Simultaneously, Germany's war luck was changing drastically. The offensive against the Soviet Union ground to a painful halt at Stalingrad. In Egypt, the Allies first stopped German advances at El Alamein in summer and subsequently won the second battle in the autumn. In August, the Danish movie trade press reported that Lauritzen had turned down a lucrative offer to direct a German-Danish co-production. And by February 1943, Karmark cancelled his 'strictly confidential' contract with Ufa and later changed the name of his company Merkur, the distributor of films from Axis countries. A couple of weeks earlier, Karmark had terminated his membership with the Danish Nazi party. He opted out on 3 February, one day after the German armies surrendered at Stalingrad. In Denmark, armed resistance was on the rise, escalating in summer 1943 to open conflict and street riots in major Danish cities. Come August 1943, the official policy of cooperation/collaboration broke down. The occupiers demanded that the death penalty be introduced to curb riots and sabotage, the Danish government resigned, and the occupation entered a harsh chapter under direct German rule. In October 1943, the Germans moved to arrest and deport the Danish Jews to concentration camps in Germany. The vast majority managed to escape to Sweden, a few of them with the indirect assistance of Henning Karmark's closest Danish ally, Lau Lauritzen, who turned a blind eye to resistance fighters stealing his boat in order to carry fleeing Jews over the narrow strait of Øresund between Denmark and Sweden. As with numerous other Danes, it was the purge of the Danish Jews and the growing number of executions of Danish resistance fighters that prompted Lauritzen to take a stand against the Germans in Denmark. From summer 1944 onwards, a resistance group including Lauritzen and members of the technical staff was active at ASA – the production company headed by Henning Karmark.

During the first three months of 1944, Nordisk, Palladium and ASA studios were subject to bombings carried out by Danish Nazis acting on German orders. The Germans did not target the film companies because they were considered hostile to the occupation; the attacks were part of a larger campaign against a variety of leisure sites and facilities, including several cinemas and the Tivoli Gardens in the centre of Copenhagen. The aim was to make life miserable for the occupied Danes, who were no longer willing to play the part of amiable hosts to the Germans. In the illegal press, the bombing of Karmark's ASA studios was met with particular glee. One article stated that now, after the bombing, Karmark was jumping for joy, having been bombed from the ranks of the traitors into the company of the righteous. Outside the searchlight of both the legal and illegal press, Karmark was eagerly trying to cut his connections to the occupiers. Alongside the ASA studio, he ran an advertisement bureau, which handled German ads for Danish papers. This company was closed down, and the accountant later stated that the profits from doing business with the occupiers were channelled into the resistance (Sørensen 2014: 243). Simultaneously, Karmark organised high-profile screenings of state-sponsored Danish short films – the very same films he had promised Ufa head von Hake to obstruct in summer 1941. The Danish daily *Politiken* publicised the screenings on 4 March 1944.

Meanwhile, Nordisk Film was quietly making a steady income from the continued export of films through German channels to the ever-shrinking number of countries under German occupation and carrying out technical work on German features and newsreels for Danish cinemas. Conditions for doing business with the Germans were deteriorating, but Nordisk did not cease its exports until the end of the occupation. The German secret police arrested Karmark in March 1945 – probably for refusing continued collaboration. Upon his release from German captivity, he fled to Sweden, having become a prize target for assassination by the Resistance. In Sweden, he was recognised by Danish resistance fighters in exile and interned by the Swedish authorities. Shortly after liberation day, Karmark was back in Copenhagen as a free man.

The Aftermath

In the wake of liberation, the Danish resistance carried out sweeping rounds of arrests. Around 40,000 suspected collaborators were interned. Now the hour of reckoning had come. None of the film bosses, however, was put behind bars. Carl Bauder of Nordisk died in 1944, and even though an investigation had been launched into the role of Nordisk Film's lab, which had hired the German national and Nazi party member Heinz Graff, it did not lead to charges or convictions. The police also carried out a year-long probe into Henning Karmark's track record but ended up dropping the case. The files show that the investigating officer had little doubt that Karmark was guilty of collaboration, but the police fell short of conclusive evidence that could lead to conviction. After a brief stint in disfavour, Karmark was back in business and became the most successful producer of folksy comedies and one of the richest, if not *the* richest, Danish film tycoon in the 1950s. His re-entry into film production was the feature *De røde Enge* (*The Red Meadows*) in autumn 1945 – a film that, ironically, glorified the Danish resistance from which Karmark had fled in the closing days of the occupation less than a year earlier. It won the Palme d'Or at the Cannes Film Festival in 1946. Apart from this highlight for Danish film, the post-war years marked a return to pre-war production levels. Competition from Hollywood was back in full force; compared to the nineteen features of the peak year 1942, which coincided with the zenith of Nazi hegemony in Europe, the number of features per year fell to the pre-war level of around ten. The golden business years of war and occupation were over.

PART II

NATIONAL GENRES

5. THE ART OF THE POPULAR: THE *FOLKEKOMEDIE* TRADITION

Niels Henrik Hartvigson

The *folkekomedie* genre was dominant in the crucial transition from silent to sound film around 1930 and initiated a popular tradition that thrives to this day. Discussing the films and prototypes of *folkekomedie*, this chapter offers insights into the popular imagination of the Danes and discusses why this happy genre has been a site of cultural conflict throughout its history. Because the term is ambiguous, *folkekomedie* will be used throughout.

With its roots in the Enlightenment comedies of the eighteenth century and the popular education movement, *folkekomedie*, meaning folk comedy or folk play, has existed as a term from the beginning of the nineteenth century. On the one hand, *folkekomedie* can be grasped in relationship to the diverse genres it has encompassed, such as comedy, sentimental comedy, satire, melodrama and realism. On the other hand, it may be understood and defined according to *the people*, which it is intended for or to which it 'belongs'. During its history, it has applied to both Danish fiction film as well as international imports (Tybjerg 1996: 77). For example, in the silent period from 1910 onwards the many stage and screen adaptations of the English author Charles Dickens as well as film imports such as *Oliver Twist* (William J. Cowen, 1933) have been referred to as *folkekomedie* (Nielsen 2009: 228). However, since the national turn of the 1930s sound comedies, the term has been used both in popular parlance and in a scholarly context to refer exclusively to Danish-themed fictions – the focus of this chapter.

Academic examination of *folkekomedie* is very scarce; there is no real tradition of dealing with the genre in any systematic or serious manner, and its study suffers from the common misconception that, because it is popular and has connotations of being simple, it is easily understood. Scholars dealing with analogous popular genres such as comedy and melodrama often make similar points (Affron 1982: 3). Making matters worse is a widely accepted tendency towards derogatory and purposefully simplified criticism.

In the first part of this chapter, the sound comedies of the 1930s are examined as a dominant *folkekomedie* prototype. It is argued that their success depended on a renegotiation of the comedy genre across media, reinventing popular theatre and its specific sociality within the new medium of sound film. The next section discusses *folkekomedie* types and the central role of popular actors, Danish locations, as well as the themes, motifs and plots of the films. Moreover, it introduces the *folkekomedie* prototypes of the family, the crew and the gang and discusses their relation to the 1930s sound comedies. Two other important cinematic *folkekomedie* prototypes are *homeland* films, which border on melodrama, and sex comedies, which are described in separate chapters in this book (see Hartvigson in Chapter 8, Schröder in Chapter 9 and Thorsen in Chapter 11). The third section investigates the role of the *folkekomedie* audience in terms of demographics, sensibility, feeling, activity and creativity, while the chapter ends with a section on how *folkekomedie* has been defined and regulated by different institutions.

It is impossible to trace the history of *folkekomedie* as a film genre without consideration of its theatrical antecedents; hence, the link between popular theatre and the cinematic *folkekomedie*, including the history and criticism of the former, will be a recurring theme in the chapter. Moreover, the Danish *folkekomedie* film will be explored with occasional reference to television. It should further be emphasised that, although it deals with the aesthetics of *folkekomedie*, this chapter is also inspired by Cultural Studies, which takes a broader sociological, cultural and psychological approach to genre.

A Decade of Musical Integration

With the coming of sound film around 1930, the hitherto internationally-oriented Danish film industry suddenly depended on little more than 3.5 million Danes – the audience who could understand the Danish language that could now be heard in the cinema. Out of this not very auspicious situation, a popular and economically viable film culture developed in Denmark, centring on singing and talking comedies in the Danish language, which drew on the *folkekomedie* genre from popular theatre.

A *folkekomedie* motif which is central in the films of the 1930s is the integration of political, regional and cultural differences. With a characteristic soft-edged populism the human conflicts are typically resolved through the intervention of offbeat, lower-class or rural characters such as the stereotypical wise old man from the mainland of Jutland, who is materially poor but emotionally rich, uneducated but insightful, and with a good dose of skepticism towards city life and everything modern.

Scholars of genre have identified a similar logic of integration in relation to American films. Thus, Thomas Schatz identifies Hollywood comedies, musicals and certain types of melodramas as genres of integration (Schatz 1981: 35), and Rick Altman argues that the American film musical can be seen as a 'cultural problem-solving device' which out of conflictual paradoxes creates a 'concordance of opposites' (Altman 1987: 27). Within American society, with its extreme cultural barriers and its history of internal conflicts, the integration achieved in the films will often feel utopian (Altman 1987: 272). Applying the same problem-solving potential to *folkekomedie* is certainly to the point. However, the small size of Denmark and its population, as well as the longevity of cohabitation makes cultural differences relatively more manageable and integration less utopian (Hartvigson 2006: 171). A specifically Danish relationship to integration as a realistic and attainable goal is concisely illustrated in journalist Jens Kistrup's reflections on how his political and personal values have been influenced by the 1930s comedies. He recounts how integration and reconciliation of differences were presented as both an ideal and the norm by the entertainment industry as well as private and public institutions: 'In my childhood we learned that the problems in society could be solved – not all at once – but step by step, with common sense and the heart in the right place. That was the indoctrination of that time – in the schools, in the homes, in the cinemas' (Kistrup 1977: n. p.). Moreover, the principle of integration is strongly reflected in political culture, especially after 1920, when negotiation and consensus became the touchstones of Danish parliamentarism (Olsen and Kaarsted 1991: 122).

With the coming of sound, films became unequivocally national. Where the streets of Copenhagen had served as metropolitan backdrop in the silent period, the sound comedies presented an unequivocally Danish land- and cityscape, showing off the capital with attention to specific social milieux: Nyhavn for the sailors, Vesterbro for the working classes, Hellerup for the upper classes and, not least, the amusement parks and department stores, where worker and socialite could intermingle and meet. In *Barken Margrethe* (*The Bark Margrethe*, Lau Lauritzen Sr, 1934),[1] the old Dyrehavsbakken amusement park north of Copenhagen unites the sailors from the quaint seaside village of Dragør and the director's daughter from Klampenborg. Their slangy performance of *Nu skal vi ud og slå til Søren* (roughly, 'We're Cutting Loose') during the horse-carriage ride through the cultural landmark, just as the oak trees are coming into leaf, is an excellent example of the films' fascination with the new-found social and cultural signification of sound and image. Also exploited for their signifying power are dialects, sociolects, archaic language and diction. In particular, the sounds of the modern technologies of radio, telephone and telegraph, as well as the singing styles, rhythms and instrumentation of swing and jazz music are used to resonate and create a modern sensibility, which serves as the backdrop for the films' themes and conflicts.

Thus, in *Provinsen kalder – !* (*The Provinces are Calling – !*, Lau Lauritzen Sr, 1935), a young man, Hans, after moving from the provinces to Copenhagen, has dropped out of his studies to become a jazz musician and has gotten his girl pregnant. Here, a classic case of inter-generational conflict is illustrated by the clash between the traditional values of the parents and Hans' modern parlance and his taste for the then divisive jazz music. The lack of successful communication is brought home by the parents' difficulties of communicating though the new medium of the telephone. Eventually, the worldwise bachelor uncle Tobias, helped by the charms of the illegitimate new-born, acts as go-between and reunites the broken family.

Emblems of inclusivity, the films harbour a strong mono-cultural vision of extended families or family-like groups. The many romantic crises pave the way for an examination of a split community and its coming together. While

Figure 5.1   In *Provinsen kalder – !* (*The Provinces are Calling – !*, Lau Lauritzen Sr, 1935) sound technologies such as the telephone are ciphers for inter-generational and regional communication difficulties. Image: Danish Film Institute.

the antagonism offered by lawyers, capitalists or authorities may be threatening on a plot level, on a dramaturgical level it functions to bring out and demonstrate the interdependence of the group members. Also, even the worst snobs and capitalist managers become infected with the community spirit. In *Der var engang en Vicevært* (*Once Upon a Time There Was a Caretaker*, Lau Lauritzen Jr and Alice O' Fredericks, 1937), a creditor becomes so caught up in the artist troupe's show, which he has desperately tried to shut down, that he becomes its backer instead *and* an actor in the troupe. Paradoxically, the popular theatre and *revues*, which so clearly inspired the performances and discursivity of *Once Upon a Time There Was a Caretaker* and many of the sound comedies, suffered financially from the films' popularity (Nielsen 2001: 150; Kvam, Risum and Wiingaard 1993: 125).

Performance Between Stage and Screen

Not only did sound cinema along with radio and gramophone compete for the audiences of theatre and *revue*, but sound comedies also appropriated the specific sociality of these theatrical forms – that is, the reciprocal relationship between stage and audience (Nielsen 2001: 182, 195; Jensen: 2001: 225, Hartvigson 2007: 74). Contemporary and later critics and scholars were baffled by how these comedies drew inspiration from popular theatre and *revues* instead of severing the ties to the old medium and creating a uniquely filmic art form (Nordin 1985: 22; Alsted 1985: 148).

Using performers and discursive strategies from popular theatre, the *folkekomedie* films unapologetically acknowledge their audience. Far from alienating and creating distance, they drew on a stage comedy tradition, which encouraged a complicity and engagement between fiction and audience (Thomsen 1986: 231, 248).

Because of the comedy's elastic ability to encompass epistemologically very different characters and elements, the genre proved perfect for epistemological clashes and the compound nature of the sound comedies (Hartvigson 2007: 123). In *Plat eller Krone* (*Heads or Tails*, Jon Iversen, 1937), such an epistemological clash is created by the collision of everyday reality and fiction of the most obvious kind, as the restaurateur couple rides through Copenhagen on their tandem bicycle doing their shopping while singing *En Sommermorgen i København* ('A Summer Morning in Copenhagen'). The musical number flaunts the high-spirited and well-sung performances of actors Ib Schønberg and Karen Caspersen, whose exaggerated acting styles, make-up and costumes in conjunction with their quaint means of transportation make them obviously staged. Three times their performance is interrupted to feature realistic sound and dialogue, as the restaurateur couple – still acting to the last row of the audience — engage with mundane and subdued non-actor Copenhageners in Vesterbro's meat quarter, Amager Torv's green market and the canal of Nyhavn. The tension between the theatricality of the performer-actors and an everyday Copenhagen is based on a compound staging of elements, which invites complicity and engagement between film and audience and in a sense becomes a porthole in and out of the fiction (Kruuse 1964: 112–13).

The reviews of *Heads or Tails* were generally critical of how the narrative, technical elements and acting styles did not fit together. Before press screenings were introduced, reviewers saw the films on opening night, and it was standard practice that they commented on the reactions of the opening night crowd, often with a skeptical and overbearing distance. The reviews nevertheless bear witness to how audience activity of both spontaneous and strategic character point to contact and complicity with the film and its actors. One reviewer of *Heads or Tails* thus notes that throughout the performance there were rounds of applause, especially when Ib Schønberg had put a snob in their place or had made a funny remark (Madsen 1937). Another reviewer, after a very negative review, condescendingly refers to a group of audience members, who through intense applause and laughter tried to get the rest of the audience going (blk. 1937).

With high-energy performances, exaggerated style and attention to type, actors such as Schønberg, Frederik Jensen, Olga Svendsen, Christian Arhoff, Marguerite Viby and Oswald Helmuth successfully simulated theatre's interaction between audience and fiction. Quite contrary to the nuance and internalisation of naturalistic playing styles, which dominated the legitimate stage and had become the norm of the silent dramas in the 1910s and 1920s, sound comedies drew on exaggeration and anti-naturalism. Such comedic acting styles stem from a long tradition of performing *for* and *in* masses and of working the life and energy of these masses into a complicity and participation in the play-acting (Kruuse 1964: 136–37, 196). The more obvious the performance, the more the audience is invited to comment, mimic and play along. Performance does not get more obvious than in the single-take performance of Liva Weel singing *Et lille kys eller to* ('A Little Kiss or Two') from *De blaa Drenge* (*The Blue Boys*, George Schnéevoigt, 1933). Surrounded by an admiring audience of touring actors, Weel's over-excited delivery and histrionic acting eagerly address both on- and off-screen audiences. Although her artistry was in a league of its own, there are certainly aspects of Weel's performance which are easily copied and invite imitation. Similarly, the thick rural dialect and meaningful glances of legendary *folkekomedie* director, playwright and actor Axel Frische functioned like a manual on how to reproduce everybody's favorite wise old man from Jutland. While the films invited the audience to join in the performance in the cinema (Jensen 2001: 127; Kjørup 1991: 16), programmes with portraits and song lyrics and the sale of sheet music and gramophones encouraged the extension of the participatory culture outside of the cinema. Thus, Danes would reproduce and recapture the looks and mannerisms of *folkekomedie*'s beloved types.

The importance of the sound comedies of the 1930s cannot be overestimated in their ability to reinvent Danish film culture in the wake of film sound; their fictions played an essential role in securing an active Danish film production in the sound era. They successfully appealed to and became common property of the small nation. Not least in their ability to assemble the broadest possible audience in cinemas across Denmark did the films in a very manifest way incarnate the cultural and social integration which they so heralded in their stories. The themes of cultural and national integration have continued into later *folkekomedie* film, theatre, as well as onto television, where recently the many seasons of the successful *Badehotellet* (*The Seaside Hotel*, TV2, 2013–) have inscribed themselves as unapologetic heirs to the *folkekomedie* of the thirties.

THE PEOPLE ON DISPLAY: FICTIONS OF THE KNOWN

The plots, characters and themes of *folkekomedie* are often referred to by critics and scholars as predictable and perfunctory, as well as recognised by fans of the genre as just for fun and not to be taken seriously. The perceived artlessness or unpretentiousness of the genre to a large degree stems from how it draws on the known, the recognisable and the relatable. On the level of subject-matter, motifs and themes, the *folkekomedie* tradition discussed in this chapter is concerned with Danish types, locations, traditions and popular superstitions of the people (Alsted 1985: 148).

In *folkekomedie* the traits of the character types, such as the work ethos of the *working girl* or the unconditional love of a mother become nationally specified, through the identification of these traits with Danishness by the audiences, or by how the films use landscapes, language, costume or history to explicate national specificity. Thus, the celebrated mother-love of *Den lille Hornblæser* (*The Little Hornblower*, Eduard Schnedler-Sørensen, 1909) becomes unequivocally Danish through the fact that it is directed at her son, who is a valiant horn blower during the Danish-Prussian campaign of 1848–52. In *Eventyrrejsen* (*The Fairytale Journey*, Ole Berggreen, 1960), which deals with charter tourism, it is the Central European setting which brings out the Danishness of travel group members such as Bodil Udsen's butcher's wife, whose healthy appetite in scene after scene battles her suspicion of foreign foods. By referring to the fairytales and stories of Hans Christian Andersen in the title, the film lends a mythical and very Danish perspective to its characters and their experiences. In the politically conscious *De frigjorte* (*Fish Out of Water*, Erik Clausen, 1993), the film's references to real political conflicts and a specific Danish socio-cultural history gives the central character's outdated worker his unequivocally national and demographic specificity.

Nowhere is the cultural meaning connected to locations and institutions more delightfully captured than in the *Olsen-banden* films (*The Olsen Gang*, Erik Balling 1968–81 and 1998; see also Schröder, Chapter 9 in this volume). In fourteen instalments filmed over thirty years, this series recounts the illegal misadventures of the Olsen gang, led by criminal mastermind Egon Olsen. His criminal intrigues rely on a seemingly arbitrary selection of culturally Danish practices and artefacts, ranging from safety matches to porn magazines and the Royal Guards. With attention to their exact cultural connotations, these are strategically staged to allow the gang entrance to management offices, vaults or bunkers. For example, a piece of second-class *smørrebrød* (a Danish open sandwich) delivered to the executive floor of the National Data Centre creates the intended upset in *Olsen-banden går i krig* (*The Olsen Gang Goes to War*, Erik Balling, 1978). Egon Olsen's most celebrated plan is set in motion in *Olsen-banden ser rødt* (*The Olsen Gang Sees Red*, Erik Balling, 1976), where the gang has to get through the armoured walls of the cellar of the Royal Theatre in Copenhagen in order to reach a red suitcase containing millions of kroner. The effectuation of the plan, which is staged with full physical comedy, suspense and attention to stereotypes, is a testament to how intelligently and subtly *folkekomedie* can draw on common and cultural knowledge. Referring to the real working conditions of the Royal Theatre, Egon Olsen in his characteristic obsessive fashion explains why the walls have been erected between the different sections of the theatre: 'The musicians hate the opera singers, the opera singers hate the ballet dancers, the ballet dances hate the actors, the actors hate each other, and the technicians are convinced that only they do any work!' Reading like an anthropological case-study, the old and respected institution is concisely and hilariously reduced to resemble every dysfunctional workplace in the kingdom. The demolition of the walls of the theatre cellar is planned to take place during the performance of the 1828 warhorse of *Elverhøi* (*Elf Hill*). Far from the destruction suggested by the dynamite and pickaxes, the explosions and crashing of walls are carried out with craft, concentration and artistry by the gang members, who synchronise every last blast with the music of the *Elf Hill* overture. The bombastic swells and reverberations create a powerful and unexpected reinvention of the overture and result in an effusive reception by the theatre's audience, musicians and conductor. Not only facilitating the concordance between artists and art forms in the National Theatre, which in itself is a sly comment on *Elf Hill* author Johan Ludvig Heiberg's strict ideas about genre-mixing, the film creates a surprising alliance between tradition, high art and the criminal creativity of the Olsen gang (see also Chapter 9 in this book).

A large part of the attraction of *folkekomedie* for the audience is being able to engage and re-engage with performers who are *folkekære* – literally, 'beloved by the people' (Alsted 1985: 148). Recreating their types in one *folkekomedie* after another, they reference prior performances, even though the role may be new. Film scholars have pointed to how comedy actors often create an irresolvable and fascinating tension between fiction and reality (see Neale 2000: 62). This is certainly at play in *folkekomedie*, where talent such as Ib Schønberg, Christian Arhoff, Erik Clausen, Marguerite Viby, Paul Reichhardt, Bodil Jørgensen, Peter Malberg and Kirsten Walther have become part of the popular imagination for seemingly bridging the gap between fiction and reality in their performances. While demographic traits help to build the type, such as the dialect of Arhoff from the island of Funen, or the working-class manners and sociolects of Viby and Walther, their performances are marked by individual traits, humour, temper and idiosyncrasies. The use of close-up and sound recording of the film medium moreover facilitates an individualisation, which pushes films' *folkekomedie* types in the direction of unique experience, a point which has also been observed in connection with filmic (as opposed to theatrical) melodrama (Affron 1982: 15–16). As noted above, the obvious and often exaggerated performance can create an audience engagement and complicity which has significant emotional potential. Even if these types are not necessarily found in real-life Denmark, the degree to which they are beloved by a national audience goes a long way to explaining why they are perceived as consummate Danish characters.

The extreme physical and vocal idiosyncrasies of Dirch Passer struck a chord with the audience, and despite his extraordinariness he came to be seen as the quintessential Danish outsider fool. In eighty films from the early 1950s to 1978, in which the performance of his type was the main attraction, his participation became genre-defining. If he was in a film, it was perceived as *folkekomedie*. Interestingly, Passer's very presence in the adaptations of international classics such as *Charles tante* (*Charley's Aunt*, Poul Bang, 1959) from the English play and the German and French operettas *Sommer i Tyrol* (*White Horse Inn*, Erik Balling, 1964) and *Frøken Nitouche* (*Mam'zelle Nitouche*, Annelise Reenberg, 1963) have been appropriated by generations of delighted audiences as examples of *bona fide* Danish *folkekomedie*. Closer to our own time, a comparable phenomenon can be seen in reality television and other genres that experiment with the combination of fiction and reality. Extreme types who have caught the fancy of the audience and come to signify Danish types include celebrity model, strip club owner and dog lover Linse Kessler of *Familien på Bryggen* (*The Family from Bryggen*, TV3, 2011–) and jet-setter and *enfant terrible* Casper Christensen of *Klovn* (*Clown*, TV2, 2005–18).

Enduring Prototypes

The family *folkekomedie* prototype broke through with *Far til fire* (*Father of Four*, Alice O'Fredericks, 1950) and a string of successful follow-ups, recounting the family life of an office worker and his four children in a modern suburban middle-class neighbourhood. Based on a cartoon strip and retaining some of its graphic stylisation, causality often gives way in these films to a comedy of types and situations with inclusion and integration as recurrent themes. Like the artist collectives and boarding houses of the 1930s sound comedies, Father's family is open to all who need somewhere to belong, from the grandfather figure of Uncle Anders to the surly neighbour, Mrs Sejersen, from lonely tenants to rescued animals. The family *folkekomedie* films are built around distinctive child performers whose significant power of attraction draws on the same irresolvable tension between proper identity and fictional role as their *folkekære* adult star counterparts, as discussed above. Arguably, the child performances are more intuitive and less reflective, and the fact that they often starred under their proper names seems to underscore a double citizenship of fiction and reality. One of the top box-office draws of the 1930s was Connie Meiling (later Linck), who as Little Connie incarnated childhood and set the standard for phenomenally popular child stars of family *folkekomedie*; examples included Ole Neumann, who played Little Per in the *Father of Four* films, and Pusle Helmuth of the series *Min søsters børn* (*Six Kids and Their Uncle*, Annelise Reenberg, 1966–71).

The family *folkekomedier* serve up an almost impudently positive vision of family, where everything from generational conflict to abuse is eclipsed by an edifying speech or sentimental moment. As such they are the very antithesis of the genre of the 'social problem film' that emerged in the early 1950s, such as *Unge piger forsvinder i København* (*Young Girls Disappear in Copenhagen*, Aage Wiltrup, 1951) and *Farlig ungdom* (*Dangerous Youth*, Lau Lauritzen, Jr, 1953), which, within the realist tradition, points to the multifaceted and intractable aspects of such problems (see also Langkjær, Chapter 6 in this volume).

The 'crew film' is another *folkekomedie* prototype which is characterised by integration and Danishness. Here, sports, infantry, navy, air force or rescue corps crew function as national microcosms, encompassing provincial and urban characters, upper and lower classes, tough guys and wimps (Nielsen 2011: 40–41). The interaction of opposing characters illustrates their parallels, conflicts and ultimate integration. In *Week-end* (*Weekend*, Lau Lauritzen Jr and Alice O'Fredericks, 1935), sports training and competition supplies the background, while in *Soldaterkammerater* (*Bugle with a Beat*, Svend Methling, 1958) and *Piger i trøjen* (*Girls at Arms*, Finn Henriksen, 1975) it is military routines and exercises with characters dressed in real uniforms and with frequent use of the national flag and characteristic Danish landscapes.

The underlying logic of *folkekomedie*, then, is that they to a significant degree refer to a known reality. This is an invitation for the audience to recognise, mirror and confirm that reality, and not least to learn to view it in a playful mode (Kruuse 1964: 136–37). Recognising the Danishness of everything from nineteenth-century mother-love to the rocking lifestyle of Linse Kessler

Figure 5.2   Danish girls at arms: uniforms and landscape lend national specificity to the characters and action in *Piger i trøjen* (*Girls at Arms*, Finn Henriksen, 1975). Framegrab.

and the cultural nuances of *smørrebrød*, a Danish audience experiences a privileged, esoteric understanding, the cultural nuances of which only they can grasp (Hartvigson 2007: 53). In *Genboerne* (*The Neighbours Across the Street*), Arne Weel's 1939 film adaption of Jens Christian Hostrup's classic 1843 *folkekomedie*, the experience of recognising and mirroring is immortalised in a naively enthusiastic outburst from the coppersmith couple. 'Herfra kan vi se vore egne Vindver', they observe – literally, 'From here we can see our own windows' – when they visit a university student in his room at the *Regensen* dormitory across the street from where they live. Seeing oneself from across the street becomes the basis for understanding the differences and similarities between neighbours, and points to the integrative logic on which *folkekomedie* plots so often draw.

Sentimentality and Farce

The often-encountered demand that *folkekomedie* must be sentimental (Tybjerg 1996: 76) places integration in an unequivocally emotional perspective, and it encourages an experience of what is *right* to be ultimately a matter of sentimental intuition for the audience. In *Far til fire i byen* (*Father of Four on the Town*, Alice O'Fredericks, 1951), the ethos of the inclusive family is exploited in a sentimental fashion, as the newly rescued dog finds Little Per at the Christmas service and, later, as they are found sleeping together in the same bed. In *Fairytale Journey* belonging and community is illustrated emotionally in the elderly professor's restrained mourning over the death of his wife, which encourages a newfound solidarity among the travellers returning home. The sentimental dimension is often highlighted as naïve and ideologically questionable by academic scholars and journalists; often referred to is a scene in *Københavnere* (*Copenhageners*, Lau Lauritzen Sr, 1933) where Ib Schønberg's character abandons all political ideals in favour of being part of the community and speaks of 'feeling something *in here*' while pointing to his heart (Kistrup 1977: n. p.).

However, the sentimental dimension and final integration are absent or played down in a number of undisputed instances of the genre, which typically play on farce and crude stereotypes. The dynamics of the *Olsen Banden* series draw on the insurmountable antagonism between the lower-class gang and the nobility, the establishment and capitalist crooks. This precludes integration, and in film after film of this series, Egon Olsen ends up behind bars, where he contemplates a new genius plan. This resistance to full-blown integration suggests that the gang film can be viewed as a separate *folkekomedie* prototype. Recent examples of this prototype are the black comedies about gangs or groups of social outcasts, criminals and maniacs such as *I Kina spiser de hunde* (*In China They Eat Dogs*, Lasse Spang Olsen, 1999) and *Blinkende lygter* (*Flickering Lights*, Anders Thomas Jensen, 2000) (see also Thomson, Chapter 13 in this volume). The theme of reconciliation of differences between the gang members is often introduced; however, no character is safe from annihilation in these films, which revel in farcical violence and coincidental killings.

In the more politically oriented instances of the genre, such as Clausen's 1993 film *Fish Out of Water*, for example, the explicit political conflicts in the plot preclude resolution of the tensions dividing the nation, even if the film's character types are drawn with warmth and off-beat charm. While Clausen's Danish types are emotionally redeemable, in the satirical *Tid til forandring* (*What's Wrong with This Picture?*, Lotte Svendsen, 2004), which denounces the lack of solidarity and humanity in modern-day Denmark, the characters are exposed as unable to connect on any meaningful emotional or ideological level.

Films for the People

While the aesthetics, themes and conflicts may vary according to historical period or *folkekomedie* prototype, supporters and critics alike agree that a determining factor is the *people*, which is the concept designated by the 'folke' of *folkekomedie*. According to this view, the dramaturgy, motifs, themes and mechanics of *folkekomedie* ultimately serve the audience's recognition and mirroring of their lives and values. As a general assumption, the term 'the people' refers to the broad, quantitative majority with limited cultural power, whose interests are not typically embraced by dominant cultural institutions. However, throughout its history, this concept has encompassed groups as different as the emerging bourgeoisie of the nineteenth century, the industrial working class or rural audiences of the late half of the nineteenth and first half of the twentieth century, and today's more segment-oriented audience, and in the nature of things this makes for very different conceptions of the genre. More than acknowledging the ability of *folkekomedie* to reflect the sensibility of the people, there is a long tradition of regarding *folkekomedie* as coming from and belonging to the people (Nielsen 2001: 193).

Using a Cultural Studies approach allows for a theoretical shift from the text as the central and determining generator of meaning and permits us to encompass *folkekomedie* as an event in a broad sociological and cultural sense, including the subjective or cultural forms which are created around it (Johnson 1986–87: 62). First and foremost, such an understanding allows us to grasp the significant openness of the *folkekomedie* texts as an opportunity to encompass the activity, sensibility, behaviour and creativity of the audience. From the actors vying for the audience's help in upholding the often obvious fictions, to the audience loudly acknowledging, meddling in or daring them, *folkekomedie* may arguably be seen as a co-creative event. In the theatre of Røde Kro, which in 1961 was one of the last *folkekomedie* theatres to close down, testimonials tell of as much acting going on in the audience as in the fiction on stage, with the audience responding to the fiction as if trying it on for size (Nielsen 2001: 193). In addition, musical numbers described the relationship between stage and audience as a 'bridge of joy' (*glædesbro*), a metaphor that splendidly encompasses the reciprocal relationship of fiction and audience as joyous mirroring engagement (Nielsen 2001: 182–84). Of course, the asynchronous film medium could not have the same direct interaction between fiction and audience. Nevertheless, with their appropriation of comedy strategies and use of actors from the popular theatre, the films acknowledged in no uncertain terms that they were direct descendants of theatrical *folkekomedie* (Jensen 2001: 127; Kjørup 1991: 16). They thereby signalled an openness to including the cultural acts of its audience, their temperament and behaviour as part of the performance – if only virtually. Testimonials of the audience activity and creativity are primarily accessible through film reviews. As witnessed by the reviews of *Heads or Tails*, the reviewers would often be baffled by the affirmative audience response and react with condescension. However, emerging from the reviews are images of a historical audience, reacting not only spontaneously, but also strategically, as they repeatedly communicate with each other and the performance of the fiction.

The emotional experience of having one's values recognised and belonging to a community goes a long way to explain such audience activity; *folkekomedie* may be said to facilitate the intuitive emotional reflection of the communal experience of recognising, mirroring and confirming the fiction. The creative activities of the audience also take place beyond the cinemas. Generations of viewers have promoted culture by singling out beloved parts of the films' imagery, such as mimicking characters, referencing dialogue and integrating these actions into their everyday lives. In this way audiences – and sometimes non-audience members – have exalted films such as *Copenhageners*, *The Olsen Gang* films and the television series *Matador* (*Matador*, Erik Balling, 1978–81) into cultural milestones. The sheer number of phrases from these *folkekomedie* fictions which have entered into everyday parlance is certainly a testament to the cultural creativity of 'the people'.

Likewise, the reverence for old culture entails a creative dimension, when the audience, actively embracing the archaic imagery, language and famous quotes, turn themselves into mediators of these classics. During the German occupation of Denmark from 1940 to 1945, a large number of film adaptations of classic *folkekomedier* by writers such as Herman Bang, Jeppe Aakjær, Johan Ludvig Heiberg and Johanne Luise Heiberg became re-canonised by the public and functioned as common cultural points of reference during the national crisis (Jørholt 2001: 123). In these adaptations, generations of fictive and historical characters stood in line to tell the Danes who they were, from the peasant lovers Lisbeth and Jochum of *En søndag på Amager* (*A Sunday on Amager*, Emanuel Gregers, 1941) to King Christian IV in *Elverhøj* (*Elf Hill*, Svend Methling, 1939). *Sørensen og Rasmussen* (*Sørensen and Rasmussen*, Emanuel Gregers, 1940), which crosses the paths and fates of a queen consort and a maid around 1850, was based on a radio play and is not a classic, but in Frederik Schyberg's contemporary review of it, he sees it as a classic in the making: 'more than simply popular; it is *of the people* (*folkelig*) and hereby it has a great potential' (Bondebjerg 2005a: 192, emphasis added). The 'great potential' suggested here is undoubtedly how the film could be activated by the people and become part of the popular imagination – which it eventually did. What determines *folkelig* and *folkekomedie* according to Schyberg's 1940s view are not the films themselves, nor the audience's enjoyment of the moment, but the public's consecration of them as cultural markers. This view of cinema represents a multilayered process between viewer, film and culture, which far transcends the film's aesthetic qualities and which pre-dates by decades the preference in Cultural Studies for studying events rather than texts.

Film Institutions and the *Folkekomedie*

That *folkekomedie's* potential far transcends that of its subject matter and aesthetics is also illustrated by how institutions actively define the genre in the light of their respective values and cultural, social and ideological affiliations.

A striking example of how much meaning is connected to institutions is the theatrical reorganisation of the mid-nineteenth century, when the newly established theatres of Casino, Dagmar and Nørrebro were allowed to perform *folkekomedier*, which until then had been the privilege of the Royal Theatre (Kvam, Risum and Wiingaard 1993: 12, 39). The new theatres achieved a formidable success, which put immense pressure on the state-subsidised Royal Theatre, which had abandoned the genre in order to distance itself from the popular theatres. This was the first of many instances where the popularity of *folkekomedie* upset the status quo and came to represent a prime site of conflict in Danish culture. Within film culture, from the 1930s onwards, the *folkekomedie* genre has repeatedly spelled out conflict, especially when it threatened the dominant position of national, state-subsidised institutions.

Unlike the state-controlled media of radio and later television, the film business was from its inception a commercial enterprise. However, with Denmark's first Film Law of 1933 and its 1938 revision under the Social Democratic government, state regulation regarding licenses for production, distribution and exhibition were introduced, along with support for films of cultural importance and public interest (Dinnesen and Kau 1983: 144). The association of 1930s sound comedies with *folkekomedie* proved extremely culturally divisive, and an emerging academic criticism followed by newspaper critics attacked the genre and demanded a more progressive output. This contributed to a critical view of the genre as such by politicians and opinion leaders, and in 1947 and then again in 1963 it came to a head: the company Saga Studios, which specialised in *folkekomedie*, came close to losing its combined production and exhibition license due to the supposedly low quality of its output (Dinnesen and Kau 1983: 244, 463; Pedersen and Klement 2016: 202). Such extreme state intervention was far from the norm in Denmark, and it is an unequivocal sign of the culturally contested status of *folkekomedie* and the studios associated with them. The Film Law of 1964, implemented as a direct consequence of the competition from television, which threatened cinema production as a whole, saw all films benefit from the state income from box-office sales tax. However, the law favoured artistic and culturally important films. The text of the law stated that film art constituted a substantial part of a country's cultural life, and economic guarantees and loans backed this claim (Dinnesen and Kau 1983: 403–4). An even harsher blow to *folkekomedie* and popular film was dealt with the revised Film Law of 1972, which introduced a state-funded film production that solely supported film of artistic or social merit (498). In practice, this meant no support for *folkekomedie* films, which were also deprived of the ticket fee subsidy (494). Established successes such as *The Olsen Gang* series still thrived, but *folkekomedie* films now had competition from the newly established entertainment department of state-financed television. The less risky production model was alluring, and the incomparable and very bankable talent of *The Olsen Gang* director, Erik Balling and his right-hand man Henning Bahs successfully applied television formats to *folkekomedie* in *Huset på Christianshavn* (*The House on Christianshavn*, Erik Balling, 1970–77) and later to *Matador* (1978–82). The massive success of both series established and redefined television as the main provider of *folkekomedie* for many years to come.

Support for popular film was re-instated with the introduction of the commercially friendly 'fifty-fifty' model of 1989 (see also Thomson, Chapter 13 in this volume), where state funding would supply the lacking 50 per cent of the budget for any film production. This model and its 'sixty-forty' follow-up from 1990 paved the way for a revival of *folkekomedie*. Especially successful were producer Ragnar Grasten's revival of the family *folkekomedie* with *Krummerne* (*The Crumbs*, Sven Methling, 1991) and the teenage-themed *Kærlighed ved første hik* (*Love at First Hiccough*, Charlotte Sachs Bostrup and Thomas Villum Jensen, 1999), which were both made into film series.

Conclusion

The renewed success of *folkekomedie* film series in recent decades is testament to the power of attraction of a simple kind of fiction that recreates Danish types and Danishness and that is characterised by integration. It also suggests cinemas' continued ability to create real and virtual meeting places, which allow viewers to investigate their national and cultural identity and interact with the fictions communally. Moreover, this chapter has shown how the phenomenon of *folkekomedie* has demonstrated a remarkable resilience and propensity to travel between old and new media, while also contributing to shaping, and being re-moulded by, emerging formats and the evolution of cultural and state institutions. We have also seen how the *folkekomedie* spawns historically-specific sub-genres, adapting its tropes and types to different times and contexts, weaving its way through Danish cinema history in various guises. Lurking at the intersection between high art and popular culture, the *folkekomedie* is a cornerstone not just of Danish cinema, but of Danish cultural history.

Note

1. Both Lau Lauritzen Senior (1878–1938) and Lau Lauritzen Junior (1910–77) are mentioned in this chapter, and both generations of Lauritzens appear in other chapters in this book. Lauritzen *père* worked for Nordisk and Palladium film companies, and Lauritzen *fils* co-founded ASA Film; both were actors and prolific directors.

6. SOCIAL REALISM OF THE 1940S: BETWEEN PATERNALISTIC CARE AND DIGNIFYING HUMANISM

Birger Langkjær

While 'realism' in film studies is an umbrella term covering a variety of meanings, 'social realism' has a more stable meaning within scholarship.[1] The prefix 'social' indicates the main theme, whereas 'realism' indicates something related to ordinary life and common people, which frequently translates into working-class people. Realism also designates a mainly serious drama (in opposition to comedy). In short, social realism addresses social issues that relate to ordinary people in a serious (non-comic) manner.

During the 1940s, a significant stream of Danish cinema engaged in a kind of filmmaking that took the trivialities of life and made them into dramas of the everyday. The motifs of these films were social, the tone was serious, and the scene often contemporary. In this broad sense, they qualify as social realism. Social realism continued into 1950s Danish cinema, but for practical reasons I will mainly focus on the 1940s.

This chapter will first establish how social realism in Danish feature film originated from different sources. These include Danish documentaries, the literary tradition of social realism and a crossover of creative people between documentary, literature, theatre and feature filmmaking. Second, I argue that there are two tendencies in social realism in Danish cinema. First, there is the 'problem film' that addresses social issues from the perspective of authorities and public institutions, in ways reminiscent of the educational intentions of the short documentary film. Second, there is the broader social realism that tends to critique social structures, yet to dignify its protagonists within a 'humanist ethos'. Furthermore, I will argue that social realism executes its 'realism' in different narrative forms and through a variety of stylistic repertoires, which can be characterised as an amalgamated style.

Taking the Trivial Seriously: From Documentaries to Feature Films

The 1940s witnessed a substantial upsurge in the production of short documentaries in Denmark, typically seven to eight minutes in duration, as the German occupation of Denmark from 1940 to 1945 increased the demand for information about public institutions and society (Jørholt 2008: 138, Thomson 2018a: 47–63). Their stylistic features had many similarities to British documentaries of the 1930s. In general, the Danish documentary of the 1940s was a highly aesthetically executed film form that combined the 'dramatisation' of scenes from the everyday, voice-over, well-composed images and distinctive and rhythmic montage sequences in a complex form, on one hand, with companies and public institutions as their protagonists in a mode of address that often combined pathos and humour, on the other hand (see Bondebjerg, Chapter 7 in this volume).

The short documentary was important for social realism in Danish feature films in several ways. Most importantly, it addressed a series of subject areas not represented in the fiction film, often tentatively captured by the terms 'the everyday' or 'ordinary life'. It also used on-location shooting and real people, thus depicting a shared reality outside the film studios. It was moreover an artistic training ground for some of the filmmakers of social realism in feature film. Ole Palsbo not only directed short documentaries such as *Spild er Penge* (*Waste is Money*, 1942) and *Papir og Pap er Penge værd* (*Paper and Cardboard is Worth a Lot of Money*, 1947) on wartime recycling, but also turned to social realism with *Diskret Ophold* (*Discretion Wanted*, 1946) (see Langkjær 2005). Bjarne and Astrid Henning-Jensen made documentaries on various subjects before directing *Ditte Menneskebarn* (*Ditte, Child of Man*, Bjarne Henning-Jensen, 1946) and *De pokkers Unger* (*Those Damned Kids*, Astrid Henning-Jensen, 1947). In addition, cinematographers moved back and forth between documentary and fiction. Verner Jensen was cinematographer on documentaries by Palsbo and the Henning-Jensen couple, as well as on features such as *Ditte, Child of Man*, *Discretion Wanted* and Johan Jacobsen's *Ta', hvad du vil ha'* (*Take Whatever You Want*, 1947) and *Tre år efter* (*Three Years After*, 1948). Another cinematographer, Aage Wiltrup, filmed documentaries in the early 1940s and feature films within social realism such as *Spurve under Taget* (*Sparrows under the Eaves*, Charles Tharnæs, 1944) and *Soldaten og Jenny* (*Jenny and the Soldier*, Johan Jacobsen, 1947). He turned director with *Unge piger forsvinder i København* (*Young Girls Disappear in Copenhagen*, 1952). In these ways, the short documentary and the fiction film are not fully separate entities, but part of a larger movement of Danish film towards realism in the widest sense of the term: an attention to and interest in ordinary life.

LITERARY SOURCES OF SOCIAL REALISM IN DANISH CINEMA

It appears natural to perceive the broader movement of social realism in Danish cinema of the 1940s in the international context of contemporary realism or 'realist' movements. Nevertheless, early social realism in Danish cinema slightly pre-dates Italian neorealism (and later British kitchen sink realism); therefore, French poetic realism is the best candidate, although its most visible influence is on the dark Danish crime films of the 1940s, beginning with *Afsporet* (*Derailed*, Bodil Ipsen and Lau Lauritzen Jr, 1942; see Sørensen, Chapter 4 in this volume). Due to the German occupation of Denmark from 1940 to 1945, access to contemporary cinemas was also restricted (Dinnesen and Kau 1983: 167–86). In 1940, 'British films were prohibited and the importation of American films was stopped. In 1942 the exhibition of American films was also prohibited' (Neergaard 1950: 226). Apart from the short documentary, an obvious source of cinematic social realism is the tradition of a critical realism in Danish literature and theatre that addresses social issues. This artistic program, originally formulated by the literary critic Georg Brandes (Brandes 1877: 17), also flourished in the Danish theatre and novels of the 1930s and 1940s (Bondebjerg 1984). This realism found its way into Danish cinema in the 1940s via adaptations for the screen. Classic realist literature was adapted to film, such as the first volume of Martin Andersen Nexø's *Ditte Menneskebarn* (*Ditte, Child of Man*, 1917–21). So too were contemporary plays like *Storken* (*The Stork*, Thit Jensen, 1929) and *Brudstykker af et Mønster* (*Fragments of a Pattern*, Carl Erik Soya, 1940), adapted respectively as *Det Brændede Spørgsmaal* (*The Burning Question*, Alice O'Fredericks, 1943) and *Jenny and the Soldier*. Novelist and dramatist Leck Fischer made Mogens Klitgaard's realist-style radio novel *Elly Petersen* (1941) into a film script (1944), and theatre actor Charles Tharnæs made his theatrical play *Spurve under Taget* (1942) into *Sparrows under the Eaves* in 1944. Furthermore, writers from the realist tradition began to work as scriptwriters, most notably Leck Fischer. He was a scriptwriter on several of the films to define social realism in Danish cinema, such as *Barnet* (*The Child*, Benjamin Christensen, 1940), *Elly Petersen*, *De røde Enge* (*The Red Meadows*, Bodil Ipsen and Lau Lauritsen Jr, 1945), *Discretion Wanted* and *Kampen mod uretten* (*The Fight Against Injustice*, Ole Palsbo, 1949). Thus, the previously addressed crossover of creative professionals between the short documentary film and social realism in the feature film mirrors simultaneous crossover activities and ideas travelling between literature, theatre and film.

ENLIGHTENMENT THROUGH FICTION: THE DIDACTIC 'PROBLEM FILM'

After the dominance of *folkekomedier* (folk comedies) in the 1930s (see Hartvigson, Chapter 5 in this volume), Danish filmmakers of the 1940s were encouraged to address serious social issues by the possibility of applying for exemption from the entertainment tax (*forlystelsesafgift*) (Jørholt 2008: 143). Record-high wartime sales of cinema tickets in combination with the ban on films from the US and Britain paved the way for a boom in the production of Danish films (Bondebjerg 2005a: 66–67), including films offering a serious treatment of social issues. This type of film, however, is not limited to the occupation period. An early example is *Skilsmissens Børn* (*Children of Divorce*, Benjamin Christensen, 1939), while a late one is *Bundfald* (*Sin Alley*, Palle Kjærulff-Schmidt, 1957), the latter on male prostitution.

Public discourse referred to this type as the 'problem film' (*problemfilm*). A reviewer of *The Burning Question* writes as follows: 'Alice O'Fredericks has made a problem film about those problems she has previously been fighting for, and it is characteristic of this problem film, like any other, that it sets up a single case and makes a generalisation from that' (M. L. 1943). In this short passage, the reviewer actually describes the overall formula of the problem film. Samantha Lay addresses a type of fiction film on social issues in 1950s British cinema that is reminiscent of the Danish problem film: 'Although fiction, these films can be seen as a continuation of the documentary movement's mission to inform and educate citizens by exploring contemporary concerns through the medium of film' (Lay 2002: 55). The Danish problem film, however, not only addressed social issues through storytelling, but also flagged its didactic or educational intention. This, however, took different forms.

The Burning Question is about a young woman who becomes pregnant out of wedlock. She persuades a doctor to perform an illegal abortion, but their crime is discovered, and they go to trial. The film then becomes a courtroom drama in which the male doctor, before the jury and the judge, argues for a woman's right to abortion in cases where the father has bad hereditary material in his family. In the courtroom, he illustrates his extensive medical and moral lecture on the principal aspects of a single woman's story with poster-size explanatory drawings. In this way, the film stages a professional authority addressing an important set of issues, yet makes it emerge 'naturally' from a given situation. Similarly, it elevates the particularity of the story of its female protagonist into a more general problematic encompassing a strange cocktail of women's rights and contemporary eugenicist ideas. This form combines devices from fiction-style storytelling and rhetorical pathos.

Svend Methling's *Det store Ansvar* (*The Heavy Responsibility*, 1944) depicts the fictional character Skipper, a well-known teacher. He is on his way to a public hall to give a radio broadcast lecture on the subject of parents' responsibility for their children. In parallel to Skipper's lecture, we follow not

SOCIAL REALISM OF THE 1940S

Figure 6.1 A poster promoting the problem film *Det brændende Spørgsmål* (*The Burning Question*, Alice O'Fredericks, 1943) is indicative of the film's blend of drama and social enquiry. Image: Danish Film Institute.

only spellbound audiences listening, but also the sad live-action stories of two young people whom Skipper has met. The main part of the film cuts back and forth between the lecture, his audiences and the stories of the two young people. In addition, the film illustrates elements of Skipper's talk with beautifully photographed and rhythmically edited documentary footage of well-functioning and modern public childcare institutions in a style aligned with short documentary film. The film's main message is upbeat: the state and its institutions are not adversaries, but helpers dedicated to making a difference for children and young people who have fallen into crime or other problems. The institutions of society are obviously not the problem, but the solution. In terms of style and narrative, Skipper's lecture allows the film to oscillate between different representational modes from fiction and documentary.

In contrast, *Café Paradis* (*Cafe Paradise*, 1950) by Bodil Ipsen and Lau Lauritzen Jr downplays the forms of direct address by authorities and public institutions. The film reflects on alcoholism as a broader issue primarily during a scene between two doctors. However, its main didactic device is to move between two parallel stories of men battling alcoholism. Formally, these plot-strings connect by audiovisual dissolves from one character to the other, emphasising the connection. Whereas the wife of the middle-class protagonist abandons him (and he dies), the working-class wife stays with her alcoholic husband and helps him stop drinking. The different outcomes teach the audience that the fight against alcoholism is heavily dependent on sustained support from close ones. Thus, *Café Paradise* is a problem film, yet with a less obvious didactic intent than the two previous films.

A final stylistic device to underline the educational purpose is the voice-over. In the opening of *Young Girls Disappear in Copenhagen*, a police officer confronts the camera and tells us about the sad 'fate' of young women coming to the city from the countryside. There then follows edited documentary footage of the town hall square in Copenhagen and people in the streets before the camera focuses on a female character entering an apartment building. During this sequence, the police officer continues as voice-over and tells the audience how an accidental meeting with a stranger (a man) became fatal for her. The past tense of the voice-over's storytelling adds a shadow of doom to her appearance.

In short, the problem film is social realism because it addresses socially defined problems in ordinary people's lives, and it often does so in a serious tone. It is a drama of the ordinary, often with a female protagonist, and it uses location shooting to embed its stories in real life. Yet, its intention to inform and educate is evident through voice-overs, authorities that lecture or reflect on a social problem and parallel storytelling.

Julia Hallam and Margaret Marshment distinguish between 'social issue films' and 'social realism' in British films: 'In social issue films, the individual's problems present a problem for society (how to educate, to police, to contain, to treat), rather than being perceived as a problem created by society, a perspective often attributed to social realism' (Hallam with Marshment 2000: 190). This difference also, to a certain extent, characterises Danish cinema. The problem film typically incorporates positive representations of social authorities. The institutions of society are often aware of the problem and actively strive to remedy it. The root of the problem is often the ignorance of citizens, or that society needs to allocate more funds for specific purposes.

Other dimensions of social realism in Danish cinema tend to adopt a more critical stance on social structures. In this kind of social realism, the hero is not society, but each and every one of the people who has to live with its unfairness. I will now turn to these films.

Critical-Humanist Social Realism: Motifs, Characters and Emotional Perspective

Elsewhere, I have argued that it is useful to characterise realism in film on the following levels: its *style* (e.g. camera style, editing and locations), its *narrative form* (how its narration unfolds), its *content* (motifs, characters, issues) and its implied *emotional perspective* on the actions, events and characters that it depicts (Langkjær 2012: 51–80). The defining features of a more critical social realism in Danish cinema, however, are on the level of content and emotional perspective, whereas style and narrative vary more. Therefore, I will first address content and emotional perspective.

The vast majority of the protagonists in Danish social realism are young women. They usually meet a man who charms and then leaves them, as in Oktober-Roser (*October Roses*, Charles Tharnæs, 1946) and *Take Whatever You Want*, often also making them pregnant, as in *Elly Petersen, Sparrows under the Eaves, Ditte, Child of Man, Discretion Wanted* and *Jenny and the Soldier*. What makes these films *social* realism, and not just personal or psychological dramas, is the way in which social elements enhance negative consequences – for example, illegal abortion (most films), stigmatisation of single mothers (*Sparrows under the Eaves*), and power relations and social inequality (all films). In these ways, the antagonist is structural and social. This 'abstract' antagonist embodies itself in particular characters, but they only become a hindrance and threat to the protagonist due to their position within a social structure. Elly leaves her countryside family behind in *Elly Petersen* to make a new life in Copenhagen as a housekeeper in a guesthouse. After a male lodger tries to rape her, the female property owner unfairly accuses her of promiscuity. Later, Elly works as a housekeeper in the mansion of a rich family. The son in the house first tries to seduce her, but soon turns his interest towards a female of his own social class, leaving Elly humiliated and without a job. In *Jenny and the Soldier*, one of several parallel stories involves Jenny, who once got pregnant by a rich man who turned his back on her, only offering her money for an illegal abortion. In sum, the antagonists in these films are specific characters in a story world, but they have certain powers due to social structures. Whereas the problem film often focuses on what society has done for the benefit of its members, critical social realism focuses on its shortcomings. Part of the emotional appeal of this is indignation in the face of injustice, yet it is a structural injustice, a systemic failure.

Copenhagen is a central motif and location. Myriads of people unknown to each other inhabit the city. This feeds into two apparently conflicting motifs: the chance event (*tilfældigheden*) and some form of fate (*skæbnen*). The chance event is the sudden meeting between two people on a street corner, in a guesthouse, or in a bar. The chance meeting, however, becomes the characters' fate, due to its grave outcome.

This emphasis on the fatal echoes the mood of French poetic realism of the 1930s. In Danish social realism, however, the main characters do not follow 'animal' instincts within their human nature, which is otherwise a tendency associated with the naturalism within poetic realism that strongly influenced dark Danish crime dramas in the period, like *Derailed* and *Besættelse*

(*Possession*, Bodil Ipsen, 1944). The heroes of Danish realism, however, are not doomed 'human beasts', as seen in Jean Renoir's *La Bête Humaine* (1938, adapted from a novel by Émile Zola), but just ordinary people in dire circumstances; they are humans with a proper human dignity. The term 'humanism' has a long but diverse history dating back to the Renaissance (Hankins 2007); yet Danish social realism embraces a humanism in the broadest sense of the term in which every single human has a worth of their own.

Social realism also has a sentimental tendency. This is different from French poetic realism, but similar to some iterations of Italian neorealism – for example, Vittorio De Sica's *Ladri di Biciclette* (*Bicycle Thieves*, 1948) and *Umberto D* (1952). The sentimental is a mixed emotion (Fridja and Tan 1999) of something both sad and positive, like looking at a picture of a beloved family member years after he or she has passed away: recognising the person in the picture creates both warm feelings for the person and sad feelings for the loss. The mixed emotion of sentimentalism in Danish social realism, however, links to the fact that the protagonists are often young women who have limited opportunities to defend themselves against the many injustices and abuses, yet they manage to maintain a certain innocence and moral integrity. The crucial dramatic test for the protagonists of social realism is therefore to develop as actors within given, limiting and predominantly negatively defined social terms. In this way, the films combine a structural adversary (the social antagonist) with a celebration of the small-scale heroism of the individual – that is, indignation and pity in combination with admiration and warm sympathy. The narrative rarely offers radical reversals of the overall situation, but a kind of inner victory that focuses on the heroic aspects of little things. This constitutes this kind of social realism's 'humanistic ethos', or its *dignifying humanism*. In the tension between a rigid social structure and an individual who can make a small but crucial difference lies the little man or woman's heroism; the heroism that social realism cultivates. Social realism in Danish cinema is a way to dignify human worth, not only through the depiction of socially imposed suffering, but also through the attitude of the hero who, despite any adversity, transcends victimisation.

Narrative Structure in Social Realism

Danish social realism executes its narratives in a variety of ways. Many films tell several stories either in parallel or in a serial mode. *Elly Petersen* uses a serial mode. It is a social odyssey from the poor countryside to an urban working-class environment and on to a high-class social milieu before it finally lets the protagonist return back home to the countryside. Other films tell their stories as parallel plot lines. *Jenny and the Soldier* makes its many characters' paths criss-cross throughout the narrative as if by accident. Likewise, a central location can connect plot lines. In *Discretion Wanted*, young girls pregnant out of wedlock stay at the midwife's home to give birth without their families' knowledge. Other narratives centre on mini-communities within the city, typically with the backyard or the local street as central locations (*Sparrows under the Eaves*, *Those Damned Kids*). These different structures tend to emphasise the broader social implications of the story: the plurality of plot lines and characters counterbalances the particularity of the film's narrative and make it an instance of a broader social phenomenon. This implied generalisation is not very different from the problem film in kind, but rather in degree.

Similar to Italian neorealism (Bazin 1971b; Thompson 1988: 197–217), Danish social realism has open endings. Some films repeat or mirror the opening scene. In *Elly Petersen*, Elly stands at a ship's rail with an expression of thrilled expectation as she arrives in Copenhagen by boat. In the final scene, she walks towards the boat on her way back home. Thus, repetition can emphasise a fundamental change in the character's situation. Repetition may also emphasise social heritage. In *Ditte, Child of Man*, Ditte is born in the opening scene whereas she gives birth to a girl in the final scene, both children born into poverty and without a father. The ending can also emphasise an entirely negative outcome, as in *October Roses*. The otherwise negligible protagonist unexpectedly experiences a love story, but she is deserted in the end. The closing scene repeats the opening scene and shows her working alone in the darkened office after hours, in a long shot that makes her look small and miserable.

Other films refrain from a circular narrative in order to end their stories on a note of moderate relief. These endings do not provide final closure to their narratives. Rather, they are the beginnings of something new made possible by, but not materialised within, the film's course of action, as in *Sparrows under the Eaves*, *Jenny and the Soldier* and *Take Whatever You Want*. These endings do not offer a firm narrative resolution, yet there is some hope for the protagonists in the future. In these ways, the narratives of social realism are not goal-driven, as in the Hollywood tradition (Bordwell 1986), but play out as a series of social challenges for one or several protagonists, imposed on them from the outside. These challenges have no definite resolution in sight, and therefore the narratives offer no positive closure. Rather, the endings are like openings to something audiences can only guess at, something to happen in the future. In this sense, it is a slice of life, a narrative in the making, never brought to a secure end.

Social Realism and Style

André Bazin praised *Bicycle Thieves* and *Umberto D* as primary examples of Italian neorealism in their use of location shooting in combination with long shots, amateur actors and a de-dramatisation of the narrative (Bazin 1971a and 1971b). Kristin Thompson, however, has shown how *Bicycle Thieves* uses three-point lighting, shot-reverse-shot patterns and other standard stylistic devices, yet combines these with elements praised by André Bazin. Thompson's argument is that default devices function automatically and go unnoticed, whereas new devices become salient in audience perception (Thompson 1988).

In similar ways, social realism in Danish cinema reveals an amalgamated stylistic form, combining standard procedures like well-lit studio sets and 'invisible editing' with elements that provide a fresh take, such as location shooting. Location shooting often occurs in opening and closing sequences that establish Copenhagen as the main setting. This is a way to embed a fictional story into non-fiction, as if the film simply dove into the world as it exists, fixated on a person on the street and followed that person into his or her private life. This also works at scene level. In a scene halfway through *Jenny and the Soldier*, the soldier walks towards the camera (long shot) on a sunny boulevard, with a cigarette in hand. He slows down and looks slightly to the left of the screen. Then he moves right towards a lamp post and (cut to a medium close-up) drops the cigarette. He closes his eyes, face fully sunlit, as the camera tracks backwards. He then turns around, moves away from the camera (into a long

Figure 6.2 Location shooting embeds fictional characters in the real-life streets of Copenhagen, in *Soldaten og Jenny* (*Jenny and the Soldier*, Johan Jacobsen, 1947). Framegrab from title sequence.

shot) and seats himself outside a bistro. After ordering, he picks up a small harmonica (medium close-up) but stops playing when he sees a small bird on the pavement. In a series of eye-line match-cuts, he looks for a piece of bread and hand-feeds the bird with a soft smile on his face, until the waiter arrives with his coffee. This part of the scene takes one minute and forty-eight seconds and is almost without dialogue. This action has no obvious dramatic importance; it is mostly a poetic scene depicting a character doing very little in a moment of simply being. In addition, the audience has no prior information about why he is in this place, which enhances the 'momentary' nature of the scene. In this manner, the film can use location shooting to embed fictional characters in real settings and slow down the narrative tempo for a poetic moment.

Some films make the countryside prominent as location, as do *Discretion Wanted* and *Ditte, Child of Man*. Furthermore, the latter film exemplifies that shooting on location does not exclude elements of stylisation. Throughout, the film uses the landscape as a poetic contributor to the narrative. Verner Jensen's cinematography captures natural lyrical moments (the wind in the grass, the fluctuating light and flocks of migrating birds against the sky) and dwells on different parts of the environment, such as the fishing village, the sea, the heath and the farm. Conversely, when Ditte and her grandmother walk around in the stormy weather at dusk and beg for food, the film depicts them as dark silhouettes against the sky. A child comments: 'There goes the witch and her child'. Thus, the expressive-symbolic stylisation through the use of natural backlighting substantiates the child's perspective, as the film briefly lets us see how the grandmother appears 'witchy'. This change of view does not diminish our sympathy for Ditte and her grandmother. However, we understand the extent of their social exclusion. The film effortlessly combines different styles that thematically depict the characters as embedded in a world in which they have very little agency. It is also significant that the film can merge location shooting with distinct stylisation. This is also apparent in its use of montage. When Ditte's grandfather goes to sea, the film moves back and forth through a series of slow visual dissolves connecting the grandmother at her spinning wheel and the grandfather rowing his fishing boat. The montage accelerates until it comes to a standstill as the grandfather dies. Thus, the film's extensive use of location shooting embodies a variety of styles such as poetic lyricism, expressionist symbolism and dramatising montage.

Most films within Danish social realism combine location shooting and studio sets. *Sparrows under the Eaves*, for example, depicts the male protagonist at work on the shipyard Burmeister & Wain through on-location footage of workers building a ship. This contrasts not only with indoor scenes, but also with those taking place in the studio-built 'back yard'. Other films use expressive techniques to enhance characterisation or underline subjective experiences in dramatic moments. *Jenny and the Soldier* and *Take Whatever You Want* both use expressionist lighting schemes such as single-source lighting to provide demonic portrayals of characters. Furthermore, *Discretion Wanted* and *Jenny and the Soldier* both underline subjectivity through voices within a character's head and by marked point-of-view shots. In these ways, style in Danish social realism is not puritan in nature. Rather, it is an amalgam of stylistic features that, nevertheless, all work to the same end: to engage audiences in the trivialities of everyday life and to dignify its small-time heroes.

Conclusion

This chapter has outlined social realism in Danish cinema with a focus on the 1940s. It has sketched out some of its many sources in the Danish documentary film, in the literary tradition of critical realism and the flows of creative people between documentary, literature, theatre and film. From this grows a cinematic social realism with at least two tendencies. First, the 'problem film' that overtly adopts the educational perspective of the documentary film, especially its intention to inform citizens about social issues of public interest and concern. This often translates into stories combining fiction-style storytelling and documentary-style informational intent that embed characters and their stories in a 'paternalistic' perspective on the state and its social institutions. Second, they espouse a broader critical-humanist social realism in which social structures, and those characters embodying them, are the main antagonists. This critical perspective on social structures, however, is combined with a humanistic ethos in which each human being has a worth of their own. The films depict not only the suffering of their small-scale heroes, but also their willingness and ability to adapt to severe circumstances in ways that dignify them as humans. In addition, the films tell their stories in a variety of ways and through what I have termed an amalgamated style. Together, these two tendencies within social realism demonstrate how Danish cinema of the 1940s expanded its motivic and stylistic repertoire in order to combine engaging storytelling with a serious treatment of contemporary issues.

Note

1. The term 'realism' has a long, yet diverse history in film scholarship (see Langkjær 2002: 15–20). Those defending a realist position in classic film theory (Andrew 1976) considered realism part of the essential nature of the medium (Kracauer 1961, Bazin 1971a), to be executed in styles that emphasised film's intimate connection to reality, such as the location shooting, long shots and de-dramatisation used in Italian neorealism (Bazin 1971b and 1971c). In the 1970s, 'realism' was an umbrella term for Hollywood-style filmmaking focusing on the 'suture' of 'invisible editing' and its 'diegetic illusion' (Baudry 1986, McCabe 1986). Finally, the term addresses different movements in cinema history, often with a prefix indicating its particular form, such as 'poetic realism', 'neorealism', 'kitchen-sink' realism (Carroll 1996), or 'social' realism (Lay 2002).

7. IMAGINING DENMARK: *DANMARKSFILM* AS DOCUMENTARY PORTRAITS OF A NATION

Ib Bondebjerg

Documentary films have explored wide-ranging aspects of Danish society, culture and everyday life since the beginning of the twentieth century. Documentaries are not just factual presentations of reality; they are also creative ways of shaping how we imagine who we are and the world we inhabit. In this chapter, I deal with how Denmark as a nation and society has been imagined and portrayed in the genre of *Danmarksfilm* (Denmark-films), films that try to capture the nation as a whole. In a way, all documentary films about Denmark contribute to how Danes imagine their nation. Documentary films deal with many aspects of Danish society and culture, and those fragments of an imagined Denmark contribute to our portrait of a nation. However, Denmark-films have the more ambitious goal of interpreting Denmark and the Danes. They are reflections on who we are – on our society, culture and way of living. Starting with the first Denmark-film in 1926, such films have often been commissioned and made for Danes themselves, but also for an international audience as an introduction or welcome to Denmark for tourists and business partners (Thomson 2018a and 2018b). The historical development of this particular genre shows an increasing focus on the global – the global influence on Denmark and the nation's place in the world.

Denmark is a small country – even if we include Greenland — but the local and regional differences are still very visible. Strictly speaking, we therefore have two types of Denmark-film: the *local-regional films* that portray specific regions and localities while stressing diversity and differences in landscapes and ways of living; and *the national films* that try to give a snapshot or a longer presentation of Denmark as a whole. Both types of film continue to be very popular with the Danish audience. One proof of this is that the Danish Film Institute (DFI) has established a streaming site for such films.[1] Another is the extraordinary success of a series of regional DVDs called *Danskernes egen historie (The History of the Danes)*. Forty-nine DVDs have been produced based on material from the regional archives in Denmark, and they have sold several hundreds of thousands of copies on DVD, while also being available in local libraries (Bach 2005). In 2015, this project was further developed at the documentary festival CPH:DOX, and the Nordea Foundation launched the 'Everyday Project' whereby Danes were encouraged to send in films about their everyday life (Nordea Fonden 2015). Both projects have contributed to historical interest in the regional past, and the success emphasises the importance of memories and visual representations of the regional as well as the national past. While my main focus in this chapter is on the national Denmark-film, the relations between the national and the regional will also be part of the analysis.

FILM AND IMAGINED COMMUNITIES

Nationality and national culture are important dimensions of identity, even in the globalised world in which we live. Danish documentaries have, from the beginning of film history, contributed to both our national and global understanding. Globalisation was already part of the story in rather early Denmark-films, but it has dominated even more so in films after 1970, and especially after 2000. The history of films that imagine Denmark is also a story about changing relations between the local, national and global. National culture and nation-states are historical constructions which often undergo changes. For example, Denmark once ruled parts of Norway, Sweden and Northern Germany; Denmark also held colonies in former times (see, for example, Østergaard 2012). Nations may change, just as national politics, culture, ways of life and the very composition and demography of a nation may change. Nations are not necessarily stable and homogenous societies, and Denmark has for centuries, and especially after 1945, seen an increase in both Western and non-Western migrants.

Theories of nation-states and nationality often stress these aspects of change and construction in the ways in which we imagine nations. Nations are of course not just imagined; they are built on a political system, on certain central institutions, and they have geopolitical borders. But they are also what Benedict Anderson (1983) has called 'imagined communities' whose construction is dominated by 'banal nationalism' (Billig 1995). Both terms refer to the mental and symbolic forms through which a national identity is communicated to us, and indeed created by us, every day. Nationality is constructed by rituals and forms of everyday life, which seem so natural that they become invisible for us, or through media images and forms of communication that frame our thinking. Our daily news positions us as citizens of a particular nation, and documentaries do the same. Media narratives make us imagine the national culture in which we are living, and they can stress cultural and social homogeneity, or they can point to diversity and difference. Such images of a nation can also create conflicts and strong public reactions: the way in which images of a nation are communicated can create ideological tensions.

PH's DENMARK

The first Denmark-film, *Danmarksfilmen* (*The Denmark Film*, 1926), was a relatively long (150-minute) silent, black-and-white film, made by three big Danish production companies (Nordisk Film, Palladium and Industri Filmen). The film is a mosaic of Danish nature, folklore, historic sites, agriculture and industry, and it takes us on a tour of the main cities and all regions of the country, including Greenland and the Faroe Islands. We also meet Danish royalty and famous Danes. The film is a rather traditional presentation of Denmark. In contrast, Poul Henningsen's film *Danmark* (*Denmark*, 1935) was meant to be a new and modern film about Denmark, the face towards the world. However, it created a scandal: the use of jazz and modern music, and a new Grierson-inspired film-style (Bondebjerg 2014b) seemed to go against what almost all the leading newspapers and the commissioning bodies imagined would characterise Denmark and Danish culture.

Henningsen's *Denmark* was produced by a special committee with representatives of the Foreign Ministry, industrial organisations, agricultural organisations, the Tourist Board of Denmark and others. There were high expectations for the film, but the choice of Poul Henningsen was rather unexpected and daring. Poul Henningsen is well-known as designer (*inter alia* of the famous PH-lamp), architect and writer, but he had not previously made a film, and he was known for his sharp social critique and satire (see Thomson 2013b). He belonged to a radical cultural group at that time (*Kulturradikalismen*), and he was not in any way a traditional nationalist. Looking at the film today, it is, however, in some ways a traditional Denmark-film. All the ingredients are there: Danish nature through the seasons and in all parts of the country; fishermen at work and the broader fishing industry; Danish agriculture, including milk, pigs and bacon, and life in the countryside; as well as many aspects of industrial production (breweries, building of diesel motors, brick production, cement production, shoe production). We visit small villages, provincial towns, big cities, islands and the coast; there is a strong visual emphasis on transport and communication (trains, bicycles, cars, ferries, radio, telephone); and we also see royalty, just as Hans Christian Andersen and his stories are used creatively.

The visual representation of Denmark is thus quite inclusive and not controversial in and of itself. However, it is clearly a film that through montage, rhythm, music and the very dry commentary (by Henningsen himself) celebrates everyday life and the mundane, rather than the more official Denmark. Occasionally there also seems to be a kind of irony, for instance, when a shot of beer bottles on a production line is succeeded by images of a great number of foreign envoys getting out of a car to visit the Danish king. There is a lot of poetry in the way in which the film is made, but the speed of the montage and the use of modern jazz music (to new Danish songs) creates an untraditional image of Denmark. The reviews in the newspapers clearly targeted these elements, and they were quite ideological in their critique. In the conservative *Dagens Nyheder*, the main critique posited that the committee had selected a man without a country and without love for his country, and that the film did not represent the love of the Danish people for their country. The film was also called flat and without poetry (Sørensen 1980: 59). But perhaps the strongest negative reaction came from Poul Henningsen's own newspaper *Politiken*. Here, too, the film was criticised for being grey and dull, for focusing too much on workaday Denmark, on the trivial. Perhaps this quote demonstrates the ideological climate of Denmark in the 1930s: 'It was not Denmark we heard and saw, it was not the beeches or the elder-flower bushes we heard singing, it was not the storks or the seagulls, not the waves of our straits that gurgled, nor our western coastal waters that roared, it was all too often just negroes [sic] that made noise' (quoted in Sørensen 1980: 55).

Poul Henningsen's film set a new aesthetic standard for how Denmark could be imagined, and the film – which was reconstructed and had a re-premiere in 1964 after having been almost forgotten – is today considered a Danish classic and the first real modern Denmark-film. But the reaction to the film in 1935 reminds us of how images of nations can trigger deep conflicts and differences in the way in which we see the nation where we live. Nations are seldom as homogenous as they seem, and the imagined community can be a cover for a much more complex, diverse and multicultural reality.

Reflexive Constructions and Images of Denmark: Post-War Denmark-Films

The German occupation of Denmark (1940–45; see also Sørensen, Chapter 4 in this volume) was in many ways a productive period for Danish documentary films. Despite censorship from the German authorities, many films were made about all aspects of Danish society, and there was a natural interest in Danish films, not least films about Danish culture and history. Very mundane subjects were treated with non-traditional aesthetics and creative energy. The British documentarist Arthur Elton described the best of the Danish wartime documentaries as being made with 'fresh, lively and human direction', 'with a gay and imaginative touch', 'imaginative and clever editing' and 'fine and luminous photography' (quoted in Thomson 2018a: 70). However, Denmark-films were not produced during the war, and those few made between 1945 and 1960 were rather traditional. Preben Frank's *Danmark (Denmark*, 1948) gives a rather comprehensive visual portrait of Denmark, but mostly consists of footage from earlier films. Arne Jensen's fine and lively film *Velkommen til Danmark* (*Welcome to Denmark*, 1951) is a short film (26 minutes) mostly made to meet the need for tourist propaganda. A slightly more innovative film is Nicolai Lichtenberg's *A Visit to Denmark* (1952) which is aimed at American academics going to Denmark (The American Graduate School). The film combines an introduction to the subjects about Denmark taught at the school with images of Denmark and Danish universities.

A much more fundamental innovation of the Denmark-film, however, developed between 1960 and 1985, a period when Danish documentary films in general gained new thematic and artistic freedom. This was due to the new film laws of 1964 and 1972 that boosted the production and distribution agency Statens Filmcentral (SFC) and created the Danish Film Institute in 1972 (see Bondebjerg 2012: 73ff, Thomson 2018a: 143ff). Henning Ørnbak's *Dejlige Danmark* (*Delightful Denmark*, 1960) and Henning Nystad's *Et par ord om Danmark* (*Introduction to Denmark*, 1962) are quite innovative. The first film tells the story of an American student arriving in Denmark where he meets two Danes and tours the country, which is thus seen from both outside and inside. The film was commissioned by Caltex Oil, which wanted to develop international understanding – and, of course, brand the company. Nystad's film is made with an ironic distance. The commentary by the narrator (Helge Kjærulff-Schmidt) and the modern music by Niels Viggo Benzon give the film a special tone and style. For example, we see a couple on a motorbike and a couple on a horse-drawn carriage, while the commentary goes: 'When you get deeper into Denmark it looks like an idyll. We only have ourselves to blame because we do everything to make things cosy and historical'. Like other Denmark-films, this film manages in only thirteen minutes to touch on most of the usual themes, but more casually, ironically and with a reflexive twist – for instance, by photographing tourists posing in front of the most famous sights. It is an elegant film about modern Denmark, told in a form void of any excessive nationalism and with a fine balance between places, landmarks and work, politics and everyday life.

However, four other films in particular illustrate the new aesthetic diversity of the modern Denmark-film: Lars Brydesen, Claus Ørsted and Klaus Rifbjerg's *Danske billeder* (*Images of Denmark*, 1970); Jørgen Leth's *Livet i Danmark* (*Life in Denmark*, 1972); Kristen Bjørnkjær's *Danmark A+B* (1976); and Jørgen Vestergaard's *Danmark dit og mit* (*Denmark Yours and Mine*, 1981).[1] In the following discussion I will concentrate on the first two of these films, but use the last two as a comparative framework. Apart from the aesthetic differences between these films, they also illustrate a shift in production forms, compared to the earlier Denmark-films. Only *Images of Denmark* is – like PH's *Denmark* – a result of a commissioning process, involving the Danish Tourist Board and other industrial organisations. The others were a result of the new type of dominant documentary production, where independent filmmakers were supported by the SFC (after 1997 by the DFI) and a film production company. Money from private sources still played a role, but the old form of commissioned films (as discussed by Thomson 2018a) was disappearing.

Images of Denmark has, however, many similarities with PH's *Denmark*: it was commissioned as an official Denmark-film by the Danish Tourist Board and the Association of Danish Banks, and the process was handled by SFC and the production company Laterna Film. By asking Klaus Rifbjerg to write a manuscript for the film, SFC and the other commissioning partners chose a modern, critical and, in some circles, controversial poet, in line with the historical tradition that PH also represented. But just as there was no direct interference in PH's project, Rifbjerg, Ørsted and Brydesen were given a free hand in making their film. The influential producer and director Mogens Skot-Hansen at Laterna Film insisted on this artistic liberty and supported the intention of creating something new (Sørensen 1980: 99). Even though there is a clear link back to PH's film and its unorthodox rhythm and irony in dealing with the image of Denmark, the two films are quite different. In *Images of Denmark*, very different Danes become central to the film: in close-ups we see a diverse portrait of Danes, all ages, all classes and from all parts of Denmark. Sometimes they tell us what they think of Denmark, how it is to live here; sometimes the camera just observes them. Another special thing is Rifbjerg's poem about Denmark, which constitutes the poetic voice-over of the film. The use of visual poetic contrasts in the film, together with the poetic voice of the narrator, gives the film a strong emotional symbolic dimension. We do not get the traditional tour of Denmark, the iconic images of nature, culture and history, nor praise for the quality of Danish agriculture and industry. The Danes themselves are put on stage in all their diversity.

In his original proposal for the film, Rifbjerg links this filmic strategy to a critical, deconstructive intention of challenging the traditional notion of nationality and nation:

> The time of grand nationalism is over, but still the love for our country lives in us. But where and how? What is it we love, what is it we hate, and what can this country offer in humanity and inhumanity? Is this a delightful country, a shit country, both/and, neither/nor or not at all? We Danes like to tease, and teasing is a mix of good nature and malice, cheerfulness and melancholia, worship and contempt. This film in many ways resembles teasing (quoted in Sørensen 1980: 102).

In line with this ambition, the film backs away from traditional national images and puts Danes at the centre, but it also uses a combination of critical discourse and contrasting montage. The music in the film clearly underlines this: together with Rifbjerg's poem read in voice-over, Pelle Gudmundsen-Holmgren's very modern, lyrical music offers a deconstruction and renewal of traditional Danish songs. The compositions refer to a national song canon but transform them and, combined with visual sequences where beautiful nature is often contrasted with ugly images of a modern Denmark of concrete, we sense the criticism. This is also the case when images of migrant workers doing the hard and dirty work in factories are contrasted with upper-class males playing on golf courses.

Images of Denmark represents a new, modern kind of Denmark-film both in style and content. The attempt to signal an imagined community as a whole or as a kind of organic network is no longer there. Instead, there is difference, contrast and a more relaxed and critical distance. The reception of the film in the Danish press was also very different from the complete rejection of PH's film. There were positive and negative reviews of the film, but all in all the reviews reflected an acceptance that it would be impossible to make a film that could capture it all.

The same recognition that a national portrait could only be partial and subjective is seen in other films from this period, which nonetheless clearly chose other strategies. Kristen Bjørnkjær and Per Højholt's film *Danmark A+B* (1976) assumed the full consequence of this tension, making a film which is basically a fight in words and images between director A (Bjørnkjær), who wants to make a film very critical of Denmark, and director B (Højholt), who wants to focus on the more positive aspects of the nation. In the film we see them sitting in the editing room arguing their case, and we also see sequences of the film made in the two modes. The film thus illustrates that point-of-view is an integral part of any film and, furthermore, how the same film footage can be manipulated for specific purposes. In a way, this is also what Jørgen Vestergaard's *Danmark dit og mit* (*Denmark, Yours and Mine*, 1981) tells us. Formally, Vestergaard's film is much more like the traditional Denmark-films. We move around in Denmark and see images from all parts of the nation – and there is a classical narrator. But the film adopts quite a distinct perspective – namely, the drastic and negative changes in Denmark following industrialisation and the growth of a mass consumer society. The underlying assumption is, in fact, that development is threatening our nation and a sustainable way of life, even though the concluding sequences of the film leave some grounds for hope, due to a new ecological way of thinking.

Jørgen Leth's *Life in Denmark*

Among the new modern Denmark-films, Jørgen Leth's very poetic-reflexive *Livet i Danmark* (*Life in Denmark*, 1972) stands out. There is a connection to *Images of Denmark* with a strong focus on concrete, individual Danes and also in the lack of any intention of capturing the essence of Denmark and being Danish. Leth has defined the approach and the chosen aesthetic form as an investigation of 'the immediate, spontaneous surroundings as if they are completely exotic' and also a 'look into the private human sphere with pseudo-ethnographic glasses' (Movin 2013: 75). His film is therefore, on the one hand, very observational: there is no authoritative voice-over, just framed images of

Figure 7.1 In Jørgen Leth's *Livet i Danmark* (*Life in Denmark*, 1972), the Denmark-film tradition is subverted, to observe Danes clinically against a black backdrop. Framegrabs.

Denmark and characters on a stage speaking about themselves and the way in which they live. On the other hand, it is all staged; everything is filmed from the same camera angle, and characters appear on a stage with a black background, not in their natural surroundings. It is as if we are observing Danes under almost clinical circumstances and in a laboratory, the framing and staging creating a certain distance.

Even though there is no underlying intention in Leth's film to represent the Danes and Denmark as a whole, we see rather different types of Danes and parts of Denmark. Some of the characters portrayed are known: a bicycle sports star, the film director and his family, four young poets appearing naked, an actor and a politician; but most of those appearing on stage are ordinary Danes, young schoolgirls, for example, or people performing different kinds of work. They tell us about themselves, but we also see them showing or doing things: for instance, a farmer with his tools, a fisherman cleaning and preparing fish, and a policeman with his motorbike. We also see people performing specific acts: dancing, having coffee and baking at home, photos of cows and pigs and awards won, pictures of families and things from their home. A special effect occurs when images of places in Denmark appear on the screen accompanied by classical music, or when the film shifts between paintings and film images of the reality from which the paintings are inspired. There is a reflexive and poetic play between frame, representation and reality. The film shows very concrete and sometimes banal images of a Danish reality, but at the same time the framing and staging of these naked forms of reality makes the viewer wonder and look in a different way. The reality is stripped of realism, yet very concrete. It is not a critical Denmark-film but a film that encourages us to draw our own conclusions and imagine Denmark in a format that we do not find in earlier films.

DENMARK-FILMS AND THE NATIONAL-GLOBAL CONTEXT

There are not many signs of the global context in the films dealt with so far. PH's film starts with a Chinese boy looking at the globe, and then we fly to Denmark; there are migrant workers in *Images of Denmark* and even an African-American. The fact that Denmark as a nation today is a much more multicultural society than before, that we are integrated into the European Union and that the global context is visible for most Danes does, however, start to influence the most recent films (Bondebjerg 2012, 2014a, 2018). We see it in films such as Joao Penaguiao and Jacob Jørgensen's *This is Denmark* (1996) which takes a global look at Denmark, starting with foreigners from several countries expressing their view on Denmark, and in Jenö Farkas' film *Danmark no. 1 – en trist film om danskere* (*Denmark no. 1 – A Sad Film about Danes*, 1990), which looks very critically at the way in which Danes encounter foreigners and Danes with another ethnic background. A more positive approach to this problem can be found in *Mit Danmark* (*My Denmark*, 2007), in which ten films, each ten minutes in length and made by a different Danish director, offer portraits of migrants and new Danish citizens of another ethnic background. It is a film trying to establish a dialogue between the many *nydanskere* (new Danes) from different parts of the world and all the other Danes.

The most original of the Denmark-films after 2000 is Max Kestner's *Verden i Danmark* (*The World in Denmark*, 2007), whose very title indicates the shift from regional-national to national-global. It is a film about how much globalisation and new communication technologies have changed Denmark and the way in which we think about our own country and the world around us (Bondebjerg 2012: 287ff and 2018: 105ff). The film was commissioned by the national television station DR2 and co-financed by the Danish Film Institute and the private fund BG Fonden. Kestner has acknowledged his inspiration from Jørgen Leth (Bondebjerg 2014c: 163f). The film uses a series of staged sequences, where characters or items are placed in front of an Excel spreadsheet, while Kestner, as the film's narrator, delivers facts and figures on Denmark and the Danes. About his project, compared to earlier Denmark-films, Kestner has said:

> The title is meant to indicate two things. The first is that we live in an era of globalisation, and that geographical borders are being substituted by other forms of borders, economic and cultural. Everything just floats into Denmark, not least through the internet. Secondly, the title refers to the fact that the film tries to capture all the things characterising Denmark right now, it is about the whole world of Denmark in itself (Movin 2006).

Taken as a whole, the film is constructed through five very different perspectives: 1) *Excel spreadsheet sequences* delivering facts and figures, sometimes with a satirical tone; 2) *sequences filmed from a bird's eye perspective* on Denmark, sequences with a high poetic and emotional quality and Danish classical music; 3) *observational sequences* from public or private institutions giving us basic insight into working Denmark, including politics; 4) four *biographic mini-narratives* of very different Danes (including a Turkish migrant) filmed in fast motion with Kestner's commentary, the images going from the present day back to childhood; and 5) some clearly *staged sequences, filmed in observational style* where different people speak with others on their mobile phones, indicating the thin barrier between public and private in our media-saturated society.

The variety of perspectives and styles used in Kestner's film makes it one of the most experimental and diverse Denmark-films ever made. The film clearly uses all the four fundamental genres of documentary film (see Bondebjerg 2014a, Nichols 2001): there is a strong *authoritative dimension* in the way in which Kestner presents facts about Denmark and the Danes, even though he sometimes gives the factual discourse an ironic twist; he uses *observational forms*, where we are allowed to see for ourselves without commentary how Danes live, work, communicate and interact; he uses *staged and dramatised forms* to compress life stories or present elements and events from daily life in a reconstructed form; and finally – especially in the eleven bird's-eye sequences of places in Denmark – he uses *a poetic-reflexive form*. Kestner's Denmark-film is more complex than other Denmark-films, although he is clearly in dialogue with Jørgen Leth and other predecessors that take a reflexive, critical approach to Denmark and being Danish. The film both plays on and questions the traditional clichés often used in classical documentary films, and it is more open to diversity in Denmark and to the global context. The message of the film seems to be that, yes, Denmark is a specific nation and Danes have their own language, culture and way of life. But we are – as the film points out very early on – children of stardust, the universe and a global context. We live in a national reality that has never been more global and influenced by media that transcend borders, cultures and nations.

Denmark-Films as Medleys

Following the history of Denmark-films from the descriptive *Danmarksfilmen* (1926), the modern, swinging and poetic portrait of the nation, *Danmark* (1935), by Poul Henningsen – causing a heated public debate – and the many creative and diverse forms in the post-war period clearly underlines the notion that nations are indeed very much, like Benedict Anderson said, 'imagined communities'. They are of course much more than that, and the modern Denmark-film also tells us a lot about how Denmark and the life of the Danes have changed from 1920 to 2020. We see images of a traditional, agricultural and fishing nation; we see the industrialised Denmark; we see everyday life in regions, local communities and big cities. We also see a nation moving into a more global and technological reality, and we see a nation where the idea of cultural homogeneity is gradually transforming into a more multicultural society. Denmark-films are very much about the reality of Denmark through time and seen from different perspectives; they also represent, however, a Denmark presented through a medley of different tunes and voices: poetic, critical, ironic and satirical.

We all somehow try to imagine the nations in which we live, but we do not see the same reality, just like we have different opinions about so many other things. Documentary films come in many modes and with many perspectives and voices, and audiences have learned to accept that there is no single one image of Denmark. The almost total rejection of Poul Henningsen's film in 1935 has been replaced by a plurality of different Denmark-films: Klaus Rifbjerg's very critical, yet poetic version, Jørgen Leth's very staged, pseudo-ethnographic film,

Jenö Farkas' angry and critical look from an outsider and Max Kestner's cosmic, global investigation of modern Danish lifestyles and institutions. Even though Rifbjerg is probably right that 'grand nationalism' is over, there is still 'banal nationalism': the reality we share by living in a country, the different forms of life within this imagined community, and the things about which we agree to disagree. Nations are imagined communities, and even though our global and mediated reality heavily influences our national reality, the ways in which we imagine this nation and its place in the world are important.

Note

1. The Danmark Paa Film project allows users to search for and view documentary and orphan films by chronology, place, or other criteria: https://filmcentralen.dk/museum/danmark-paa-film.

8. RURAL DREAMS: LANDSCAPE, FAMILY, SEXUALITY AND QUEERNESS IN HOMELAND CINEMA

Niels Henrik Hartvigson

Just as Germany has its *Heimatfilm,* Denmark possesses its own homeland tradition. The extremely popular 'homeland films' constitute cinematic myths of Danes and Danishness, which tell of farmers and country folk – and in rarer cases fishing folk – who fight to save their farms or livelihood and sustain their lifestyle. Dealing with themes such as the plight of the land and the fateful interconnections between humans, animals and nature, they are set in characteristic national landscapes featuring fertile farmland, heaths, rolling hills and inner seas. Often adapted from national plays and literature and catering exclusively to a Danish audience, homeland cinema is nevertheless part of an international movement with examples in several Central, East and North European countries (Beindorf 2001: 21). Danish Homeland films were directly inspired by our nearest Scandinavian neighbour Sweden's successful run of *landsbygdsfilm* in the 1930s, and in 1950 the watershed success of *De røde heste* (*The Red Horses*, Alice O'Fredericks and Jon Iversen, 1950) coincided with the success of the German Heimat film *Grün ist die Heide* (*The Heath is Green*, Hans Deppe, 1951). With approximately forty such films made during the 1950s and 1960s, homeland cinema was at the centre of Danish film culture and eclipsed the sophisticated, darker and more international cinematic trends which had characterised the 1940s (see Langkjær, Chapter 6 in this volume). The explanation by film critics and historians for the surge of homeland cinema was that the genre was a nostalgic response to the urbanisation taking place during the 1950s and 1960s. Although that explanation has some merit, it has tended to reduce the films to being regressive modernism-rejecting kitsch. Moreover, the severe and uncompromising Copenhagen-centric critics, who were weary of the association with the German Heimat films, eagerly castigated homeland cinema as reactionary, regressive, escapist exploitation of a potentially dangerous ideology (Villadsen 1997: 110, 177; Neergaard 1960: 140; Ulrichsen 1960: 152; Andersen et al. 1977, 9–10). However, its many fans hailed homeland cinema not just for its subject-matter, theme and aesthetics, but also because it constituted a cultural demarcation in opposition to a state-subsidised urbane and academically defined cinema. In later years, some academic criticism, inspired by reception theory and cognitive theory, has moved from an emphasis on the genre's backwardness and problematic ideology towards a view of homeland cinema as a nostalgic cinematic re-imagining of the old and the modern (Bondebjerg 2005a). Moreover, readings drawing on post-structuralism and queer theory have explored the ambiguity of the genre's sexual politics (Hartvigson 2016).

A New and Yet Traditional Film Experience

As discussed in Chapter 5 of this volume, with the conversion to sound around 1930, Danish films were suddenly dependent on an audience of circa 3.5 million Danish speakers, and the hitherto extremely internationally oriented film culture turned to an exclusively national perspective. Musical comedies, which celebrated the conciliation of urban classes and featured popular performers from *revue* and theatre, catered to all audience groups and dominated the market to the near exclusion of other genres. As an alternative to the Copenhagen-based urban comedies, however, two dramatic homeland films of the late 1930s proved commercially very viable alternatives: *Den kloge Mand* (*The Quack*, Arne Weel, 1937) and the Jeppe Aakjær adaptation *Livet paa Hegnsgaard* (*Life on Hegnsgaard*, Arne Weel, 1938). The socially conscious Aakjær (1866–1930) is to this day the country's most celebrated rural author; his plays were among the first to be adapted as homeland films and his rural songs feature prominently in the homeland genre and in Danish films in general. With their descriptions of rural life in a characteristic Danish landscape and featuring dialogue in dialect and songs from a strong national tradition, the sound film medium facilitated a completely new cinematic experience. With the landscape and country life becoming more nationally and regionally specific, the dramatic visions attained stronger potential as mirrors for identity and history. During the 1940s a dozen homeland films were produced, some of them following that decade's trend towards the dark and sinister, such as the highly-strung erotic melodrama *Møllen* (*The Mill*, Arne Weel, 1943) or the grittily realistic *Ditte menneskebarn* (*Ditte, Child of Man*, Bjarne Henning-Jensen, 1944). The latter was based on a literary work by the internationally renowned left-wing author,

Martin Andersen Nexø, and remains one of the few homeland films to have been enthusiastically received by critics; it also enjoyed a successful international festival run.

However, works by the most popular contemporary Danish homeland author, Morten Korch (1876–1954), were not being adapted. Since the 1920s, Korch's works about the plight of farmers and pre-industrial entrepreneurs had filled the bookcases of a hitherto non-literary rural folk. Vilified by literary critics and institutions, who regarded his oeuvre as second-rate and populistic, the Korch literature was a site of cultural conflict, as witnessed by the heated debate during the 1940s about whether his books belonged in public libraries. Korch had long sought for his work to be adapted, but studios were wary of being identified with someone who was regarded as the antithesis of artistic and cultural value. It would eventually be Henning Karmark (1907–1989; see also Sørensen, Chapter 4 in this volume), already a producer of homeland films, who bought the rights to Korch's stories, which were adapted into contemporary dramas in collaboration with the production company ASA and director Alice O'Fredericks. The first installation of the series, *De røde Heste*, became the highest grossing Danish film ever, seen by 2.4 million out of a 1950 population of 4.28 million Danes. That the film opened in provincial Odense, thus celebrating Korch on his native island of Funen, sent an unequivocal statement about the power and imagination of popular culture to a Copenhagen-based intelligentsia (Bondebjerg 2005b: 116–17). Due to the continued popularity of his adaptations, and due to his strong public presence, it is not uncommon – if imprecise – to identify homeland films as Morten Korch films.

ASA followed the spectacular success with a string of highly popular Korch adaptations by O'Fredericks, who developed an unpretentious house style with acting styles ranging from the sombre and melodramatic to comically stylised portrayals. From the second film, *Mosekongen* (*The King of the Marshes*, Alice O'Fredericks, 1951) the cycle came to feature Sven Gyldmark's hit songs performed by the film's stars, in particular Paul Reichhardt and Peter Malberg, which certainly contributed to the continued popularity of the cycle.

While the larger companies like Nordisk Film and Palladium would eventually try to latch on to the success of the homeland genre, it was the relatively young studio SAGA that successfully rivalled ASA with its own cycle of homeland films. Directed and scripted by Annelise Reenberg (see Hartvigson 2017a), SAGA films such as *Bruden fra Dragstrup* (*The Bride from Dragstrup*, 1955) and *Den Gamle mølle på Mols* (*The Old Mill on Mols*, 1953) served up contemporary folklore in an expertly sophisticated film style, characterised by the flowing camera's seamless investigation of the rural locations.

It is a striking occurrence that in the 1950s two women, O'Fredericks and Reenberg, were at the creative helm of the country's most popular – in both senses of the word – film franchises. In this perspective it is also relevant to call attention to the influential Grethe Frische, who after a short directing career at SAGA became Alice O'Fredericks' right-hand woman at ASA (Hartvigson 2017b).

Homeland and *Folkekomedie*

Homeland cinema is an extension of *folkekomedie*, or folk plays (see Chapter 5 in this volume), and many of the films explicitly position themselves as such. For example, *Naar bønder elsker* (*When Peasants Love*, Arne Weel, 1942) was marketed as a *Tonefilms-Folkekomedie*, a 'talkie' or sound film *folkekomedie*. Whereas the homeland genre may be said to be determined by its semantic elements such as folk life and traditions, different historical conceptions of *folkekomedie* define it according to what audience group is addressed (as fictions for the people) and to what avail they are made (to evoke an original and intuitively understandable cultural identity). As Chapter 5 in this volume explains, at several historical junctures the *folkekomedie* became a site of intense cultural conflict in Denmark. Similarly, a major cultural conflict was sparked by the formidable cross-medial homeland tradition cemented by the combined efforts of Reenberg at SAGA and by Korch, Karmark and O'Fredericks at ASA, because the homeland films were antithetical to the progressive and artistic potential of the film medium in the eyes of progressive left-wing critics. The success of the homeland film and its affiliation with *folkekomedie* would play a significant role in the development of a film industry that was increasingly supported by the state, culminating in the establishment of the film consultant system under the Film Act of 1972, with little love or money for homeland films and other genres connected with *folkekomedie*. As an active popular cultural phenomenon, the homeland genre was effectively put on hold until the 1980s, when the advent of the video market facilitated a resurgence of the old homeland films.

When films with distinct homeland sensibilities such as *Der er et yndigt land* (*Land of Plenty*, Morten Arnfred, 1983), *Pelle Erobreren* (*Pelle the Conqueror*, Bille August, 1987) and *Fruen på Hamre* (*The Lady of Hamre*, Katrine Wiedemann, 2000) were made within the system and by directors trained at the auteur-oriented, state-run National Film School of Denmark, the generic frame was social and psychological realism favored by the system (Langkjær 2002: 15). In the films' marketing, the visionary strength of the directors was emphasised despite the homeland *folkekomedie* genre. In an instance of poetic justice, it was the homeland spoof *Kampen om den røde ko* (*The Fight for the Red Cow*, Jarl Friis-Mikkelsen and Ole Stephensen, 1987) that broke the patent-like hold of the consultant support system. A fifty-fifty funding system was introduced, which obligated 50 per cent of a film's budget to be state-funded, regardless of the content, if half of the budget could be raised independently.

This acknowledgement of the value of popular taste in film culture paved the way for modern homeland films such as the wartime Resistance-themed *Hvidsten Gruppen* (*This Life*, Anne-Grethe Bjarup Riis, 2012) and the racehorse biopic *Tarok* (*Catch the Dream*, Anne-Grethe Bjarup Riis, 2013). Both were produced by Regner Grasten, who was also a driving force behind *The Fight for the Red Cow*. In contemporary film production, homeland films are few and far between, but the genre's themes and sensibilities have successfully crossed over to television with series such as *Landsbyen (The Village*, DR, 1991) and the Morten Korch adaptation *Ved Stillebækken* (*Still Brook*, Finn Henriksen, Henrik Sartou and Lone Scherfig, TV2, 26 episodes, 1999–2000) produced by Zentropa. Recently, *Badehotellet* (*The Seaside Hotel*, TV2, 2013–), which draws heavily on the homeland themes, motifs and aesthetics, has achieved a popularity reminiscent of *The Red Horses*. Also, during the 2010s, the homeland sensibility has with great popular success made inroads into television-formats such as documentary and reality series such as *Bonderøven* (*The Farmer*, DR, 2008–), *Landmand søger kærlighed* (*Farmer Wants a Wife*, TV2, 2012–) and *Hjem til gården* (*The Farm*, TV2, 2017–).

Generic Bindings

While the landscape, the character types, the extended families and the care for property and livestock may determine the homeland *folkekomedie*, these semantic elements are activated within different narrative syntaxes and generic modes such as that of melodrama and comedy, as well as musical lyricism. The melodramatic homeland films set the scene for identity-related struggles, which are unequivocally linked to a place, region or farm of origin. The theme of identity is emphasised by the many stolen or lost deeds, birth certificates and last wills. In the melodramatic tradition, the universe is morally polarised, as victimised characters defend themselves against human and non-human aggressors who are obsessed with their destruction (Brooks 1976: 28ff). Also in a melodramatic vein, the climactic physical challenges – when characters are threatened by dangerous marshes or runaway horses – display the characters' fight for their identity in a very corporeal sense. The dominant emotional viewer response to the hardships of brave and pressured melodrama characters is one of pathos (Neale 1986: 10). While pathos features prominently, it often coexists with comedic and lyrical elements, which imply both more detached and aesthetically oriented responses. Thus, the melodramatic structure and theme are almost inevitably tempered by a sunnier, less dramatic outlook through the presence of characters with a positive disposition, presenting a happy parallel to and being a source of relief against the brooding main characters. Moreover, central characters will often balance the hardship in some parts of the film with joyful musical expressions in other parts. As such, the homeland films of the 1950s are part of a broader international cinematic strategy of integrating musical numbers and landscape, combining language, lyrics and identity. At SAGA, whose homeland output did not feature musical performances to the same degree as ASA, the quaint interaction of a large number of comedic side characters effectively tempers the darker side of melodrama.

In some homeland comedies, imbalance between rich proprietors, sharecroppers and outsiders in a rural society is regulated with wit and cunning through the intervention of a wise mediator character, who understands the hearts and traditions of the land and its people (Alsted 1985: 150). Most often these films recount the redemption of victims of fate or wrongdoing. However, in the humanistic tradition of Jeppe Aakjær, even the self-righteous and hurtful may be accorded their share of understanding. Thus, in the Aakjær adaptation *When Peasants Love*, the wealthy parish officer, who has forced a young woman's hand in marriage and knowingly accused her innocent beloved of arson, is also presented humanely as a victim of his emotions and temper. In other films such as *Historien om Hjortholm* (*The Story of Hjortholm*, Asbjørn Andersen and Annelise Reenberg, 1950) and *Baronessen fra Benzintanken* (*The Baroness from the Gas Station*, Annelise Reenberg, 1960), rural tradition and ethos manifest themselves as providential occurrences or ghosts. Such fateful interventions underscore the comedy aspect of the films (Neale and Krutnik 1990: 30–31) and place them as direct descendants of the supernatural literary and theatrical *folkekomedie* of the mid-nineteenth century. A modern member of this *folkekomedie* tradition is *Bornholms Stemme* (*Gone with the Fish*, Lotte Svendsen, 1999) which delightfully combines homeland themes and supernatural events with a comedy of manners set during the historical fishing quota crises of the 1980s, which heavily affected the island of Bornholm.

Landscapes Ripe with Meaning

As the most successful homeland director, it often fell to Alice O'Fredericks to explain and justify homeland cinema, and she would repeatedly draw attention to how filming on location allowed the audience to see beautiful Danish landscapes. It was also what attracted her to the genre in the first place: 'I could catch it all: the fields, the woods, the dykes, the mills and the animals with lots of sun and air and clouds' (Pedersen 2012: 137). What may on the surface seem a trite statement nonetheless points to an insight into the role that landscape plays in homeland cinema. Much more than beautiful backdrops for stories and characters, the landscapes are integral to plot, theme and dramaturgy and thus often incarnate the fictions. Martin Lefbvre has argued that the narrative potential of cinematic landscapes, or their *narrational mode*, is paralleled by a non-narrative potential, *a spectacular mode*, where the landscapes are released from their function as setting for plot and characters and instead are to be enjoyed and contemplated on an emotional and philosophical level. The shifts between the two conceptions of landscape are determined both by the cultural knowledge and the sensibility of the individual spectator *and* by the individual film's presentational strategy (Lefebvre 2006: 29). Through repeated and lengthy panoramic shots of characteristic landscapes devoid of character and plot, underscored by melodies and lyrics from the national song tradition, an exclusive meeting between audience and landscape is established. This creates a viewing experience with philosophical and emotional implications, as the audience is invited to contemplate their own relationship to the landscape. For a mid-century Danish audience who had lived through the country's transition from a predominantly rural to urban culture, homeland film's cinematic landscapes most probably served as emotional emblems of cultural history and memory, and for the rural class mirrored a lived experience. Contemporary audiences, most of whom are far removed in time and logic from the fictions, continue to be attracted to these filmic landscapes, whether they serve as setting for characters and plot, or whether they manifest themselves as a landscape to engage with on a personal level.

The Nexus of Landscape and Character

The characters' engagements with the land signal an indisputable rural ethos, not only in terms of diligently and respectfully working the fields and livestock. They are also constantly examining and being drawn in by the mystical force of the natural surroundings, from recognising a spectacular landscape as a bridge between past and present, to the smallest of wonders, as when the central couple in *The Red Horses* are pondering the characteristics of typical Danish crops: wheat, barley, rye and oats. The genre's manner of letting characters emerge from landscapes, be couched in them and recede into them at the closing of the films, invites interpretations of a mystical interconnection between character and landscape traits. In *The Quack*, Carl Alstrup's title character is constantly in tune with the natural surroundings, whether philosophising in the fields with his dog or singing the praises of the rye, while standing in the middle of a field, as he becomes one with the crop. When Ole Offor walks to the run-down farm of Enekær, which he has been sent to salvage in *The Red Horses*, he discovers the characteristics, beauty and dangers of the natural surroundings. Upon reaching the farm, the audience instinctively understands that a process of osmosis between character and nature has taken place. He is now one with Enekær, and his former traits as a traveller, scholar and lover retreat into the background. When Offor and the landscape become mutually defining, psychological nuance gives way to an epistemologically complex and emotionally potent nexus of natural surroundings and character, which is underlined by visual style and music. Homeland cinema thus draws on the same intuitively graspable linkage of human psyche and nature as the Old Testament's High Song of Solomon.

Figure 8.1 Carl Alstrup in *Den kloge Mand* (*The Quack*, Arne Weel, 1937). Here we see a mythical and instantly relatable interconnection between landscape, human and animal. Image: Danish Film Institute.

Figure 8.2 The interconnection between landscape, human and animal suggests a mythical connection in this framegrab from Anne-Grethe Bjarup Riis' biopic of the racehorse *Tarok* (*Catch the Dream*, 2013). Framegrab.

Natural Forces and Narrative Agency

The landscapes, farms, fields and livestock that the characters work to salvage are integral to the plot and conflict in very manifest ways, as they represent the characters' goal in a structural sense and – as argued above—the character traits of its inhabitants. Moreover, the homeland genre often distributes agency to human and non-human characters, as well as to natural phenomena, effectively creating a mystical world where reason gives way to emotional intuition. Landscape or natural phenomena may stand in for the deceased, as the beautiful and dangerous marsh does for the drowned mother in *The King of the Marshes* or the stormy shoreline for the fratricidal victim in *Flintesønnerne* (*The Flint Sons*, Alice O'Fredericks, 1956). When the land benevolently discloses natural wealth or buried treasures to save farms, as in *Det gamle guld* (*The Ancient Gold*, Alice O'Fredericks, 1951) in which a gold treasure is ploughed up by the protagonist in need, it takes up agency in its own right. The agency of nature may also be fatally dangerous, as exemplified by marshes, streams, or storms, which at dramaturgical high points threaten to swallow or smother characters. Whether good or bad, the non-human agents first and foremost offer up alternatives to logic and reason, paving the way for fate and providence. Thus, in *The Bride from Dragstrup*, the human intrigues of a grandmother and her maid – along with the old mansion coming to life, the beauty of the summer night and the musical procession of the townspeople – conspire to unite the unmarried lovers in the wedding chamber of the old mansion. Precisely through the intervention of natural and non-human agency, the nominal illegitimacy of the union is transformed into a natural and providential one, which trumps conventional morals. Even if this film draws somewhat on romantic comedy, its homeland identity is cemented by how the union of the lovers is established through nature, community and tradition.

Household Families

In contrast to the biologically determined nuclear family, which was the dominant family form in 1950s Denmark, the rural households of earlier times cut across family and class, with farmhands, grandparents and relations making up the households together with immediate blood relations (for a historical overview, see Rosenbeck 1987). In addition to portraying such extended or 'household families', homeland cinema's households are systematically presented as incomplete or broken as a result of disappeared or dead family members. The practical project of finding heirs to take over is unambiguously connected to an emotional need stemming from loss. Thus, in *Fra den gamle købmandsgård* (*From the Old Merchant's House*, Annelise Reenberg, 1951) the motherless Anne is raised by five elderly and single characters from all walks of life: her manager father, the maid, the grandmother, the station manager and the postman, all of whom regard her romantic development as a communal project. When she chooses the clerk with work ethics and morals over money and class, it serves both the continuation of the household and emotional compensation for the dead mother-figure for all involved. A characteristic feature of the genre, which is connected to the emotionally incomplete households, lies in their willingness and desire to include cultural outcasts, the unmarried, the childless, the old and orphans. This reaches a touching apex in Jon Iversen's *Ta' Pelle med* (*Take Pelle with You*, 1952) which sees two illegitimate orphans being integrated into rural society and giving life and hope to their new and hitherto broken families.

A Crisis of Heterosexuality

Personal emotional needs and wants are almost always portrayed as extremely complicated for homeland characters, who are naturally attuned to rural activities, but often emotionally not self-conscious in regard to romance and sexuality. A paradoxical sexual inability of these physically attractive and able characters is shown as romantic unassertiveness and restraint, or juvenile or unserious love-making. Often the emotional demands that marriage and romantic fulfilment entail are not met, and veritable sexual crises ensue, resulting in an inability to produce the heirs on whom the rural lineage traditionally depends. In *The Red Horses*, the young couple marry out of a sense of duty and struggle to convert the relationship into love. In *Husmandstøsen* (*The Smallholder's Lass*, O'Fredericks, 1952) and *Ild og jord* (*Fire and Earth*, Kai Wilton, 1955), characters who are initially sexually conscious and active become restrained to the point of abstinence, as they align their fate with the land (Hartvigson 2016: 110). In *The Flint Sons*, successful procreative sexuality is suspiciously connected to mental illness, social climbing and brute force. The poor Jesper marries a mentally ill heiress to become master of the Flintegården farm, and while his entrance into the family bodes well for the farm, tragedy on a personal level is in store for bride and groom. In one of the most striking scenes in homeland cinema, which thematises sexual fulfilment, rape and sexual sacrifice, Jesper sees no other way out but to use sexual force to calm down his bride during their wedding celebration. The marriage's sole procreative act results in the mother dying in labour with twins, one of whom will continue the emotional and sexual suffering.

Sexualised Innocence

Even if the central rural characters in general have a low awareness of sexuality and romance, their able and working bodies are put on display, and they are systematically sexualised on a thematic and dramaturgical level and in terms of plot. The sexually and romantically unassertive characters are constantly being pursued by over-sexed city girls, unruly farmhands and lecherous landowners. In terms of plot these sexual predators are evidently antagonists, but on a dramaturgical level their violent and immoral physical and sexual attacks have a surprising community-sustaining potential, as they seem to facilitate a sexual awakening of the central characters. Thus, it is often – and paradoxically – these sexual predators who are key to the central characters' development from innocent to sexually assertive and producers of heirs and heiresses (Hartvigson 2013: 114). The sexual interdependence between heroes and villains certainly represents a complication of the viewers' moral, emotional and sexual engagement with the characters. Far from being able to make an easy choice between good and evil, the audience may find themselves rooting for the rural characters, while at the same time they are drawn to the shady morals and destructive sexuality of the villains. Such a response not only amounts to guilty pleasure, but in a sense is morally fitting.

The character-landscape nexus described above allows us to contemplate a connection of identity between humans and their surroundings, and we may

Figure 8.3 Sexualised innocence: working bodies on display. Poul Reichhardt in *De røde heste* (*The Red Horses*, Alice O'Fredericks and Jon Iversen, 1950). Image: Danish Film Institute.

well invite interpretation of rolling hills, fertile fields and nightly storms which render the rural characters projections of a benevolent or dangerous sexuality. Certainly, the prominently featured horses serve as dramaturgical parallels for the characters, as their emotional and physical characteristics, from docile to wild, are projected as imagined animal libido or libidinal potential smouldering under the restrained countenances of the homeland characters. Strikingly similar observations have been made about the cinematic genre of the Western (McGillis 2009: 111–12; 152). The mercy-killing in *Der brænder en ild* (*A Fire Burns*, Alice O'Fredericks, 1962) sees the hero shoot his beloved horse trapped in the burning barn. His actions represent a wildly complicated mixture of violence, love and mercy, which mirrors the emotional and sexual control which he has demonstrated every day of his adult life, renouncing his love for the married woman he can never have.

The coexistence of an almost conspicuous sexual reticence on the part of the characters with these possible corporeal and sexual interpretations of the films makes for an ambiguous viewing experience, suspending the audience between visions of a natural world that is both quietly benevolent and dramatically sexual. The striking corporeal and sexual aspects of homeland cinema suggest that it is sexually a much more complicated and ambiguous genre than is acknowledged by critics and historians, who generally ignore this aspect or only acknowledge it on a very superficial level (see Hartvigson 2013).

Queer Couples and Queer Nurture

Homeland cinema presents us with an impressive roster of queer characters, whose sheer quantity means that the heterosexual plot and themes are constantly developed in their vicinity. The sexually and emotionally restrained heterosexual relationships of the central couple often coexist with a same-sex relationship consisting of one half of the heterosexual couple and a character of the same gender. In *The Baroness from the Gas Station*, an emotionally complex relationship between a grandmother and her granddaughter, who only meet as adults, dominates the film with scenes of conflict and reconciliation. To the point of eclipsing the excitement for characters and audience of the romantic union between the granddaughter and her beau, it can be interpreted as a non-heterosexual or lesbian narrative competing with the heterosexual one (Hartvigson 2016: 260; see also Doty 2000: 41).

The same-sex coupling typically serves as a more playful, joyous, or emotionally intense mirror for the restrained heterosexual relationship, which it often seems to imbue with joy and energy. In the Korch cycle, Peter Malberg's characters – whether a goofy farmhand, small-time criminal, or circus artist – strike up relationships with Paul Reichhardt's heroes, letting him develop emotionally and creatively. Moreover, the homosocial relationships are crowned with musical performances, which establish a privileged extra-fictional meeting place between audience and performers, positioning them as a star couple, something which is much more rarely the case with heterosexual couples.

Queerness is prominently and positively featured in a broad collection of couples, families and parent figures with unconventional gender appearances and lifestyles. These have typically been described as alleviating the melodramatic tension (Bondebjerg 2005a: 105; Troelsen and Andersen 1980: 245), but only recently have their roles as vessels for sexual and gender experimentation, whether homoerotic or latently homosexual, been acknowledged (Hartvigson 2013: 117–18). A staple of the genre are the relationships between old eccentric and similarly dressed males, who behave like married couples and have no interest in or little success with women. Also, mixed-gendered adult brother-sister pairings or single figures sport attire, attitudes and lifestyles that place them squarely outside the logic of reproduction. Often displaying a playful, comic, or absurd approach to life, their rural priorities are emphasised by their solidarity and emotional relationship with the land. This is witnessed by the many queer nurturing parent figures who stand in when biological parents disappear or fail to care for their young. Homeland cinema reminds us that, while heterosexuality begets children, their nurture and care may very well be queerly determined, thus establishing queerness as a conservative and community-sustaining phenomenon.

Conclusion

Homeland cinema's potential for meaning and power of attraction is much greater than the standard accounts of film critics and historians allow. While nostalgia for an experienced or imagined past certainly is leveraged and generated by the films, they also offer contemplation of the philosophical aspects of landscape, and they open up a space for representation and interrogation of both traditional and queer images of body, gender and sexuality. Moreover, homeland cinema, which has retained an extraordinary popularity among generations of Danes, continues to serve as a clear marker of cultural identity, concealing behind its sunny disposition profound and surprisingly progressive rural visions.

9. THE OLSEN GANG IN DENMARK – AND ABROAD

Stephan Michael Schröder

In the 2016 test for applicants for Danish citizenship, one of the questions that aspiring Danes had to answer was whether the first *Olsen-banden* (*The Olsen Gang*) film was released in 1971, 1970 or 1968 – an inclusion which illustrates the extent to which *The Olsen Gang* films are considered an integral part of the collective memory in Denmark. The fourteen films, released between 1968 and 1981 with a follow-up in 1998, are surely a prime example of popular films of the 1970s, but their penetrating cultural power transgresses the realm of cinema. The longevity of these films is even reflected in spin-offs, such as prequels about the childhood of the Olsen Gang, animated films, a lively fan club, the use of quotations from the films in everyday language, commemorative stamps, a musical version, exhibitions and, since 2004, a street named after the eponymous gang leader Egon Olsen – not to mention all kinds of merchandise (Monggaard 2018: 324–29).

However, the popularity of the films has fostered rather uncritical publications about them, more indebted to national idealisation and/or fandom culture than to academic scholarship. Furthermore, the widespread veneration of the films as an epitome of Danishness and as 'arch-national' (Monggaard 2018: 299) evokes the question of how to explain their international success: in Eastern Bloc states, they found an eager audience, and although it proved impossible to export the Danish films to the neighbouring countries of Norway and Sweden, the films nevertheless became a template for successful national versions, in the Norwegian case even by recycling most of the original scripts (in Norway: *Olsenbanden,* fourteen films 1969–99; in Sweden: *Jönssonligan,* nine films 1981–2000 and 2015).

The Olsen Gang Recipe

From a film-historical perspective, the first Olsen Gang film with the plain title *Olsen-banden* (*The Olsen Gang,* 1968) was, to begin with, just another attempt to deal with the crisis of cinema and Danish film production in the 1960s. The arrival of television had taken its toll: 70 per cent of Danish households paid for a television license in 1969 (Nielsen and Halling 2006: 337), and cinema admissions fell by a third between 1964 and 1971 (Nissen 2001b: 238). However, the narrative about the relationship between cinema and television in the 1960s is not simply about the decline of Danish cinema, but rather about differentiation. As the public service television schedule was heavily dominated by high-brow content (Bondebjerg 1997a, Agger 2006), there was still a substantial market for popular entertainment in the cinema. At Nordisk, the director Erik Balling (1924–2005) tried to serve this popular segment, *inter alia* with two successful James Bond parodies: *Slå først Frede!* (*Strike First Freddy!*, 1965) and *Slap af, Frede!* (*Relax, Freddy!*, 1966). There was also a sailor's film, *Martha* (1967), which already drew on actors and a crew later re-used in the Olsen Gang films, most notably his co-author and production designer Henning Bahs (1928–2002) and the three main actors, Ove Sprogøe (1919–2004), Morten Grunwald (1934–2018) and Poul Bundgaard (1922–98). The first Olsen Gang film was a prolongation of these attempts to counter black-and-white television by offering popular entertainment, colour and (at least in the first Olsen Gang film) sex – quite a successful attempt, as it turned out to be the start of a whole series and helped to save Nordisk economically in the long run.

It took Balling and Bahs a few films to develop the characters, the basic narrative pattern, the specific visual language and the recurring motifs, but generally an Olsen Gang film is as follows: Egon Olsen is released from prison, where he has conceived an ingenious, meticulously planned heist worth millions; he is met outside the building by the other two gang members. With his worn-out pinstripe suit, bowler hat and perpetual cigar butt, Egon is the dictatorial head of a motley gang of small-time crooks, which further consists of Benny Frandsen, an unabashed optimist with yellow socks who has never really grown up, and finally timid, un-manly, stout Kjeld Jensen with his eight-piece cap and brown velvet jacket. Kjeld has to carry around the necessary heist utensils in a midwife bag, and at home he is totally under the thumb of his wife, the fancy and 'grotesque petty bourgeois' (Gentikow 1994: 1) Yvonne (Kirsten Walther, 1933–87). The execution of Egon's plan inevitably involves an ensemble of disparate things – for example, a crochet needle, balloons, stockings and a flagpole.

During the flow of events, the audience can look forward to Egon opening a safe either built by the company Franz Jäger in Berlin or by one of the company's international branch offices, to a domestic lecture by Yvonne and to a cascade of imaginative invectives by Egon during a crisis in the cohesion of the gang, which is overcome by restoring the true spirit of the three musketeers. The Olsen Gang's adversaries always belong to the world of high finance and international capitalism, protected by compliant politicians and incompetent policemen afraid of losing opportunities for advancement. Although the initial heist is often successful, the gang loses the loot again in the long run. In the end, the hapless Egon Olsen has to return to prison, only to be released again at the beginning of the next film, reuniting with his gang and stubbornly trying to rob big business of shady money.

The Olsen Gang and Danish Silent Film Comedy

Usually, the films are characterised by commentators as crime comedies or as farces, a term even Balling and Bahs used in 1968 when describing *The Olsen Gang* as 'an attempt to make a good old-fashioned farce' (quoted in Larsen 1993: 130). Other obvious inspirations are the Danish *folkekomedie* or folk comedy (as discussed by Hartvigson, Chapter 5 in this volume); the Olsen Gang films have been described as 'homeland comedies taking place in Copenhagen's Valby' (Arnedal 2006: 107).

Another precursor is the strong Danish tradition of silent film comedy. Although the term 'slapstick comedy films' (Lange-Fuchs 1997: 7) is sometimes applied, it is worth noting that slapstick elements became less prominent after the first film which, tellingly enough, ended with *the* iconic slapstick scene: a policeman slipping on a banana. The silent film tradition to which the Olsen Gang films refer is less the slapstick comedy à la Hal Roach and more of the Danish variety, notably the Fyrtaarnet-og-Bivognen (Long-and-Short) films of the 1920s with their less grotesque humour. Indeed, the poster for the first film *Olsen Gang*, showing the three gang members as black silhouettes walking in file (a recurrent shot in all the later films), cites a famous poster for the Long-and-Short film *Film, Flirt og Forlovelse* (*The Film and the Flirt*, Lau Lauritzen Sr, 1921). The Olsen Gang actor Poul Bundgaard claimed, incidentally, that his film debut was as a baby in the Long-and-Short film *Professor Petersens Plejebørn* (*The Smugglers*, Lau Lauritzen Sr, 1924) (Bundgaard 1988: 19).

The silent film tradition is discernible everywhere in the Olsen Gang films: one encounters intertitles as well as a heavy reliance on 'sight gags' (Carroll 1991), whole scenes filmed through glass panes so that the dialogue is not perceivable and the action becomes pantomime-like, and a multitude of cinematic quotations from easily recognisable films. Among them are Charlie Chaplin's

Modern Times (1936) or Jacques Tati's films, which are heavily indebted to the silent tradition, and the famous clock scene in Harold Lloyd's *Safety Last!* (1923) is even surpassed in a tongue-in-cheek way in *Olsen-banden går i krig* (*The Olsen Gang Goes to War*, 1978), when all three gang members have to cling to the clock of the Copenhagen town hall at the height of the action. There are good reasons for calling the films 'shadows from the silent film era', as the German author Uwe Tellkamp does (Tellkamp 2014).

HIGH-BROW AND POPULAR CULTURE

It is surely no coincidence that a still picture of Nordisk's silent film star Gunnar Tolnæs (1879–1940) is visible on a wall in the best-remembered scene of all Olsen Gang films: in *Olsen-banden ser rødt* (*The Olsen Gang Sees Red*, 1976), the gang is pounding and blasting its way through walls in the catacombs of the Royal Theatre in Copenhagen in such a carefully choreographed way that the noises and bangs correspond to the well-known overture of Friedrich Kuhlau's *Elverhøj* (*Elf Hill*, 1828), while the piece is simultaneously being performed in the theatre, thereby enhancing the performance of the musicians. The ingenious scene can be read as an assertion about the relationship between high-brow and popular culture: 'It is these walls we have to break down to reach the public', as Egon states when describing the task for his companions, both delivering a guide to actual action and a meta-commentary at the same time. And the performance of the musicians – uninspired at the beginning of the scene – merges into a higher unity with the perfectly timed craftsman-like performance in the rooms below so that both spheres benefit from the interference. The scene thus serves as an allegory of true *folkelighed* (roughly translatable as 'folksiness') as it was understood by Balling (Schepelern 2006a). Balling did not aim for 'artiness', but neither did he aim at chumming up to the audience, because 'there is a difference between ingratiating oneself with the audience and soliciting the audience' (quoted in Monggaard 2018: 10) (see also Chapter 5 in this book).

Despite his success with the audience, in the early phases of his career Balling seldom convinced the critics with this tricky balancing act. But the Olsen Gang films helped to persuade most critics on both sides of the political spectrum that popular culture indeed could be more than vulgarised, run-down high-brow culture. In hindsight it is symbolic that the first Olsen Gang film was released the same year as Fiedler's famous appeal to 'Cross the border – close the gap' between high-brow and popular culture (Fiedler 1977, first published 1968). Significantly enough, however, a reviewer who wrote a goodbye article to the Olsen Gang after the thirteenth film in 1981 (which at that time was supposed to be the last one) still assumed that his readers might shake their heads because he sacrificed two whole pages to a 'Danish folk comedy' in the film periodical *Kosmorama* (Lindberg 1982: 33).

However, the general appreciation of the films is not just due to the gradual acceptance of popular culture in the 1970s, the convincing acting, the elaborate, sophisticated scripts, or the perfect craftsmanship, all of which distinguish the films. Just as important was the overall narrative: the common man bearing commonplace Danish surnames like Olsen, Frandsen and Jensen, revolting against 'the system', but abstaining from violence. 'We would actually like to promote a little suspicion of authority', Balling stated in 1973 (quoted in Monggaard 2018: 237). Accordingly, scholars have underlined the 'subversive' character of the films (Lange-Fuchs 1997) and their 'satirical criticism of the unsightly sides of capitalist society' (Iversen 1997: 12). Robbing, like Robin Hood, only the rich, the stockbrokers, bankers and multinational capitalists, the Olsen Gang is up against the 'pillars of society', as Henrik Ibsen had it, as the politicians and the state authorities are mostly just marionettes in the hands of high finance. Although nearly every film ends with an illustration of the saying 'little thieves are hanged, but great ones escape', the films themselves are a wistful celebration of a rebellion – albeit futile – against a world of international big business (when Egon cracks safes made abroad with the help of a stethoscope, symbolically treating the money inside like a patient), but also against an increasing socialisation under the auspices of the welfare state and against modernity.

Figure 9.1   In *Olsen-banden ser rødt* (*The Olsen Gang Sees Red*, Erik Balling, 1976), the gang members consult the score of Friedrich Kuhlau's *Elverhøj* overture to calibrate the noise from their safe-cracking with the music from the orchestra playing in the theatre above them. Framegrab.

Socio-Cultural Change and Nostalgia

Parallels in the films to societal and political developments in Denmark at that time are by no means coincidental. The rising burden of taxation due to the development of the welfare state, the controversial legalisation of pornography in 1967 and 1969 (see Thorsen, Chapter 11 in this volume), the youth revolt and the closely-tied 1972 referendum on the decision to become a member of the European Communities all contributed to the so-called 'landslide election' in 1973, when 44 per cent of voters shifted their votes, not only severely punishing the reigning Social Democrats, but eroding the traditional party system as a whole and making the newly founded party Fremskridtspartiet (fighting against taxation and later to become the cradle of the right-wing populist Dansk Folkeparti) the second-largest party in parliament. The fundamental consensus about Danish society was gone, and if one casts a sideways glance at how the welfare state is dealt with in the literature of the time, the phase from 1968 into the 1970s has accordingly been characterised as a stage of crisis and dystopianism (Kjældgaard 2011: 22–24).

The Olsen Gang with its anarchistic fight against big business and authorities resists the current of modernisation – assiduously, but sure to lose. The new world of high finance, the modern headquarters of the EEC far away in Brussels and the advance of computers in *Olsen-banden deruda'* (*The Olsen Gang Strikes Again*, 1977) is juxtaposed with a petty bourgeois world (cf. Nissen 1980) in a quaint Copenhagen, which was already a nostalgic echo of a past time. Kjeld's family lives in a building that has fallen out of fashion, Benny drives a rusty Chevrolet, Egon is dressed in bygone grandeur. Even the film music with its swinging dixieland theme evokes former times. The centre of resistance in the Olsen Gang films is a cosy petty bourgeois milieu, Kjeld's home, where the ultimate ambition is to be able to keep up in the consumer race, to finance a family feast or a fur coat for Yvonne, or to take a trip to Mallorca. The Olsen Gang's world is still small, traditional (also with regard to gender roles) and predictable. Quite significantly, Egon's announcement 'I have a plan!' (precisely fifty-two times in fourteen films) (Monggaard 2018: 58) in a way inevitably anticipates the failure of this plan, as the modern world no longer lends itself to planning (and perhaps the old one never did anyway, because more often than not it is the human factor that sabotages the careful planning).

In one of the few critical engagements with the films, Nissen has called them 'a regressive utopia about a petty bourgeois organisation of society' (Nissen 1980: 345). But they are, rather, a eulogy and at the same time a wistful swansong about clinging to an easily understandable, still manageable, more human, even humanistic world which, however, is at odds with the present – as were many Danish voters at the same time, and not just those voting for Fremskridtspartiet. This overarching narrative is even mirrored in the use of the farce genre and in the serial character of the films. The characters are generally two-dimensional, easily recognisable stereotypes: policemen look like Sherlock Holmes parodies, Italian criminals look like Mafia bosses (and are called 'Motzarella'); bankers wear their bowler hats indoors; barons are always dressed for hunting; Germans wear either Bavarian *lederhosen* or look like SS officers; and so on. In the Olsen Gang films, characters are who they appear to be. The seriality of the films further contributes to an aesthetic experience of soothing orderliness and reliability, as it implies the return of the familiar, not at least with regard to the actors: watching an Olsen Gang film is like a family reunion, as even the minor characters are often played by the same crew of well-known popular actors. The dialectic of repetition and variance as structural pattern in the Olsen Gang films – for example, the introduction scene when Egon is released from prison and meets the expectant gang members outside – never allows true contingency, because variance (the receiving committee is absent or not complete, Benny is obviously displeased with something and so on) can only be something *conditionally* new, as it still hinges on expecting the reiteration of the familiar.

The Olsen Gang in the Eastern Bloc

When asked in 1972 about the saleability of the Olsen Gang films abroad, Balling was rather sceptical: 'They're very specifically Danish. [. . .] The films are so attached to a familiar milieu that they don't really say anything to foreigners. They are local. [. . .] Nothing is as different as humour [. . . It] is very, very national' (quoted in Lindberg 1972/73: 243). But in spite of this assessment, and although the films were explicitly made for a Danish audience, the films became quite a success in several Eastern Bloc states as well (see the corresponding entries in Eberlein 2001), especially in the German Democratic Republic (GDR). Here, the films gained cult status. Sprogøe, Grunwald and Bundgaard even made their appearance in a popular television show in 1982, and to this very day the films are cherished in the Eastern part of Germany. It is no exaggeration to say that the recognition value of the films is quite as high in East Germany as in Denmark – and their cult status factor perhaps even higher. The films are still successfully shown on television and screened in cinemas; they are the subject of several publications and exhibitions drawing a large number of visitors; they have their own fan club; the neologism *mächtiggewaltig*, a rather imaginative translation of Benny's rather vulgar *skidegodt* (roughly 'bloody great'), entered East German language use; and since the fall of the Berlin Wall in 1989, three theatre plays have been written and performed, which updated the deeds of the famous gang as 'secondary texts' *à la* Fiske (for more information on the

East German reception, see Breitenborn 1994, Eberlein 2001, Monggaard 2018: 254–73).

This popularity calls for an explanation – not just with regard to Balling's doubts about exporting the films because of their 'Danishness', but also because the films flopped in the Federal Republic of Germany (FRG) (and were never even shown in the rest of Western Europe). To this very day, knowledge about the Olsen Gang's deeds works quite reliably as a litmus test for discerning Germans with an Eastern socialisation from those with a Western one. One could, of course, point out that the silent film elements in particular are 'transnationally comprehensible' (Gentikow 1994: 152) – the cultural barrier in slapstick comedy tends to be rather minimal. Other decisive factors (cf. Breitenborn 1994, Gentikow 1994, Lachmann 1997) were the congenial GDR dubbing, the attractive origin of the films from the West, the arch criticism of capitalism and, perhaps most importantly, the ridiculing of authorities and an overlap with the experience structures in the secluded GDR. Here, one was much too familiar with an economy of scarcity and improvisation, with diffuse ideas of happiness and escape, with the inevitable failure of big ambitions and plans as a consequence of 'the illusion of rational omnipotence and the idea of long-lasting, constant functional contexts' (Breitenborn 1994: 130). While the government untiringly launched five-year plans on the road to a brighter future, doubts prevailed among the population about the 'projected linearity of the idea of progress' (137): 'The multifaceted scepticism towards "new-fangled stuff" appears like a continuous line in the sympathetic alignment of the Olsen Gang films and the cosmos of experiences in the GDR, an indication of delayed modernisation' (136). The audience in the FRG, however, would have lived in a world characterised by 'abundance and dominance of modernisation', so that 'the apparent "losers" of the Olsen Gang could not represent a sympathetic pattern' (126).

Such explanations are, however, partly problematic, not only because of a much too homogenous, simplified understanding of the FRG, but also because of the implicit thesis about significant societal similarities between the GDR and Denmark. But if the GDR reception of the films was not founded on a 'negotiated reading' (Hall 1999), how can this enthusiastic reception in a dictatorship shed light on the films and the construction of society that they project?

Danishness and its Others

It is worth noting that the 'people-versus-elite' dichotomy in the Olsen Gang films, surely attractive for an audience in a dictatorship but expressing a rather populist picture of society in a democracy, is additionally intertwined with an ever-present discourse on Danishness and its Other. Numerous and beloved in Denmark are the scenes self-ironically depicting Danish symbols, institutions, peculiarities and national stereotypes, mocking, for example, the self-centred Copenhagenism of the characters and their disdain for Jutland – blatantly in *Olsen-banden i Jylland* (*The Olsen Gang Plays for High Stakes*, 1971), but also a recurring gag in later films – or the inedibility of the traditional Danish brown sauce in *Olsen-banden over alle bjerge* (*The Olsen Gang over the Hill*, 1981). But while Danish culture is tinged with mild self-irony, other cultures are portrayed less favourably, sometimes even in a defamatory way typical of nationalist discourses. Notably, Germany is constructed as the Other of Danishness, as the films teem with Nazi and even SS connotations as well as German backers of international shady finance plans, trying to subdue Denmark once again with the help of the EEC and to turn the country into a gigantic holiday resort. Not surprisingly, the Olsen Gang takes on the task of defending Denmark (*The Olsen Gang Goes to War*) because, as explained in the title of the next film, which alludes to a slogan from the occupation period during the Second World War (Gentikow 1994: 154), *Olsen-banden overgiver sig aldrig* (*The Olsen Gang Never Surrenders*, 1979). Even the opportunistic, cynical policeman Jensen, normally trying not to interfere at all with the assumed expectations of his superiors and turning a blind eye to big business crime, declares: 'Here I draw a line!' In the Olsen Gang films, the octopus of international financial capitalism and the EEC more often than not have an ugly German face (Pinkert 2011), and when *The Olsen Gang Never Surrenders* counterfactually ends with the exclusion of Denmark from the EEC, this is merrily celebrated by the population, with obvious parallels to 5 May, the liberation day from the German occupation.

In this context, Egon Olsen's specific ability to open safes of the brand 'Franz Jäger, Berlin', one of the recurrent motifs, is not just a demonstration of the fact that a Danish petty criminal can open German quality work without any problems (Pinkert 2010: 92). Taking into consideration that the safes in the films were built no later than 1944, Egon's mastery of the safes symbolises his personal successful resistance to an overpowering, albeit long-gone Germany which nowadays has other means of exercising power.

As is generally known, the construction of identity relies on the construction of alterity. In the Olsen Gang films, two Others are intertwined in a way typical for populist stances: the internationalist elite of big business, supported by politics and state authorities and associated with modern times (the power dimension), and Germany in its traditional function as the Danish arch enemy (the national dimension), partly substituted by the EEC. In the GDR, this was obviously no obstacle to an enthusiastic reception, as the GDR defined itself in discontinuity with the 'old', fascist and capitalist Germany (and was not a member of the EEC anyway), but it might have been another factor explaining why the films never became a success in West Germany.

Conclusion

Aesthetically, Balling and Bahs succeeded in creating popular films in the best *folkelig* sense, perhaps more than any other Danish films contributing to tearing down the walls between high-brow and mass culture, as well as in creating authentic 'popular culture' as opposed to pure culture industry products. Politically, however, the Olsen Gang films reflect the dissemination and acceptance of populist thinking in the 1970s and 1980s (which did not seem to have bothered the Danish audience), when Denmark was faced with the necessity of transcending the nation-state in order to cope with the ongoing challenges.

But then one might even interpret the films as already providing an ironic commentary on their own populist ideology of defending Danishness against 'the system' more or less controlled from abroad. In a self-reflexive turn, the adversary insurance company Høje Nord (High North) with the witty motto *In Calamitate Fidus* (We trust in bad luck) in *Olsen-bandens flugt over plankeværket* (*The Olsen Gang Jumps the Fence*, 1981) has the same logo as Nordisk Film itself. This playfully identifies the films as products of commercial interests in their own right, thereby ridiculing the basic Manichaean opposition in the filmic narrative. And whenever Egon and his gang occasionally succeed, as they do in the films *Olsen-bandens sidste bedrifter* (*The Olsen Gang's Last Escapade*, 1974) and *Olsens-bandens sidste stik* (*The Olsen Gang: Final Mission*, 1998), what do they do? They turn their back on Denmark and settle down abroad.

10. MAKING A LIFE OF YOUR OWN: FILMS FOR CHILDREN AND YOUNG PEOPLE IN THE 1970S AND 1980S

Christa Lykke Christensen

Stolen Spring is the English title of a classic Danish novel, *Det forsømte forår* by Hans Scherfig, first published in 1940. The novel enjoyed considerable success and has often been included in the reading syllabi for schools, high schools and universities. Still widely read today, the book has been translated into nine languages and was made into a film by the same title in 1993 (directed by Peter Schrøder), becoming an instant hit with more than 400,000 tickets sold in Danish cinemas that same year. The novel and the film are about the ways in which an authoritarian society, represented by the old-fashioned school system with its emphasis on discipline and punishment, systematically erodes the independence and self-esteem of young people. The key figure is a despotic teacher who, by means of malicious and powerful psychological and physical violence, is able to humiliate and terrorise his pupils. He crushes their spirit and stunts their imagination, so that as adults they end up looking back at their younger days as a time of abandoned dreams and wasted opportunities; in other words, a life characterised by stolen springs.

The novel is mentioned in this context because it critically examined the consequences of the denial of young people's personal freedom under an authoritarian, patriarchal education and played a substantial role in the general public discourse about the reforming of educational styles in the period in which it appeared. It suggested that those who lost out were the children and young people who failed to lead good and meaningful lives as a result of being bullied when they were young. Many of the Danish children's and youth films from the 1970s and 1980s can, in several respects, be regarded as drawing inspiration from a similar critique of a traditional, hierarchical society and of a harsh disciplinary mentality that privileged conformity over individuality, a process which was so exemplarily described in *Stolen Spring*.

Confronting the dark shadow of the past that this novel depicted formed a precursor to the kind of alternative cinema that Danish films for children and young people represented in the 1970s and 1980s – featuring strongly independent children and young people revolting against the obduracy of their parents' generation and articulating their own dreams for the future. Thus, this so-called golden age of Danish children's and youth film involved a number of films that thematised the new social and cultural position that children and young people were in the process of establishing as representatives of a rebellion against the old, patriarchal world.

Danish films for children and young people in this period set a new agenda for the portrayal of their intended audience. Their social and psychological realism alone distanced the films from previous film genres such as the family film and the popular comedy, in which children and young people also appeared but played quite different roles (see Hartvigson, Chapters 5 and 8 in this volume). In particular, the family film series *Far til fire* (*Father of Four*, Alice O'Fredericks, 1953–61) was popular among children, as the films portrayed children as funny, innocent characters always displaying a positive attitude and having a good time in a safe and idyllic environment. In the new films of the 1970s, children and young people consistently played leading roles representing a new earnestness that did not simply connote innocence, victimhood, or 'maladjusted youth'. Rather, children and young people represented an independent agency characterised by critical thinking and inward-looking reflection. In many films, they demonstrated an emotional sensibility related to the new roles and opportunities in their more liberated position *as* children and *as* young people. In this chapter, I will take a closer look at this earnestness and how it can be seen as constitutive of children's and young people's new roles as independent actors. We will see how social, psychological and magical realism became crucial to this depiction and to the relationships that children and young people have with other people. Before we proceed, however, it is important to outline the particularly favourable production conditions prevailing at the time of this heyday of Danish children's and youth film.

Cultural Modernisation and State Subsidies

These films gave voice to young people and, as a genre, made contributions to cinematic realism; but it is also important to see them in the context of the cultural politics of their time. Danish children's and youth films of the 1970s and 1980s were created in an especially child-friendly cultural environment. They were inspired by the radical pedagogical and cultural trends of the time, which argued that the child should have more influence in the family, in school and in culture and society as a whole (Drotner 1997: 143). Equally, they were inspired by the ongoing youth revolution, by young people struggling against authority and expressing hope for a new freedom. Apart from these cultural trends, economic and institutional changes in society also played a crucial role in the new film productions for children and young people. In 1972, legislation was passed in Denmark to guarantee state subsidies to films that were considered worthy of support based on a politically independent assessment of their artistic qualities. As a result of this legislation, film subsidies became an important culture-political issue, not merely an industry-specific subsidy to a sector having financial difficulties.

This in turn led to discussions in the public and political spheres, in which arguments were put forward for introducing a focus on children's film (Breuning 2002: 26). The arguments were based on ideas of the importance of showing the world from a children's perspective, as children look at things differently and often have an alternative approach to the world when compared to adults. Children should be taken seriously as small citizens having the opportunity, in the form of films, to be confronted with the situations or experiences of other children, and perhaps identify with them or recognise them from their own lives. They should be presented with stories of children's dreams, rebellions, friendships and ways of tackling problems. Films for children and young people were considered a cultural means of enlightening and raising awareness among children about their particular value and importance for culture and society, and throughout the 1970s and 1980s in general, there was a cultural-political will to support this agenda. Moreover, in light of the expanding influence of American film and pop culture, it was argued that it was crucial to present children and young people with films that took place within a recognisable Danish environment and used the Danish language.

In 1976, this discussion resulted in the appointment of a special children's film consultant, which from an international perspective was unique at the time; this institutionalised recognition was in itself an incentive to produce high-quality films aimed at young audiences. Thus, the annual amount of targeted subsidies gradually increased throughout the 1970s, and new Danish film legislation introduced in 1982 went even further. It was decided that at least 25 per cent of all state subsidies for film production and film import should be allocated to the production of children's and youth film. This provided a good basis for the development of children's and youth film, which had been gaining momentum from the mid-1970s onwards and continued to do so throughout the 1980s. It was a trend that resulted in increases in both the number of films produced (Bondebjerg 1997b; Breuning 2002) and the size of the audiences watching them (Synnott 1997). In addition, children's and youth films had a significant impact on the rest of Danish film realism over the two decades (Langkjær 2012), and from the end of the 1970s onwards, according to Ib Bondebjerg (1997b: 20), an aesthetic and generic change started taking place in Danish film culture, resulting in popular genre film, such as melodramas and comedies aimed at adult audiences, becoming less prominent than before.

CHILDREN AND YOUNG PEOPLE AS MAIN CHARACTERS

As Ulrich Breuning argues, the films for children and young people produced over these two decades had a lasting impact on what was perceived as being a 'good' quality Danish children's or youth film (2002: 31). First of all, film realism was dominant, be it social, psychological, or magical realism, taking children and young people seriously as citizens who should also have a voice in culture and society. The same values were encouraged by the influential public service broadcaster Danmarks Radio (DR), which had a monopoly at the time (Christensen 2006, 2013). Several directors of the period started their careers making series and programmes for children's and youth television at DR, including Søren Kragh-Jacobsen, who directed the television series *Guldregn* (*Showers of Gold*, 1986) and was the scriptwriter on the TV series *Omsen og Momsen* (*Omsen and Momsen*, 1987). In his early career Bille August (director of 1988 Oscar-winner *Pelle the Conqueror*) made television productions for children – for example, his film *Busters verden* (*Buster's World*, 1984), which was originally made as a television series for DR in 1983. Both Søren Kragh-Jacobsen and Bille August went on making film for an audience of both young people and adults, thereby carrying realism with them in their further careers.

Taking a closer look at children's film of the period, some films were retrospective and focused on the experience of being a child or a young person in the 1950s and at the beginning of the 1960s in the context of family, friends and school. This genre includes films such as *Johnny Larsen* (Morten Arnfred, 1979), *Kundskabens træ* (*The Tree of Knowledge*, Nils Malmros, 1981), *Zappa* (Bille August, 1983), and *Tro, håb og kærlighed* (*Twist and Shout*, Bille August, 1984). Other films were set in the contemporary world of the 1970s and 1980s and tried to capture moods, emotions and sensations specifically related to individual experiences of and problems with being a child or a young person. Here we find children's films such as *Gummi Tarzan* (*Rubber Tarzan*, Søren Kragh-Jacobsen, 1981) and *Busters verden* (*Buster's World*, Bille August, 1984), as well as youth films such as *Mig og Charly* (*Me and Charly*, Morten Arnfred and Henning Kristiansen, 1978), *Vil du se min smukke navle?* (*Wanna See My Beautiful Navel?*, Søren Kragh-Jacobsen, 1978) and *Du er ikke alene* (*You Are Not Alone*, Ernst Johansen and Lasse Nielsen, 1978). Some of these are discussed in the next section.

Regardless of whether the films were set in Denmark of the 1950s or 1960s, or unfolded in a contemporary Danish context, they all had a common starting point: namely that children and young people were special and experienced the world in ways that were unique to them. Accordingly, children and young people were entitled to films specifically aimed at them. The idea was to portray children and young people as seen from their perspective. They themselves therefore were the lead actors in films that focused on the particular challenges and dilemmas peculiar to children and young people. The films tried to depict the emotional reality of being a child or young person in order to communicate, within the fictional framework, an authentic picture of what characterised such experiences. And they always did so from a humanistic viewpoint in solidarity with the characters, trusting in their potential for development and change; also, they were marked by a redemptive sense of humour.

A Child's Perspective on the World

Characteristic of children's films was that they represented children as being in a particular phase of their lives, unaffected by the normative rules of the adult world. Children were portrayed as having specific emotions, and as having ideals and expectations of the future which often differed from those of adults. In that sense, they often represented a kind of silent rebellion. One film that presaged both the theme and tone of the children's films to come was the animation film *Bennys badekar* (*Benny's Bathtub*, Jannik Hastrup and Flemming Quist Møller, 1971). The film is about an ordinary boy, Benny, who is very lonely. His rather dreary childhood is spent in a dull high-rise building. The adults are always nagging him about making a mess and, as punishment, send him outside. One day Benny finds a tadpole that turns out to be an enchanted prince. Benny brings it home to his bathtub, and when he dives into the water it turns into a huge ocean with brightly coloured fish. Benny's bathtub becomes a haven where he can find fun and excitement. Using his fantasy to escape into this magical undersea world, he forgets his feelings of being unwanted and lonely.

Benny's Bathtub became a source of inspiration for many later children's films, which drew on its theme of a child's sense of loneliness and point of view, the use of alternative ways of visual presentation and the use of experimental music. It was based on the idea that children and adults belonged to two separate worlds: the magical, fantasy-creative world, on the one hand, and the material world with a focus on work and wealth, on the other hand. Children were assumed to possess a natural curiosity and creativity, which was under threat from adults and society in general. Thus, *Benny's Bathtub* paid tribute to the power of fantasy and laid the foundation for the idea that imagination needs to be stimulated, as it is an important utopian element in how children deal with problems.

The idea of fantasy as both a natural and utopian element in children's lives also features in Søren Kragh-Jakobsen's live-action film *Rubber Tarzan*. This was a film adaptation of a 1975 children's book by the author Ole Lund Kierkegaard. The film is about a boy, Ivan Olsen, who is somewhat weak and backward at school and bullied by the bigger boys. Moreover, his father, who thinks of Tarzan as the ideal man, thinks that Ivan is a wimp who cannot do any of the things a real boy should be able to do. Ivan is only happy and carefree when he can play by himself and fly his kite. Like the red balloon in the film *Le ballon rouge* (*The Red Balloon*, Albert Lamorisse, 1956), Ivan's kite becomes a symbol of joy and freedom. In the harbour Ivan meets the crane driver Ole, who teaches him how to operate a crane; he takes Ivan to a container that gives him magical powers and makes all his wishes come true. In this magical and fantastical world, Ivan manages to live up to his father's ideals of masculinity and get the better of the bullies and his father. The main point, however, is not this magical and joyful revenge against his father and the other boys, but his friendship with Ole the crane driver, who helps Ivan believe in himself by telling him that he has to find out what he is good at, because, as Ole explains, there is always something you are good at; you just need to find out what it is.

Children's films like *Lille Virgil og Orla Frø-Snapper* (*Little Virgil and Orla Frog Face*, Gert Fredholm, 1980) and *Otto er et næsehorn* (*Otto is a Rhino*, Rumle Hammerich, 1983) are also about small boys who are bored, bullied, or repeatedly told off by their vociferous fathers. The former is based on the books *Little Virgil* (1967) and *Orla Frog Face* (1969), the latter on the book *Otto is a Rhino* (1972), all three authored by Ole Lund Kierkegaard. The films take place in a realistic setting combined with magical elements to overcome boredom, deal with bullies, or to make their fathers realise that they should not castigate their sons but treat them compassionately.

Another popular film that was inspired by magical realism was *Buster's World*. Buster is a small boy, and his world is characterised by the family's social problems, the rigidity of the school, its humourless authority and the big, nasty boys who continuously bully the small boys. However, Buster manages to keep his spirits up by using his magic and conjuring tricks. As with the above-mentioned films, *Buster's World* represents the child and its alternative approach to the world. Buster is a bit of an outsider, but he never places himself completely outside the rules of reality; he merely provokes and challenges them. Thus, where the film might have focused on children as a special group of people, it does not represent them as entirely different from adult people; rather, it portrays Buster as a boy who feels solidarity with his family and friends. In *Buster's World*, fantasy does not, however, represent an escape from reality. Imaginative power belongs in the real world and has to be used inventively and constructively, just as Buster does in several unexpected ways. The film shows that, in many ways, children should be regarded as mini versions of adults, with the same worries and cares as adults. The main message, however, is that the capacity of children to be open-minded creates valuable potential for change.

Danish children's films of the 1970s and 1980s had strong narratives and easy-to-understand dramaturgy. They were designed to support children's and adults' understanding of both the vulnerability and the strength of children. Boys in particular were put in the role of being able to create 'fantastic' alternatives to the authoritarian structures represented by adults, especially the fathers. It was not until the late 1980s that girls acted as lead characters in Danish children's films, such as *Negerkys og labre larver* (*Tootsiepops and Candyfloss*, Li Vilstrup, 1987), *Skyggen af Emma* (*Emma's Shadow*, Søren Kragh-Jacobsen, 1988), *Tarzan Mama Mia* (*Me and Mama Mia*, Erik Clausen, 1989) and *17 op* (*Sallys Bizniz*, Brita Wielopolska, 1989). This relatively late emergence of narratives led by girls seems all the more remarkable given that television series had been broadcast on DR since the late 1960s starring girls in the lead roles (Christensen 2002). In both social and magical realist forms they portrayed strong and independent girls trying to find their own ways and agendas in relation to the parent generation, such as *Super Carla* (Thomas Winding and Lulu Gauguin, 1968), *Sonja fra Saxogade* (*Sonja from Saxo Street*, Jytte Hauch-Fausbøll, 1968, produced by Nordisk Film for DR) and *Farvel, jeg hedder Kurt* (*Goodbye, My Name Is Kurt*, Thomas Winding, 1969).

Thus, children's films of the period portrayed children from the point of view of the child, but they also addressed an adult audience. Generally, at least if we look at the protagonists, the films communicated a somewhat romanticised view of children as unspoiled representatives of a better and more human world. One could, like Birgitta Steene, argue that the child was represented 'partly from a realistic adult perspective as a representative of a young person, partly as a potential fulfiller of the future [. . .] both as an individual child and as a personification, both as a concrete socially formed person and as a mythical or emblematic common figure' (Steene 1992: 33). Such duality was dominant in children's films of the period. Yet, one can argue, the films actually showed children confronting rigid authoritarian structures, primarily represented by fathers or male contemporaries. As Anders Lysne points out, children were given a voice, for example, in the form of internal 'monologue as narrative device' (Lysne 2016: 138). Children were given agency, and as agents they stirred things up. They were not portrayed as victims; on the contrary, they were empowered, and as such they represented opportunities for change and hope for the future.

Danish Films for Young People

Compared to the children's films of the period, Danish films for young people were more obviously characterised by presenting the viewpoint of the young people themselves. This was not only different from children's film, but also a departure from earlier films about young people from the 1950s such as *Farlig ungdom* (*Dangerous Youth*, Lau Lauritzen Jr, 1953) and *Blændværk* (*Delusion*, Johan Jacobsen, 1955), which presented young people as being surrounded by danger and temptation, such as sex, alcohol and crime. The message was clear here: young people had to be morally advised by their parents' generation so they would not get into trouble, but they could take part in and identify with the traditional way of life followed by their parents.

In contrast, youth films in the 1970s and 1980s were not produced from the point of view of a worried and concerned adult generation. In the 1970s especially, films were aimed at being young people's 'own' films, with young people as the primary audience, and they were about groups of ordinary, young people and their typical problems, such as friends, love, sex and identity. To underline the collective atmosphere of young people as a special group of people, music and lyrics played a central role in most youth films, such as in *Måske ku' vi* (*Could We Maybe*, Lasse Nielsen, Morten Arnfred and Morten Bruus, 1976), *You are Not Alone* and *Me and Charly*. The music featured was the 'young music' of the time, and the lyrics often referred to young people rebelling against adult authority, sticking together and representing an alternative to a society that suppressed individual freedom and independence.

Young Alternatives

Parents and those of the older generation were, if not absent, then often present without any importance, as in the group of films that can be described as *robinsonades* (Linnet 1983). These films were often about boys who ran away, Robinson Crusoe-like, from the problems that they experienced with parents and teachers, to remote locations outside the immediate urban and cultural environment. Nature played an important role as a setting for realising their utopian ideas and for love and friendship. This group of films includes *La' os være* (*Leave Us Alone*, Lasse Nielsen and Ernst Johansen, 1975), *Could We Maybe* and *You Are Not Alone*. For instance, in *Leave Us Alone* a group of young people leave the grey and dreary city for a summer camp on a deserted island in order to experiment with alternative lifestyles and realise utopian ideas of solidarity. *You Are Not Alone* takes place in a school for boys and in particular focuses on two boys who discover and experiment with their homosexuality.

Wanna See My Beautiful Navel? takes place in a remote area in the Swedish countryside and portrays social relations among fifteen-year-old school friends. The film has a realistic, episodic form that supports the atmosphere and emotions of the characters. The episodic here-and-now-structure or its 'fluttering mosaic form' (Langkjær 2012: 302) connects directly to the individual experiences of the young people and reinforces the aim of presenting a subjective viewpoint. While the film is about the social interactions among a group of

Figure 10.1   Søren Kragh-Jacobsen's *Vil du se min smukke navle?* (*Wanna See My Beautiful Navel?*, 1978) follows the subjective experiences of a group of teenagers on a camping trip with a mosaic-like narrative strategy. Framegrab.

young people, it focuses primarily on one teenager, Claus, in his search for love. For brief moments we receive a casual impression of the young people in the camp, at the same time as we are getting involved in Claus' feelings of uncertainty and insecurity, his emotional confusion and the ups and downs of connecting with the girl with whom he might be in love. All in all, the film gives an intimate psychological portrait of a teenager trying to deal with all sorts of conflicting emotional reactions. It portrays youth as an exciting phase in life, but a difficult one. It shows that young people not only fight against society for alternative utopias, but also have to come to terms with their own inner world of conflicting emotions.

Another group of youth films takes place in a well-known and ordinary everyday setting, such as on the streets of a small town, at school, or at home. In *Me and Charly*, a friendship develops between the local good guy, Steffen, and the rough diamond, Charly, a teenager who has run away from an orphanage. Using a social realist, episodic format, the film follows Steffen as he faces emotional dilemmas between his pretty, rich girlfriend, his lovely but often frustrated mother and his new friendship with the cheeky but good-hearted Charly. Like Claus in *Wanna See My Beautiful Navel?* Steffen is a young innocent teenager, who is emotionally confused in his attempts to negotiate his identity among different people to whom he feels a connection. Unlike *Wanna See My Beautiful Navel?*, *Me and Charly* takes place in various social arenas, pulling Steffen in different directions so that he feels caught between several social situations that each attract him in different ways. The film thereby makes the point that people can have very different social motivations for being the people they are.

Blaming and Shaming

Another specific group of films about young people from the 1980s became very popular. They did not share the aim of the films just discussed, of being young people's 'own' films and with young people as the primary audience. They were *about* young people, and the characters were seen from the perspectives of both young people *and* adults. The films deal with the typical problems that young people experience with parents and teachers, love, friendship and sexuality. Moreover, in a Danish context, they are regarded as being among the most successful psychological, realistic films from the 1980s *about* children and young people. In contrast to the youth films of the 1970s, they do not take place in a contemporary setting, but in the recent past. These films thus tend to be based on the memories that the directors had of what it was like to be a teenager in the 1950s and 1960s. Among the most popular of these directors were Nils Malmros and Bille August, the former considered one of Denmark's few auteurs; almost all of Malmros' films tell stories about children or adolescents.

Figure 10.2   Nils Malmros' historical drama *Kundskabens træ* (*The Tree of Knowledge*, 1981) reconstructs school life in 1950s Aarhus. Its inclusion in the 2006 Danish Cultural Canon for Film speaks to Malmros' auteur status and to the status of films for children and young people in Denmark. Framegrab.

In contrast to the youth films of the 1970s, most of Malmros' and August's films have a stronger, linear narrative, although poetic elements often function to stop time temporarily in order to accentuate the moods and feelings of the characters. Another difference is that the films do not have an improvised character; the dialogues are clearly carefully prepared. Nils Malmros' *Kundskabens træ* (*The Tree of Knowledge*, 1981) focuses on a group of teenagers and their internal relations. The group ends up bullying and insulting one of the girls in class, the implicit message being that, away from the influence and interest of adults, young people are left at the mercy of friends and schoolmates, who are often just as annoying and cruel as, or even worse than, their parents and other figures of authority.

Bille August's film *Zappa*, based on a popular novel by the author Bjarne Reuter, is a realist youth drama about power relations among three fifteen-year-old boys set around 1960. One of the boys is very destructive and exerts his powerful influence over the other two in order to manipulate them to carry out criminal acts. The film focuses on the different social backgrounds from which the boys come and thematises questions such as: what is a real friend? How do you avoid being an opportunist? And, in particular, how do you preserve your self-respect and individual identity in a group of friends with differing moral values? August's subsequent film *Twist and Shout* is partly a sequel, as the main character is one of the boys from *Zappa*. Even though the boy is a few years older, he still has problems with his friends, especially with two girls, with one of whom he is expected to fall in love, and the other with whom he actually falls in love.

Characteristic of both Malmros' and August's youth films are their psychological realism, their focus on the constitution of friendship, and the problems involved with establishing social relations with peers, parents and other figures of authority. Moreover, as Langkjær points out, their films on youth often have open endings (Langkjær 2012: 320). Thus, they not only offered an interpretation of what it meant to be young in the 1960s; they also encouraged the audiences of the 1980s to dare to imagine that things can change for the better.

Conclusion

As several film scholars point out (Nordin 1984, Breuning 2002, Langkjær 2012), Danish films for children and young people of the 1970s and the 1980s supported the development of Danish film realism. In particular, psychological realism was strengthened in portrayals of children's and young people's emotional life and their close social relationships. Often combined with social and magical realism, psychological realism was used to portray children and young people as being historically and culturally in the process of setting a new agenda in relation to what it meant to be a child or a young person in modern culture and society. The films embraced humanistic ideals and articulated values and visions on behalf of the young generation: they espoused independence from authority, individual freedom, solidarity and social responsibility, and they promoted a new openness about emotions, love and sexuality. However, they also thematised complicated problems and dilemmas that young people could easily identify with, such as the loss of innocence, vulnerability and loneliness. Yet, most of these films did so in such a way that the audience was left with a feeling of optimism and hope for the future for the young generation. In common with other cultural trends in literature, television, music and theatre, children's and youth film helped articulate a new attitude towards children and young people as independent, psychologically interesting, resourceful and active human beings, none of whom deserved to experience a single 'stolen spring'. The films therefore helped to create a culturally legitimate public forum for discussions about this new perspective.

The 1970s and 1980s are regarded as the golden age of Danish children's and youth film. They succeeded in depicting children and young people in ways that kept abreast with the modernisation of Danish culture and society. The period became a point of orientation for future film producers who wanted to realistically portray the ups and downs of the lives of children and young people. Thus, the heritage of the period was carried into the next decades and still serves as an inspiration for realist depictions of children and young people in the twenty-first century. Simultaneously, children's and youth film have evolved into new genres, such as road movies, action films and adventure movies, giving much higher priority than previous films to entertainment, including suspense and comic effects. Especially with regard to youth film, after the millennium a starker realism manifested itself, focusing on violence, drug abuse and victimisation (Christensen 2008).

Moreover, in the 1990s, Danish films for children and young people were challenged by the global and commercialised film and media industry. In particular, children's film was challenged by Disney's re-launch on VHS and later DVD format of both their classic and new animation movies, making them readily available to most children. From the 1990s onwards, the highly successful Danish film director Lars von Trier and the *Dogme* movement (see Thomson, Chapter 13 in this volume) set a new film agenda, which consequently drew attention away from children's and youth film. After the millennium, films made in Denmark for domestic audiences were first and foremost cosy family film series, such as the remakes of *Min søsters børn* (*My Sister's Kids*, seven films 2001–15) and of *Far til fire* (*Father of four*, ten films 2005–18).

However, there is no doubt that among children and youth audiences both serious and entertaining fiction films remain a hit. This is especially evident when looking at how the heritage of the Danish tradition of children's and youth film has enjoyed a revival in recent years, in the form of a burgeoning production of short film formats and television web series which, like their forerunners, focus on realist psychological and social dramas about children and young people.

11. PORNOGRAPHY AND CENSORSHIP

Isak Thorsen

In the summer of 1969, Denmark was the first country in the world to abolish censorship on picture pornography. The new law was initiated by the conservative Minister for Justice, Knud Thestrup, and it did not come out of the blue. Thestrup's argument was not merely to liberate a forbidden subcultural phenomenon, but also to restrain it (Thestrup 1976: 282–85). In 1967, the repeal of the obscenity clause on literature had led to a decrease in the sale of erotic and pornographic literature, and the hope was that the 1969 law would have a similar effect (Kutchinsky 1973: 277). But the law on picture pornography worked in quite a different way, causing a wave of pornographic pictures and films. This placed Denmark in a unique position internationally, and for a few years the small nation became synonymous with sex and pornography. Taking a historical perspective, this chapter gives a brief account of film censorship in Denmark and of the circumstances leading up to the decriminalisation of visual pornography, addressing how the mainstream Danish feature films of the late 1960s and 1970s incorporated sex and pornography.[1]

CENSORSHIP BEFORE 1969

From the very arrival of film in Denmark in 1896, it was subject to regulations and legislation. At first the new media fell under the laws for traveling markets and fairs, but when Nordisk Films Kompagni released the violent *Mordet paa Fyn* (*The Murder on Funen*, 1907), based on a then recent murder case, it caused a scandal, and the Minister of Justice passed a censorship notification. From then on, the theatre censor in Copenhagen and the individual local commissioners of police throughout the country became responsible for censoring films. The consequence was that a film could be banned in one town and shown in a neighbouring town; even in the capital, Copenhagen, a film could be released in different versions. In 1911 the censor in Copenhagen, P. A. Rosenberg, publicly declared that Asta Nielsen's infamous Gaucho dance in *Afgrunden* (*The Abyss*, Urban Gad, 1910; see Allen, Chapter 2 in this volume) could be shown in the city centre due to the mature and well-educated audience, while the dance was cut when the film was shown in the suburban areas because the audience there consisted mainly of children and young people (Sandfeld 1966: 270). Rosenberg's statement is in line with the overall idea of censorship: to protect the innocent and uneducated audience from the medium's potential to influence the viewer's heart and mind. In 1913 this uneven censorship system was replaced by a national film censorship system, which became law in 1922. The Ministry of Justice appointed three censors for the whole country, and a minimum viewing age of sixteen years was introduced for films not suitable for children. The law that the censors had to follow was not very specific, and so decisions were often taken on the basis of the current social and cultural values of society. It was subjects like crime, murder and sex which drew the attention of the censors, and American films in particular were seen as cynical and brutal. For instance, Howard Hawks' *Scarface* (1933) was banned, and scenes were cut from Orson Welles' *Touch of Evil* (1958) before its release (Dinnesen and Kau 1983: 275–83).

Sex in the Cinemas

Attitudes towards sex and pornography gradually changed in the western world during the 1960s. Eric Schaefer, writing in an American context, has pointed out that what has become known as the 'Sexual Revolution' was something that actually started decades prior but became visible through the media in the late 1960s and 1970s (Schaefer 2014a: 3). In the decade leading up to 1969, erotic and sexual themes became more prominent in Danish feature films, and some of them actually tested the borders of mainstream culture and legislation. One of the first films to do so was Johan Jacobsen's psychological drama *En Fremmed banker på* (*A Stranger Knocks*, 1959), which included a controversial scene with a female orgasm. Originally the film was banned but eventually released with a seventeen-second outtake, featuring shots of feet caressing. Although it was mainly in comedies such as *Det tossede paradis* (*Crazy Paradise*, Gabriel Axel, 1962), *Halløj i himmelsengen* (*Two Times Two in the Fourposter*, Erik Balling, 1965) and *Sytten* (*Seventeen*, Annelise Meiniche, 1965) that erotic and sexual themes were present, other films addressed the new currents of the 1960s. The Danish-Swedish production *Jeg - en kvinde* (*I, a Woman*, Mac Ahlberg, 1965) told the story of the emancipated nurse Siv who has an active and vigorous sex life and avoids committing herself to one of her lovers. *I, a Woman* can be perceived, on the one hand, to exploit the erotic and, on the other hand, as portrait of a modern, sexually liberated woman. The film was widely shown in the USA and, together with *A Stranger Knocks*, paved the way for more lenient censorship laws in certain states. It heralded a shift from France to Denmark and Sweden as the nationalities equated with 'sexy', a shift that gained pace in the summer of 1969 when Denmark decriminalised pornography (Petersen 2013; Schaefer 2014b: 215–17, 221).

One individual who saw the signs of the time as a decline in morals was the culturally conservative director Knud Leif Thomsen. His film *Gift* (*Venom*, 1966), including footage from a hardcore stag-film, was a moral warning against pornography. *Venom* was immediately banned by the censors, but the ban caused public discussion, and the film was later released in cinemas with a white cross over the pornographic scenes. On the other side of the debate, the future Academy Award-winning director Gabriel Axel contributed to the ongoing discussion, arguing for an open-minded attitude towards pornography with *Det kære legetøj* (*Danish Blue*, 1968), which mixed documentary and fiction sequences. A film that deliberately tested the bounds of the censorship laws – still within the limits of softcore pornography – was Annelise Meineche's *Uden en trævl* (*Without a Stitch*, 1968), a story about an apparently frigid young woman who is helped by her doctor to discover and explore her sexuality. *Without a Stitch* was released twice. First it was banned, then released with four minor cuts in 1968, and later re-released in an uncut version after the legalisation in 1969. This kind of testing of the Danish censorship laws can be seen as a natural development. Erotic and pornographic literature was fairly easy to access, and pornographic magazines such as *Weekend Sex* with explicit graphic illustrations and images were published regularly from 1967 onwards, although they were technically prohibited. The dismantling of the ban on picture pornography seemed inevitable.

Certain underlying currents in Danish culture can be considered as reasons for the new law. One of these is the Danish *frisind* (liberalism, literally 'free mind'), which is not easily translated, but refers to a general liberality and tolerance coinciding with the underlying liberal virtues from the Age of Enlightenment, privileging individual liberty, freedom of expression and an underlying belief that as a principle the state should not interfere in the lives of adults and what they choose to read and watch (Stevenson 2010: 5; Rasmussen 2017: 92–97; Birkvad 2020). An ongoing argument in the debate about Danish film censorship in the 1940s and 1950s concerned the limitations of freedom of speech (Dinnesen and Kau 1983: 278). As argued by Schaefer (2014a), the sexual revolution became visible in the 1960s but had actually begun decades earlier. In the Danish context, the influence of Cultural Radicalism was still a strong current leading to the decriminalisation of pornography (Birkvad 2020). A prominent figure in the cultural radical movement, the architect, writer and social critic Poul Henningsen – known as PH in Denmark and internationally renowned for his lamp designs – wrote about the 'pedagogical value of pornography' as early as 1928 (Henningsen 1928). Although cultural radicalism went through different phases historically, one can summarise some of its core values as being in opposition to religion and inherited norms and as a criticism of Victorian sexual morals. As I will argue below, some prominent cultural radical figures were among the first to embrace the possibilities of the new law of 1969.

SEX 69

One of the first results of the new law of 1969 was the world's first sex trade fair, *Sex 69*, held in Copenhagen in October 1969. Over 300 journalists, many from abroad, flocked to the six-day-long event, together with nearly 50,000 visitors (Kutchinsky 1970: 28). Among the many foreign guests was the American filmmaker Alex de Renzy, who shot the documentary *Pornography in Denmark – A New Approach* (1970). The film combined interviews with Danes discussing pornography and sex, traditional travelogue images of Copenhagen, as well as erotic images and hard-core scenes. Since de Renzy had shot the sex scenes straight from the projection screens, he could claim that the film was a documentary and not a pornographic film, and the film passed the strict censorship laws in the USA. A similar film was John Lamb's *Sexual Freedom in Denmark* (1970). Both films used Denmark as a prime example to argue for decriminalising the American obscenity laws, insisting, as in de Renzy's film, that 'pornography and sexual stimulation do not necessarily lead to antisocial or criminal behaviour'. Denmark's special status as the 'Wild wild west of xxx-rated porn' (Heidenry 1997: 54) attracted other foreign filmmakers. Most notably, these included the American psychologist couple Eberhard and Phyllis Kronhausen who lived in Denmark for a couple of years from 1970 onwards. With the backing of the Danish production company Palladium, they made the film *Hvorfor gør de det?* (*Why?*, 1971), in which three couples, one of them lesbian, have sex in front of hundreds of bystanders. The action on the mattresses is crosscut with interviews, testimonies and re-enactments from the performers, as well as a kind of Q&A session between the Kronhausens and the bystanders. The underlying message from the Kronhausens was that 'sexual activity in public was the inevitable manifestation of a higher, freer consciousness' (Stevenson 2012: 295). The Kronhausens went on to direct *Porno Pop* (1971), a feature-length compilation of old stag-films, and the Swiss-Danish co-production *Sex cirkusse* (*The Hottest Show in Town*,

1974), shot in Denmark with mainly Danish actors about a circus on the verge of bankruptcy spicing up their acts with hard-core sex. *Why?* also includes scenes with the Danish porn celebrity Bodil Joensen having sex with animals on her farm. Sex with animals was allowed in Denmark until 2015; much more controversially, so too was child pornography, as long as it was produced outside of Denmark, until 1980. A majority of the Danish Parliament supported legal child pornography, reasoning that, if it were allowed, sex crimes against children would decrease.

One company that used Denmark's brief porn monopoly as a stepping stone to a leading position on the world market was Rodox, established in 1966 by the brothers Jens and Peter Theander. From their second-hand bookshop in the centre of Copenhagen, the brothers sold and distributed illegal material, and in 1968 they founded the magazine *Color Climax*, followed by a film production company, Candy Film, in 1969. In the following two decades, it is estimated that Rodox produced more than 140 million magazines, nine million Super 8 films and one million VHS cassettes for the world-market (Rasmussen 2017: 40–41). The Theander brothers' company is probably one of the most successful film companies in the history of Danish film. The estimated total retail turnover of the Danish porn industry in 1969 was $50 million; 50 to 60 per cent of the material produced was smuggled into other countries, for instance, to Britain, hidden in refrigerated trucks transporting Danish bacon (Kutchinsky 1970: 15; Carter 2018: 422).

Criminologist Berl Kutchinsky, who conducted several empirical studies of pornography and crime from 1969, predicted a prosperous future for the porn industry as long as Denmark could uphold its unique position. However, Sweden removed its obscenity clause in 1971, and more permissive legislation in the early 1970s gave rise to adult cinemas and the production of pornography in the USA, West Germany and other countries. Based on the falling prices of pornographic commodities and observations made in porn shops, it seems that the Danes' interest in pornography quickly dwindled. Less than four years after the legalisation of pornography, Kutchinsky concluded that the porn wave had peaked in Denmark in 1969 and was now merely a splash in the local village pond (Kutchinsky 1973: 273). But pornography did not disappear: the splash in the pond sent ripples into mainstream cinema.

Sex and Porn in Cinemas

Linda Williams has called the 1970s 'the "Classical" Era of Theatrically Exhibited Porn', in which a comparatively mixed audience watched pornography together in cinemas (Williams 1999: 296). It is worth noting that feature-length pornographic films were shown all over Denmark in established cinemas in the 1970s – something which seems to be limited to Denmark and, later, Sweden.

The screening of porn was good business for the cinemas. The owner of the local cinema in the small village of Brørup could report that 'a midnight screening of a porno film earned as much as a full week of screenings of "films of the decent kind"' (Anonymous 1970).

Besides *Without a Stitch*, which was shown in the uncut version, the first feature pornographic films to emerge in Danish cinemas in August 1969 were the Swedish *Som havets nøgne vind* (*One Swedish Summer*, Gunnar Höglund, 1968) and the American *Romeo og Julies hemmelige sexliv* (*The Secret Sex Lives of Romeo and Juliet*, Peter Perry Jr, 1969). Both were softcore films with nudity and simulated sex and would hardly be considered pornographic by today's standards. Even at the time some reviewers found the labelling of the films as pornographic misleading (see, for example, Lej– 1969). *The Secret Sex Lives of Romeo and Juliet* was shown in the cinema Carlton, which had been the main Copenhagen Art House cinema in the 1960s and which had introduced the French New Wave films to the Danish audience; the porn film was programmed alongside a Japanese thriller directed by Akira Kurosawa, *Tengoku to Jigoku* (*High and Low*, 1963). Carlton was owned by Ove Brusendorff, the former head of the Danish Film Museum. Brusendorff had also edited and published several books on pornography from a cultural-historical perspective, among them *Erotikkens historie 1–3* (*The Complete History of Eroticism*, 1961–62), edited together with the cultural radical Poul Henningsen. Brusendorff was also involved as producer of what must be considered the first genuine Danish feature-length porn film *Pornografi – en musical* (*Pornography – A Musical*, Ole Ege, 1971) to be shown in cinemas. The film was a compilation of ten short stag-films shot before 1969 by the photographer and director Ole Ege, and the original score for the film was partly composed by the famous US jazz musician Dexter Gordon, who lived in Denmark at the time, testifying to the fashionable aspect of porn. This corresponds to the *Porn Chic* wave, which captured the free spirit and open-mindedness of the period during which pornography migrated into mainstream American culture and became visible outside the adult zones and X-rated cinemas. What had previously been forbidden by mainstream culture was suddenly becoming fashionable and tolerated as a by-product of the sexual revolution (McNair 2013: 40–42).

Despite Denmark's reputation as the sex-centre of the world, only ten to fifteen Danish feature-length porn films were produced in the 1970s, and several of them were compilations of short films. Others were co-productions, such as *Liderlige Lisbeth* (*The Birthday Party*, Unknown, 1971) or *Vilde pornolyster* (*The Blue Balloon*, Unknown, 1971), aimed at the international market and not released in the Danish cinemas until years after their original release. As other countries decriminalised pornography, the feature porn films filling Danish screens in the 1970s came from the USA, West Germany and France.

Non-Fiction Porn

Beside the genuine porn films, one can find explicit and graphic sex in a few non-fiction feature films that took a more sociological or pedagogical approach to sex and pornography. One of the first films to include explicit sex in Danish cinemas was *Et døgn med Ilse* (*24 Hours with Ilse*, Annelise Hovmand, 1971), a part-fiction, part-documentary film about a day in the life of the stripper Ilse, played by real-life stripper Ilse Damsgaard. The episodic and mostly improvised film was based on veteran director Hovmand's own curiosity about a stripper and her liberated approach to love and sexual relations. New family structures and ideas of free love were much-discussed topics in the 1970s; such issues were also explored from a female perspective in mainstream non-pornographic fiction films of the decade, such as *Christa* (*Swedish Fly Girls*, Jack O'Connell, 1971) and *Violer er blå* (*Violets are Blue*, Peter Refn, 1975). This tendency also corresponds to themes present in films such as *I, a Woman* and *Without a Stitch*.

An educational and pedagogical approach to sexuality can be found in four Swedish-produced films, beginning with *Ur Kärlekens Språk* (*Language of Love*, Torgny Wickman, 1969). The Danish sexologist couple Inge and Steen Hegeler were the main recurring experts in the films. The couple had a pioneering and influential correspondence column about sex in the largest Danish newspaper *Ekstra Bladet*. The Hegelers received letters from all over Scandinavia, as their column was reprinted in major newspapers in both Sweden and Norway. The illegitimate son of Poul Henningsen, Sten Hegeler was a figurehead in sexual education and can be considered to be affiliated with the cultural radical current to which his father also belonged. As early as in 1948, he wrote an introduction to reproduction aimed at children, *Hvordan, mor?* (*How, Mother?*), and in 1961 the Hegelers published *Kærlighedens ABZ* (*The ABC of Love*), which was reported to the police for violation of the laws against pornography but was not banned and became a huge success. *The Language of Love* films combined round-table discussions with the Hegelers and Swedish sexologists with re-enactments depicting the difficulties and problems people faced in their sex life, as well as scenes of actual intercourse. As the series of *Language of Love* films progressed, the sexually explicit scenes became increasingly dominant. Sten Hegeler was well aware of the sensational aspect of showing couples having sex on screen, saying 'It may well be pornographic as far as I am concerned [. . .] but of course, preferably healthy and good porn' (Bjørklund 2012: 192). Although the *Language of Love* series never gained a large audience in Denmark, the films were exported widely and frequently met with censorship and protests; at the instigation of British pop singer Cliff Richard, thousands of Brits protested against the film on Trafalgar Square (Stevenson 2010: 134).

Finally, we should mention the observational documentary *Sex en gros* (*Sex Galore*, 1971), in which director Niels Vest captured the new porn industry behind the scenes as well as various effects of the new phenomenon. Although the film was made with the intention to enlighten, it was promoted by several cinema owners as porn. *Sex Galore* still stands as a unique document of the Danish porn scene around 1970.

Sexy Comedies

As mentioned, many Danish comedies from the 1960s included erotic themes, and it was the combination of sex and *folkekomedie* or folk comedy (see Hartvigson, Chapter 5 in this volume) which led to the most visible and successful pornography shown in Danish cinemas. In 1970, the well-established production company Palladium released *Mazurka på sengekanten* (*Bedroom Mazurka*, 1970), the first instalment of a series of eight 'Bedside' films made between 1970 and 1976. The tremendously popular *Bedroom Mazurka* told the story of the sexually innocent teacher Max Mikkelsen, who is destined to become the new headmaster of a boys' boarding school, but to do so he has to be a married man. The somewhat bewildered Mikkelsen, who manoeuvres innocently and helplessly through a world filled with sexual temptations, was played by Ole Søltoft. The chubby Søltoft had participated in several erotic comedies in the late 1960s and became the epitome of the Danish sex comedies. The Bedside films are very similar to the trend of softcore comedies found in many other Western European countries in the 1970s. The British *Confessions of a Window Cleaner* (Val Guest, 1974) and its successors, the Italian sex comedies, as well as the more than forty German 'Bavarian sex films' are all examples of this trend of unsophisticated humour and gross sexual stereotypes combined with nudity and simulated sex.

Bordellet (*The Bordello*, Ole Ege, 1972) was a period film set at the beginning of the 1900s and combined comedy and hardcore sex. It was a huge success, apparently earning over a million Danish kroner during its first run in the cinemas (Rud 1972). Producer Anders Sandberg was behind the production; inspired by the success, he began the production of the Zodiac films. As the name suggests, this project was originally conceived as a series of twelve films, one for each of the zodiac signs, but ultimately only six were completed between 1973 and 1978. The first of the Zodiac films, *I jomfruens tegn* (*In the Sign of the Virgin*, Finn Karlsson, 1973), was marketed as a sex comedy similar to the Bedside films but took the sex comedies to a new level. Within the first ten minutes of the film, the generic conventions of hardcore porn films were evident: two lesbian sex acts, masturbation, oral sex and a 'money-shot' of male ejaculation. Ole Søltoft also participated in the Zodiac films, together with treasured popular Danish actors such as Poul Bundgaard, Arthur Jensen and Karl Stegger, although the professional actors did not take part in the hardcore sex scenes. Within the framework of the Danish *folkekomedie*, the Bedside and Zodiac films allowed a mainstream audience to view soft- and hardcore pornography at their local cinema, which helped to legitimise pornography. In general, the films were not a success with the critics; they were seen as half-hearted pornography disguised as popular comedy. But even though box office data are sparse on Danish films in the early 1970s, the available figures indicate that the Bedside and Zodiac films were among the most-watched films of the decade.

Coda: How to Shock a Dane

Although all censorship for adults ceased to exist with the 1969 law, a famous incident in the history of Danish cinema showed that the Danish *frisind* also has some limitations. The artist and provocateur Jens Jørgen Thorsen had been one of the first to include shots of penetration in his adaptation of American author Henry Miller's novel *Stille dage i Clichy* (*Quiet Days in Clichy*, 1970). Thorsen's film took a bold approach to sexuality and was fairly successful. On the basis of the film's success, the Danish Film Institute in 1973 granted Thorsen funding for a film about the human side of Jesus, which would also include his sex life. The reaction was overwhelming: demonstrations took place in the streets, and letters of protest were received from all over the world, together with threats of boycotting Danish goods, while the pope condemned Denmark for being the pigsty of Europe. The protests led to an ongoing political discussion, and in 1976 Niels Mathiasen, the Social Democratic Minister of Culture, withdrew the grant – not because of the obscenity, but because Thorsen violated the *droit moral* of the Bible; in other words, Thorsen had violated the authorship rights of the Bible. The decision was challenged in court, and in 1989 the case was finally settled to Thorsen's advantage. Thorsen never realised his original Jesus film, but he went on to direct a film about Jesus two decades later, *Jesus vender tilbage* (*The Return*, 1992). However, the provocative element of combining Christianity and sex was gone, and the film sold only 7,461 tickets (Nørrested 1997).

By the end of the 1970s, feature porn films gradually disappeared from ordinary cinemas in Denmark and tended to concentrate in specialist porn cinemas in the major towns. With the coming of home video in the early 1980s and subsequently the internet, pornography migrated from the public back into the private sphere. One enduring legacy of the liberalisation of pornography in 1969, however, was a relaxation of social attitudes towards nudity and pornography. In this sense, the media, and particularly cinema, played an important part in changing the national attitude towards sex.

Note

1. This chapter is partly based on my previous published research, for instance, Thorsen 2015, 2016a.

PART III

AUTEURS AND INSTITUTIONS OF THE NEW GOLDEN AGE

12. INTO THE DARK FOREST: THE CINEMA OF LARS VON TRIER

Peter Schepelern

At the end of each episode in his breakthrough TV serial *Riget* (*The Kingdom*, DR, 1994–97), Lars von Trier addresses the audience on camera in a clear imitation of *Alfred Hitchcock Presents* (CBS/NBC, USA, 1955–65). Trier comments on the plot and asks the spectator 'to take the good with the evil'. His manner is sarcastic and humorous, but there is no mistaking that this is a filmmaker branding himself.

Going His Way

From the very beginning, Trier built up his auteur persona – at times, a *persona non grata* – with a deliberateness that has given him a special position in both Danish and world cinema. Trier is Denmark's most influential and admired filmmaker since Carl Th. Dreyer. He also stands out as a controversial innovator who has repeatedly surprised with his artistic provocations. These include intellectual sharpness, a touch of perversity and an unremitting urge to find new expressions in film style and film technology.

He has often compared his artistic vocation as an auteur to that of a scout on an unknown island who is told to go south, no matter what. 'A stringency, is what this is called. And therefore, I still fancy that I work my way south. [. . .] And that, perhaps, is what *auteurism* is to me; it has perhaps something to do with going in the direction you are called upon to follow' (Schepelern 2004: 120).

He was born in 1956 as Lars Trier (the 'von' invented in his younger days was a joke). He grew up in a well-to-do neighbourhood north of Copenhagen, in a left-wing 'cultural liberal' home. His parents were both academics and civil servants working in ministries.

Most young filmmakers start imitating others, gradually finding their own original voice. Trier began his career with a central focus on creating a special look. In 1970 (when he was fourteen), he made two small, significant 8-mm fiction films, *Hvorfor flygte fra det du ved du ikke kan flygte fra?* (*Why Run Away From What You Know You Cannot Run Away From?*) in which a boy is killed in a traffic accident, turns into a ghost and pursues his friend who had run away in a cowardly fashion. The other is *En blomst* (*A Flower*) in which a boy experiences an apocalyptic situation, perhaps the end of the world. Trier was a rare example of a teen auteur.

During his student years at the University of Copenhagen, he made two half-hour 16-mm fiction films (both in black and white), *Orchidégartneren* (*The Orchid Gardener*, 1977) and *Menthe – la bienheureuse* (*Menthe – The Happy One*, 1979). The films, which Trier has kept out of distribution, were not part of the university curriculum but grew out of his own initiative. They are decadent, modernist stories with characteristic Trier elements – *The Orchid Gardener* a bizarre story of a tormented artist (played by Trier himself) and his relation to two women (or the same woman in two personifications), and *Menthe* an unofficial version of (parts of) Pauline Réage's erotic novel *Histoire d'O* (*The Story of O*, 1954).

At the National Film School of Denmark, he worked deliberately to give his films a look very different from that of other student films. His short, the allegorical *Nocturne* (1981), about a young woman's journey into death, created by Trier with his fellow students, cinematographer Tom Elling and editor Tómas Gislason, in a dreamlike, hypnotic style won a prize at the Filmschoolfest in Munich. This gave Trier a special cachet, intimating the unique position he would soon obtain in Danish cinema.

With Elling and Gislason, he continued the exploration of this style in both his graduation film *Befrielsesbilleder* (*Images of a Relief*, 1982), set during the last days of the German occupation of Denmark when a German soldier finds his martyrdom and goes to Heaven, and his first feature film, *Forbrydelsens element* (*The Element of Crime*, 1984). Like most of his films, it is in English, signaling his international rather than local Danish ambitions.

European Underworld

The Element of Crime is set in a decayed, post-apocalyptic Europe, presented in sallow colours, a mesmerising vision of the European darkness. Police detective Fisher (Michael Elphick) is called in from his Egyptian exile to solve a series of cases involving murdered girls. In the process he gradually comes to realise that he must follow in the footsteps of the assumed murderer, finally completing the murderous pattern himself.

After *The Element of Crime*, which received the Technical Grand Prix in Cannes, Trier prepared *The Grand Mal*, a drama about the rivalry of two gangster families in the divided Berlin. The manuscript was completed but the film never found the necessary financial backing and remains unrealised (this was the only time a fully developed Trier project had to be abandoned).

Frustrated by the long delay, Trier made a bet with a film consultant at the Danish Film Institute which grants state support for film production in Denmark, claiming that he could make a feature film for one million Danish kroner (the equivalent of $145,000 at the time). The result was *Epidemic* (1987), a production featuring mostly a stationary camera without an operator for a majority of scenes. This resulted in a deliberately faulty-looking, sloppy style, while other shots (representing the film-within-the-film) were shot in an aesthetically distinguished, perfectionist style by Henning Bendtsen, Carl Th. Dreyer's cinematographer for his last two films.

The film tells the double story about a film director and a scriptwriter who must write a new manuscript in five days, interrupted by scenes from the film on which they are working – about a young idealistic doctor in the early twentieth century who tries to fight an epidemic, but only manages to spread it further. The film culminates with the outbreak of a deadly plague, not in the past but in the present. The mid-1980s was of course the period when HIV-AIDS was clinically discovered and named. Although *Epidemic* was a success neither with audiences nor critics, it contains some characteristic Trier moments: the downfall of the idealist, the defeat of good intentions and the anti-perfectionist, 'faulty' style; the meta-layer; the use of a financial limitation as creative stimulation, all of which foreshadow Dogme 95 a decade later.

After the television film *Medea* (1988), a daring video experiment based on Dreyer's manuscript for a never realised film version of the Greek tragedy (see Thomson 2017), Trier could complete the final part of what he called his Europa Trilogy, *Europa* (1991, distributed in the US as *Zentropa*), a melodrama on the grand scale. In this film, an idealistic young man, Leo (Jean-Marc Barr), returns to a ruinous Germany in 1945. A sleeping car attendant, he falls in love with the daughter of the railroad company owner – only to find that he has been trapped in a fatal maze of intrigue and conspiracy. The film uses back projection and an original mixture of colour and black and white cinematography.

'Nazism is the greatest visual gift Europe has received', Trier had stated provocatively some years earlier (Trier 1985). For him, Germany was the extreme European case (both *The Element of Crime* and parts of *Epidemic* take place in Germany), seen as a kind of apocalyptic underworld. At the end of the film, when the drowned Leo floats through the rivers, the narrator tells him to 'wake up, to free yourself of the image of Europa, but it is not possible'. *Europa* was Trier's personal farewell to his Jewish identity. Shortly before her death in 1989, Trier's mother confessed to her son that his late father, Ulf Trier, who had a Jewish but non-religious background, was not his biological father. She had wanted a child with 'artistic genes', and it was her boss from the ministry where she had worked at the time who was Lars's biological father. Members of his family had been important figures in Danish music for several generations. The patriarch in *Europa* bears the name of the biological father, Hartmann.

Zentropa Kingdom

Europa was produced by Nordisk Film (established 1906), the oldest production company in Denmark and the symbol of old-fashioned and provincial film culture (see Thorsen, Chapter 1 in this volume). The following year, in 1992, Trier together with his producer on *Europa*, Peter Aalbæk Jensen, established his own company, Zentropa, the fictitious name of the railroad company in the film. In the years that followed, it became Scandinavia's largest production company, so far involved in more than a hundred Danish or international feature films; it garnered a reputation as daring and innovative, especially in the years up to 2008, when half of its stock was acquired by the arch enemy, Nordisk Film.

Riget (*The Kingdom*, 1994), a four-part television serial, was made by Zentropa on commission from DR (Denmark's Radio, the traditional state television channel in Denmark), written by Trier with co-author Niels Vørsel (who also co-wrote The Europa Trilogy). In Copenhagen's National Hospital (Rigshospitalet, popularly called Riget, which could be translated as The Kingdom) the clairvoyant Mrs Drusse (Kirsten Rolffes) makes contact with a ghost haunting the place, little Mary (Annevig Schelde Ebbe), who was murdered by her demonical father decades earlier. Meanwhile, the conceited Swedish chief physician Helmer (Ernst-Hugo Järegård), who tries to conceal his responsibility for a medical mistake, constantly ridicules Denmark and the Danes. The manuscript was considered too long for the shooting period available, but rather than trimming the script, Trier chose to simplify the production methods. He employed the handheld camera in a loose, seemingly improvised style and also disregarded the usual rules of lighting and continuity editing, giving the serial a highly untraditional look.

The Europa Trilogy had made Trier quite well-known with the Danish and international arthouse public, but it was not until *The Kingdom*, mixing horror with comedy, soap opera and satire, that he managed to attract and entertain a large audience. *The Kingdom,* which was followed by four more episodes in 1997, *The Kingdom II*, attracted worldwide attention, making it possible for him to find backing for his most ambitious project.

Golden Hearts

Breaking the Waves (1996) marked an important change of focus in Trier's work. In the early films, the protagonist is a man, typically a disillusioned idealist whose downfall is furthered by a deceitful or marked woman. Beginning with *Breaking the Waves* where Trier is sole writer, as he has been since, the protagonist is a woman, emotional and naïve. It is interesting to observe that Trier hit worldwide fame when he replaced the male protagonist with a female.

Breaking the Waves is a highly emotional melodrama, set in a remote part of Scotland in the 1970s, about the young woman Bess (Emily Watson) who, in a mysterious deal with God, accepts sexual abuse and finally death as a sacrifice that will rescue and redeem her disabled husband in an ending that refers to both Dreyer and Andrei Tarkovsky. The film daringly connects religion with eroticism. It focuses on sexual perversity and female martyrdom, issues that will continue in Trier's later work. And issues that have challenged critics and commentators who see the self-sacrificing, submissive heroine as a misogynist cliché. The character of the unselfish woman took inspiration from a children's book that Trier loved in his childhood. An ordinary colouring booklet, *Gold Heart* presents a simplified version of a Brothers Grimm fairy tale, *The Star-Money*, in which a little girl gives away all her things to needy persons but is rewarded at the end. Trier would follow the theme in two more films, together constituting his so-called Gold Heart Trilogy, with *The Idiots* and, more clearly, *Dancer in the Dark*.

Breaking the Rules

Trier has always been fascinated and inspired by self-imposed rules and systems. It was his experiences from the making of *The Kingdom* that led Trier to the concept of Dogme 95. The Dogme Manifesto – advising an ascetic and minimalist approach to filmmaking with technical obstructions and limitations used as a creative incentive – was written in collaboration with the young filmmaker Thomas Vinterberg just after the premiere of *The Kingdom* and presented in Paris in March 1995, at a conference celebrating the centenary of the first *cinématographe* screenings by the Lumière brothers in France.

Trier's contribution to the movement was *Idioterne* (*The Idiots* or *Dogma #2: The Idiots*, 1998), a Danish-language film set in contemporary Denmark (a rarity in Trier's work). A woman in crisis – she has left her bourgeois family after the death of her child – joins a group of young people spending a summer of communal living in an old villa, as they pretend to be mentally challenged, confronting the 'normal' world to 'find their inner idiot'.

Although only ten Danish Dogme films were made between 1998 and 2004 (and some twenty-five certified international Dogme films), Dogme had great impact internationally and cemented Danish cinema's reputation abroad (see, for example, Hjort and MacKenzie 2003, and Thomson, Chapter 13 in this volume).

Trier continued with Dogme-related projects. The bizarre *D-Day* (1999–2000), four parallel films, shown on four television channels, shot and aired live on the last night of the twentieth century, was a joint venture for the four Dogme brothers (Trier, Vinterberg, Søren Kragh-Jacobsen and Kristian Levring) (see Roberts 2003; Schepelern 2003). In 2003, he made *De fem benspænd* (*The Five Obstructions*) with veteran filmmaker Jørgen Leth. The starting point is a short experimental film, *Det perfekte menneske* (*The Perfect Human*), made by Leth in 1967. Leth proceeds to remake the film five times according to special rules that Trier conceives. The result is a most original experimental film, subtly dissecting both ethical and aesthetic issues, a virtuoso game exploring artistic engagement and detachment (see Hjort 2003, 2006).

Singin' in the Dark, and a Trilogy in Two Parts

Trier's final variation on the Gold Heart theme was *Dancer in the Dark* (2000). Selma, played by Icelandic singer Björk, who also composed the music, is a young immigrant woman in the US in the 1960s. Due to a hereditary illness, she gradually loses her eyesight and works in a factory to earn enough money for her son's surgery, so that he will not go blind, too. When her landlord, a deceptive policeman, steals her savings, she kills him. After making sure that the boy will be rescued, she accepts that she will be hanged for her crime. The film, which gave the musical genre a new dimension, won the Golden Palm at the prestigious Cannes festival where Björk also received the prize as Best Actress.

Trier's next project was a trilogy about the USA, *Land of Opportunity*, although he has never visited the country (he has a phobia of flying). *Dogville* (2003) takes place during the great depression of the 1930s. A young woman, Grace (Nicole Kidman), is on the run from gangsters and finds refuge in a small Rocky Mountains village. At first the villagers show understanding for her situation, but gradually they turn against her, exploiting and abusing her. For a long time, she submits to the humiliations, like the self-sacrificing heroines of *Breaking the Waves* and *Dancer in the Dark*, but in the end she takes gruesome revenge.

The striking formal and visual element of the film is its theatrical style. Trier had earlier made a theatre experiment, *Psychomobile #1: The World Clock* (1996), one of his more bizarre projects: the characters in a building with many rooms followed instructions from lamps activated by computer impulses which in turn were controlled via satellite by the activity in an ant hill in New Mexico! In *Dogville* the entire film takes place on a sound stage, where the buildings and streets are indicated with white lines. Here and there we see a wall, or some furniture, but everything is open so that we can survey the entire community at all times. It may resemble a classic of American theatre, Thornton Wilder's *Our Town* (1938), unknown to Trier, but the inspiration came partly from Bertolt Brecht and his so-called *Verfremdung* (alienation) technique, where the realist illusion is deliberately broken, and partly from a famous television version of the Charles Dickens novel *Nicholas Nickleby* (*The Life and Adventures of Nicholas Nickleby*, Channel 4 and Royal Shakespeare Company, UK, 1982). The film also uses a voice-over narrator in the style of an old-fashioned novel and is a didactic fable, giving us an ambiguous allegory about society and its refugees, about the establishment and the outsider.

Dogville was followed in 2005 by *Manderlay*, in which Grace (now played by Bryce Dallas Howard) comes to an estate in the South, where slavery has continued. Her attempt, however, to give the slaves their freedom and create a new social order fails. The projected third part of the trilogy, *Wasington* (deliberately misspelled), has never been realised. Thus, the US Trilogy is a trilogy in two parts!

The End of the World, and Murder as Art

Ironically, after completing a light-hearted comedy, *Direktøren for det hele* (*The Boss of It All*, 2006), about a company boss who pretends that he is only following the orders from the real boss, Trier, who had battled with anxiety attacks since his childhood, was hit by depression. This complicated his work on *Antichrist* (2009), which he called 'the most important film of my entire career' (Zentropa 2009). His most vulnerable and haunted work, it points back to his beginnings, both personal and artistic. The film has connections to European *fin-de-siècle* culture – Nietzsche and Freud, the Swedish author August Strindberg (1849–1912) and the Norwegian painter Edvard Munch (1863–1944), all admired by Trier in his early years, as well as to filmmakers such as Andrei Tarkovsky (to whom the film is dedicated) and Ingmar Bergman.

In the prologue, a couple has sex while their two-year-old son crawls out of his bed and falls out of the window to his death. The scene is shot in black and white and extreme slow motion with a Handel aria as the only sound. She is devastated by grief and cannot get over the accident. He and She (both nameless) go to their cabin in the woods, where he – a therapist – tries to cure her anxiety and depression. However, the treatment is not successful, and the plot takes a drastic turn. The psychological chamber play becomes a horror story with the following provocative premise: woman is nature, and nature is evil.

Trier's next film, *Melancholia* (2011), is also an intimate chamber play, a story about two sisters, but also a story about the end of the world. Justine (Kirsten Dunst, who won the Best Actress prize at Cannes) is celebrating her wedding, but is seized by a strange melancholy, seemingly connected to the sudden arrival of a giant planet that is approaching Earth. In the disturbing prologue we see the collision in haunting visuals, accompanied by intense music from the Wagner opera *Tristan and Isolde*.

The third part of Trier's Depression Trilogy (not his own term, but accepted by him) is the two-part *Nymph()maniac* (released in a four-hour version with less explicit sexual material in 2013 and in the five-and-a-half-hour Director's Cut version in 2014). This film tells the life story of a self-declared nymphomaniac from childhood to maturity, in a digressive style, filled with sardonic wit and daring use of CGI (in the sex scenes the torsos of the actors/actresses are digitally combined with the lower bodies of adult performers).

Trier's latest film, *The House That Jack Built* (2018), returns to the male protagonist in the story of a serial killer who insists that his cruel murders are works of art. The film, which quotes from Trier's own films, can be seen as his definitive outlook on human evil – but with Jack, who is also an architect, obsessively building and tearing down models and construction sites, appearing as a perfidious personification of the artist who creates and destroys in a continuous process.

Twisting Genres

In the early *Epidemic*, Trier states (in the film and repeated as a motto in the press kit): 'A film ought to be like a pebble in your shoe' (Element Film 1987). He is not one to please, and he insists on contradicting traditions, as is seen in his attitude towards genre and genre patterns. Usually, mainstream films follow genre patterns while art films go their own way. Although Trier's work unmistakably belongs to the art film tradition – with demonstrative styles and allegorical and ambiguous elements that invite very different interpretations – he has repeatedly taken a genre, a formula with its traditions, and twisted it into something new. 'It is partly because genre films are well known', he says. 'People who go to the cinema know it. My thought is that if you want to do something that is really different, then you have to do it in one "track" of the film only' (Schepelern 2018).

His work can be seen as a nearly systematic revision of genres, often with a postmodern irony: the detective film (*The Element of Crime*), the meta-film (*Epidemic*), the historical melodrama (*Europa*), the hospital soap/horror show (*The Kingdom*), the religious melodrama (*Breaking the Waves*), the musical (*Dancer in the Dark*), the chamber play (*Antichrist*), the disaster epic (*Melancholia*), the porno (*Nymphomaniac*) and the horror/thriller (*The House That Jack Built*).

According to Trier, there are two different things one can do with a camera: you can *frame* or you can *point* (Schepelern 2000: 233). Framing – as in *Europa* – means seeking perfection in the carefully planned and controlled recording that takes place within the camera's accurately calculated image frame. Pointing – as in *The Kingdom* and *The Idiots* – means letting go of control and impulsively letting the handheld camera point to an action that seems exciting and relevant here and now. The framing method – with its full control – creates formalism, while the pointing method – with its loss of control – creates realism.

It is part of the same ambition of challenging the traditional elements in filmmaking, when Trier, as a continuous tendency in his work, uses a stylistic and/or technical speciality in each film: the yellowish sodium lighting in *The Element of Crime*, filming without a cinematographer for the major part of *Epidemic*, the handheld camera in *Breaking the Waves* and *The Idiots*, the 100 video cameras in *Dancer in the Dark*, the white lines and minimal sets on the stage in *Dogville*, the challenging of his colleague Jørgen Leth in *The Five Obstructions*, the Automavision – letting a computer randomly decide angles and image sections – in *The Boss of It All*, the 'Digressionism' – with short essays on various topics interrupting the plot line, mostly using archive material – in *Nymph()maniac* and *The House That Jack Built*.

THE DARK FOREST

Two dominant themes in Trier's work are sex and death. The fascination with sexuality as a dark, demonic power is quite visible in *The Orchid Gardener* and *Menthe – The Happy One* with chains and whips and lustful punishment, clearly anticipating both *Antichrist* and *Nymph()maniac*. Sexuality in Trier's universe is mostly a painful and detached experience.

His depiction of women and sexuality has always been controversial. In the early films, as in *The Element of Crime* and *Europa*, the women are shown as false and threatening. In his later films, as in *Breaking the Waves* and *Dancer in the Dark*, they are self-sacrificing and submissive. 'She' in *Antichrist* starts as a grieving mother, lost in despair, but turns into a murderous monster. She is both a victim and a threat.

Most of his films have fatal outcomes and abundant amounts of murder and cruelty, suggesting a demonstrative touch of nihilism. There is Fisher's strangling of the little girl in *The Element of Crime*, the suicide in the bathtub and the assassination of the mayor in *Europa*, the hanging of the sons in *Medea*, the murder of Little Mary in *The Kingdom*, Selma's killing of the policeman in *Dancer in the Dark* and her subsequent execution, the massacre of the villagers in *Dogville*, the execution of the old woman in *Manderlay*, the strained physical violence with wrench, hand drill and scissors ending with the strangulation of She in *Antichrist*. Joe is beaten up in a dark alley in *Nymph()maniac* and eventually uses a gun herself. And in *Melancholia*, the entire Earth and its people are destroyed, but at least in a very beautiful way, leaving a clean slate.

The fascination with evil reaches its culmination with *The House That Jack Built*, which focuses on a serial killer and ends in Dante's *Inferno*. 'More than anything, there are more images in evil. Evil is based far more on the visual, whereas good has no good images at all', Trier has said (Björkman 1997).

Recently asked about the new technical potentials of Virtual Reality, he expressed how he basically sees the role of the filmmaker: 'Precisely because Virtual Reality gives the spectator a freedom', he says, 'I don't think that is the way to make art. I believe that all good art has been created under dictatorial conditions. People must enjoy being led. I've said earlier that it's a dark forest that people must go through, and they are scared to. But if they have a friend who says, "I know the forest", they will happily follow. And then they enjoy this dark forest. And that, in a small way, is my principle' (Schepelern 2018).

Lars von Trier's accomplishment could be summed up as his building up and tearing down the role and the myth of the artist, tirelessly searching for new styles, revising genres and using new technical approaches, while confronting us with a universe of downfall and anxiety, sexuality, death and darkness.

13. 'I AM NO LONGER AN ARTIST': HERITAGE FILM, DOGME 95 AND THE NEW DANISH CINEMA

C. Claire Thomson

'Tonight I have learned that in this world anything is possible' (Dinesen 2001: 62–63). Accepting the Oscar for Best Foreign Language Film at the 60th Academy Awards in 1988, Franco-Danish director Gabriel Axel quoted this line from the novella from which he adapted Denmark's first Oscar-winning feature film: Isak Dinesen's *Babettes gæstebud* (*Babette's Feast*, 1987) (oscars.org 1988). A year later, it transpired that anything was possible twice over, when Bille August's *Pelle erobreren* (*Pelle the Conqueror*, 1987) won the same award. Diagnosing the significance of this double miracle for the Danish film industry, Mette Hjort has commented wryly: 'The fact of two Oscars in successive years was [. . .] the kind of statistically unimaginable and thus quasi-prophetic event that could truly galvanize an entire milieu and make it an irresistible magnet for new talent' (Hjort 2005: 5).

It would be another two decades before Susanne Bier won the same Oscar in 2011 for *Hævnen* (*In a Better World*, 2010), but in the meantime the Danish film industry had changed beyond recognition. Bier herself was emblematic of the 'New Danish Cinema', a new generation of filmmakers and a new constellation of institutions that emerged in the 1990s in the wake of Axel's and August's Academy Award success, as well as Lars von Trier's international breakthrough in the mid-1980s (Hjort 2005: 4–6; see also Chapters 12 and 14 in this volume). Central to this narrative of renewal and renaissance for Danish cinema was the Dogme 95 movement – not really a movement at all, but a manifesto and a set of rules. Launched by Lars von Trier in 1995 at the Paris celebrations of the centenary of cinema and co-signed by the up-and-coming director Thomas

Vinterberg, Dogme 95 would serve as a framework and label for some thirty-five certified (and countless uncertified) films made in Denmark and around the world over the next decade.

Towards the end of the Dogme 95 Vow of Chastity, the signatories declare: 'I am no longer an artist'. The filmmaker is challenged to refrain from 'personal taste' and from 'aesthetic considerations' and to regulate their filmmaking according to the ten rules of the Vow (Trier and Vinterberg 1995). Clearly, the creativity engendered by engaging with the constraints of the Vow entails artistry, skill and expertise (Hjort 2003: 32–37). This irony is only superseded by the Vow's other great paradox: this is a self-defining genre whose eighth rule forbids genre films. In this chapter, I want to unpack this rather neglected sentence in the Vow – 'I am no longer an artist' – and use it to try to understand what Dogme 95 was purportedly rebelling against in Danish cinema and Danish film policy of the 1990s. While Dogme 95 self-consciously wrote itself into global cinema history, not least by its launch at the Paris celebration of the centenary of cinema and its allusions to earlier movements in the text of the Manifesto (Thomson 2013a: 38–41), its origins and its repercussions are very much part of the story of Danish cinema before and after the turn of the millennium.

Heritage Film: The Sacred and the Sensual

On the ground floor of Filmhuset, the 'Film House', in central Copenhagen in which the Danish Film Institute is located, is a high-end restaurant. In early March 2016, just after that year's Oscars, a screening of *Babette's Feast* was held, with accompanying supper. On the menu were blinis Demidoff with caviar, *cailles en sarcophage* with truffle sauce, cheeses from the Auvergne and rum baba with glazed fruit salad – recognisable to any aficionado of Isak Dinesen (the pseudonym of Karen Blixen) as the dinner served by Babette to her guests. This lavish event is indicative both of the 'popularized cinephilia' (Hjort 2005: 6) that has taken root in Danish culture over the last two decades and perhaps also the growing esteem in which *Babette's Feast* is held. In its day, the film's reception by the Danish critics was lukewarm at best (Mørch 2008: 429–31). Gabriel Axel's daughter recounts his fourteen-year-long struggle to get the film funded; he applied repeatedly via the Danish Film Institute's consultant system, as well as to Nordic and French television companies, and met one rejection after another (Mørch 2008: 200–10), before securing funding via the DFI in 1985 (Forbes 1988: 106). This may have been in part due to Axel's inconsistent career in Denmark, encompassing experimental and popular film (Thorsen 2012), as well as a controversial documentary about pornography, *Det kære legetøj* (*Danish Blue*, 1968; see Thorsen, Chapter 11 in this volume), and perhaps also his bicultural identity and peripatetic career as a respected television director in France. 'No one is a prophet in his own country', mused Axel

(Forbes 1988: 107). Indeed, the fate of *Babette's Feast*, this film about fate, has been to serve as a historical marker in recent narratives of the turn-of-the-millennium renaissance of Danish cinema, and as an exemplar of the parochial state of Denmark's film culture in the 1980s.

'I am a great artist!' exclaims Babette in the novella (Dinesen 2001: 66). Babette had been head chef at the Café Anglais in Paris; after her family was killed in the aftermath of the Commune, she fled to Norway to live with two sisters, Philippa and Martine, the daughters of a local pastor. In Gabriel Axel's adaptation, the setting is moved to Denmark, to the north-west coast of Jutland. This allows him to bring together two forms of art: Babette's cuisine and Danish painting. This is a fine recipe for a heritage film. 'It's just a series of portraits', the director explained (Forbes 1988: 107). Indeed, in composition, if not always in colour and tone, many shots echo the work of the late-nineteenth-century Skagen artists who painted the shoreline, landscape and light of northern Jutland, where the film was shot (see Hirschsprung Collection n. d.). More striking is the resemblance of many shots to the paintings of Vilhelm Hammershøi (1864–1916). As Babette pauses to enter the sitting room, her back to the camera, her dark form echoes one of Hammershøi's portraits of women from behind. Shafts of weak daylight on white and grey walls, dark furniture, looming portraits; all of this is Hammershøi and, via him, the auteur Carl Th. Dreyer, whose evocation of the same painter's still spaces and peculiarly Danish architectonics is so developed as to have been the subject of a museum exhibition (Hvidt 2007).

When Babette wins 10,000 francs in a lottery and decides to cook a feast for her Danish hosts and their religious neighbours, the portraiture continues, in close-up. The enormous turtle which is turned into soup; Babette's skilful hands forming pastry, spooning caviar, arranging fruit. What such filmic portraiture can do is capture the ambivalence of the guests' experience, in a way that the novella is too ascetic to articulate. As Lutherans, they have vowed not to enjoy or even taste the food and drink. But Axel's unwavering attention to his actors' faces (Forbes 1988: 107) delineates their struggle to suppress pleasure in a meal so luxurious that they cannot grasp its artistry, only sense it. The look of uncomprehending wonderment after a mouthful; the tiny, insuppressible smile on a wrinkled face. As philosopher Julian Baggini (2020: 5) has recently written of the film, '*Babette's Feast* does not present a systematic argument for collapsing the sacred/secular distinction, rather it shows us why the distinction is a false one. Similarly, it does not systematically describe what is sacred in the sensual world but it does very carefully attend to it'. The tragedy and naive joy of this experience are redoubled for a viewer familiar with Dreyer's great works, for the faces we are watching are those of actors such as Lisbeth Movin, Birgitte Federspiel and Preben Lerdorff Rye, familiar from *Vredens Dag* (*Day of Wrath*, 1943) and *Ordet* (*The Word*, 1955), and now grown old. *Babette's Feast* feels like the end of an era – and yet it was the beginning of a new one.

Figure 13.1 In *Babettes gæstebud* (*Babette's Feast*, Gabriel Axel, 1987), the pastor enlightens his guests from the head of the table with a revelation. Framegrab.

Figure 13.2 In *Festen* (*The Celebration*, Thomas Vinterberg, 1998), Christian looks down the table towards his father and prepares to make his own revelation. Framegrab.

Righteousness and Bliss: Dogme 95, Dogma and Art

'Righteousness and bliss shall kiss one another' (Dinesen 2001: 59). A little drunk on vintage Veuve Clicquot and giddy at the sight of his long-lost love, General Lorens Löwenhielm gives a speech to his fellow diners in *Babette's Feast*. He is declaiming the transcendent experience of savouring world-class cuisine in a humble pastor's house, but the sentiment could just as well describe the often exquisite films created by adherence to the Dogme 95 Vow of Chastity. And appropriately enough, the first film from the Dogme 95 stable, Thomas Vinterberg's *Festen* (*The Celebration*, 1998; usually referred to as *Festen* in English) is also structured around a dinner party during which etiquette, ritual and scandal are held in productive tension (Rukov 2002: 202–3).

In *Festen*, the main protagonist, Christian, has returned to Denmark from his successful restaurant in Paris, echoing Babette's trajectory and artistry. However, Christian's mission is to confront his father who had abused him and his late sister in their youth. He chooses to reveal the secret in a speech during his father's sixtieth birthday dinner. While Babette's guests struggle to suppress their reaction to the gourmet food, the guests at this party face a struggle to suppress their reaction to Christian's shocking revelations. They make small talk (is the soup lobster or tomato?), drink themselves insensible and stubbornly persevere with the well-worn rhythm of a formal dinner party. Here, too, the camera is complicit in capturing and evoking the emotional journey of the actors, but the revelation comes from the tension between their rictus grins and evasive stares, and the jerky dynamism or 'emotional movement' (Kelly 2000: 100) of the digital handheld camera – a camera which at times is operated by the actors themselves, all the better to enter into and co-create the space of the event (Thomson 2013a: 73–90).

The Dogme 95 Manifesto self-consciously critiques the French New Wave for its reliance on artistry ('a ripple that washed ashore and turned to muck') and declares itself a 'rescue action', combating 'the film of illusion' and 'the individual film' (Trier and Vinterberg 1995). Its accompanying Vow of Chastity, in an obvious gesture to religiosity, consists of ten rules, and filmmakers were encouraged to confess to any breaches (MacKenzie 2003: 54–56). While the obvious intertext consists of the Ten Commandments, another is the Scandinavian Law of Jante, which specifies ten ways to keep the ego in check (Booth 2014: 88–97). The ten rules are designed to strip out the crutches used by experienced directors (Hjort 2005: 38–39), bringing filmmaking back to the ascetic basics:

1. Shooting must be done on location. Props and sets must not be brought in (if a particular prop is necessary for the story, a location must be chosen where this prop is to be found).

2. The sound must never be produced apart from the images or vice versa. (Music must not be used unless it occurs where the scene is being shot.)
3. The camera must be hand-held. Any movement or immobility attainable in the hand is permitted.
4. The film must be in color. Special lighting is not acceptable. (If there is too little light for exposure the scene must be cut or a single lamp be attached to the camera.)
5. Optical work and filters are forbidden.
6. The film must not contain superficial action. (Murders, weapons, etc. must not occur.)
7. Temporal and geographical alienation are forbidden. (That is to say that the film takes place here and now.)
8. Genre movies are not acceptable.
9. The film format must be Academy 35 mm.
10. The director must not be credited.
(Trier and Vinterberg 1995)

Certain moments in the resulting films can be traced back to one or another of the rules. For example, towards the end of *Idioterne* (*The Idiots*, Lars von Trier, 1998), a slap in the face is rendered more distressing and visceral by a whip pan on the part of the handheld camera (Rule 3). In *En kærlighedshistorie* (*Kira's Reason*, Ole Christian Madsen, 2001), the same rule facilitates a startling opening sequence in which the frantic handheld camera performs a manic episode experienced by the titular character. In *Festen*, variations in sound levels are retained (Rule 2) and edited together to create a sense of disorientation, for example, when the protagonist, Christian, is losing consciousness; and later, a rising level of ambient sound invests the final shot with a sense of abstract drama. Out of constraints comes creativity; out of righteous dogma comes transcendent bliss.

The Legacy of Dogme 95

A quarter-century after the launch of the Dogme 95 Manifesto, what remains to be said about it? Such was the immediate impact of the first few Dogme films that, as early as 2003, a scholarly anthology of essays analysing Dogme 95 and its impact had appeared, under the title *Purity and Provocation* (Hjort and MacKenzie 2003). Other books interviewed figures associated with Dogme 95 in its heyday (Kelly 2000), followed 'the gang who took on Hollywood' to the USA (Stevenson 2003), or examined the changes to filmmaking practice occasioned by the Manifesto and Vow (Hjort 2010a), as well as the role of the earliest Dogme films in the digital turn (Thomson 2013a). As Schepelern (2013) remarks, the inclusion of Dogme 95 in general film studies works and primers is also a sign of its impact on filmmaking practice and film historiography. And even if none of the big-name directors of the era took up the invitation to make a film under the Dogme rules – Ingmar Bergman, Steven Spielberg and Akira Kurosawa were invited, but declined – many notable indie films of the 2000s bore the visual traces of Dogme's influence, including *The Blair Witch Project* (Daniel Myrick and Eduardo Sánchez, US, 1999), *Bamboozled* (Spike Lee, USA, 2000) and *Full Frontal* (Steven Soderbergh, USA, 2002) (Schepelern 2013).

Beyond its creative and academic impacts, Dogme 95 contributed to re-shaping the film industry in the first years of its new century, and not only in Denmark. Assessing the legacy of Dogme 95 for the catalogue of a 2017 exhibition on Lars von Trier's work, Mette Hjort credits the movement with stimulating meaningful debate on the nature of cinema in the twenty-first century, with inspiring decision-makers to innovate in supporting sustainable conditions for filmmaking, especially in small-nation contexts, and with reiterating the contribution of actors to compelling film narratives (Hjort 2017: 115). The second of these points – the impetus to consolidate film policy and institutions to build on the domestic and international success of the Dogme films – is arguably of most import. There are two dimensions to this, which I will now explore in more depth: firstly, the re-fashioning of Danish film institutions in the 1990s, which Dogme helped to accelerate; and secondly, a more diffuse influence on the international marketing and reception of small-nation cinemas.

New Institutions and a New Generation

The 1972 Film Law established the principle that films of cultural value that were not commercially viable should be supported by the state. This system was facilitated by a cadre of consultants, usually academics or critics, who would select film projects to support (for a description of the consultant role in the Nordic context, see Wiedemann 2009). By the 1980s, this system was creaking, and Danish film production showed all the signs of a moribund, state-financed film culture producing work that Danish audiences had no interest in viewing (Bondebjerg n. d.; Hjort 2007: 27–28). While a new Film Law proper would not be promulgated until 1997, two significant developments in a 1989 revision to the existing law paved the way for meaningful change. First, a new system of financing supplemented the consultant system, offering 50/50 match funding to projects commercial enough to raise a portion of production costs. Second, the language criterion for state funding was lifted, freeing the way for Lars von Trier and others to receive support for films that were not necessarily in Danish, but which 'made a clear artistic or technical contribution to film art and film culture in Denmark' (Hjort 2007: 27). Further internationalisation came in the form of the Nordic Film and Television Fund, established in 1990 to provide top-up funding for high-quality productions in the Nordic region, thus leveraging economies of scale (Nordisk Film & TV Fond 2020).

Professor Ib Bondebjerg, who at that time served as chair of the Danish Film Institute Board, relates that changes to support structures were underway by 1990, but were helped along by Dogme 95 (cited in Schepelern 2013). Ironically, the first four Danish Dogme 95 films did not benefit from the financial structures being built up in the mid-1990s. The then Minister of Culture, Jytte Hilden, allegedly promised Lars von Trier financial support at a party, only to have to rescind the offer when it was realised that it fell foul of the 'arm's length principle' whereby consultants sat between the government as a source of finance and the funding decisions (Schepelern 2013). Instead, the first four Dogme films were commissioned by the national public service broadcaster, DR, for its new channel DR2.

A new Film Law of 1997 consolidated the mid-1990s gains. The Danish Film Institute (established 1972), the Danish Film Museum and the National Film Board were amalgamated and moved to a dedicated building in central Copenhagen, ensuring that expertise in film policy, production, marketing, distribution, archiving, a cinema and other functions were all located in one place. The very effective Henning Camre was appointed CEO, and negotiations with the government in spring 1998 – fortuitously coinciding with the premieres of the first two Dogme 95 films – resulted in a net increase in funding of 75 per cent (Hjort 2007: 29). The 50/50 scheme was expanded to a 60/40 arrangement, and a pipeline of new filmmaking talent was secured by low-budget, short-film programmes such as New Fiction Film Denmark and New Danish Screen (for more on talent development, see Hjort, Chapter 16 in this volume). Independently of the DFI, the production company Zentropa, founded by Lars von Trier and Peter Aalbæk Jensen, established Filmbyen (Film Town) in an old army barracks in 1997, providing studios and offices for small companies and film practitioners, thus encouraging collaborative innovation.

These institutions helped to achieve a critical mass of film professionals who are inter-connected in ways typical of a small-nation network with one National Film School. From the relatively small pool of actors that a small nation can sustain, a number of Danish actors have become familiar to international audiences over the past two decades: Trine Dyrholm, Paprika Steen, Sidse Babett Knudsen, Ulrik Thomsen, Thomas Bo Larsen, Nikolaj Coster-Waldau, Mads Mikkelsen and Lars Mikkelsen. While it is difficult to speak of a star system in a small country where even the royal family is often sighted out shopping or cycling, such actors have attained stardom 'in terms of visibility elsewhere, somewhere in the transnational beyond' (Hjort 2005: 4). Anecdotally, such status is regarded with proud bemusement at home in Denmark; I was amused in 2014 to notice a spoof newspaper headline pinned to a fridge door in the Danish Film Institute, announcing a rare new film in which Mads

Mikkelsen did *not* have a starring role. Directorial stardom is another factor, and Hjort (2005: 5) posits that it is the graduation, year after year, of young filmmakers from the National Film School in the 1990s, and their subsequent breakthrough films, that constitute the New Danish Cinema. In many cases, but not all, the breakthrough films were Dogme 95 films: Thomas Vinterberg's *Festen* (1998), Lone Scherfig's *Italian for Beginners* (2000), Susanne Bier's *Elsker dig for evigt* (*Open Hearts*, 2002). Others fall into the category of genre films: the comedy gangster film *I Kina spiser de hunde* (*In China They Eat Dogs*, Lasse Spang Olsen, 1999) and Anders Thomas Jensen's dark action comedies, *Blinkende lygter* (*Flickering Lights*, 2000) and *De grønne slagtere* (*The Green Butchers*, 2003). (For an account of the international trajectories of some of these filmmakers, see Shriver-Rice, Chapter 14 in this volume, and for interviews with this generation of directors around the millennium, see Hjort and Bondebjerg 2001).

Nation-Branding beyond the Heritage Film

Mette Hjort has argued for an understanding of Dogme 95's rejection of 'art' as a rejection of a particular kind of globalised and globalising cinematic art, 'a middle-brow or standardised entertainment involving cost-intensive visual and narrative styles' (Hjort 2003: 45). *Babette's Feast* and *Pelle the Conqueror* are obvious examples of films falling under this rubric. By providing a new model that could facilitate filmmaking in marginal, small and less well-funded national contexts, Dogme 95 provided an alternative to the heritage film as a reassertion of cultural heterogeneity (Hjort 2003: 42–45). Hjort sees this as a case-study in grassroots globalisation; while the Dogme 95 Manifesto is more playful than political, its effective political thrust lies in its crafting of a mode of production alternative to neo-liberal, big-budget Hollywood (Hjort 2005: 37–46).

Despite its bumpy start in terms of state funding, the value of Dogme 95 for nation-branding Denmark abroad was quickly recognised by the Danish government. A 2010 report commissioned by the Ministry of Culture singled out 'the Dogme wave' as a key factor in Danish film's reputation, and thereby in Denmark's wider 'brand' or soft power as a 'creative and innovative cultural nation' (Kulturministerens udvalg om dansk film i udlandet 2010: 16). It is striking that, in its definition of the 'auteur tradition' to which it ascribes Dogme 95, the report repeatedly uses terms related to the notion of the 'artist'. The Vow of Chastity insists that the filmmaker renounce the mind-set and status of artist; but for the consultants charged with mapping the Dogme 95 'brand' in the outside world, key phrases include 'kunstnerisk vision' (artistic vision), 'banebrydende kunst' (ground-breaking art), 'kunstnerisk fornyende' (artistically innovative) and 'kunstnerisk fotografering' (artistic cinematography) (15). It is instructive to read this report in the wake of the Cultural Canon published four years earlier, discussed in the Introduction to this volume. Published in both Danish and English by the Ministry of Culture and listing a dozen examples of the best that the nation had to offer across a range of art forms including film, the Canon functioned both as a primer in cultural heritage for the domestic audience and as a means of marketing Danish culture to the anglophone world (Committee for Film 2006). The first two Dogme 95 films, *Festen* and *The Idiots*, are included in the Canon for Film and thus incorporated into the national pantheon of auteurial and arthouse works, along with the Oscar-winning heritage films *Babette's Feast* and *Pelle the Conqueror*.

The national film 'brand' that Dogme had helped to establish was so strong, in fact, that the same report warned that diversifying the image of Danish film beyond its reputation for 'auteur' cinema might prove challenging (15), a concern that would soon be laid to rest with the unexpected international breakthrough of Danish television serials such as *Forbrydelsen* (*The Killing*, DR, 2007–12) and *Borgen* (DR, 2010–13) (see Redvall, Chapter 15 in this volume). Indeed, while the stylistic, cultural and economic impacts of Dogme 95 are hard to overstate, the movement did not appear out of nowhere and in the eco-system of Danish cinema did not function in isolation at home or abroad.

Style and Genre in the New Danish Cinema

The report for the Ministry of Culture compares and contrasts auteur cinema with 'high-concept' cinema. Although it does not reference the source directly, 'high concept' is discussed along the lines of Justin Wyatt's definition: films with a marketable concept, clear narrative, star power and perhaps associated merchandise (Wyatt 1994: 8–12). The report tries to locate a strategy for Danish film between the two concepts, but that middle ground had already been mapped out by film scholar Andrew Nestingen. He adopted the term 'medium-concept' to describe a particular constellation of style, narrative and institutional context that had characterised Nordic cinema since 1987 (Nestingen 2008: 53). Such films, he argues, 'use the dramaturgical structures and continuity style of genre film and the excess characteristic of the art film' (73). By 'excess', Nestingen means marked stylistic features that are not necessarily motivated by the plot. Some Dogme 95 films, he thinks, can be construed as medium-concept films, because they adopt the features of the family melodrama while selling themselves as Dogme films: examples include the hugely successful *Italiensk for begyndere* (*Italian for Beginners*, Lone Scherfig, 2000) and Annette K. Olesen's *Forbrydelser* (*In Your Hands*, 2004) (Nestingen 2008: 119).

A similar point is made by Ib Bondebjerg, who sees Dogme 95 as just one iteration of a broader turn towards new forms of realism in Danish cinema from the mid-1990s onwards. He observes similarities of genre, acting style, theme and visuals across Dogme and non-Dogme films (Bondebjerg 2003: 70).

One tendency that emerged in parallel with Dogme 95 was a new kind of extremism, 'a more modern, fast-paced action style cinema [. . .] characterised by a strong use of digital colour manipulation and an aggressive use of music, camera style and editing with shock-like effects' (74). Foundational films in this stream include the precocious Nicolas Winding Refn's *Pusher* (1996) and *Bleeder* (1999), both gritty, stylised, self-aware portraits of violence, featuring the youthful Mads Mikkelsen and Kim Bodnia. Winding Refn's subsequent international career is a rare example of a successful, if patchily so, transatlantic trajectory for a director emerging from the New Danish Cinema (see also Shriver-Rice, Chapter 14 in this volume). Another watershed film, Ole Bornedal's thriller *Nattevagten* (*Night Watch*, 1994), exemplifies the traffic in expertise between the Danish film and television industries that was just as crucial to the New Danish Cinema as the 1990s generation of Film School graduates; Bornedal left his position as Head of Fiction at DR to make *Night Watch* (see also Redvall, Chapter 15 in this volume).

The other tendency in 1990s Danish cinema identified by Bondebjerg is a dramatic, everyday realism, featuring 'a much more intense psychological and social portrayal of characters and reality compared to the realism of the 70s' (Bondebjerg 2003: 75). This is the sensibility to which *Festen* belongs, he thinks, as well as Ole Christian Madsen's Dogme film *En kærlighedshistorie* (*Kira's Reason*, 2001). Beyond Dogme, an arresting example of this tendency can be found in Per Fly's trilogy exploring three social classes in Denmark, the underclass with *Bænken* (*The Bench*, 2000), the upper class with *Arven* (*Inheritance*, 2003) and the middle class with *Drabet* (*Manslaughter*, 2005), respectively.

We can observe, then, that the literary adaptations so typical of Danish cinema up to and including the Oscar triumphs of the late 1980s are conspicuous by their absence from the New Danish Cinema. Rather, the position of the heritage film has been usurped by original stories largely set in the present day, although the influence of generic tropes on medium-concept productions may engender situations, characters and events that are somewhat more akin to 'superficial action' than Rule 6 of the Dogme Vow would allow, or more 'scandalous' than realist, as screenwriting supremo Mogens Rukov would put it (Rukov 2002: 200). This is a realism that can often be psychologically intense, but that is also based on stringent attention to form.

Screenwriting as Dogma

A notable phenomenon in the New Danish Cinema is the director-screenwriter: Anders Thomas Jensen, for example, won an Academy Award for Best Live Action Short Film for his debut short, *Valgaften* (*Election Night*, 1998), in the wake of which he directed and wrote *Flickering Lights*; he has continued to direct films at roughly five-year intervals. However, Jensen is most renowned for his screenwriting, having contributed as writer or script consultant to an astonishing array of Danish films of the last twenty years. A recurring collaboration has been with Susanne Bier, not least on *Brødre* (*Brothers*, 2004), the Oscar-nominated *Efter brylluppet* (*After the Wedding*, 2006) and the Oscar-winning *Hævnen* (*In a Better World*, 2010). While Jensen is an autodidact, his contemporary Kim Fupz Aakeson graduated from the screenwriting programme at the National Film School of Denmark in 1999. Aakeson has also collaborated with Susanne Bier and Lone Scherfig; a recurring partnership has been with director Annette K. Olesen, among others on *Små ulykker* (*Minor Mishaps*, 2002), the Dogme film *In Your Hands* and the compelling *1:1* (2006), an interracial teen romance that plays out in the concrete spaces of the planned suburb of Avedøre. A notable collaboration was the trans-gender romance *En soap* (*A Soap*, Pernille Fischer Christensen, 2006), on which Aakeson shared writing credit with Anne Cathrine Sauerberg, and another on Henrik Ruben Genz's *Kinamand* (*Chinaman*, 2005), a vivid tale of an arranged marriage marketed as 'a Danish/Chinese melodrama' and co-funded by Shanghai Film Studio.

The culture of screenwriting has thus been central to the New Danish Cinema. As explained by Eva Novrup Redvall (Redvall 2013, and Chapter 15 in this volume), this culture cannot be understood in isolation from the policies and practices of public service broadcasting in Denmark in the same period. However, the emphasis on writing was also fostered by a strong emphasis on storytelling at the National Film School (Hjort 2005: 11–12), not least under the leadership of Mogens Rukov, who co-founded the screenwriting programme at the school in 1985 and led it until 2008. Rukov co-wrote seminal films already mentioned such as *Festen*, *Kira's Reason* and *Inheritance*, as well as Omar Shargawi's breakthrough feature *Gå med fred Jamil* (*Go with Peace Jamil*, 2008, discussed by Eva Jørholt in Chapter 18 of this volume), and has numerous credits as script consultant. However, the influence of his screenwriting dogma can be discerned across the broad sweep of New Danish Cinema.

The core principle for Rukov is not to mirror reality, but to craft a more existential truth through form. Constructing a film, for him, means 'a collision between form and existence. It is form that makes a film a film. That's what makes a film worth watching. Exciting, surprising, gripping, purifying [...] The core of reality. Existential conditions. The rules of the game of existence that form can contain' (Rukov 2002: 198). His screenwriting favours public rather than private spaces, places that are misunderstood or mis-used 'scandalously' by the characters. The characters themselves, however interested the audience might be in their psychology, are functions of form (199–200). Nonetheless, says Rukov, a writer must remember that the film always somehow belongs to the director – even at manuscript stage (78).

Conclusion

Interviewed in 1996 about the Dogme 95 concept, which at that point had not yet spawned its first films, Lars von Trier insisted that the project was not a protest against the current state of Danish cinema. 'If you want to protest about something', he said, 'then the thing you're protesting against has to have a certain amount of authority' (Björkman 2003: 202). A decade later, the warm critical reception of Danish cinema – the burgeoning 'brand' – was apparent in remarks by film critics and professionals. Reviewing Nikolaj Arcel's political thriller *Kongekabale* (*King's Game*, 2004), the veteran British film critic Philip French said that '[a]t the moment, Denmark is producing the most thoughtful and interesting films not only in Scandinavia but in western Europe' (French 2005). Quotations adorning the first page of the Ministry of Culture's report on Danish film abroad include an assessment by Sean Farnell of Hot Docs Toronto: 'Danish films stand out; they represent real energy and openness to the world. They are breaking rules and pushing forms. Definitely a strong brand value' (quoted in Kulturministerens udvalg om dansk film i udlandet 2010: 2).

Other metrics are often cited to hammer home the dramatic difference in Danish film culture achieved through a combination of sustained effort and serendipity over the past three decades: annual feature film production has increased from ten to about twenty-five films; Danish-produced films account for about 27 per cent of cinema tickets sold (Budtz-Jørgensen 2019). But as Claus Ladegaard, CEO of the DFI, remarks in his introduction to the institution's annual 'Facts and Figures' publication for 2019–20: 'Cultural significance cannot be expressed in a formula. It is more dynamic and evolves in tune with the times [. . .] to keep films relevant, we have to get better at talking about their deeper cultural impact' (Ladegaard 2019: 3).

There is an echo in Ladegaard's words of what Babette explains to her friends after she has given her all to the feast: the ineffable value of art and the value of self-actualisation. 'Throughout all the world there goes one long cry from the heart of the artist: Give me leave to do my utmost!' (Dinesen 2001: 68). By renouncing their status as artists, the Dogme 95 Brethren helped to craft the conditions of possibility for their fellow Danish filmmakers to do just that.

Indeed, in April 2021, Vinterberg himself accepted an Oscar for Best Foreign Language Film: *Druk* (*Another Round*, 2020). Co-written with Tobias Lindholm, and starring Mads Mikkelsen, *Another Round* was filmed in the wake of the tragic death of Vinterberg's daughter Ida. The film is about learning to live again with the help of friendship – and alcohol. In the final frame, Mikkelsen is frozen in mid-air, drunkenly re-discovering his artistry as a jazz dancer. Like Gabriel Axel's puritans tasting wine for the first time, he, and we, are lifted 'off the ground, into a higher and purer sphere' (Dinesen 2001: 57) and reminded that 'in this world, anything is possible' (62).

14. STORIES OF SCANDINAVIAN GUILT AND PRIVILEGE: TRANSNATIONAL DANISH DIRECTORS

Meryl Shriver-Rice

For a small national cinema that draws from a population of only 5.77 million and produces only twenty-six fiction films per year (in 2018), it is not a stretch to say that Danish filmmakers have been wildly successful on the international film festival circuit. It has been argued that directors from small nations face unique challenges and must navigate competitive production contexts in an increasing global age of media convergence (see Hjort and Petrie 2007). From a relatively monocultural national cinema of the 1980s, the 1990s produced two major changes to Danish film culture: a move towards Hollywoodisation (recognisable in films such as *Smilla's Sense of Snow*, Bille August, 1997) and the emergence of the Dogme 95 movement (see Thomson, Chapter 13 in this volume). Dogme inspired socially 'truthful', realistic and intimate storylines in direct opposition to highly marketable and ethically questionable Hollywood-style movies (Schepelern 2006b); it was an effective, non-nationalist and anti-Hollywood response to the 1990s rapid rise of globalisation. Rather than exhibit the cultural backlash of intensified localism (which might have resulted in a plethora of new Danish heritage films), Dogme directors instead chose to employ new digital technologies to innovate the cinematic art form (Hjort 2003: 38). As a result, Dogme spurred significant artistic development and international visibility for its directors and writers, including Lars von Trier, Anders Thomas Jensen, Susanne Bier, Lone Scherfig, Thomas Vinterberg, Åke Sandgren and Annette K. Olesen (among others), who have since been recognised for their contributions to the New Danish Cinema of the post-Dogme

2000s (for a definition of 'New Danish Cinema' see Hjort 2005, and Thomson, Chapter 13 in this volume).

As a production strategy involving strict rules (hence the polemical moniker 'Dogme'), Dogme challenged directors to craft superior stories using low-budget filmmaking practices that would allow for greater freedom in multiple areas of production (see Hjort 2010a). Not surprisingly, former Dogme directors still favour intimate narratives that are overwhelmingly focused on the psychological and social realism that the rules of Dogme cultivated (Bondebjerg 2003: 84). This emphasis on story over marketability is also apparent in Danish film funding schemes. Today most Danish films are publicly funded, at least partially, through the subsidy system managed by the Danish Film Institute. About half of films funded by the Danish system are funded for a general public (the 'market scheme'), while the other half eschew solely economic evaluations of a potential film's worth, instead selecting 'artistically valuable' films, which rose in number from fourteen to sixteen films a year in 1999 and to twenty-five to twenty-seven feature films by 2009 (Hjort et al. 2010: 26). The Danish film industry also encourages extraordinary screenwriting collaborations uncommon in other national cinemas. Most, if not all, film scripts are co-written by the writer and director. Eva Novrup Redvall's scholarship on the unusually prolific collaborations between writers and directors in the Danish film industry argues that these collaborations cultivate an environment in which the story remains the critical focus of each film (Redvall 2010: 67). This distinct approach to screenwriting resembles the collaborative dynamic often exhibited by competing Danish production companies. Mette Hjort's *Small Nation, Global Cinema: The New Danish Cinema* has interpreted the production culture of New Danish Cinema as a Maussian 'gift culture' where stakeholders trade off social debts. This unique production context has been described as the creative machinery of a cinema that is intentionally structured to nurture artistic vision over marketability (Hjort 2005: 23). While extraordinary, this commitment to collaboration is logical for a national culture that is known to exhibit an 'unshakable commitment to egalitarianism' (Hjort 2005: 4). It is within this unique film industry context that women directors such as Susanne Bier, Paprika Steen, Lone Scherfig, Pernille Fischer Christensen and Hella Joof (among others) have received support for their film projects (although this is changing; see Hjort 2018).

Furthermore, New Danish Cinema has allowed for the production of narratives that combat social marginalisation through morally positive representations of gender, sexuality and immigrant identity (Shriver-Rice 2015, 2018). This consistency of themes and values across filmmakers is not especially surprising given that many Danish directors are graduates of the notoriously 'socially-aware' National Film School of Denmark (Stevenson 2003: 162, 201).

And yet this does not limit these films' success to a small national market: as many high-profile film festival nominations and wins over the past two decades have highlighted, New Danish Cinema has produced compelling works with local and transnational appeal (Hedling 2018b). Much of contemporary Danish cinema self-consciously engages in psychologically difficult narratives that adopt a normative stance supporting political action as opposed to privileged and irresponsible detachment.

This chapter assesses the international careers of contemporary Danish directors in this light, asking whether, and how, their individual and collective commitment to interrogating ethical quandaries in their narratives has had an impact on their reception abroad. The first part of the chapter discusses the emergence of a generation of Danish auteurs from Dogme 95, examining a typical pattern in their careers: perceived failure in Hollywood, followed by a renaissance at home. Focusing on Vinterberg, Bier and Scherfig, the discussion also touches on other Danes who have achieved global fame but whose careers have taken a different trajectory: Lars von Trier, Nicolas Winding Refn and Nicolaj Arcel. The second half of the chapter looks more closely at the ethical concerns that typify the work of Vinterberg, Bier and Scherfig, not least their interrogation of Scandinavian privilege.

Post-Dogme: Four Globally Visible Auteurs

Three of the four most internationally successful Danish auteurs of this century – Susanne Bier, Lone Scherfig and Thomas Vinterberg – ironically launched their globally recognised directorial careers during the Dogme 95 experiment. This is ironic since the Dogme 95 Manifesto banned each individual director from being credited in the opening or closing film credits and from exercising personal aesthetic taste, all with the explicit intention of avoiding the notion of individual directorial authorship as venerated by the post-war French New Wave and *Cahiers du Cinéma* concept of the auteur. Nevertheless, insofar as Dogme 95 positions itself as reacting to earlier movements in film history, the movement ensures that 'the role of the director as intellectually and ideologically ambitious cinephile is reiterated, and his [or her] influences are picked over in ways that, again, redouble the focus on the director' (Thomson 2013a: 44). Indeed, despite the collaborative efforts behind Dogme productions, the directors garnered far more international attention than the actors or scriptwriters. Four Danish Dogme alumni made international waves at Cannes (Lars von Trier repeatedly being nominated or winning the Palme d'Or) and at the Academy Awards, in particular at the start of the second decade of this century. In 2010, Lone Scherfig was nominated for Best Picture; in 2011 Susanne Bier won the Best Foreign Language Film (she was also nominated in 2006); and in 2014 Thomas Vinterberg was nominated for Best Foreign Language Film.

Until quite recently, Lars von Trier was easily the most globally recognised contemporary Danish director, in equal parts due to the repeated celebration of his films at the Cannes Film Festival and the highly controversial nature and divisive reception of his fictional narratives (for example, during the Cannes screening of *The House That Jack Built* in 2018 100 people walked out, but there was also a ten-minute standing ovation; see Mumford 2018). Despite having never left the context of Danish production, von Trier's English-language films have had wide appeal with both film festivals and popular global audiences (see Schepelern, Chapter 12 in this volume). Part of this global visibility is also due to the internationally famous actresses that have headlined von Trier's films (including Björk, Nicole Kidman, Emily Watson, Kirsten Dunst and Charlotte Gainsbourg). As the co-founder of his own production company Zentropa (with Peter Aalbæk Jensen in 1992), von Trier has maintained complete control over his films (despite his overall political belief in collectivism), rendering him the 'ultimate auteur' of Danish cinema, a fact that has fascinated both journalists and film studies scholars for over two decades (Bell 2005). His penchant for collectivism has largely aided fellow Danish filmmakers working in Denmark through the loaning of sets, collaborative screenwriting efforts and help with production deals (Hjort 2005: 23). In terms of his own cinematic work, von Trier has never worked in Hollywood, nor with any other large international production companies outside Scandinavia (although Zentropa has co-produced films with other European production companies, including several with the small Scottish production company Sigma Films). He has self-reported in multiple interviews that his choice to remain working in Denmark hinges on two main factors: first, his disdain for Hollywood and American politics generally, and secondly, his aviophobia or fear of flying (Preston 2014). Von Trier has also been outspoken about the fact that he does not desire to comment on (nor think about) the social politics of his films; rather, he prefers to think of them as 'art for art's sake' (Badley 2010, Preston 2014, Bell 2005).

Thomas Vinterberg's wild international success with *Festen* (*The Celebration*, 1998), the groundbreaking first film released with the Dogme 95 certificate, landed him a high-profile US-Danish-British-French-German-Swedish-Japanese-Dutch English-language production deal with leading Hollywood stars (Joaquin Phoenix, Claire Danes, Sean Penn) for *It's All About Love* in 2003. Despite the hype surrounding the five-year Hollywood-style production (New York City setting, Hollywood star cast, runaway production, Hollywood-level budget), *It's All About Love* was very poorly received by both critics and viewers (see Thomson 2007b). Afterwards, Vinterberg remarked multiple times that the success of *The Celebration* was like an albatross around his neck: having reached a pinnacle of cinematic success at such a young age, critics made it clear that his later films were viewed as embodying failed potential.

His early auteur status thrust high expectations onto his post-Dogme work, which seemed impossible to fulfil (Thomson 2013a: 46). His later international success with *Jagten* (*The Hunt*, 2012), still marketed with the tagline 'Director of *The Celebration*', came after his return to Danish production contexts and Danish-language filmmaking.

After her Dogme film *Elsker dig for evigt* (*Open Hearts*, 2002), Bier completed two high-profile, Danish-language dramas focused on masculinity and crisis (co-authored with Anders Thomas Jensen) – *Brødre* (*Brothers*, 2004) and *Efter brylluppet* (*After the Wedding*, 2006), the latter of which was nominated for an Academy Award for Best Foreign Language Film. After the success of *After the Wedding* Bier was invited to direct her first Hollywood-backed (by Dreamworks-Paramount presentation of Neal Street Production) English-language film, *Things We Lost in the Fire* (2007). During this time, the script for *Brothers* was also optioned by Hollywood and adapted as an American English-language remake in 2009, which brought Bier's name further international visibility. *Things We Lost in the Fire* was allotted a star-studded 1990s Hollywood cast that included David Duchovny, Halle Berry and Benicio del Toro, but despite the popularity of the all-star cast, the film failed to find a significant audience. After the film's weak reception, Bier returned to Denmark to make the third film in her world-renowned masculinity-in-crisis trilogy, *Hævnen* (*In a Better World*, 2010), to follow *Brothers* and *After the Wedding*. Returning to Denmark and to her collaboration with Thomas Jensen proved fruitful when *In A Better World* won the Academy Award for Best Foreign Language Film in 2011.

Lone Scherfig's *Italiensk for begyndere* (*Italian for Beginners*, 2000) was arguably the most circulated and seen Dogme film, as it found a wide international audience with its 'feel-good' reputation (Hjort 2010a: 121). Scherfig's next film *Wilbur Wants to Kill Himself* (2002) was an English-language film shot in Scotland with a Scottish cast as part of a new relationship between Zentropa and Scottish Sigma Films. This film marked the foundation of Scherfig's lasting and rewarding career working in the United Kingdom. After the success of *Wilbur Wants to Kill Himself*, Scherfig returned to Denmark and Danish-language production to make what was viewed as a failed production experiment (Ebert 2004). In an effort to lower her directorial sense of control, Scherfig made a production rule for *Hjemve* (*Just Like Home*, 2007) that stated that directorial decisions on character and location were to be made at the very last moment prior to shooting, so that no one would know what was happening until two days beforehand. Refusing the term 'improvisation' in reference to her work, Scherfig's unconventional production mode was an attempt at continuing the 'practice of openness' and 'conditions of possibility for spontaneity' that Dogme 95 had taught her (Hjort 2010a: 35, 38). After the lukewarm reception of *Just Like Home*, Scherfig returned to the UK to make her next English-language film, *An Education* (2009), which would prove to be the critical pinnacle of her directorial career to date, widely praised by international audiences and critics and nominated for Best Picture at the 2010 Academy Awards.

Hollywood Failure and Danish Renaissance

In the short history of Hollywood and Hollywood-adjacent studios extending invitations to Danish directors in this century, few directors have made the transition to Hollywood a critical success. Nearly all returned to the Danish film industry, where directors have more creative control, where the content of a film matters more than the box-office numbers and where the industry is so highly collaborative that Lone Scherfig has commented: 'Every time a Danish film succeeds, things become that much easier for everyone else' (Hjort, Jørholt and Redvall 2010: 230). As critics, film festival awards and ticket sales have attested – and as has been played out across Bier and Vinterberg's careers—a smaller industry context and a smaller budget have often equated to greater creativity and mastery of a film project. In a similar vein, after his Academy Award nomination for *En kongelig affære* (*A Royal Affair*, 2012), Nikolaj Arcel directed the *The Dark Tower* (2017), based on the Stephen King novels of the same name, casting major Hollywood stars. *The Dark Tower* garnered impressive cumulative worldwide ticket sales (likely due to the popularity of Stephen King's novels) but was lambasted by reviewers (Kelley 2017). The next film Arcel was to direct in Hollywood was promptly cancelled; public speculations abounded about the failure of *The Dark Tower* and included Arcel being 'plagued with creative differences, test screenings gone awry, and reshoots', the same sort of industry quicksand that affected Susanne Bier's 2014 film *Serena* (Kelley 2017).

This is the trajectory of most Danish filmmakers in Hollywood, unless, like Nicolas Winding Refn, directors develop their own production companies to continue making films that appear to be Hollywood films (big budget, packed with Hollywood stars, reliant on violence and spectacle). Winding Refn provoked Hollywood studio attention in the same manner that Arcel, Bier and Vinterberg had, through international film festival awards and nominations, including a Grand Jury Prize nomination at Sundance in 2009 for *Bronson* and a Golden Lion nomination for Best Film at the Venice Film Festival for *Valhalla Rising*, also in 2009. Winding Refn's Hollywood indie film *Drive* (2011) was a favorite with film festivals and most critics but received a mixed reception from general audiences due to its ultra-violence and 'extreme brutality' (Bradshaw 2011). It was also recognised in Denmark (non-ironically) that year as the Best American Film (Årets amerikanske film) at the 2012 Robert awards. Winding Refn has gone on to make *Only God Forgives* (2013), which competed for the Palme d'Or at Cannes, and *The Neon Demon* (2016), both of which were criticised for their superficially violent and vapid plots, but highly praised for their glossy fashion-ad aesthetic.

Winding Refn is one of the few internationally successful Danish directors who did not attend the National Film School of Denmark, which is made clear by his overwhelming emphasis on artifice and spectacle over 'real' human stories. His 'stylish glitterbombs of sex and death' stand in direct opposition to the penchant for psychological realism in New Danish Cinema (Leigh 2016). Most graduates of the National Film School are inspired by the institute's 'strong commitment to the pursuit of film as something more or other than a purely commercial undertaking' (Hjort 2010a: 22). His last two films were made without Hollywood support, as French-German-American Indie productions backed by Winding Refn's own production company Space Rocket. Winding Refn's obsession with glossy visual aesthetics has led to his directing branded fashion content for Gucci and Hennessy (Leigh 2016). After the *Neon Demon*, Winding Refn did not continue making Hollywood-inspired films and has instead (like Bier's work with Netflix and the BBC) entered a collaboration with Amazon Productions to make an American crime mini-series *Too Old to Die Young* (2019).

Like Arcel, Susanne Bier has dealt with the heavy-handed interventions of Hollywood studio productions and, as with Winding Refn, working in large-nation productions has led her to choose to work with new content-streaming production houses (Amazon, Netflix, Hulu) that allow for greater directorial control over her work. While neither *Things We Lost in the Fire* (2007) nor *Serena* (2014) are strictly Hollywood productions, both are widely understood as Bier's 'Hollywood films' due to their Hollywood star casts, massive budgets and production contexts. Missy Molloy has argued that Susanne Bier's lukewarm reception for *Things We Lost in the Fire* was due in part to the very aesthetic (reminiscent of *Brothers* and *After the Wedding*) that critics speculated must have motivated its production with the aim of generating award nominations (Molloy 2018: 56). Reviews of the film specifically criticised these unique art-cinema stylistic features that had been praised in Bier's Danish-language international hits (Whipp 2007, Ebert 2007, Molloy 2018: 56). One review of *Things We Lost in the Fire* indicated that its failure lay in ultimately making 'the connections too honest, hopeful, and human, to induce guilt on the part of any open-hearted moviegoer', a cutting criticism that would later be aimed at both Vinterberg and Scherfig's films shot in New York City (Lawson 2007). After the lukewarm reception of *Things We Lost in the Fire*, Bier returned to Danish filmmaking and her creative collaboration with screenwriter Anders Thomas Jensen, which resulted in massive critical acclaim for *In A Better World*. Her directorial success led to her invitation to complete *Serena* with massive Hollywood stars Jennifer Lawrence and Bradley Cooper when another

Hollywood director backed out of the project at the last minute. *Serena* was a commercial failure that generated the worst reviews of Bier's career. Thus, as Molloy has commented, 'despite overcoming setbacks related to her nationality and gender', the Hollywood industrial context 'impacted the extent to which Bier was able to make her authorial mark visible in bigger-budget productions featuring Hollywood stars' (Molloy 2018: 57; see also Agger 2015).

The year 2014 represented a commercial and critical low point in Bier's career. While *Serena* was in post-production, Bier returned to Danish-language dramas, releasing *En chance til* (*A Second Chance*, 2014) in the same year that *Serena* premiered; *A Second Chance* is undoubtedly Bier's least successful Danish-language film of this century (Van de Velde 2018: 181). When interviewed about the failure of *Serena*, Bier has accounted for that film's incoherent narrative by pointing to the fact that Jennifer Lawrence's stardom skyrocketed as *Serena* was in post-production, and as a result her agents and managers were suddenly and unexpectedly highly concerned with the way in which her stardom might be affected by her violent role in *Serena*. This debacle resulted in Bier being asked, as director, to re-edit the film about 120 times over a two-year timespan, when her usual editing regime averages eight to ten times on any film. She remarked that her usual 'compass for what is right or wrong' and 'what beats will affect' an audience went 'numb' throughout the process (Molloy, Nielsen and Shriver-Rice 2018: 273). Ultimately, it is clear from this interview that the greater Hollywood studio machinery hijacked *Serena*'s post-production and potential success as a film.

Rather than return to making feature films in the comfort of a Danish context, Bier chose next to try her hand at a BBC-produced transnational television mini-series, *The Night Manager* (2016), where she chose to switch the gender of one of the *The Night Manager*'s protagonists from male to female (Leonard Burr in the novels became Angela Burr in the mini-series), a choice that did not impede the series' popularity, which amassed viewing numbers that well surpass her theatrical releases (Patten 2016). That BBC and AMC co-produced the John le Carré adaptation, combined with its categorisation as a thriller, underscores Bier's generic versatility and her willingness to experiment in varied production environments and media formats (Molloy, Nielsen and Shriver-Rice 2018: 4). Her willingness to work in various industrial milieus and across genres is further demonstrated by her unexpected and provocative collaboration with Netflix on the psychological thriller *Birdbox* (2018), which made international headlines as the most watched film on Netflix with over 45 million accounts watching it in its first week (Perez 2018). To date, Bier has been remarkably prolific and generically diverse, particularly when compared to research on women directors that suggests that they often experience notable career gaps and produce fewer films than their male counterparts. Bier has proven exceptional in this respect, directing fifteen feature-length films, a TV movie, *Luischen* (1993), and two transnational television series (*The Night Manager* and *The Undoing*, 2020) in the two decades since graduating from the National Film School of Denmark. Thus, factoring in her work in television, Bier has averaged nearly one major work per year, which makes her the most prolific in the small cohort of internationally visible women directors helming big budget productions in contemporary film and television (Molloy, Nielsen and Shriver-Rice 2018: 5).

Similar to Susanne Bier recovering from the tepid reception of *Things We Lost in the Fire* by returning to Danish production and to the massive critical acclaim of *In a Better World*, Thomas Vinterberg returned to a Danish production context and the genre of psychological realism after the failure of his English-language big-budget, transnational psychological sci-fi thriller love story *It's All About Love* (to which we will return presently). His career did not bounce back immediately, as did Bier's; instead, his next two films *Dear Wendy* (2005, written by Lars von Trier) and *En mand kommer hjem* (*When a Man Comes Home*, 2007), were compared with resounding disappointment to *Festen* by the reviewers (the latter in particular due to its title seeming to reference the plot of *Festen*). A later collaboration with screenwriter Tobias Lindholm proved fruitful with *Submarino*'s (2010) positive reception and *The Hunt*'s (2012) global success, surpassing even the critical reception of *Festen*, with an Academy Award, Golden Globe and BAFTA nomination for Best Foreign Language Film and a Palme d'Or nomination at Cannes.

The complete failure of *It's All About Love*, Vinterberg's star-studded English-language Hollywood-style film set in New York City, concerned not only its complicated plot line involving cloning, climate change, a mysterious heart disease, the loss of gravity over Uganda and a central love story, but it also garnered the same criticism that Susanne Bier had received for *Things We Lost in the Fire*; ultimately, it was far too sentimental and earnest for American audiences in 2004. Critics recalled loud snickering during the 2003 Sundance premiere, and most critics' reviews reported total confusion over the film's narrative complexity (O'Sullivan 2017), although a few reviewers acknowledged that they could grasp a faint outline of the deeper, dramatic point and philosophical questioning that appeared to be the film's main point (McCarthy 2003). Returning to Danish-language film and Denmark-based production was ultimately the key to Vinterberg's directorial renaissance: since the smash hit *The Hunt*, he has completed a UK/American English-language co-production *Far From the Madding Crowd* (2015), another Danish-language film written by Lindholm, *Kollektivet* (*The Commune*, 2016), in connection with which he was billed as 'the director of *The Hunt*', and the highly transnational production (of the true story of a Russian submarine) *The Command* (2018). All three films were critical successes, with *The Commune*'s festival awards standing as further proof of the overall success of Vinterberg's smaller Danish productions (*The Commune* won the Robert Award for Best Adapted Screenplay and the European Film Award for Best Editor). Not surprisingly, his further work with screenwriter Tobias Lindholm on another Danish-language drama, *Druk* (*Another Round*, 2020), won the 2021 Academy Award for Best International Film.

In direct contrast to Vinterberg and Bier, Lone Scherfig's post-Dogme cinematic victory occurred after exiting Danish production, rather than returning home to it. In fact, her least well received film was made in Denmark. She credits her ascendancy as a director to her Danish Dogme roots, and Scherfig has continued – like Bier – to be part of a minority of globally visible female directors, except her successes have all been within largely British production contexts (some of which have included collaborative transnational production companies), including the films *One Day* (2011), *The Riot Club* (2014) and *Their Finest* (2016). Her next film, *The Kindness of Strangers* (2019), marked her return to Danish production schemes (including the Copenhagen Film Fund and the Danish Film Institute) – aside from the fact that the film is another English-language film, has a leading cast from the UK and Hollywood and is shot in New York City rather than Denmark. Given that she is one of the few Danish directors (other than Lars von Trier) who solo-authors her own scripts (when not directing scripts adapted from novels), as opposed to working in collaborative director-screenwriter duos, it is not surprising that *The Kindness of Strangers* tackled themes similar to those in her scripts for *Italian for Beginners* and *Wilbur Wants to Kill Himself*. An initial critical review stating that 'there's a palpable urgency to the film's kindness, and a real despair to the film's inability to make us believe in it' (Ehrlich 2019) was a harbinger of the criticism directed at Scherfig's latest project, the same critique received by both Vinterberg and Bier's first North American films: that they employed too much sincerity.

Danish Privilege and Responsibility

There is a larger trend in the New Danish Cinema of the twenty-first century, in which cinematic narratives act as sites of ethical negotiation and epistemic rupture for spectators in the position of privileged welfare state citizens. When Danish films do not miss the mark concerning an emotional register of sincerity and believable kindness, this cinematic space is capable of confronting contemporary ethical issues head-on, by positioning the spectator to relate to the ethical demands of the film with appropriate passion and self-reflection (Shriver-Rice 2015: 4). When Danish films are not criticised for their sincerity (see Bradshaw 2003 versus Ebert 2004) and find wide international audiences, they are often viewed as masterful because their narratives are capable of generating ontological shifts in the ways in which individuals see their place in the world (Shriver-Rice 2018: 255). This probing of moral worlds in socially-informed narratives has brought particular success to Bier's transnational trilogy (consisting of *Brothers*, *After the Wedding* and *In a Better World*), all of which she directed from co-authored Jensen scripts. Bier and Jensen's trilogy does not self-reflexively mock or explicitly acknowledge its sincerity; instead, its protagonists embody earnest humanitarian aid workers who profoundly believe in the benefits of their actions. This sincerity springs from a Danish educational system where many Danish children grow up attending schools in which local, regional and international equality and global social justice issues are integrated into daily classroom lectures. Although Bier is explicitly concerned with transcending cultural specificities so that global audiences 'get the point' of her films (Smaill 2014: 12), they do not ignore her Danish viewers – they star Danish actors, use Danish language and depict Danish families on Danish soil. This narrative strategy is used to reach audiences who are aware of and concerned with difference in class and agency, but who are perhaps unwilling to dedicate two hours of their lives to a social documentary. Consequently, Bier's drawing from non-Western narrative sites in her internationally acclaimed trilogy has more to do with speaking to the privileged-world guilt in the Danish viewers and reminding them of the world beyond Western space. This is a world from which the Danish cultural imaginary is not cut off, an imaginary that has reached a wide Western audience but has typically been stifled when attempted in the context of Hollywood productions (see Hollywood's adaptation of *Brothers*, Shriver-Rice 2011).

Bier and Jensen's trilogy is not unique among recent Nordic cinema, nor amidst Danish film, for narratives that evoke the guilt of privileged nations; instead, the trilogy is part of a wider trend in twenty-first-century Nordic entertainment to incorporate people and spaces that lie outside of the relative stability and affluence of Northern European social democratic nations. Within Scandinavian cinema, Swedish directors Lukas Moodysson and Roy Andersson are known for narratives that portray intense experiences of palpable privileged-world guilt. Comparing these two Swedish filmmakers, one can get a glimpse of the wide-ranging styles and genres that have incorporated notions of privileged-world guilt. Moodysson's films are dark, intense 'melodramas of demand' that invoke shame in the spectator (Nestingen 2008: 114), while Andersson's work relies on dry, Scandinavian existentialist humour in his Ingmar-Bergman-meets-Monty-Python-style comedies (Yang 2013). In the Danish context, a number of powerful films since the early 2000s have dealt with issues of industrialised nation guilt, particularly in terms of immigration and citizenship (Shriver-Rice 2018). Films such as *Kinamand* (*Chinaman*, Henrik Ruben Genz, 2005), *Lille Soldat* (*Little Soldier*, Annette K. Olesen, 2008), *Broderskab* (*Brotherhood*, Nicolo Donato, 2011) and the Academy Award-nominated *Krigen* (*A War*, Tobias Lindholm, 2016) dive headfirst into issues of belonging, identity, race, class and citizenship. Over the past two decades, Denmark has demonstrated the viability of film as a vehicle to negotiate and reinforce cultural ethics and political values, while also navigating the ongoing and mounting forces of digital communication and globalisation (Shriver-Rice 2015). There has been little reason for Danish directors to tone down the social justice issues in their narrative content, since for many Danish directors, such as Bier, embracing politically or ethically charged content has not diminished their films' critical success at highly visible film festivals like Cannes and Berlin. As the rise of exclusionist, populist and isolationist western governments occur in the second decade of this century (Brexit in the UK, the election of Trump in the US, the rise of populist parties in the Netherlands, France, Denmark and so forth), screen narratives that contend with issues of migration and resource allocation and address the 'us versus them' paradigm speak to the historical moment.

Ethics and Humour

Lone Scherfig's films tend not to grapple with such obvious ethical qualms, but Mette Hjort has contended that films written by Scherfig take an *ethical perspective* on 'how people construe their connection with others' that is manifested through a pervasive attitude of kindness and a careful use of humour (Hjort 2010a: 144, emphasis original). Anthropologist Mary Douglas defined humour as a thin line separating an insult from a joke, with a joke expressing something a community is ready to hear, while an insult expresses something it does not yet want to consider (Douglas 1991: 292). Thus, interpreting humour often involves exchanging judgements about the world and defining oneself either with or against others. Through an anthropological lens, humour is not strictly a matter of taste, but rather a vehicle by which people validate and articulate their ideas about the world. Seen as such, Scherfig's veiled contribution to social justice issues lies in her pervasive sense of humour that specifically avoids the type of social violence that humour often elicits through scornful or humiliating views of others, a strategy often used in popular film to generate laughter. Instead, Scherfig's humour takes a normative stance in which incongruity results in eliciting sympathy (Hjort 2010a: 148, 149). Crowd-sourced jurors recognised this ethical stance in *One Day*, which won the 2013 Jury Prize at the Global Non-Violent Film Festival. This festival is an inclusive, crowd-sourced digital festival that 'showcases nonviolent motion pictures to show that these movies are not only capable of great international success but they are also in high demand by the public' (Pischiutta and Trifu 2012).

In an inversion of this strategy, other dramatic examples of contemporary Danish psychological realism have employed scornful mockery of the un-virtuous and self-interested, with selfish characters openly ridiculing other characters' attempts to be socially conscious citizens. This form of mockery is rampant in *Little Soldier* and *Brotherhood*. The protagonist of *Little Soldier* is cruelly taunted by her father for trying to save the world by becoming a soldier and going off to Afghanistan, and even further for having what he calls a 'bleeding heart' over the fate of the father's African sex workers. In *Brotherhood*, neo-Nazi characters openly deride anyone who, like the Danish majority, believes in human equality between different racial and ethnic groups. In these two films, socially violent humour is specifically employed as an ethical weapon to alienate the 'bad' characters and their corresponding value systems from viewers.

Conclusion: Globalisation from Within

Many believe that fiction film can be a springboard for political analysis to further global awareness of problematic issues that affect others in unequal ways. Before *The Day After Tomorrow* (Roland Emmerich, USA, 2004) successfully affected audience concern about climate change (Leiserowitz 2004), Vinterberg's *It's All About Love* attempted to use imaginative fiction as a discursive ethical space to enter into conversation with global viewers about issues of human worth and dignity, climate change and the violation of everyday life

Figure 14.1 Characters from *It's All About Love* (2004) sidestep another person who has died from loss of love. Framegrab.

by rapid technological progress. The plot clearly took on too many subjects at once, and even Vinterberg in all of his interviews on the film admitted that it was terribly rendered and nearly incomprehensible, but the central aim is not to be scoffed at: viewers should be entrenched in global awareness instead of caught up in the whirlwind of neoliberal capitalist values and pace of life. In Vinterberg's failed epic, climate change is causing record low temperatures all over the world as water glasses freeze indoors and snow falls on the Eiffel Tower in July. At the same time, people are dropping dead on the streets of New York from an unknown heart condition caused by loss of love in their lives. To highlight the indifference that the public sphere has for these tragic deaths, characters in the film mindlessly step over bodies on airport escalators and on subway steps as they go about their day.

In discussing transnational publics and emerging new concepts concerning globalisation, Torill Strand has pointed out that the contemporary theoretical turn in art, cinematic narrative and literature signifies an innovation in global awareness and new habits of thought. Strand refers to this process as globalisation from *within*. She points out that, while people from New York to Beijing have long been living in existing relations of interdependence, 'what's new is

Figure 14.2 The closing shot from Vinterberg's *It's All About Love* (2003). Ugandans are tethered to their houses during an unexplained loss of gravity. Framegrab.

not forced mixing but *global awareness* of it, it is self-conscious political affirmation, its reflection and recognition before a global public via mass media, in the news and in the global social movement of blacks, women, and minorities' (Strand 2010: 234, emphasis original). Like Vinterberg's *It's All About Love*, much of contemporary Danish cinema self-consciously engages in psychologically difficult narratives that adopt a normative stance supporting political action as opposed to privileged and irresponsible detachment.

As Denmark's leading auteurs continue to pursue transnational production preferences and sensibilities that do not marry themselves to narratives that depend heavily on specific, local meanings, their films will continue to reach global audiences. Hopefully, these directors will continue to ask searching ethical questions while their films entertain, allowing their audiences to grapple with difficult issues brought about by increasing globalisation. As Sean Penn's character says at the end of *It's All About Love*, 'the disorder of the world [. . .] it's all connected somehow'.

15. DANISH TELEVISION DRAMA IN THE TWENTY-FIRST CENTURY: NEW SYNERGIES BETWEEN FILM AND TELEVISION

Eva Novrup Redvall

While Danish cinema has seen directors and actors who managed to build international names for themselves throughout the course of film history, Danish television drama was a very nationally oriented endeavour until the first decade of the twenty-first century. There are many reasons for this. For many years, only the national public service broadcaster Danmarks Radio (DR) produced television drama, and this was specifically targeted at the domestic, license-fee paying audience. Moreover, with a few exceptions, television drama was produced on rather small budgets and built on a television theatre tradition with limited production values and appeal in terms of attracting international viewers. The question of language has of course also been a recurrent issue, with little tradition of seeing subtitled television drama travel in a way similar to art cinema fare at film festivals or through limited cinema releases.

While Danish television has created highly popular national productions over the years (Agger 2005) – such as the historical family saga *Matador* (DR, 1978–82), which still enjoys re-runs with staggering viewing figures – it was only in the twenty-first century that international audiences started paying attention to Danish stories produced for the small screen. Since the founding of the Nordic public service media partnership Nordvision in 1959, there has been substantial programme exchange and collaboration between the Nordic countries, and quite a few Danish series have been shown on Nordic public service television. However, during the 2000s German audiences developed an appetite for Danish crime fare, such as the Emmy-award winning series

Rejseholdet (*Unit One*, DR, 2000–4), *Ørnen* (*The Eagle*, DR, 2004–6) and *Livvagterne* (*The Protectors*, DR, 2009–10). When the screening of *Forbrydelsen* (*The Killing*, DR, 2007–12) on BBC4 managed to create substantial hype around Danish series and 'Nordic Noir' in the UK in the 2010s (Redvall 2013: 163), this was a game-changer in terms of how to think about Danish series as content that might potentially travel. Since then, a number of series have been made with more international co-funding, based on the belief that they can appeal outside of the national realm (Jensen et al. 2016), and there has been export of not only directors and actors, but also writers and other crew, who have managed to build successful international careers based on their television track record (Redvall 2019).

Studies of the recent success of Danish television drama have analysed some of the reasons why the Danish series were suddenly able to compete: an overall professionalisation of the writing and production framework when trying to create entertaining serial storytelling with high production value based on public service ideals (see, for instance, Redvall 2013, Hochscherf and Philipsen 2017) and the incorporation of narrative and stylistic trends from American series (see, for example, Nielsen 2016). Without getting into a detailed discussion about what might define 'cinematic television' (see, for example, Mills 2013, Restivo 2019), this chapter argues that a fruitful meeting between the otherwise quite separate production worlds of film and television has been crucial for creating Danish high-end television with a look that equals international primetime content. This meeting grew out of deliberate attempts to create a so-called 'crossover' between film and television in the DR production framework, leading to the hiring of a long list of talent from the National Film School of Denmark – not only directors, but also cinematographers, editors and sound designers who could help improve the audiovisual aspects of the Danish series in combination with a strong focus on improving screenwriting and storytelling strategies.

Taking Lars von Trier's *Riget* (*The Kingdom*, DR, 1994) as a starting point (and using the series' opening credits as an example of how this sequence sets a particular tone for the following content), the chapter thus discusses how this ground-breaking mini-series legitimised working in television for aspiring filmmakers and how, accordingly, DR deliberately set its sights on working with upcoming talent from the National Film School of Denmark. To illustrate what can be regarded as an approach to television drama that calls for the more concentrated 'cinematic gaze' rather than the more casual 'televisual glance' (Ellis 1982: 50), the chapter then analyses the opening of the third season of *The Killing* as an example of what this kind of visual storytelling for the small screen can look like. The chapter ends by discussing how Danish television drama in the late 2010s is marked by a diversity of players, genres and approaches, as well as of talent moving back and forth between platforms and formats more than ever before, while the boundaries between cinema and television have become even more blurred.

Lars von Trier's *The Kingdom* as the Pathway for Crossover

Lars von Trier was asked by DR to try his hands at television drama in the early 1990s, coming off his arthouse 'Europa trilogy' consisting of *The Element of Crime* (1984), *Epidemic* (1987) and *Europa* (1991), which had earned him international recognition. At the time it was not common for film directors to work in television drama, and there was still a strong sense within the Danish film industry that cinema was the artistic medium and television the more popular and low-brow medium. This was not least the case among graduates from the National Film School of Denmark who were only taught to work in film and not in television until the school established a collaboration with DR on developing TV series with a so-called 'TV term' in 2004 (Redvall 2015). However, the resulting series from von Trier – who approached this task in a highly unconventional manner (as described in Schepelern 2000: 165–92; see also Chapter 12 in this volume) – nuanced these industry perceptions of film and television by showing young talent that one could in fact make television with an artistic voice and also appeal to television critics and mainstream audiences.

Stylistically, *The Kingdom* was inspired by popular US crime series from the late 1990s, such as *NYPD Blue* (ABC, 1993–2005) and *Homicide* (NBC, 1993–99), but this was combined with what can be regarded as a more mysterious art cinema layer about the haunted history of the Danish hospital, Rigshospitalet or 'Riget' (meaning 'The Kingdom', which gave the series its title), with clear visual ties to von Trier's previous films. The opening credit sequence of the series illustrates this eclectic combination beautifully. Somewhat pretentiously, the series opens with the caption 'Lars von Trier presents', pointing to how this is his personal work, rather than that of an institution such as DR. The yellow-tinted and foggy sequence over which this is stated starts with a slow-motion tracking shot of bleachers working in the ancient marshlands where the hospital, The Kingdom, was later built while this area was part of rural Copenhagen. A slow voice-over tells us, almost like a secret, about the history of the place before the camera moves down into the marshland water and then further down, into the ground. Here we see a pair of hands emerging from the soil before blood bursts through the image with the title of the series, accompanied by spooky choral voices.

Only a few seconds after the title of the series is washed away by blood, this is followed by a more traditional television credit sequence from a present-day hospital where one gets to see the doctors and patients and the names of the actors intercut with images of an ambulance driving in what appears to be a hazardous way. This sequence is frantically edited with many different angles

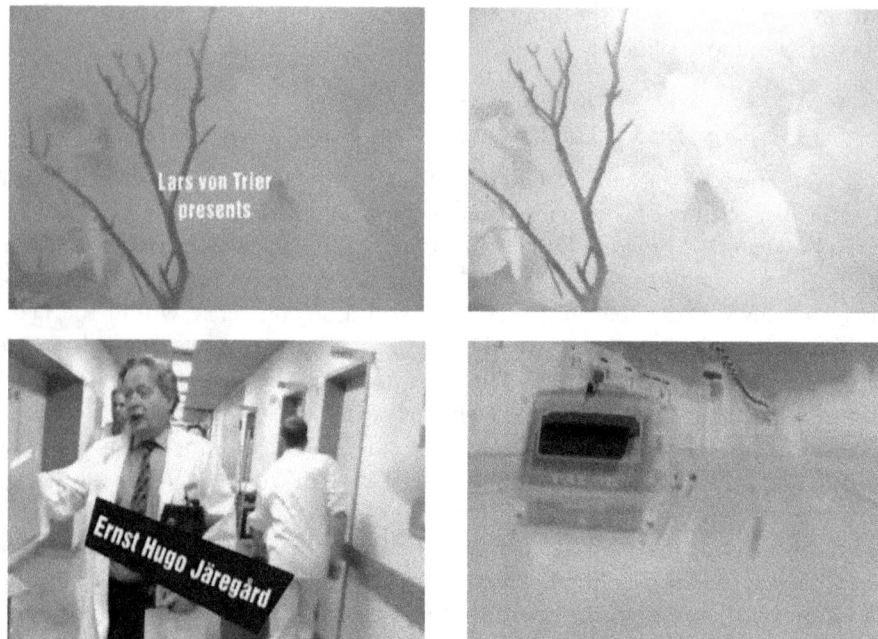

Figure 15.1A–D Four framegrabs from Lars von Trier's *Riget* (*The Kingdom*, 1994) produced by Zentropa for DR. The opening credit sequence illustrates the meeting between Lars von Trier's previous art cinema work and the inspiration from US crime series such as *NYPD Blue* (ABC, 1993–2005) and *Homicide* (NBC, 1993–99).

and lots of movement, while a modern song accompanies the stressful introduction of the main arena and all its characters. The two very different parts of the opening credits are in stark contrast to each other and mark von Trier's playful approach to trying to move into television drama with his own voice. In film as well as in television, title sequences are crucial for establishing a certain sense of expectation for the following content among audiences (e. g., Stanitzek 2009, Davison 2013). The title sequence for *The Kingdom* helped set a certain tone for the series, while also communicating to audiences that, even though von Trier was coming from the cinema scene and making a series with some 'arty' content, this would also be an entertaining series in a more traditional style, with many highly popular Danish actors in the story.

Moreover, knowing that his mini-series might be a challenging cocktail for some mainstream audiences, von Trier added a personal epilogue to each episode where he, tongue-in-cheek, asked viewers 'to take the good with the evil' while assuring them that *The Kingdom* is a story that we can all relate to, about helping one's next of kin – and of which, accordingly, we should all watch the next episode. It was a clever touch – which also made him famous outside of the art cinema circuit in Denmark – and the overall impression of *The Kingdom* was a sense that one could create fun, ambitious and engaging television drama with a personal touch that was remarkably different from the previous Danish television drama fare.

The Kingdom helped legitimise television drama production as an interesting opportunity for young talent to make a name for and express themselves, a strategy that was also adopted by film director Ole Bornedal in the wake of his acclaimed thriller *Nattevagten* (*The Night Watch*, 1994); he made the road movie mini-series *Charlot og Charlotte* (*Charlot and Charlotte*, DR, 1996) two years later. Lars von Trier and Ole Bornedal reinvigorated Danish television drama, and when film director Rumle Hammerich was hired as Head of DR Drama, insisting that television series should be the flagships of DR as highly entertaining public service television, this led to the otherwise rather separate film and television industries starting to converge in the late 1990s. DR hired several young directors from the film school for their new flagship serial *Taxa* (*Taxi*, DR, 1997–99), among them Niels Arden Oplev as the 'conceptualising director' and episode directors such as Ole Christian Madsen, Per Fly and Lone Scherfig who all went on to become major names in Danish cinema.

Several of the directors from *Taxa* have stressed the value of working with television drama early in their careers, since the TV series served as a 'boot camp' and helped professionalise Danish cinema (Ole Christian Madsen, interviewed in Hjort et al. 2010: 169), through the possibility of getting many hours of on-set experience and learning how to handle large teams and working at a fast pace (Niels Arden Oplev, interviewed in Hjort et al. 2010: 212). For DR, drawing on ambitious film school talent improved the look and sound of the series, while producers – based on what DR called 'the producer's choice' principle (Redvall 2013: 71) – were able to hire the best team for each series rather than having to work with in-house staff.

Through the 2000s, the DR series became ever more visually impressive, not least because of German co-financing that was sometimes specifically targeted at ensuring added production value (Redvall 2013: 65). In the 2010s, the Danish production framework was regarded as an example of best practice in Europe, with several industry events focusing on the DR mode of production and European series, such as *The Team* (2014–), a co-production between eleven media organisations from eight European countries (involving six public service broadcasters), trying to export this particular production framework (Redvall 2020).

Insisting on the Cinematic Gaze

An important reason why international audiences started appreciating the Danish series was their high production values and their focus on how storytelling for the small screen should be visually ambitious and demand the attention of the viewers in a way similar to watching a film in the darkness of a cinema. As discussed by John Ellis, when comparing the viewing situations of cinema and television (1982: 50), the concentrated viewing situation in a cinema has led to scholars arguing that spectators engage with content in this particular setting with a concentrated 'gaze'. In contrast, television has traditionally been discussed as marked by a more casual 'glance', when people watch programmes in their everyday surroundings, often marked by interruptions and sometimes while performing other tasks such as cooking, cleaning or concentrating on other screens, such as cell phones.

Most of the scholarly literature on what has been labelled 'high-end TV drama' (Nelson 2007), 'quality TV' (McCabe and Akass 2007), 'complex TV' (Mittell 2015) or 'complex serial drama' (Dunleavy 2017) focuses on how a new kind of primetime television drama has been marked by narrative complexity. This complexity forces viewers to pay careful attention if they want to follow the action, while also allowing for a more visual 'show, don't tell' approach rather than the old-school televisual tradition of TV being marked by 'talking heads'. This aspect is only enhanced when series are in a foreign language, where viewers have to read subtitles to understand what is being said. Engaging with what Sam Ward has described as 'subtitled oddities' (Ward 2013) calls for viewers to sit down and pay attention, investing themselves in the viewing situation rather than casually glancing at the small screen.

The opening sequence of the third season of *The Killing* is a good example of how certain series ask viewers to pay close attention by insisting on visual storytelling, and of how this kind of television drama complicates traditional ideas of what is cinematic and what is televisual. From the outset, the creators of *The Killing* had many notions of how to create an arena that would be powerful and interesting enough to keep a whodunnit murder mystery going for twenty episodes. One of the metaphors behind the main idea of the series about solving the case of a girl gone missing was that the city of Copenhagen has fallen under a spell similar to the one in *Oedipus* where the city of Thebes cannot be liberated until the riddles of the sphinx are solved. Based on this idea, the series portrays Copenhagen as a city where the sun never shines (all seasons were shot in the dark and dreary month of November) and the main character, Sarah Lund (played by Sofie Gråbøl), basically never smiles (Redvall 2013: 167–69).

There was no concept of 'Nordic Noir' when developing *The Killing*, but it is easy to see why the cold, winter darkness and the hardships of the main character while solving the gritty crime branded the series as a core example in this crime category. Several scenes in the series have so little lighting that one basically cannot see what is going on without turning down the light in the room where one is watching. *The Killing* is a series made for the modern 'big-screen versions' of the television screen that render colours faithfully and, preferably, in HD resolution. The series asks viewers to simulate the way in which they watch films in a cinema, concentrating on the storytelling in a room where what is happening on screen should be the main attraction.

To keep the character of Sarah Lund interesting and somewhat mysterious for the entire series, another notion during the making of *The Killing* was to often shoot her character from the back. This is not common in television where the traditional approach is to focus on the faces, and mouths, of actors talking. One important reason for this practice is to avoid the classic viewer complaints about dialogue in present-day dramas being hard to follow because of the actors' naturalistic use of everyday language and diction. In the UK, there has been ongoing discussion of 'Mumblegate' in relation to UK television drama series (e. g., Harrison 2017) and the BBC has frequently had to explain the sound quality and dialogue approach of major productions, such as *Happy Valley* (BBC, 2014–) (Brown 2016). In Denmark, there have been similar complaints about the audibility of drama dialogue and criticism of a new generation of 'mumbling' actors, but this is not an issue for foreign audiences who are watching with subtitles and are thus more open to accepting creative decisions such as filming characters more from behind.

The opening sequence of Season 3 of *The Killing* has almost no dialogue, but it has a complex sound design as part of the chilling set-up. The location is a big industrial ship that is first shown from the outside in the dark of night. The camera then takes us on board, slowly moving around empty locations inside the ship, accompanied by an old Danish song (about sailors being fond of girls) that at first seems to be non-diegetic, but then appears to be coming from a rusty speaker on the ship. The camera then finds the back of a man who seems to be maybe masturbating in front of a blurry TV screen, but then we find that his bloody hands are tied behind his back. The man manages to free himself from the ropes and frantically runs through the claustrophobic spaces of the ship, closing the doors behind him. This is first filmed from above, as if an omni-present camera is catching everything, and then the camera is with him in the hallways until he arrives at the bridge of the ship where he tries to call for help, only to find that the cord of the phone has been cut. A smoking cigarette shows us that someone was just there, and we then see a shadow passing the camera in the foreground, which the man also notices. Terrified, he runs for his life, now accompanied by the ship's emergency alarm, and decides to jump into the water to escape whoever he saw on the ship. The sequence has been intercut with the names of the main actors of the series; following the splash of the man hitting the water, the title 'Forbrydelsen III' appears. The sequence is markedly dark with the little light on the ship used for dramatic effect in a blueish-green colour scale, with occasional red from the blood on the man, emergency buttons, or the floor of the deck. The sound design emphasises the cold and metal setting in stark contrast to the Danish song heard on the speakers. The camera angles are varied and used to create a sense of unease while small clues, such as the smoking cigarette, are used for dramatic effect. The man is silent. There is no dramatic yelling telling us that now is the time to watch for a possible shadow, nor any begging for his life. From the outset, the series insists that we need to watch closely if we want to follow the action and not miss crucial clues.

A lot of effort has clearly gone into making this unsettling, thoroughly composed opening that ambitiously sets the scene for the following crime investigation. This is far from the more realist rendering of crimes in the Danish series of the 2000s where everyday life is captured in a more naturalistic manner, and it is a sequence that insists on creatively working with images, sound and production design to create the sense that we are about to watch something special. The sequence illustrates how the meeting between film and television in Danish production culture definitely had an impact and how Danish series at this point in time were able to compete on production values in an international context. Both national and international audiences responded positively to *The Killing* (e. g., Hansen and Waade 2017), paving the way for future high-end DR series in other genres. The political drama *Borgen* (DR, 2010–13) and the family inheritance drama *Arvingerne* (*The Legacy*, DR, 2014–17) would have had a much harder time finding viewers outside of the Nordic countries without the established interest in Danish drama.

Crime is the genre that most easily crosses European borders (e. g., Bondebjerg et al. 2017), but being exposed to what was perceived as several high-quality crime dramas from the Scandinavian countries, such as *The Killing*, international audiences seemed to be more willing to also take a chance on other kinds of 'subtitled oddities' (Ward 2013) in the 2010s. As repeatedly stated by the head of DR Drama, Piv Bernth, Danish public service television drama is made first and foremost for domestic audiences (see, for example, Redvall 2013: 79), and no one expected that a series such as *Borgen* might in fact interest international audiences when writing and developing what was perceived as a nationally oriented series on domestic politics (Redvall 2016).

The crossover between talent and traditions from cinema and television has thus helped a wide range of series find success outside of Denmark through what some have discussed as a meeting between 'national specificity' and 'Americanization' (Nielsen 2016). While this kind of crossover started as a DR strategy, many players are now making series with A-list talent from Danish cinema that are from the outset deliberately targeting international audiences in a variety of genres.

DANISH TELEVISION DRAMA IN THE TWENTY-FIRST CENTURY

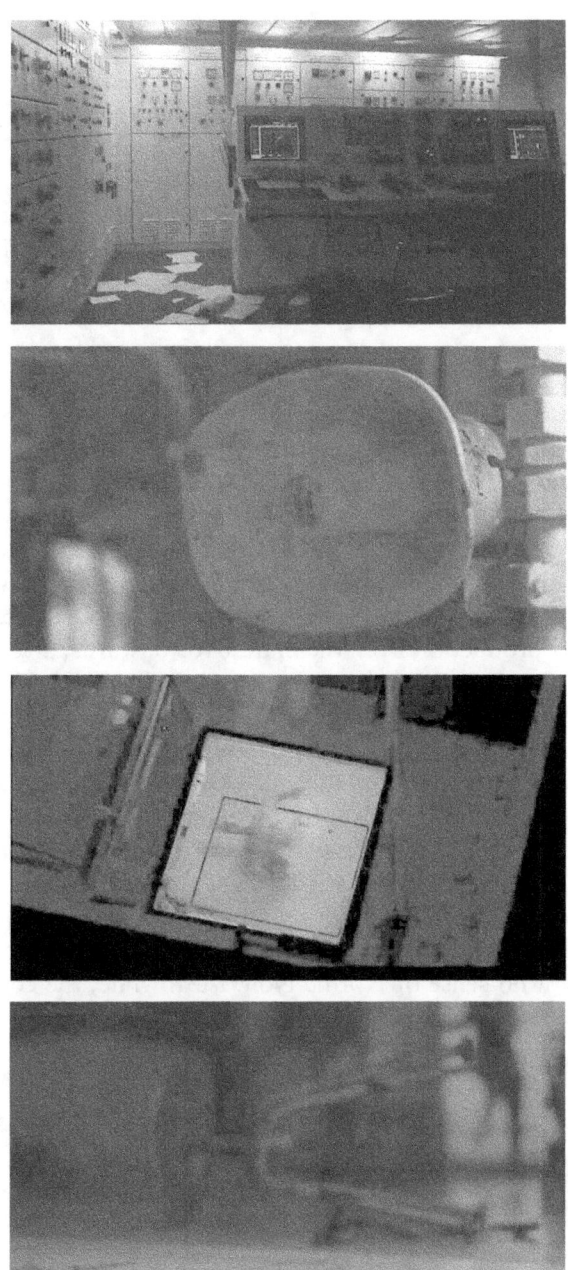

Figure 15.2A–D Four framegrabs from the opening sequence of *Forbrydelsen* (*The Killing*, DR, 2007–12), illustrating its unsettling and ambitiously cinematic composition.

Concluding Remarks and Cliffhangers

The international success of television series from a small nation such as Denmark in the 2010s is remarkable, and it is important to keep in mind that these quality series did not suddenly emerge from nowhere. As discussed in previous research (Redvall 2013, Hochscherf and Philipsen 2017), they were the result of many years of hard work on changing the general approach and production framework for making television drama. As illustrated in the two main examples in this chapter, *The Kingdom* and *The Killing* bear witness to the visual journey that has taken place from the mid-2000s to the late 2010s, with an insistence on creating not only engaging and entertaining public service stories, but also visually ambitious dramas marked by high production values.

Since DR's *Taxa* in the late 1990s, there has been a remarkable crossover of talent between film and television in all professional roles, and it is now common and respectable to work for the big as well as the small screen. While the main strategy of DR in the 2000s was to focus on serials with several seasons at the expense of more experimental fare or mini-series – a fascinating exception being Per Fly's highly original and somewhat overlooked mini-series *Forestillinger* (*Performances*, DR, 2007) – there seems to be a more diverse approach to television drama production from the mid-2010s onwards, and a more auteurist approach is returning, with directors directing all episodes of mini-series or shooting content as both serial fiction and feature film.

As an example, in 2014, Ole Bornedal returned to television with the big-budget historical mini-series *1864* (produced by Miso Film for DR, 2014) with impressive battles and an epic approach to telling the story of a legendary national defeat. After having focused on original stories written for the screen in the 2000s, DR started also moving into adaptations, such as the mini-series *Liberty* (DR, 2018) after a bestseller by the Danish writer Jakob Ejersbo, telling the story of a Scandinavian expat community in Tanzania in warm and lush colours with no sense of Nordic Noir. Meanwhile, the competing public service broadcaster, TV2, started focusing still more on television drama, commissioning, among many other things, veteran filmmaker Bille August's adaptation of Henrik Pontoppidan's classic Danish novel *Lykke-Per* (TV 2, 2018) as both mini-series and feature film, while also getting the largest national viewing figures for the sunny mainstream drama *Badehotellet* (*The Seaside Hotel*, 2013–). As in many other countries, international streaming services such as Netflix and HBO Nordic are now ordering still more 'original content', such as *The Rain* (Netflix, 2018–), while commercial national broadcasters are also confident that Danish television drama can be a good investment with the new potential for international sales.

Much has changed since DR was the only provider of Danish television drama for the domestic national audience, and while international audiences may still primarily associate Danish television series with 'Nordic Noir' or 'Scandi crime', the Danish television production landscape of 2020 features many different players, genres and approaches and is marked by talent moving back and forth between platforms and formats, more than ever before. While the challenge of Danish television drama in the mid-2000s was to find talent that could reinvigorate national television series, the challenge going into the 2020s seems to be to hold on to this talent in an ever more international and competitive production landscape (Redvall 2019). The boundaries between what is film and what is television, and who might be working in which medium, are increasingly blurred. Overall, this exchange was fruitful for both Danish film and television in the 2010s. The 2020s will show whether the Danish production culture will manage to keep national talent focused on the domestic realm, or whether the success of Danish series will make it harder to retain the best people in the industry, with the global film and television industries suddenly calling.

Acknowledgment

This chapter was written as part of the research project 'What Makes Danish TV Drama Series Travel?' (danishtvdrama.au.dk), headed by PI Anne Marit Waade at the University of Aarhus. The author would like to thank the many good project colleagues for discussions and feedback on content for this chapter. Moreover, sincere thanks go to the institution San Cataldo for a writing stipend to work on this chapter and other projects in the spring of 2019.

16. NEW DANISH SCREEN AND THE SKETCH: THE ROLE OF IMPOSED AND SELF-IMPOSED CONSTRAINTS IN TALENT DEVELOPMENT

Mette Hjort

The concept of creativity under constraint has long played an influential role in the Danish filmmaking milieu. The idea that constraints of various kinds can be strategically transformed into a productive scaffold for facilitating creativity became especially salient in the wake of Lars von Trier's and Thomas Vinterberg's Dogme 95 initiative, launched in Paris in 1995 as part of a centennial celebration of film (Hjort and MacKenzie 2003). As is well known, the global movement that was spawned by this duo's provocative intervention was a manifesto-based one that prescribed filmmakers' abidance by ten rules, codified in a 'Vow of Chastity', as the *sine qua non* of inclusion (see also Thomson, Chapter 13 in this volume). The relevant constraint-based approach has rightly been traced back to well-established practices at the National Film School of Denmark (Philipsen 2005), where both Vinterberg and von Trier were trained. With the success of Dogme 95, however, the concept of creativity under constraint became common coin beyond the environment of the film school, including in institutional milieus devoted to policy formation and the disbursement of public funds earmarked for film.

It is this institutional context that is of interest here, with particular reference to talent development. There is much at stake, particularly for small nations (Hjort 2015), in getting talent development right, for arguably the successful nurturing of future filmmakers is the basis for a given film ecology's persistence and thriving, as well as for its very viability and capacity to generate different types of value. Such value – be it aesthetic, artistic, cultural, or societal – is itself a decisive factor for the welfare state's continued commitment to motion pictures as part of a public good. The aim here is to examine the role of constraints in nurturing talent, by focusing on a particular talent development initiative, namely the Sketch, a well-circumscribed project of limited scope and duration that nonetheless has had a lasting impact on the landscape of Danish talent development.

Launched in 2017, the Sketch was an initiative of the Danish Film Institute's talent development programme, New Danish Screen (henceforth NDS). Although principles at the heart of the Sketch have made their way into Danish talent development more generally, the initiative has been neglected in research on talent development. This is regrettable, for there is considerable interest, in a variety of filmmaking milieus, in coming to grips with the approach that informed the Sketch, which is clearly seen as transferable to other production environments, some of them having dynamics very different from those driving the Danish film industry. Examples of international interest in the Sketch include the 'Danes Do It Better' programme at the 2019 Neuchâtel International Fantastic Film Festival (NIFF). *NIFF Extended*, a series of interventions by experts on the 'future of cinema and the audiovisual industry', offered a workshop, keyed to 'Danes Do It Better', by former NDS talent developer Johnny Andersen. In his talk Andersen explored the ramifications of giving priority to audiovisual form, rather than to words, when developing a given film and, through this, the talent of the relevant filmmakers (NIFF 2019). The priority given to audiovisual expression from the very outset is a distinctive feature of the Sketch initiative, the value of which has also been underscored by Andersen in film milieus outside Europe. Andersen has, for example, collaborated with FilmLab Palestine, in the context of solidarity-based talent development on a transnational basis (Hjort 2019). In 2017, he offered an industry-oriented workshop in Ramallah, during FilmLab Palestine's film festival, then known as Days of Cinema. The write-up for the talk echoes the central premises of the Sketch:

> One of the keys to a successful low-budget feature film is that you find a strong artistic and production concept during the development of the film, a concept that goes hand in hand with the writing of the script [. . .] Andersen will talk about how you can find your own method when developing your film. The examples are *visual pre-studies of the concepts* (FLP 2017, emphasis added).

Practitioner's agency figures centrally in the research underpinning the present analysis, attention having been given to the self-understandings of two key categories of practitioners, that of the film director and that of the talent developer. Practitioner interviews were conducted by the author of this chapter with the director of New Danish Screen, Mette Damgaard Sørensen, talent developer for Christian Tafdrup's *En frygtelig kvinde* (*A Horrible Woman*, 2017); with one of the NDS talent developers, the above-mentioned producer Johnny Andersen; and with Rasmus Kloster Bro, director of *Cutterhead* (2019). Kloster Bro was selected for an in-depth interview on account of his research-oriented work with audiovisual sketches in the wake of his experience with *Cutterhead*. Interview questions addressed to Kloster Bro focused on his creative intentions and processes, his reflective assessment of his Sketch film, the institutional parameters (encompassing both the funding body's ethos and the constraints that it imposes) and the articulation of self-imposed constraints in response to an overarching economic constraint. Questions addressed to the talent developers emphasised the criteria used to select projects and the core values underpinning the process of nurturing talent through the development of a specific film.

New Danish Screen: Talent as the Outcome of a Successful Development Process

A few words about the origins of NDS as well as the Sketch are in order. In 2014 the DFI's talent development programme NDS celebrated its tenth anniversary, releasing a boxed set of materials for the occasion (Danish Film Institute 2014). Included in the package is a 'Welcome' sheet with prefatory reflections by then CEO of the Danish Film Institute, Henrik Bo Nielsen, a small volume entitled 'Perspectives' featuring assessments and vision statements from five international experts (Wendy Mitchell from *Screen International*, Canadian producer Todd Brown, American film critic Robert Koehler, former HotDocs programmer Sean Farnel and Mike Goodridge from the British production company Protagonist Pictures), and a second and third volume, 'Processes' and 'Frameworks', both of which are designed to capture the first-hand experiences of filmmakers, institution builders and talent developers associated with NDS's then ten-year history.

Nielsen's framing text (Nielsen 2014) effectively highlights the institutional context and concept of NDS. Talent is seen here not as a natural, pre-existing phenomenon that merely requires discovery – an ideology favoured by the televised talent shows to which Nielsen contrastively refers – but as a phenomenon that emerges through, among other things, sustained hard work supported by appropriate interactions and processes of development within a particular kind of institutional environment. Referring to NDS's mission statement, Nielsen (2014) highlights the intended cultural and societal contributions of the talent development programme, the goal of 'supporting and inspiring the development of the language of film and film narrative', the overarching aim being to ensure that Danish film remains dynamic and diverse in the longer term and, thus, sustainable.

In brief, the NDS programme combines funding for a specific film with the relevant film practitioners' development, where the latter is achieved through interaction with a supportive commissioner who also wears the hat of talent developer. The conceptual specificity of NDS is the result of a cluster of clear commitments spanning the entire course of its existence. Foremost among these is the commitment to producing various forms of value (most notably aesthetic and artistic value) through low budgets; the insistence on giving new and emerging talents access to the film industry; the strong desire to enable already established talents to renew themselves and their creative practices through the relatively risk-free experimentations that low budgets afford (Redvall 2012; for the DFI's earlier initiative involving limited risk, see Hjort 2005: 16); the emphasis on bringing together a more personal concept of authorship (with the attendant notions of voice and individual style) with effective teamwork; and, finally, the clearly articulated idea that 'persons and processes' at all times must be given priority over 'marketable products' (Nielsen 2014). Marketable products being trumped by persons and processes does not, however, mean that audiences are left out of the equation. An important structural feature of NDS is the collaboration, from the outset, with DR (the Danish Broadcasting Corporation) and TV2, the point being to ensure that 'Danish viewers continue to be exposed to interesting, challenging, and unusual stories, even after the light of the projector has been dimmed' (Nielsen 2014). It is clear that the collaborative arrangement has a role to play in creating access to the industry, and thus in the provision of professional opportunities for new talents.

The poster in the boxed anniversary set provides an overview of the films, directors, scriptwriters, producers, production companies and commissioners/talent developers whose collective work constitutes the achievements of NDS over a ten-year period. A remarkable 133 titles are listed, the vast majority of them directed by different directors (exceptions include Omar Shargawi and Manyar Parwani, both of whom received support for more than one film). While especially well-established production companies, most notably Zentropa, figure prominently in the overview, newer companies (such as Adomeit Film, Dencik Film, Fridthjof Film and Beofilm Productions) also found support through NDS, confirming Mette Damgaard Sørensen's (interview 2019) claim that the programme has helped to diversify the production landscape for Danish film. The talent developer/film commissioner category encompasses five names only: Jakob Kirstein Høgel, Kim Leona, Marie Schmidt Olesen, Peter Schønau Fog and Vinca Wiedemann. Vinca Wiedemann, the first Director of New Danish Screen and Rektor (President) of the National Film School of Denmark from 2014 to 2019, is listed as the talent developer/film commissioner for thirty-three films. What is evident in the numbers is the possibility of the talent developer herself learning from experience, refining the processes and practices of talent development over time, so as to achieve the core aims of NDS.[1]

NDS has its origin in a dialogue between Vinca Wiedemann and then Chief Executive of the Danish Film Institute, Henning Camre, at the Berlin International Film Festival in 2002 (Yde 2014). Wiedemann and Camre recall their dissatisfaction with Novellefilm (New Fiction Film Denmark), a funding scheme established in 1994 for the purposes of facilitating film school graduates' transition into the film industry, through short film productions with restricted budgets. What was needed, claimed Camre, was a new scheme that offered scope for feature film production and gave 'people the possibility of making what they needed to make', instead of requiring them to make yet another short film, something they had already achieved during their film school years (Yde 2014: 17). New Fiction Film Denmark was indeed eventually phased out in favour of the new talent development scheme, NDS, which was to be defined by its prioritisation of talent over product, and by an unshakeable conviction that 'radical and anything but conventional films' (Yde 2014: 19) could be made cheaply. Interestingly, as Wiedemann and Camre debated the possibilities, a guiding question was whether Jørgen Leth's modernist film *Det perfekte menneske* (*The Perfect Human*, 1968) – a film that was to enjoy newfound attention in 2003 with the release of Leth and von Trier's collaborative work, *De fem benspænd* (*The Five Obstructions*) – would have been able to secure state support in the context of 2002. In a sense, then, Leth's *The Perfect Human* was seen as the very embodiment of the kind of radical, unconventional filmmaking for which NDS was to create a supportive and protected space.

The Sketch

As director Rasmus Kloster Bro (interview 2019) points out, NDS's Sketch initiative, launched in 2017, was in many ways a constructive response to filmmakers' recurring frustration over the years with existing development protocols, which typically called for a *purely verbal articulation* – in treatments and scripts – of what is essentially an irreducibly audiovisual work. The whole point of the Sketch was to give priority to the *audiovisual* articulation of a film's central concept from the very outset. What was prioritised was *showing*, through actual audiovisual properties, not mere dialogues or descriptions on the page. The Sketch was launched through an open call that offered filmmakers and producers a budget of 500,000 Danish kroner (about £60,000) to produce an audiovisual study and treatment for a film with a budget of 3 million kroner (about £350,000). NDS received seventy applications and allocated initial support to nine or ten of them (interview Andersen 2018). The recipients were then given four months to produce a twelve-minute audiovisual study and to write a treatment, and five of the submissions were subsequently selected for further development as feature-length films.

The five films that were a response to the call and thus qualify as fully fledged Sketch films are *A Horrible Woman* (a drama directed by Christian Tafdrup, 2017), *Usynligt hjerte* (*Neon Heart*, a drama directed by Laurits Flensted-Jensen, 2018), *Christian IV – Den sidste rejse* (*Christian IV – The Last Journey*, a historical drama directed by Kasper Kalle as Kasper Skovsbøll, 2018), *Lifeboat* (a drama and thriller, directed by Josefine Kirkeskov, 2018) and *Cutterhead* (a thriller directed by Rasmus Kloster Bro, 2019). *A Horrible Woman* offers an excoriating critique of a manipulative young woman, presented as typical of our times, the plot being driven by the dynamics of a pathological relation between just two characters, Marie (Amanda Collin) and Rasmus (Anders Juul). *Neon Heart* restricts its action to three characters – the former porn worker Laura (Victoria Carmen Sonne), the recovering addict Niklas (Niklas Herskind), who is her former boyfriend, and Frederik (Noah Skovgaard Skands), his younger brother – within the timeframe of a single day. In *Lifeboat* the action unfolds within a carefully circumscribed space, that of a sailing vessel. The conflict concerns three central characters, Iben (Sofia Helin, known for her role as Saga Norén in *The Bridge*) and Thomas (Pål Sverre Valheim Hagen), two lovers on a sailing holiday in the Greek archipelago, and Amal (Sebnem Hassanisoughi), a Syrian refugee whom Iben, motivated by self-conscious heroism, plucks from the sea in the middle of the night. *Cutterhead* tells the story of Bharan (Samson Semere), Rie (Christine Sønderris) and Ivo's (Kresimir Mikic) drive to survive, following an accident deep underground, in the construction site of the Copenhagen metro which serves as the film's only setting. *Christian IV* also limits its story to a single setting, a horse-drawn carriage taking the Danish king to his deathbed at Rosenborg Castle in 1648. Within this carriage, the dying king interacts, in his imagination, with his former wife (Kirsten Munk, played by both Karen Lise Mynster and by her daughter, Rosalinde Mynster), whom he divorced and imprisoned years earlier for her putative infidelity.

While only the above-mentioned films qualify as Sketch films, it is important to note that their production histories overlap with those of later NDS films. The continuity in question has to do with the perceived success of the Sketch's emphasis on the early audiovisual articulation of a given film's central concepts. The relevant practice of developing an audiovisual study as the first step in a project's development has thus been adopted more widely by NDS. Indeed, as Mette Damgaard Sørensen (interview 2019) puts it, 'we now develop sketches on nearly all our films'. Ulaa Salim's award-winning drama and thriller about political extremism, more specifically about Muslim radicalisation and extreme ethnic nationalism, *Danmarks sønner* (*Sons of Denmark*, 2019) is an example of a post-Sketch film 'that actually begins as a sketch, that is, has a sketch as the starting point for the film' (Damgaard Sørensen 2019).

In the institutional environment of the Danish Film Institute and its overarching talent development programme, the Sketch is regarded as a resounding success. On 6 September 2019, Nikoline Riget, Film Coordinator for New Danish Screen since the very beginning, shared NDS's call for Skitsen2 (the Sketch2) on Facebook. Included in the call published by the DFI was a rationale for revisiting the initiative, four years after the original Sketch:

> We wanted to get away from the word as the most important tool for examining one's material – and instead combine it with a visual exploration in which narrative devices and an artistic production concept served to establish a quite different and far more cinematic starting point for the development of the story.
>
> The initiative met with great enthusiasm and became the beginning of a wave of strong new artistic voices in the Danish film world. *They have shown how a strict economic framework can sharpen the artistic expression*, when concepts and aspirations are successfully fused with artistic production frameworks from the very beginning (Danish Film Institute 2019, emphasis added).

Commenting on the call the same day, also on Facebook, Kloster Bro's reaction was one of unmitigated enthusiasm:

> It is truly fantastic that New Danish Screen once again is offering the possibility to create the foundation of the entire film and process, in the language of film. Because film can effect something quite different – through the body, aesthetics and time – compared to what we can do by speaking and writing. Indeed, it can be really hard to get through the eye of the needle with an idea that one cannot talk or write about. Hurrah for New Danish Screen and the Sketch vol. 2.

Imposed and Self-Imposed Constraints

Philosopher Jon Elster's (1992; 2000) influential discussion of imposed, chosen and invented constraints with reference to creativity drew attention to the phenomenon of creativity under constraint, to the idea that constraints, far from impeding creativity, may be the very condition of creativity, understood as novel and valuable achievements. In a study of Lone Scherfig's *Italian for Beginners* (Hjort 2010a), I argued that, when it comes to creativity, constraints are by no means created equal. Some can be highly conducive to creativity, whereas others have little creative impact. If the productive connections between creativity and constraint in the context of film are to be properly understood, I claimed, the variations that arise in connection with different kinds of constraints cannot be ignored. For example, empirical research on the implications of the Dogme 95 Manifesto's ten rules for the practitioner's agency associated with specific roles within the production process revealed that Dogme's rules were highly effective in stimulating the creativity of actors and of entirely dubious value in this regard to film editors (Hjort 2010a: 40–99).

The approach adopted in the Sketch, which is fully consistent with a philosophy of creativity under constraint, is seen by NDS and others as having been effective in stimulating film practitioners' creativity, allowing especially directors to explore, manifest and develop their talent. In what follows, the aim is to pinpoint the nature of the relevant constraints and the factors that allowed them to play a positive role in the creative, developmental process. The focus is on Mette Damgaard Sørensen's guiding principles as Director of New Danish Screen, and on the particular case of Rasmus Kloster Bro, director of *Cutterhead*. The claim is that New Danish Screen's Sketch imposed two framework constraints that were decisive for the creative success of the films. The filmmakers were to envisage a film with a budgetary ceiling of three million Danish kroner (about £350,000). In and of itself, such a constraint, well known to all low-budget filmmakers, is no immediate spur to creativity. Yet, this master constraint was accompanied by a more specific condition – namely, that the project was initially to be developed by relying on audiovisual modes of expression, and not primarily on words.

In addition to the Sketch's two framework constraints, invented self-imposed constraints contributed to the dynamics of the filmmakers' creativity and, through this, to the talent development process. That is, the directors who succeeded in securing funding for their feature films on the basis of their audiovisual sketches all demonstrated an ability to invent further highly effective self-imposed constraints in response to the institutionally mandated master constraints. Expressed in the twelve-minute audiovisual sketches, these invented, self-imposed constraints were seen as signs of the directors' creativity and thus as providing reasons for selecting their projects. Yet, these self-imposed constraints also became the cornerstone for the development of the filmmakers' talent through interaction with the NDS talent developers. That is, the process of developing a selected film and, through this, the talent of the filmmaker was in each and every case a matter of respecting the invented, self-imposed constraints and of finding ways of further exploring and, indeed, heightening the quality of their artistic value for a given cinematic work.

To capture the impact of imposed as well as invented, self-imposed constraints for creativity in the context of the Sketch project *qua* talent development initiative, the changing role of the talent developer and timing of funding decisions require attention. During the process of assessing the submitted audiovisual sketches, the talent developers wore the hats of gatekeepers charged with selecting the projects that were to be developed into feature films. At the heart of that selection process was an assessment of the relation between the master constraints and the invented, self-imposed constraints, of the extent to which the filmmakers had managed to produce a concept that was fit for purpose, given the overarching economic constraint of producing a film with a low budgetary ceiling. However, the role of gatekeeper was quickly replaced by the far less intimidating one of supportive interlocutor, for a defining feature of the Sketch initiative is that funding for the five feature films was allocated immediately following the positive assessment of the audiovisual sketches.

With their projects funded at an exceptionally early stage in the development process, the selected filmmakers found themselves interacting with supportive, dialogic talent developers, who saw their task as being one of assisting the directors with the further exploration of the very constraints that they themselves had invented. As Mette Damgaard Sørensen (2019) puts it, the approach adopted essentially eliminated, very early on, the feeling, and indeed the typical reality, of 'having to prepare for a high-stakes grilling each and every time there was a meeting with the funders'. The set-up of the Sketch had the effect of making trust, rather than doubt, a core element of the process of development. This trust itself was the outcome of the interaction between imposed and self-imposed constraints, as manifested in the audiovisual sketches that created a sound basis for the film commissioners'/talent developers' faith in the selected projects.

The five Sketch films are stylistically very different, a claim that cannot be made of the Dogme films, where the constraints of the Vow of Chastity encouraged a particular audiovisual style (grainy, shaky images produced by a handheld camera, for example). Yet, in spite of their differences, the Sketch films do share at least one trait, one derived from an effective match between an economic master constraint and the films' constitutive audiovisual concepts. According to Mette Damgaard Sørensen, the films clearly reflect a series of *radical choices* in response to the overarching economic constraint, a deliberate process of cost-cutting exclusions. Whereas low-budget filmmaking is often marred by a discernible, unrealised desire to make a film of far greater scope and cost, the Sketch films give evidence of a properly creative engagement with a non-negotiable need for cost-cutting exclusions. In this sense, the Sketch initiative appears to offer an attractive model, readily transferable to other jurisdictions, for heightening the *quality* of low-budget filmmaking and for producing audiovisual works of high artistic, aesthetic and cultural value.

On the Ethos of the Talent Developer as Gatekeeper

The success of the Sketch project undoubtedly had much to do with the clarity of the ethos, clearly articulated by Mette Damgaard Sørensen, that accompanied the low-budget initiative. That is, during the initial phase of selection, the talent developers were clearly looking for certain elements, some of which were seen as necessary, others as optional yet highly desirable.

Included in the category of the necessary, as indicated above, was a clear audiovisual concept that translated the budgetary constraint into production-related delimitations. An example is the decision to have a film's story be set in a single location, as is the case with *Christian IV*, *Cutterhead* and *Lifeboat*. The category of the necessary also encompassed a genuine *proof of concept*, in the form of a twelve-minute audiovisual sketch that was integrally connected to the proposed feature-length film. Damgaard Sørensen underscores the significance of requiring filmmakers to produce audiovisual sketches, not as mere evocations of a work, but as sequences that could actually be incorporated into it:

> They have to take it seriously, in all sorts of ways. That is, the whole production set up, the actors who are involved, everything has to be as though it's for real. [. . .] Often, when you're trying to test something, people come back with something that has all sorts of provisos attached to it. The actor won't be in the actual film, or the editor wasn't available that week, so someone else did the editing, and so on. And what this means is that the material is really of limited use, in terms of trying to draw conclusions about what does and does not work. With the audiovisual sketch, the filmmakers had to really mean it (Damgaard Sørensen 2019).

Damgaard Sørensen cites the case of *Christian IV* to make the point about the efficacy of the audiovisual sketch as a tool for exploring the filmmaker's central audiovisual concept and testing its viability. Following Damgaard Sørensen, the focus of Kasper Kalle's investigation, in his twelve-minute audiovisual sketch, was on whether the physical space of a single carriage could become the basis for an 'expanded mental space' linked to the memories of a dying king. What the audiovisual sketch actually demonstrated was that an additional temporal dimension was needed, in the form of interaction, as recollected or imagined by the dying king, between him and his wife as a young couple. The audiovisual sketch, in sum, clearly showed that the concept of limiting the setting to the single location of a moving carriage was workable, even creative and ingenious. At the same time, it made it evident that the concept required refinement, with the core cast of two being thus doubled to four, and with actors both young and old eventually performing in the single setting of the moving carriage. In this case the audiovisual sketch offered a proof of concept, on the condition that certain adjustments and refinements were undertaken.

Although marketability, understood in terms of box office numbers, was not a factor in the context of the Sketch, clarity of thinking regarding a film's addressee was non-negotiable and thus necessary. Damgaard Sørensen's view is that talent is best developed by remembering that storytelling necessarily involves an audience, whether small or large. The point, she claims, is to encourage filmmakers to make films, not 'for their own sake' (be it the filmmakers themselves or the films), but in order to communicate 'something to someone'. An additional requirement is that the telling in question should have a sense of subjective urgency, the teller being invested in the significance of the story, in the relevance of its telling (Damgaard Sørensen 2019).

In terms of story content, the guiding ethos allowed for considerable diversity, although the option of developing 'new stories for dramatic times' (Damgaard Sørensen 2019) was seen as highly desirable. Referring to the work of New Danish Screen and the Sketch, Damgaard Sørensen has on occasion made reference to an ideal role for films, as 'artistic seismographs' (Danish Film Institute 2016b) with a precious ability to respond to and, indeed, capture the complexities of an increasingly dramatic world. While several of the Sketch films tell contemporary stories – for example, about migrant workers (*Cutterhead*) and refugees (*Lifeboat*) in Europe today – Damgaard Sørensen insists that a focus on the here and now, as was the case with Dogme 95, was by no means seen as necessary. What was emphasised throughout, however, was the desirability of supporting filmmakers who wished to engage with the world in rather direct ways, and not merely with film as a largely autonomous reality:

> You often encounter a certain amount of nostalgia, I mean nostalgia for the cinema, in the first applications of young talents, with the filmmakers referring to earlier masterpieces that they would like, in one way or another, to recreate. And I actually try to avoid those kinds of projects, because they typically lead to highly self-referential films that might end up having a certain impact on the festival circuit but won't actually be that meaningful (Damgaard Sørensen 2019).

Developing an Audiovisual Concept through Self-Imposed Constraints

Rasmus Kloster Bro, director of *Cutterhead*, has especially well articulated views on the value of the audiovisual sketch, having continued to work with the relevant approach following the completion of his first feature film. Kloster Bro, more specifically, has since received funding for a research project titled 'Video Sketches as a Fundamental Artistic Tool' within the context of the National Film School's new mandate to engage in film-related research. In brief, the aim of Kloster Bro's project is to investigate the extent to which the process of developing a film, as well as the completed film itself, are affected by an exclusive focus on video sketches during the phases associated with pitches, treatments and scripts. A key goal for Kloster Bro is to understand the distinction between a sketch and a work, just as he seeks to explore the possibility of developing a 'work in an iterative and *purely audiovisual manner*, through a cycle consisting of shooting, editing, and reflections' (Kloster Bro 2019a, emphasis added).

In his application for research funding, Kloster Bro's response to the question regarding the principal investigator's qualifications makes direct reference to NDS's Sketch:

> The project builds on the experience of developing and producing the feature film *Cutterhead*, which was developed on the basis of a twelve-minute collection of video sketches. The sketches were first and foremost an examination of the physical experience of the progression through the spaces of the film [. . .] Through the sketches we discovered the key concepts in the film's anatomy of production, and these became decisive for the film's shape and style (Kloster Bro 2019a).

Kloster Bro goes on to underscore the extent to which this development process deviated from standard practices: 'The script for the film was only written after the sketch process had been completed and after the shape and style of the film had been defined' (Kloster Bro 2019a). Kloster Bro situates his research in relation to the work of a number of other filmmakers whose practices also give priority to sketch-like approaches: Hlynur Pálmason with *Vinterbrødre* (*Winter Brothers*, 2017; see Bigelow, Chapter 19 in this volume), Annika Berg with *Team Hurricane* (2017), Jørgen Leth with *Det Perfekte Menneske* (*The Perfect Human*, 1968) and *De Fem Benspænd* (*The Five Obstructions*, 2003), and the VFX supervisor Peter Hjorth in connection with Lars von Trier's *Dancer in the Dark* (2000), *Dogville* (2003), *Manderlay* (2005), *Antichrist* (2009), *Melancholia* (2011) and *Direktøren for det hele* (*The Boss of It All*, 2006). Especially significant in the present context are Kloster Bro's references to the work of Harvard's Sensory Ethnography Lab, for it is indeed ideas about motion pictures as enabling a haptic, tactile, synaesthetic and full sensory experience that inform Kloster Bro's exploration of physical space in the *Cutterhead* sketch, and thus his articulation of self-imposed constraints based on choices in response to the overarching budgetary constraint.

Kloster Bro claims to have been operating with two main foci during the production of his audiovisual sketch *qua* exploration of his film's constitutive concepts:

> The twelve-minute audiovisual sketch focused on a spatial investigation and on an investigation of the characters [. . .] What really drove the process was the spatial aspect. What is the smallest imaginable space? Perhaps it's that oxygen machine that Rie is taught to use on the train on her way to the cutterhead [. . .] What's the smallest imaginable space, if the idea is that the spaces should become smaller and smaller. Well, it must be the oxygen that Rie and Bharan share through that machine (Kloster Bro 2019b).

Figure 16.1 Bharan eyes Rie in the ambulance, following their underground struggle to breathe through a single shared device. Framegrab from *Cutterhead* (Rasmus Kloster Bro, 2019).

Kloster Bro is firmly convinced that it would have been impossible to articulate convincingly the results of his spatial investigation, so important for the film's synaesthetic and tactile effects, through a mere verbal description on the page, in the manner of a standard treatment, for example:

> The scene where they share the oxygen machine is not even really in the final script. There's just a remark about how they take turns breathing through the oxygen machine. That's a really good example of something that would have raised all sorts of dramaturgical or production-related questions if I'd tried to use words to describe it. If I'd written that an enormous drill comes crashing through a cement wall somewhere, they would have said, 'Right, ok, so now you've spent all the money and what are you then going to do?' (Kloster Bro 2019b).

For Kloster Bro, the proof of concept that the audiovisual sketch delivered was highly enabling. As he puts it, the sketch had a 'double or even triple function', for it demonstrated the viability of his concept in aesthetic terms, but also with reference to the sheer practicability of its implementation in a production process. Just as importantly, however, the third function of the sketch was to allow the filmmaker and his team to 'detect the way in which the audiovisual

Figure 16.2 *Cutterhead* opens with a scene of the drill penetrating a thick wall. Framegrab.

articulation of our concept resonated with us, so that we could be sure that it really belonged in the work' (Kloster Bro 2019b).

Kloster Bro's audiovisual sketch is remarkably close to the actual film, with some scenes having even been incorporated into it. In this sense, Kloster Bro can undoubtedly be said to have accepted the talent development scheme's requirement that the audiovisual sketch be taken seriously, in the sense of being genuinely continuous, in terms of audiovisual style and the involvement of specific practitioners, with the envisaged final film. The role of Rie, the PR coordinator for the Metro construction project, is played by Christine Sønderris in both the audiovisual sketch and the film, just as Samson Semere assumes the role of Bharan, the migrant worker from Eritrea, throughout. In the film, Ivo, the highly specialised tunnel worker charged with operating the cutterhead, the device that drills through rock and cement, is played by Kresimir Mikic, while the audiovisual sketch features the actual operator. More striking than this continuity of two out of three main actors is the inclusion in *Cutterhead* of actual scenes from the sketch – for example, the briefing that Rie receives on how to use an emergency oxygen mask, as she is taken through the tunnel to the cutterhead. The decision to re-use material from the audiovisual sketch was linked, so claims Bro, to the master constraint of a low-budget production. More specifically, the reasoning on the part of the director and his team was that, given a perfect continuity of one single location from the sketch to final film, useable material from the audiovisual sketch should be re-deployed. The knock-on effect was that the sketch determined the selection of costumes for the final film in some scenes.

A comparison of Kloster Bro's audiovisual sketch and his final film brings to light a series of relatively minor differences that nonetheless have the effect of significantly heightening the drama and emotional tension of key scenes in *Cutterhead*. For example, in the audiovisual sketch, Rie, trapped underground with Ivo and Bharan following a serious accident in the tunnel, shares her concern about being prevented from picking up her daughter from kindergarten. In the film, this same concern is prompted by an alert from her phone, telling her that it is time to collect her child. The use of the phone in the film facilitates the development of Rie's character, for in addition to explaining what the alert means, she confesses to being surprised that her daughter has been absent from her thoughts throughout the crisis. This confession in turn prompts a condemnation from the Croatian migrant worker Ivo who claims to think about his children and wife constantly, although he hardly ever sees them: 'What kind of person are you?' he asks, lying on his side – in order to save on the limited oxygen that the three must share – and with his back to Rie. Reflecting on the differences between the audiovisual sketch and the final film, Kloster Bro underscores the role of the audiovisual sketch in a Mike Leigh-style approach, with the script, far from being present at the very beginning, in fact being the outcome of a series of improvisations and, crucially, debriefings with the actors. Providing access to the actors' interiority, to their subjective experience of a given scene, these debriefings motivated decisions leading to a script and film that, when compared to the audiovisual sketch, evidence the clarifying effect of a properly developmental process.

Conclusion

The Sketch strongly suggests that imposed and self-imposed constraints have a significant role to play in the development of film talent. In the case of the Sketch, the relationship between the imposed and self-imposed constraints was key, as was the priority given to one of the two types of constraints throughout the talent development process. More specifically, the imposed constraints set the stage for the articulation of a number of self-imposed constraints that, in turn, provided the real focus for the talent development process. The priority given to the self-imposed constraints was well-reasoned and judicious, for it was in these constraints that the guiding concepts of the filmmakers, indeed their agency, found expression. Inasmuch as significant emphasis was placed on the self-imposed constraints from the moment of selection and funding, the talent development process was to a large extent a matter of working supportively and dialogically with the filmmakers' own concepts and agency. The role of the imposed constraints should not be underestimated, however, for it made precision necessary and mandated a proof of concept. The clarity and precision encouraged by the imposed constraints served to create the conditions needed for a trusting relationship between the filmmaker and the funder-*cum*-talent developer. Trust was a defining feature of the Sketch and one of the main reasons for the scheme's success. Indeed, arguably the ingenuity of the Sketch lies in the use of constraints to create a robust basis for trust, trust being essential to the process of developing a film of genuine value as well as the talent of the filmmaker.

Acknowledgment

I am indebted to Nikoline Riget at New Danish Screen for having contacted the producers of the Sketch films on my behalf, and to the producers themselves, for granting me access to the works in question. The interviewees – Rasmus Kloster Bro, Mette Damgaard Sørensen and Johnny Andersen – were all exceptionally generous with their time and ideas, for which I am deeply grateful.

Interviews

Andersen, Johnny (2018), interviewed by Mette Hjort. Copenhagen.
Damgaard Sørensen, Mette (2019), interviewed by Mette Hjort. Skype. Hong Kong/Copenhagen.
Kloster Bro, Rasmus (2019b), interviewed by Mette Hjort. Skype. Hong Kong/Copenhagen.
Stephen, Mary (2019), interviewed by Mette Hjort. Hong Kong.

Note

1. An interview with Hong Kong-born film editor, director and talent developer Mary Stephen (2019) brought to light the extent to which talent development, in the best of all possible worlds, is a two-way process. That is, the talent developer is part of a creative exchange that is enriching, transformative and valuable for all parties.

PART IV

DECENTRING AND DIVERSIFYING DANISH CINEMA

17. DANISH DOCUMENTARY PRODUCTION: AN ALL-FEMALE COMPANY

Anne Jerslev

The company Danish Documentary Production was founded in 2007 by three experienced and internationally acclaimed female documentary filmmakers together with a female producer. The founding filmmakers were Phie Ambo (b. 1973), Pernille Rose Grønkjær (b. 1973) and Eva Mulvad (b. 1972), soon joined by Mikala Krogh (b. 1973) and producer Sigrid Dyekjær (b. 1969).[1] Since 2007, these five women have played a prominent role on the international documentary scene and received a range of prizes at international documentary film festivals. Right from the start, Danish Documentary Production aimed to reach international audiences and work internationally; yet, the company also reflects a particular Danish documentary-making culture, largely because the directors all graduated from the Danish Film School's four-year documentary film line more or less at the same time (Phie Ambo in 2003, Mikala Krogh and Eva Mulvad in 2001, and Pernille Rose Grønkjær in 1997).[2] They brought to the company a personal approach to their subjects, fundamental to the training they had received from Arne Bro, head of the school's documentary line, as well as the school's methods of supporting the development of individual talent through collaborative work processes and collective discussion. In a Danish film-historical context, Danish Documentary Production is an unprecedented example of female filmmakers working together to create an internationally successful production and distribution company. Moreover, the company is an illuminating example of the significance of the training at the Danish Film School and its importance for creating and sustaining film talent in Denmark.

Finally, as an example of the generally strong position of female Danish documentary filmmakers, this chapter provides insight into the workings of Danish Documentary Production and particularly into its films. It offers some answers to the following question: what kind of creative thinking about documentary and the making of documentaries has made the company so successful?

The chapter begins by situating the company and the directors within the wider context of women in contemporary Danish (documentary) filmmaking, based on reports from the Danish Film Institute (2016a, 2018a) and interviews with the five women (Hjort 2014; Redvall 2014a, 2014b, 2014c; Jerslev 2018). It then proceeds to discuss films by the four directors (including those made before the company's founding). The chapter investigates which production strategies and documentary visions characterise Danish Documentary Production. I conclude by arguing that what unites the directors' otherwise rather different authorial approaches and themes is their enquiring and curious approach to the social world – a *modus operandi* that has laid strong artistic foundations for this flourishing production company.

Women in Danish Documentary Film Production – and at 'Danish Documentary Production'

According to a report from the DFI (Danish Film Institute 2016a) on gender distribution in the Danish film industry, men are generally over-represented (56 per cent men and 44 per cent women), relative to the gender composition of the Danish population as a whole. If we consider the various occupations within the industry, gender distributions resemble the imbalances seen internationally (for US figures, see Lauzen 2017; Women's Media Center 2018, 2019). For example, in Denmark, men represent 90 per cent of photographers, 64 per cent of editors, 66 per cent of directors and 93 per cent of sound directors, whereas women represent 85 per cent of casting professionals and 100 per cent of those employed in costume and makeup (Danish Film Institute 2016a: 6). However, when one examines these figures in greater detail, the picture is more complex. If we look at applications for funding to the state support system for development and production, the Danish Film Institute (2018a) shows that two-thirds of directors and scriptwriters applying for project development support under the New Danish Screen system (the DFI's talent development programme, see Chapter 16) were men, whereas a little over half of the people applying as producers were women. Regarding applications for a production grant, the gender distribution was somewhat more equal among scriptwriters and directors, although men were still in the majority (approximately three-fifths of applicants), whereas the reverse gender distribution is present for applications by producers.

When it comes to applications for grants within the state support systems for fiction films, the general pattern for the period of 2012–17 is the same.

The gaps between female and male scriptwriters and directors are even greater than under the New Danish Screen programme. This is especially the case among directors, with three out of four applicants being male, but almost the same disproportion is evident between male and female scriptwriters (Danish Film Institute 2018a). There is no difference between the percentage of male and female producers applying.

However, turning to applications for the funding of documentaries, the pattern is somewhat different. Three times as many women as men were granted funding under this programme overall (75 per cent vs 25 per cent). When it comes to producers' applications for development funding during the period of 2012–17, 63 per cent were women and 37 per cent men. As for applications for production grants, almost four out of five grants were given to women (79 per cent vs 21 per cent), with female producers being granted the most (for the 2010–15 figures, see Danish Film Institute 2016a). Moreover, in contrast to the sizes of grants awarded to fiction films in terms of development support for producers and production support for male directors and producers, female documentary filmmakers on average received more money in grants than did male applicants (Danish Film Institute 2018a: 27). A recent DFI report (2018a) concludes that 30 per cent of directors who were granted production support for fiction films in 2017 were women, whereas the same percentage for documentaries was 59 per cent: since 2014, the percentage of grants given to female documentary filmmakers has markedly exceeded the percentage of applications by female filmmakers.

Part of the explanation for this gender imbalance between documentary and fiction film is that during the entire period from 2003 to 2015, there were more male than female graduates emerging from the Danish Film School's fiction film line (71 per cent men vs 29 per cent women) and more female than male graduates from the documentary line (63 per cent women vs 37 per cent men).[3] It was against this backdrop that the four documentary filmmakers decided to join forces and create their production company together with producer Sigrid Dyekjær, who has produced all the films made by Krogh, Mulvad and Grønkjær in recent years, as well as most of the films made by Ambo. Ambo, Krogh and Mulvad knew each other from the Danish Film School, where the four directors had been part of a creative educational environment that supported partnerships, collaboration, mentoring and a dialogic feedback system. 'You really learn to collaborate during those four years', as Mikala Krogh put it in her conversation with Mette Hjort (2014: 188). This collaborative, dialogic and artistically inspiring culture has been transferred to Danish Documentary Productions. Moreover, the four directors have each established long-term collaboration with photographers and editors, which are also a result of networks established at film school. This is an advantage of coming from a small film nation, as the directors often emphasise.

Although Danish Documentary Production was established by five women, it was not a feminist endeavour. Mulvad describes it as a coincidence that they were five women (Redvall 2014b: 282). It was partly because the directors had all worked with the same producer, because of mutual dissatisfaction with the poor distribution of their internationally acclaimed films and because they were not receiving enough money for their films. 'The idea behind this company is to spend as much money as possible on actually making films', Krogh said, 'so it's quite simply really because it's all about giving the power back to the directors' (Hjort 2014: 202). Grønkjær likewise says: 'Our hope with this company is that the money that might otherwise have gone to a production company will end up going to the directors' (Redvall 2014a: 123). In addition, Sigrid Dyekjær lists the company's 'house rules': firstly, that they wanted from the start to make documentaries for the big screen; secondly, that each director should have her own camera; and thirdly, that the directors should research their films through the camera and pitch them in images instead of in writing: 'Back in 2003–2004, we were the first to make a three minute visual pilot – which is common today when you apply for money' (Jerslev 2018; see also Hjort, Chapter 16 in this volume).

'We do not have an editorial line', Dyekjær emphasises: 'What is important to us is whether the film is important to the directors and, besides, our interest in storytelling' (Jerslev 2018). This accords with Pernille Rose Grønkjær's statement that '[w]e really put a lot of effort into the story and are genuinely interested in being entertaining' (Redvall 2014a: 122). Moreover, Mulvad highlights the partnerships with cinematographers and editors who are working within both documentary and fiction film and are therefore engaged in discussing narration and artistic expressions, contributing to documentary 'the feel of a fiction film' (Redvall 2014b: 273).

Even though Dyekjær agrees with Mulvad that there was nothing to prevent a male documentarist from having been a co-founder of Danish Documentary Productions, she emphasises that the company's policies and its smooth functioning are connected with its all-female character (Jerslev 2018). It is company policy to actively remove obstacles to female documentary filmmakers' work – because 'otherwise: female documentary filmmakers stop making films':

> Documentary filmmaking is a very intensive and lonely creative process. You have to cut a whole story in your head but try to dig it out of reality and understand how to shape it. A lot of women also want to have children. My role as a producer is to help women combine the two. Many documentaries made by women would not happen if we producers would not create the right environment for them (Sigrid Dyekjær in Pham 2015b).

Even though the directors do not consider themselves feminists, they work actively to overcome obstacles for women to succeed in the business. Dyekjær takes pride in the fact that, at the company, 'we hire the men as the nannies' – 'for which we are also internationally renowned' (Jerslev 2018). With this remark, she refers to the company's hiring of Mikala Krogh's husband as a production assistant during the period when Krogh went to the Philippines to make *A Year of Hope* (2017): 'Basically he took care of the children, so that she could make a film'. The company also seeks to diminish the structural insecurities regarding employment in the industry and maintain sustainability as a business by pooling money to finance 'interim periods', the intervals between projects: 'How do you survive two years of nothing? But by pooling earnings, we are able to buy ourselves time' (Jerslev 2018). There have thus been strong creative, economic and organisational incentives for establishing Danish Documentary Production. In what follows, I consider the films made by Mulvad, Ambo, Krogh and Grønkjær – many of which have been produced by Dyekjær. In my discussion of the films, I include three focus points: the creation of presence, documentary aesthetics and themes.[4]

Documentary Moments of Encounter

In terms of the production process, in which a strong element of collective discussion characterises the company ethos, I would label the films made by the four directors as 'collective auteur films'. Yet, each director's films are different from those of the others, and each director has a distinct 'authorial identity' and mode of 'self-inscription' (Sayad 2013), which leads each of them to follow their own documentary vision when it comes to themes and aesthetics. Moreover, the four directors have each made very different films and performed authorship (see Sayad 2013) in very different ways over the years. They are, however, united in shared documentary interests and ways of addressing the world. They share a curiosity about reality and privilege, asking hard questions to get straight answers. Furthermore, they are – albeit in very different ways – engaged in staging *moments of encounter*, to borrow the term Stella Bruzzi uses to describe the essence of direct cinema (2002: 72). On the one hand, these moments of encounter are created by the various social actors' address to the filmmaker's off-screen presence and their inclusion of the filmmakers in their thoughts and world, not only as observers, but also as fellow human beings. Many of the films thus blur the boundaries between the framed world and that which is outside the frame, between the world of the social actors and the process of filming, embodied by the director and/ as cinematographer. On the other hand, moments of encounter can also take place between participants within the films, who discuss, talk, quarrel, or just sit together and think for themselves.

Accordingly, the moments of encounter are unlike direct cinema's moments 'when the filmmaking process disrupts and intrudes upon the reality of the world it is documenting' (Bruzzi 2002: 72). Rather than 'disrupting' and 'intruding', they demonstrate the connection between two parties who have come to know each other well over the course of the many months – even years – it takes to film a documentary: the woman with the camera and the social actors whose world she seeks to understand and who perform their reality in front of her. Accordingly, many of the films may be labelled 'performative' (Nichols 1995, Bruzzi 2002, Jerslev 2005, Sayad 2013). I do not use the term in the same manner as Nichols, to mean documentaries that 'deflect our attention from the referential quality of documentary altogether' (Nichols 1995: 93). I instead use it for films which simultaneously observe, are involved in and construct a narrative reality, a 'doing documentary' on the part of the filmmaker and the social actors alike, as they come together and create a referential quality through this very encounter (see Jerslev 2005). The embodied presence of the filmmaker – or the 'authorial self-inscription', as Cecilia Sayad (2013) would call it – is strongly felt in many of the directors' films, even when the filmmaker is not seen in the image frame. In contrast to the documentary films discussed by Sayad, the director never plays a central role in these films, but she is clearly communicated with and heard answering. A feeling of presence and intimacy is constructed through snippets of communication between a documentary character, who in a sense expands filmic space by addressing the filmmaker, and the often slightly delayed and mostly short responses from the director. This is a recurrent method of showing that 'doing documentary' basically means creating and filming an encounter between two parties who are interested in each other.

Phie Ambo claims in an interview with Eva Novrup Redvall (2014c: 32) that she 'wasn't at all interested in journalistic stories. I wanted my own voice to be included'. As a result, a prominent voice characterises all her films, regardless of whether they concern her own projects or other people's lives. In contrast to Mulvad's and Grønkjær's more restrained voices, Ambo often engages directly with her characters' actions and decisions in conversation and discussion, for example in *Family* (2001, made together with Sami Saif before she graduated from the Danish Film School), in which she is heard from behind the camera in the film's opening scene, trying to persuade her reluctant boyfriend to go to the national register in order to start the search for his absent father – which is the whole point of making the documentary. Likewise, in *Mechanical Love* (2007), she cautiously interrogates Japanese robotics scientist Hiroshi Ishiguru's experiment with exposing his daughter to a robot model of himself. But equally, in Pernille Rose Grønkjær's *The Monastery* (2006), *Love Addict* (2011) and *Den anden side* (*The Other Side*, 2017), as well as in Eva Mulvad's *Det gode liv* (*The Good Life*, 2010) and *A Modern Man* (2017), the directors are positioned by their social actors as interlocutors and faithful acquaintances, who are continuously present and to whom they can speak freely, almost as if no camera was present. The solitary, old Jørgen Laursen Vig in *The Monastery*, who is preparing his decaying castle for a visit by a group of Russian orthodox nuns who will decide whether the castle is usable as a monastery, seeks Grønkjær's advice as to which decorations nuns might like or dislike, whether the rooms are warm enough, and what to do about the sheets on the beds: 'Don't you have any opinion on that?' he asks the director directly.

Both the extremely popular Danish stand-up comedian Anders Matthesen in *Den anden side* and the internationally acclaimed violinist Charlie Siem in Mulvad's *A Modern Man* use the director to vent their frustrations and insecurities regarding their futures. This is the case even though Matthesen is surrounded by his family and people organising his tour, while for Siem the director and her camera seem to create a kind of stability in a life of constant travel from concert to concert. In Phie Ambo's portrait of the biodynamic farmer Niels Stokholm in *Så meget godt i vente* (*Good Things Await*, 2014), as she films the difficult labour of a cow giving birth to a bull calf, Stokholm at one point says: 'Couldn't you drop that camera and come here and help?' At this point Ambo immediately and obediently abandons her position behind the camera. In Ambo's philosophical science film . . . *Når du kigger væk* (. . . *When You Look Away*, 2017), in which she initially asks how we can understand consciousness and whether our mind can be in several places at once, Buddhist monk, doctor and scientist Bhikkhu Samahita interrupts a conversation with poet and theoretical physicist Astri Kleppe concerning the relationship between subjectivity and conscience, turns toward Ambo and asks her: 'What do you think? What is consciousness?' Ambo replies: 'Well, I don't know, and this was exactly the reason why I decided to make this film'.

Likewise, in Mulvad's *The Good Life*, which presents the portrait of a mother and a daughter who once lived a life of luxury thanks to a large inheritance but are now completely broke and do not know what to do, the film continuously shows scenes in which the daughter aggressively accuses the mother of never having prepared her for the present situation. After a particularly heated outburst, which ends with the daughter slamming the door, the mother, who rarely defends herself, turns to Mulvad and confides resignedly that 'this is how it goes very often'. The same confidence is performed in Mikala Krogh's behind-the-scenes portrait of a Danish tabloid, *Ekstra Bladet uden for citat* (*The Newsroom: Off the Record*, 2014), when the inexperienced trainee journalist puts down her telephone and, somewhat shocked, turns toward Krogh, telling her that *Ekstra Bladet* is going to be sued for bad conduct because of an article she wrote. Finally, in Mulvad's *Den sidste dans* (*The Last Dance*, 2005) which takes place in an old-age home in which the inhabitants include her in their lives, thoughts, fears and failures of memory, one of the women orders Mulvad to film her grandson on his motor bike as he leaves following a visit. She then asks Mulvad, 'did you get it', as if the elderly woman herself were the director. These documentary moments of encounter thus employ a range of moods and always create a sense of the presence of an embodied director, even though she is mostly neither seen nor heard.

THEMES AND DOCUMENTARY FILM AESTHETICS EXPANDED

'I'd always been fascinated with people who are a bit apart from society and live in their own world', says Eva Mulvad (in Knegt 2010). What unites Mulvad's films is an interest in human beings situated at a threshold, whether it be the elderly people approaching death in the old-age home in *The Last Dance* or the trial against a young man charged with having murdered his best friend with a samurai sword in *Med døden til følge (Death as a Consequence*, 2011). The portraits of Charlie Siem and the lonely, desperately longing love addicts in Grønkjær's *Love Addict* (2011) also concern being 'a bit apart from society', albeit in different ways. Another group of films portray idealists, such as Afghan politician Malalai Joya in *Enemies of Happiness* (2006) and her struggle to gain election to the Afghan parliament as a woman, in the face of constant death threats; Mr Vig in *The Monastery*, who fights to achieve his dream of transforming the run-down castle into a convent; and Niels Stokholm in Ambo's *Good Things Await*, who despite being fined by the certified ecological authorities, fights for his right to use the biodynamic methods he believes to be best when it comes to protecting nature and animals. Mikala Krogh's films about a group of women who try to solve garbage disposal problems in a Cairo neighbourhood in *Cairo skrald (Cairo Garbage*, 2009) falls into this group of films as well.

In a third group of films, mostly made by Phie Ambo (*Mechanical Love, Free the Mind* [2012] and . . . *When You Look Away*), but also by Pernille Rose Grønkjær (*Genetic Me*, 2014), Ambo and, in *Genetic Me*, Danish science journalist Lone Frank embark on a quest for answers to abstract and existential questions about definitions of robots and humans, the brain, the body and the mind, as well as the role that genes play in determining our lives. These films are characterised by their personal points of departure – for instance, a question asked by Ambo's child or Lone Frank's quest for self-understanding. Moreover, characteristic of the films is their deployment of a sensual visual language to explore these philosophical questions. A final group of films turns toward broader societal questions such as Mikala Krogh's participation in a series of documentaries about infrastructural problems in the world's largest cities (*Cairo Garbage*) and a film about a social project to help Filipino boys escape the streets of Manila (*A Year of Hope*, 2017). There are also films about social conflicts in Denmark, such as Phie Ambo's slightly satirical depiction of community mediation of neighbourly disputes in *Hjemmefronten – fjenden bag hækken (The Home Front*, 2010) and about the bailiff in action in *Kongens foged – sat på gaden (Royal Bailiff: Out on the Street*, 2012).

Besides funding from the Danish Film Institute, many of the directors' films are made with financial support from the Danish public service provider DR and broadcast on television. However, all four directors and their producer have been interested in making documentaries for cinema screenings as well and in expanding the visual confines of documentary aesthetics; consequently, their endeavour has translated into a variety of aesthetic expressions. Parts of Grønkjær's *Love Addict* employ thriller aesthetics (Redvall 2014a: 119), as well as dream-like staged scenes. Ambo uses simple, almost child-like animation in her later films to provide accessible illustrations of the complex philosophical questions that her films are exploring. Eva Mulvad creates a kind of Armani advertisement aesthetics in *A Modern Man*, in the scene in which Charles Siem himself is posing for an Armani ad. The most intimate and grittiest aesthetics are used in Mikala Krogh's *Beths dagbog* (*Beth's Diary*, 2006), in which the drug addict Beth in part has filmed herself confiding to the camera her story of a life of prostitution, drugs and fear of committing to her relationship with her boyfriend. However, the film is made in collaboration with Swedish photographer Kent Klich who has followed Beth for a couple of decades, and Klich's black-and-white photos are delicately animated and interspersed with the video diary recordings. Photography, animation and video recordings thus work together to create a mix of portrait and self-portrait. Beth is simultaneously seen from the outside and the inside, and a poetic layer is added to her harsh story, thereby supporting the love story and the slight hope she dares to express.

In contrast, the most explicitly performative documentary is Phie Ambo's *. . . When You Look Away*, the director's personal 'research project' (Dam 2018) into whether we have a consciousness apart from the body and how this question relates to quantum physics and her daughter's occasional feeling of being an animal. The film in a sense encapsulates many of the preoccupations of this group of directors: the personal quest for knowledge, expressing curiosity, asking questions, being open to the world and taking nothing for granted, exploring documentary film storytelling and imagery. Ambo allows the film to be formed by coincidences, lets knowledgeable people come to her instead of seeking them out herself and listens to all of them with an open mind. Ultimately, the film ends up focusing on water. It transforms into a portrait of the power and mystery of water and of the mind, emphasised by recurrent, almost abstract close-ups of water in different shapes, movements and colours. Similarly, the simple animated sketches of the people whom Ambo encounters offer no definite answers regarding the workings of the mind, even if the meetings have been truly mind-blowing. Aesthetically, then, many of the directors' films can be labelled *portraits*, at least in art historian Cynthia Freeland's (2010) understanding of the term as dialogic encounters, the collaborative combination of authorial self-inscription and performance. Moreover, Freeland stresses that portraits are 'proofs of presence or

Figure 17.1 A portrait of an ageing farmer in Phie Ambo's *Så meget godt i vente* (*Good Things Await*, 2014). Framegrab.

Figure 17.2 A very different ageing face in Pernille Rose Grønkjær's *The Monastery: Mr Vig and the Nun* (2006). Framegrab.

"contact"' (Freeland 2010: 74), which is another way of labelling documentary moments of encounter.

Conclusion

The contemplative close-ups of ageing faces in Mulvad's *The Last Dance*, Grønkjær's *The Monastery* and Ambo's *Good Things Await* tell rich but unfathomable stories of long lives lived and invite the audience 'to think about the other's thinking' (Cowie 2011: 93). Similarly, the curiosity and desire to understand that seem to drive the various documentary projects which have emerged from the creative, authorially supportive and collaborative environment at Danish Documentary Productions – and from the directors even before the founding of the company – is not rooted in a wish to prove, but instead in a desire to understand, in a desire to avoid preconceptions and seek out questions about people, their thinking and their worlds. This curiosity gives rise to a range of approaches, stories and journeys; to encounters with idealists who want to make the world a better place, with artists, scientists and ordinary people; with affective outbursts, contemplative moments and talk; with people who desire to communicate. From the interviews with Danish Documentary Production's directors and producer, it is evident that discussions and mutual support for ongoing projects are essential to the company's working environment. Moreover, because this is an all-female company, the general gendered imbalance in the film industry has been consciously attended to, so that the financial means for supporting family life across the long periods of filmmaking are integrated into the production budget. Hence, Danish Documentary Production's female filmmakers – producer Sigrid Dyekjær and directors Mikala Krogh, Eva Mulvad, Pernille Rose Grønkjær and, until 2014, Phie Ambo – have through a combination of talent, training from the Danish Film School, creative curiosity and a strong company ethos managed to create a vibrant company, produce important documentary films and achieve international recognition.

Interview

Jerslev, A. (2018), Personal interview with Sigrid Dyekjær in Danish Documentary Production's office in Copenhagen, December 21.

Notes

1. Co-founder and director Phie Ambo left the firm as an owner in 2014, in order to establish together with her husband the Green Free School, which focuses on sustainability at all levels. She is still closely connected with Danish Documentary Production.
2. Pernille Rose Grønkjær graduated from the first two-year documentary line; the other four attended the four-year line.
3. The general numbers are very small: the Danish Film School has only enrolled six students in each line every other year.
4. Many of the directors' films have original English titles, probably because of their ambition to secure international distribution. Films produced by Danish Documentary Production since the time of writing (2019) can be explored at https://www.danishdocumentary.com

18. WELCOME TO DENMARK: IMMIGRANTS AND THEIR DESCENDANTS IN DANISH CINEMA

Eva Jørholt

On 1 July 2018, twenty-year-old Jens Philip Yazdani, former president of Danske Gymnasieelevers Sammenslutning (National Association of Danish High School Students), watched the FIFA World Cup match between Denmark and Croatia on a giant screen at the Roskilde music festival, amid thousands of cheering Danish fans. Being a Dane, Yazdani wanted to cheer along with the crowd, only he suddenly felt nauseated: 'How could I stand there, deeply immersed in the match, and alternately fear and cheer for Denmark – this Denmark that shits on, denigrates and vilifies me and my people on a daily basis?' (Yazdani 2018a). Yazdani – who was born in Denmark to a Danish mother and an Iranian father – later went on to explain how the Danish political debate on immigration and the increasingly harsh policies towards citizens with an immigrant background have made him, and people like him, feel unwanted in Denmark:

> We all feel that our very presence in Denmark is problematised by the country's leaders. 'Immigration is a burden that is bringing the country to its knees; a disaster; an error that must be corrected'. And the people they talk about are me, my dad and all the rest of us. As problems – *the* problem – for our society. These are not just abstract political issues, but real people, in flesh and blood. For whom such an attitude has real consequences (Yazdani 2018b).

In order to better understand Yazdani's nausea, let's take a brief look at Danish immigration policies. Overall, immigration to Denmark follows the pattern of most Western European countries: invitation of foreign manual labour for the construction of the welfare state during the 1960s; a halt to labour immigration in the mid-1970s due to high unemployment rates in the wake of the oil crisis but, nonetheless, a steadily increasing number of immigrants entering the country owing primarily to family reunification and the reception of refugees from various international conflict zones (see, for example, Bjerre et al. 2019: 2).

Unlike neighbouring Sweden, which since the 1970s has had a multiculturalist approach to immigration, the official policy of shifting Danish governments has been one of assimilation. Immigration was not at the top of the 1970s political agenda, but that changed in the early 1980s when Mogens Glistrup, the leader of the populist, far-right Fremskridtspartiet (Progress Party), called for a 'Mohammadanian-free' Denmark. While his opinions were considered extreme by most Danes back then (see, for example, Bergmann 2017), the idea that Muslims are not welcome in Denmark stuck with the Progress Party's successor, Dansk Folkeparti (Danish People's Party), which has played a pivotal role in Danish politics since its creation in 1995 (see, for example, Christiansen 2016). Even though the Danish People's Party has distanced itself from the Progress Party's explicit racism, its main political objective is to 'keep Denmark on the right track' and 'safeguard our values, tradition and culture' (Dansk Folkeparti 2020). Maintaining immigration at an absolute minimum and making sure that those 'foreigners' who have nevertheless succeeded in establishing themselves in Denmark will adopt all aspects of the Danish way of life are the chief strategies to reach this goal. At the 2015 general elections, the Danish People's Party obtained 21.1 per cent of the vote, which made it the second-largest party in parliament (see, for example, Bergmann 2017). Paradoxically, perhaps, the fact that the party's share of the vote was drastically reduced to a mere 8.7 per cent at the 2019 elections only testifies to its success in influencing the entire political spectrum, left and right, who in recent years have followed the Danish People's Party's xenophobic lead and tried to surpass each other in ever harsher immigration policies. And, in a reaction to this mainstreaming of the party's anti-immigrant line, new and even more extreme right-wing nationalist parties such as Nye Borgerlige (The New Right) and Stram Kurs (Hard Line) have come to the fore, thus challenging the Danish People's Party from the right as well (see, for example, Jupskås 2019).

It is against this background – and the resultant legislation (Abend 2019), including a ban on burqas and niqabs, a 'ghetto law' which, among other things, doubles the penalty for offences committed in those socially vulnerable areas where many immigrants live, in addition to a plan to isolate rejected asylum-seekers on a deserted island – that one should see Yazdani's feeling of ambivalence towards his native country.

This chapter will discuss whether Danish cinema can be said to contribute towards making Yazdani and people like him feel more welcome in Denmark, and to which extent, if at all, the 'official' Danish attitude towards immigrants and their descendants is reflected in the way they are portrayed in the country's cinematic output.

Danish Immigration Cinema: A Brief Historical Overview

As the vast majority of Danish films representing immigrants are made by filmmakers who have no immigration background themselves, the following will rely on the concept of 'immigration cinema' as defined by Isolina Ballesteros: 'a thematic, wide-ranging category that [. . .] refers to the variety of films that depict and address the lives and identities of both first-generation immigrants and children of the diaspora, whether they are authored by immigrants themselves or by white Europeans' (Ballesteros 2015: 14). Also, it should be noted that the chapter's main focus will be on immigrants (and their descendants) from non-Western countries, not only because they are the ones who are at the heart of the heated debate on immigration to Denmark, but also because Danish immigration cinema is predominantly concerned with this group, with a few asides to immigrants from Southern or Eastern Europe.

With a single exception – the film *Gæstearbejdere* (*Guest Workers*, Voja Miladinovic, 1968) about an illegal Yugoslav immigrant's encounter with a sexually liberated but largely cold and unwelcoming Denmark – post-World War II immigrants first made their appearance in Danish feature films in the late 1970s, typically in minor parts with little or no dialogue, and when they did speak, their accent or limited command of the Danish language was usually emphasised. An example of this is provided by Astrid Henning-Jensen's *Vinterbørn* (*Winter-Born*, 1978), an adaptation of Dea Trier Mørch's eponymous novel about a group of women in a maternity ward. The characters are carefully selected so as to represent a microcosm of the (female) Danish population at the time, which, interestingly, includes a Turkish woman, Habiba, who has recently joined her husband in Denmark. Habiba does not speak a word of either Danish or English, but the women succeed in communicating through sign language, and Habiba is admitted as a natural part of the little community of women.

Another early case in point is *Firmaskovturen* (*The Factory Outing*, John Hilbard, 1978) – a comedy about a group of colleagues who go on a company picnic and soon get extremely drunk. Among them is a young Greek named Georgius (sic) who does not partake in the general drinking and, at the end of the day, is the only one who manages to maintain a certain amount of dignity.

Not only does Georgius function as a wholesome counterpoint to a dubious Danish alcohol culture, but he is also singled out as different from his colleagues in the way that he is discriminated against by his male colleagues and wooed by the women. In this latter respect, the film thus initiates what was later to become a kind of trend in Danish immigration cinema: the depiction of immigrants as presenting a certain exotic attractiveness.

What stands out, however, is that in the 1970s, immigrants were not – yet – represented as a problem, and to the extent that their 'difference' was highlighted at all, it was only insofar as they had a somewhat darker complexion, did not speak Danish fluently and, in the case of *The Factory Outing*, did not adhere to Danish drinking habits. And as for *Winter-Born*, it arguably made a point of emphasising Habiba's human sameness in regard to the other women, rather than her difference from them.

While immigrants were still very sparsely represented in Danish cinema during the 1980s, the end of the decade saw the release of two films that gave some prominence to immigrant characters: Erik Clausen's *Rami og Julie* (*Rami and Juliet*, 1988), a magical realist transposition of Shakespeare's *Romeo and Juliet* to a suburban housing estate which provides the setting for a doomed romance between blonde Dane Julie and Palestinian refugee Rami; and *17 op* (*Sally's Bizniz*, Brita Wielopolska, 1989), a bleak social realist depiction of life in yet another concrete desert, focusing on the friendship between Sally, a destitute but entrepreneurial Danish teenager, and headscarf-wearing Turkish Zuhal – a friendship that comes to an abrupt halt, however, when Zuhal is shipped off to Turkey and a forced marriage.

Through their respective stories of love and friendship between a Dane and an immigrant, both films can be said to foreground the point already made by *Winter-Born* – namely, that at a basic human and individual level native Danes and immigrants can get along very well. At the same time, however, the stories of both films are inserted into a context of violent (neo-Nazi) xenophobia that was completely absent from the 1970s films. If the two films clearly distance themselves from any anti-immigrant sentiment and even voice some criticism of Danish immigration policies, it should be noted that they also, each in their own way, contribute to an understanding of insurmountable cultural differences between Danes and immigrants – in *Sally's Bizniz* primarily through the issue of forced marriage, in *Rami and Juliet* arguably through the very choice of Shakespeare's play and the transformation of the original family feud into a clash of cultures.

While the Romeo and Juliet motif was carried on in later films such as *Halalabad Blues* (Helle Ryslinge, 2002), *Fighter* (Natasha Arthy, 2007) and Pernille Fischer Christensen's short *Habibti min elskede* (*Habibti My Love*, 2002), all of which also touch on the issue of forced marriage, the 1990s saw the advent of yet another – and, as it turned out, particularly robust – trope in

Danish immigration cinema: the criminal immigrant. First was Nicolas Winding Refn's *Pusher* (1995) in which Croatian-born Zlatko Buric played a Yugoslav drug lord in Copenhagen's shady underworld, a role that Refn and Buric later extended and deepened in the third film of the trilogy, *Pusher III* (2005). Meanwhile, Ole Christian Madsen took up so-called 'second-generation immigrants' in the short *Sinans bryllup* (*Sinan's Wedding*, 1997) and, two years later, in the feature *Pizza King* which is set in Nørrebro, a particularly multi-ethnic part of Copenhagen, and portrays a motley group of youngsters who engage in petty crime and are largely stuck between their parents' traditional culture and Danish 'modernity'.

'The criminal immigrant' was to return in a number of films ranging from (social) realist depictions in the vein of *Pizza King* – for instance, *1:1* (Annette K. Olesen, 2006) which despite its attempt at problematising the trope arguably sustains it, in that the falsely accused Tareq actually has a criminal record – to a string of what can perhaps be best termed 'juvenile bad boy comedies' such as *I Kina spiser de hunde* (*In China They Eat Dogs*, 1999) and *Gamle mænd i nye biler* (*Old Men in New Cars*, 2002), both of which were directed by Lasse Spang Olsen and written by Anders Thomas Jensen, as well as, to some extent, the latter's own *Adams æbler* (*Adam's Apples*, 2005). The juvenile bad boy comedies typically feature lowlife, rather dumb and unsuccessful (white) small-time crooks who bully an even dumber immigrant and fight a heavily stereotyped rival immigrant gang who wear ostentatious gold chains and drive potent BMWs.

A Politically Incorrect Cinema?

Despite the undeniable fact that some immigrants and their descendants do turn to crime and that forced marriage does exist in some immigrant families, all of these films can, especially when combined, be criticised for bolstering exactly those kinds of xenophobic stereotypes that are, arguably, at the heart of the widespread Danish opposition to immigration.

While forced marriage is also a theme in Swedish immigration cinema – for example in the immensely popular comedy *Jalla! Jalla!* (Josef Fares, 2000) – the 'bad immigrant' trope has been much less prominent in Sweden where, overall, negative representations of immigrants have been deemed inappropriate. According to Swedish film scholar Olof Hedling, Swedish cinema has mainly depicted immigrants in accordance with the country's official multicultural and anti-racist stance – that is, they have, in general, been taken seriously and presented as an overall enrichment of Swedish culture, yet also to some extent as victims of discrimination and ethnocentrism (Hedling 2007). Against this background, Hedling sees Swedish immigration cinema as (too) politically correct.

On the other hand, Danish cultural sociologist Mehmet Ümit Necef praises Thomas Vinterberg's *Festen* (*The Celebration*, 1998) for being the only politically correct Danish film seen from an immigrant point of view (Necef 2003: 184), presumably because a black character, Gbatokai, who attends the film's cataclysmic birthday party is depicted neither as victim nor as 'bad immigrant'. And in what, to my knowledge, is the only investigation of what actual immigrants think of Danish immigration cinema, Golrang Ranjbar's survey among Iranian immigrants (Ranjbar 2015), the respondents point to another Vinterberg character, the protagonist's girlfriend Nadja in *Jagten* (*The Hunt*, 2012), as the only 'normal' (that is, non-stereotypical) immigrant character which they have encountered in Danish feature films (Ranjbar 2015: 45).

It can, however, be argued that many of the 'politically incorrect' Danish films, especially the juvenile bad boy comedies, actually aim to undermine the 'bad immigrant' stereotype through irony and exaggeration. As the white Danish characters in these films are typically as one-dimensional and stereotyped as the immigrants – dumb, weak, self-righteous and often violent, especially towards immigrants – the films can be said to present a humorous but severe critique of the overall Danish attitude to immigrants. Yet, stereotypes are not easily subverted, for, as argued by Mireille Rosello (1998), they feed on repetition; from the point of view of the stereotype, it does not matter much whether it is caricatured or just reiterated. Danish immigration films like these are thus walking a tightrope between the politically correct and its opposite, for if they do attempt to undermine immigrant stereotypes, they also risk reinforcing them.

Not unlike Swedish as well as (the early phases of) British and German immigration cinema, many Danish films do, however, also present immigrants and their descendants as victims – of discrimination, exclusion and, especially, their own or their parents' traditional culture and religion – which is another point of criticism raised by the Iranian immigrants in Ranjbar's survey. While the respondents' own lives in Denmark had not been without difficulties, they had also experienced happiness and good moments, but they did not find any instances of the latter in Danish immigration cinema. In this respect, the Danish films come close to the 1970s and 1980s British 'cinema of duty' (Malik 1996) and German *Kino der Betroffenen* ('cinema of the affected', Burns 2007), both of which were 'frequently criticised for reducing their protagonists to stereotypes, portraying the migrant as victim and focusing excessively on conflict of an intercultural or intracultural kind' (Burns 2007: 3). But whereas British and German immigration cinemas largely moved on to celebrate cultural and ethnic hybridity from the 1990s onwards, the vast majority of Danish films on immigrants and their descendants continued to reduce their protagonists to either stereotypes or victims, or both.

Filmmakers with an Immigration Background

Thus far, all the films under consideration here were made by Danish filmmakers with no personal experience of migration, but, as Ole Christian Madsen has rightly pointed out, 'the problem was that nobody else was making films about immigrants' (in Hjort et al. 2010: 162). Barring the above-mentioned film *Guest Workers* and, since the 1980s, some short films, mostly workshop productions, immigrants in Denmark did not really get their own filmic voices until the 2000s – decades after their counterparts in the UK, Germany and Sweden (cf. Malik 1996, Burns 2007, and Hedling 2007).

Most of the recent Danish filmmakers with immigration background were born abroad and brought to Denmark by their parents at a very early age. As such they all have an intimate knowledge of Denmark, as well as of what it feels like to either *be* or be treated as an immigrant. Some of them studied at the National Danish Film School, others at the alternative film school Super 16, while a third group is self-taught, but they all typically work within low-budget formats, in most cases subsidised not by the Danish Film Institute's primary support schemes, but by the talent development programme New Danish Screen which is devoted to the production of low-budget films, fiction as well as non-fiction (see Hjort, Chapter 16 in this volume).

First out was *Ma salama Jamil* (*Go With Peace Jamil*, 2008) by Omar Shargawi who was born in Denmark to a Danish mother and a father who had fled Palestine in 1948. Like the self-taught Shargawi's subsequent films – the documentary *Fra Haifa til Nørrebro* (*My Father from Haifa*, 2010), in which the filmmaker persuades his father to revisit Palestine; ½ *Revolution* (2011), a personal documentary about the Arab Spring uprising in Egypt; the feature film *Al Medina* (2015), in which Shargawi plays a Danish Arab who plans to settle in the Middle East with his pregnant Danish wife but is sucked into a maelstrom of evil; and his most recent documentary *Western Arabs* (2019) that once more revolves around his father's background – *Go With Peace Jamil* is about Arabs living in the West and the Middle Eastern history, culture and traditions that they carry with them. *Go With Peace Jamil* tells the story of a young Danish Arab who is caught up in the ancient war between Sunni and Shi'a Muslims as it plays out in present-day Copenhagen – a Copenhagen whose physical aspects are made barely recognisable through colour grading and tight framings, and where the Danish language plays second fiddle to Arabic. While this powerful drama won six prizes at international festivals, it was accused by some Danish observers, including Birgitte Rahbek in the newspaper *Information*, of reinforcing prejudices about Arabs by depicting them in a way that 'fits perfectly into the image many Danes already have of them' (Rahbek 2008). She could be right, but it could also be argued that the very wording of her criticism contributes to widening the gap between a Danish 'us' and an immigrant 'them', a gap to which Shargawi himself drew attention in an interview he gave on the occasion of the premiere of *Western Arabs*, but from the point of view of an Arab in Denmark:

> It's tough, because you don't really fit in anywhere. To an Arab, you'll always be Danish. And to a Dane, you'll always be Arab. That's just the way it is. You just have to get used to not fitting into any of the categories and accept that you're an outsider (Larsen 2019).

Next to Shargawi, Fenar Ahmad – who was born in Czechoslovakia after his parents had fled their native Iraq and then brought to Denmark in 1986, at the age of five – is the most experienced of these new filmmakers. Ahmad graduated in 2010 from the Super 16 film school and has since directed two relatively successful films, the low-budget rap film *Ækte vare* (*Flow*, 2014) and the high-octane action thriller *Underverden* (*Darkland*, 2017) which was produced by Nordisk Film. Unlike Shargawi, Ahmad's focus is first and foremost on the concept of integration, particularly as it applies to the 'second generation'. Indeed, integration was already the topic of *Den perfekte muslim* (*The Perfect Muslim*, 2009) – a documentary he made while still in film school – in which a professional survey company investigates what the term 'integration' actually means in the eyes of 'indigenous' and so-called 'new' Danes, respectively. Unsurprisingly, Danishness and integration are very diversely defined, both within and between the two groups. This insight may have been the starting point for *Flow*, which turns most preconceived notions about 'them' and 'us' upside down: it is, for instance, about a white rapper who looks like a skinhead but is an integral part of a multi-ethnic group of youths in a suburban housing estate that has the air of an idyllic allotment garden (see Jørholt 2020). And in *Darkland*, the Iraqi-born Danish actor Dar Salim – who made his breakthrough in *Go With Peace Jamil* – plays a yuppie heart surgeon who has severed all ties to his immigrant family. When, however, his younger brother is killed by a gang of criminals from the concrete suburb where his parents still live, the surgeon is transformed into a dark avenger. If a heart surgeon with an immigration background does present a radical break with the usual immigrant stereotypes, it could be argued that Ahmad's recurrent focus on (more or less) criminal gangs contributes to nourishing the 'bad immigrant' trope. His latest film, *Valhalla* (2019), however, represents a new departure for Ahmad, based as it is on Norse mythology.

Charmøren (*The Charmer*, 2017), the first feature film by Iranian-born Milad Alami, is an arthouse film about an Iranian immigrant, Esmail, who persistently tries to seduce Danish women in order to obtain an official Danish partner who can be his ticket to a residence permit. Alami, who arrived in Sweden at the age of seven and has been living in Denmark since 2007, graduated from the Danish National Film School in 2011. While *The Charmer* does address the issue of immigration and the stereotype of the 'exotic Other', it does so in a fashion that does not pit immigrants against 'indigenous Danes' but rather focuses on the desperation that may lead (in this case) an Iranian to engage in what really amounts to prostitution. At the same time, however, the film also distinguishes itself by offering those instances of happiness and good moments within the Iranian community in Denmark which the Iranian respondents in Ranjbar's survey (2015) found to be lacking in Danish immigration cinema up to that point.

Ali Abbasi, another Iranian-born director, has followed much the same trajectory as Alami; he even graduated from the Danish Film School the same year. Abbasi's first feature film, *Shelley* (2016), however, has nothing in common with *The Charmer*. It is a horror film about a young Scandinavian couple living in a remote Swedish forest (without electricity or running water) who hire a Romanian girl as their housemaid and eventually pay her to carry the couple's child. If the film pays clear homage to the romantic Gothic tradition, it can also be interpreted as a (metaphoric) reflection on the treatment of guest workers as disposable tools.

Mens vi lever (*While We Live*, 2017), on the other hand, is an intense existential drama. It is the debut film of the so-called Avaz Brothers – Mehdi (director), Milad (script writer) and Misam (producer) – who were born in Iran but have lived in Denmark since their early childhood. Compared to the other filmmakers mentioned here, the Avaz Brothers stand out in several ways: they neither attended any kind of film school, nor did they receive any kind of public financial support for *While We Live*. In addition, the film does not address immigration at all and has no 'brown' characters, barring a medical doctor in a tiny part. It is indeed a very 'Danish' film, with blue summer skies, rolling wheat fields and a score by Bent Fabricius-Bjerre, who to many Danes stands out as *the* national Danish film composer. The film's style, however, owes more to Hollywood than to traditional Danish realism, an approach that the brothers carried on in their second film, *Kollision* (*Collision*, 2019), which, again, is not about immigration at all but can more aptly be described as a 'white' Danish family melodrama, this time supported by a budget of roughly 1 million Euros from the Danish Film Institute.

Similarly, May el-Toukhy, who was born in Denmark to a Danish mother and an Egyptian father, does not address immigration in her films – at least as it pertains to immigrants from non-Western countries. Her latest film, the Oscar-shortlisted drama *Dronningen* (*Queen of Hearts*, 2019) does contain a Swedish character living in Denmark, but his status as an immigrant is never highlighted.

By contrast, *Danmarks sønner* (*Sons of Denmark*, 2019) by Dar Salim's younger brother Ulaa Salim (who was born in Denmark) provides the most

WELCOME TO DENMARK

Figure 18.1 Ulaa Salim's *Danmarks sønner* (*Sons of Denmark*, 2019) offers a frightening and visually stunning vision of a future marred by extreme nationalism. Framegrab.

unrelenting portrait thus far of the effects of extreme nationalism, not only on Denmark's immigrant communities, but also on the country at large. Set in 2025, it depicts a deeply polarised Danish society in which harassment of Danes with an immigration background has become normalised, to the extent that even Ali, a fully integrated policeman working undercover to prevent violence on both sides, is targeted by white nationalists. In the end, he comes to doubt whether his choice to protect Danish society and Danish values was the right one.

Towards Increased Inclusion?

To sum up, it is clear that something new is taking place in Danish immigration cinema right now. Until very recently, the cinematic depiction of immigrants was mainly in tune with the 'official' Danish attitude towards immigration, from the generally benign welcoming of the newcomers in the 1970s through the following decades' consistent othering of immigrants and their descendants. To the extent that Danes with an immigration background saw these films at all, they will hardly have felt like an integral part of the Denmark depicted on screen; rather, the films are likely to have made them feel even less wanted in Denmark.

Today, however, Danish cinema appears to be in the process of parting ways with the current, increasingly hateful political discourse against immigration and 'foreigners'. While a report on ethnic diversity published by the Danish Film Institute in 2015 made clear that Danish cinema did not reflect the multi-ethnic composition of Danish society, a second report from November 2018 shows considerably more encouraging results. Whereas there is still room for improvement, the number of what the reports refer to as 'new Danes' (that is, according to the DFI, Danes of a 'different ethnic origin', whether immigrants themselves or descendants) working both behind and in front of the camera has increased significantly since 2015, and the percentage of 'new Danes' watching Danish films is now almost equal to the rest of the population (Danish Film Institute 2018b).

It could be taken as a further sign of inclusion that the scope of subject-matter addressed by filmmakers 'with an immigration background' has widened to include topics unrelated to immigration. While this could also be seen as an expression of assimilation taken to the extreme, it is probably more reasonable to understand it as a recognition of these directors as, simply, directors rather than 'immigrant filmmakers', on the part of the Danish Film Institute as well as in the eyes of the directors themselves.

A cause for concern, however, are the generally dismal box office results obtained by their work. Except for Ahmad's two feature films *Flow* and *Darkland* which sold 32,868 and 180,643 tickets, respectively, as well as *While We Live* (100,150 tickets) and *Collision* (241,385 tickets), these films have been seen by remarkably few Danes: from 5,310 in the case of *Go With Peace Jamil* to a mere 448 for *Shelley* (Danish Film Institute 2020). By way of comparison, the internationally acclaimed *En kongelig affære* (*A Royal Affair*, Nikolaj Arcel, 2012) sold 515,000 tickets in Danish cinemas. This lack of popularity may be due primarily to the low-budget and/or art film format of most of these works – formats that rarely attract large audiences (Lars von Trier's *The House that Jack Built* [2018], for example, sold fewer than 30,000 tickets), especially when designed to 'push the boundaries of cinema' which is the declared aim of New Danish Screen. The relative success of *Darkland* and *Collision* suggests that this may indeed be the case, and that if more of these new directors were given the chance to work with more substantial production budgets, their box office results might improve significantly.

Yet, the reason for the modest numbers of tickets sold may also be that the majority of Danes are simply not curious about films that, in one way or the other, reflect Denmark as a multi-ethnic society. If that is so, one may fear that films by directors 'with an immigration background' – even when they do not take up the subject of immigration in their work – will remain 'ghettoised' as a kind of niche cinema mainly for 'new Danes', whereas 'old Danes' will find their cinematic thrills elsewhere. While the increasing ethnic diversity in Danish cinema may contribute to making Jens Philip Yazdani and others like him feel more welcome in Denmark, audience segregation of this sort is hardly helpful.

19. DIRTY FILMS: GRIMY MATERIALISM AND ECOLOGICAL AESTHETICS

Benjamin Bigelow

Ecology has become an increasingly crucial critical lens to use as one considers contemporary film and media. This is especially true in the Nordic region, where a sense of environmental urgency, activism and state-supported sustainability initiatives have become pillars of a powerful regional identity based on an exceptional commitment to environmental causes in the Nordic societies. Within the Nordics, Denmark has been at the forefront of sustainable energy development, investing in massive offshore wind farms as early as 1991, well before broad international consensus on the urgency of such initiatives had been reached. This move to wind energy in Denmark has been part of a larger national energy strategy that aims to reach 100 per cent renewable electricity by 2035 and to cover all of its energy needs in all sectors through renewable sources by 2050. This Nordic 'environmental exceptionalism' (Hennig et al. 2018: 5) is not free from nuance, of course, as realities such as Finland's nuclear energy program and Norway's long-time economic dependence on petroleum exports suggest. Despite these inconsistencies and mixed records on environmentalism, the Nordic region's worldwide reputation as leaders in global efforts to combat environmental degradation is as solid as ever.

As ecological awareness and climate activism have become matters of extreme urgency, such perspectives have therefore also become crucial aesthetic and critical tools in contemporary film culture. In the face of pressing global urgency on climate change, terms such as environmental film studies, ecocriticism and ecocinema[1] have all become notable (though still not dominant) modes of scholarship over the last decade. There are differences in terms of intellectual priorities and political intents within these academic fields, but one fundamental premise from which they all proceed is the inseparability of 'nature' and 'culture'. While the most fundamentalist forms of poststructuralism and postmodernism tend to treat culture as part of an isolated, self-contained domain, ecocritical approaches all proceed from the same premise as the broader field of cultural materialism, by dissolving the supposedly impermeable boundaries between culture and nature. Cultural artefacts (such as films) are therefore subject to the same material forces as any other material object, so art can never be fully severed from the material context of its production or reception. Films of today are produced within a context of rapid ecological change and a global awareness of (possibly unavoidable) environmental catastrophe. Like any other cultural objects, films made in such conditions will be inherently marked by that pronounced ecological awareness (and perhaps even marked in disavowal of material concerns). By the same token, films produced many years before such concerns became widespread are currently *received* within that same climate of heightened ecological awareness. For instance, an ecocritical lens allows us to see the underlying ecological implications of Swede Arne Sucksdorff's remarkable documentaries of the 1940s and 1950s. Films like *Vinden från väster* (*Wind from the West*, 1942) or *Människor i stad* (*Rhythm of a City*, 1947) are revealed as more than poetic ruminations on human habitation and place, and can instead be seen as highlighting and documenting the dynamic interdependence of living organisms (human and more-than-human) and their material surroundings. And while the role of natural landscapes and the wilderness have arguably been less crucial to Danish cinema history than they have been in Iceland, Norway and Sweden, the obvious ecological themes in films such as Max Kestner's dystopian sci-fi epic *QEDA* (*Man Divided*, 2017) or Daniel Joseph Borgman's survivalist coming-of-age drama *Harpiks* (*Resin*, 2019) suggest a recent turn toward directly confronting ecocritical questions in Danish film.

This chapter argues for the continued relevance of materiality in film studies today, despite the less obvious tangibility of the largely digital production technologies, distribution networks and exhibition platforms of recent years. The broader case I make here on maintaining critical focus on materiality in film studies is anchored in an analysis of one particular contemporary Danish film – Hlynur Pálmason's *Vinterbrødre* (*Winter Brothers*, 2017). The film won a spate of prizes at various film festivals,[2] as well as several Bodil Awards (including Best Film) in 2018. More importantly, *Winter Brothers* and its singular aesthetic brought widespread critical attention to Pálmason, a still recent graduate of the Danish Film School, who was immediately hailed as one of the most promising young film talents in the Nordic region. Examining Pálmason's debut feature in the context of a volume on Danish cinema also has the advantage of acknowledging the transnational and transcultural realities of Danish film culture today. As an Icelander who was educated at the National Film School of Denmark and has made Danish-language films in Denmark, Pálmason joins the ranks of other young Icelandic filmmakers such as Dagur Kári and Rúnar Rúnarson, a trend that points to the ways in which Iceland's longstanding political ties to Denmark have persisted in the cultural realm today. Examining *Winter Brothers* thus not only suggests timely ecological and material considerations, but also allows for a broader understanding of what 'Danish cinema' actually entails at a time when questions of globalisation and the reassertion of national boundaries are matters of extreme political and humanitarian urgency.

In his debut feature, Pálmason develops an aesthetics of grimy materiality, which manifests itself in a fixation on accumulations of particulate matter. In other words, *Winter Brothers* underscores the 'filminess' and haptic materiality of the medium against a more pervasive sense that cinema has become less tangible and anchored to the material world in an era of digital film production and distribution. This materialism is important not only for how we understand the human dynamics in the story, but also for understanding the ecological implications of the film.

As this chapter will argue, the growing field of material ecocriticism has developed robust critical tools for understanding the way in which culture and human life are not just shaping (and often threatening) the 'natural' world, but also the ways in which humans themselves are enmeshed in material ecosystems, despite the pervasive humanist fantasy of somehow inhabiting a space distinct from 'nature': a space of human mastery and superiority. Material ecocriticism argues that human concerns – enmeshed as they are in material and more-than-human forces and agencies – are fundamentally ecological concerns as well.

How then to proceed with a material-ecocritical reading of a film like *Winter Brothers*, a film that does not immediately present itself as overtly engaged with environmental issues or 'natural' spaces? I argue that we must start with the way in which the human stories in the film are played out by human figures situated in overtly material ways in relation to their environments.

Hlynur Pálmason uses a consistent phrase when describing *Vinterbrødre*. He calls it a 'lack of love' story.[3] This bit of art-house branding extends to the post-theatrical promotional materials used to market the film, some of which include the subtitle 'A Lack of Love Story' under the main title (this is the case on the cover of the DVD packaging in US distribution, for instance). The film centres on Emil, a young worker at a limestone mine in rural Denmark, who lives in the shadow of his older brother Johan, also a mine worker. Emil is regarded as an oddball within the hyper-masculine work environment of the mine. His only social capital within the small community of workers derives from his coveted moonshine, which he covertly sells to his fellow miners – only later do we find out that the homemade concoction is distilled from chemicals that Emil and Johan routinely steal from the mine. It is therefore no surprise when the liquor seems to have poisoned one of Emil's co-workers, who suddenly falls mysteriously ill. After being beaten and literally tossed out of the mine by his boss – who confronts him over the missing chemicals and Emil's apparent poisoning of his co-worker – he finds out that Johan has been sleeping with Anna, the local girl with whom Emil had fallen hopelessly in love, having already begun to think of her as his girlfriend. Following this discovery, the brothers engage in an intense wrestling match (in the nude), during which Emil is overpowered and nearly asphyxiated. After the near-death experience, the brothers make up, and Emil and Anna end up on friendly terms. The film ends in the same place where it began: down in the darkness of the underground mine. Instead of Emil, we now follow Johan and the rest of the workers who labour in the dark under the earth, while the unemployed Emil finally sparks up a friendship with Anna above ground.

Centred as it is on human desires, labour and rivalries, *Winter Brothers* would never be mistaken for a *naturfilm* (nature film), and few viewers would immediately categorise it as an environmental or posthumanist work. But to get a sense of the film's ecological awareness, one good place to start is a remarkable image from the title sequence. After a pre-credit scene set within

Figure 19.1 This tableau emphasises the brothers' materiality and transcorporeality, and references Sigurður Guðmundsson's work *Mountain* (1982). Framegrab from *Vinterbrødre* (*Winter Brothers*, Hlynur Pálmason, 2017).

the underground chalk mine, where we see Emil and his fellow workers hacking away at the earth and taking nips of his moonshine during a break, all the workers emerge from the shaft and shed their calcium-caked work helmets on their way out of the mining facility at the end of the day. The roughly 8½-minute segment is jarringly punctuated by a cut to an arresting image: a stationary shot, almost completely devoid of movement, showing Emil and Johan lying head-to-head in their work clothes, encased within a carefully arranged pile of chopped wood and rocks, all of which is set atop a pedestal of boulders in front of a mountain of mined limestone looming as a backdrop. At first glance, the viewer may instinctively take this as an iconic representation of death and burial, perhaps presaging the later demise of one or both of these characters. This initial sense of tragedy and foreboding is reinforced by the apparent dark stain running down the side of Emil's uniform, the most obvious visual difference between Emil and Johan as they lie there. Is it blood? Will this character end up being shot and killed? This sense may later seem to be reinforced by the appearance of a gun, which Emil procures through a trade with a neighbour in exchange for some jars of Emil's coveted moonshine. But this gun-death speculation turns out to be a narrative blind alley. In what amounts to an almost parodic overturning of the famous Chekhovian axiom, we are presented in the first act of the film with a loaded gun that never figures in the narrative resolution in any substantive way. The gun remains a narrative red herring that almost frustratingly lingers as a motif that is repeatedly invoked, but never actually used by any of the characters to fulfil its *raison d'être*. Not only that, but – to return to the shot of Emil and his brother lying encased in a pile of wood and rock – Emil's hand noticeably moves as he lowers it ever-so-slightly within his wood-and-rock cocoon, so that the viewer realises that they are not, in fact, looking at an image of corpses, but evidently living, moving bodies that just happen to be enclosed within an assemblage of material objects.

What to make of this (not quite) still image that Pálmason lingers on for several seconds right before cutting to the title shot? I propose that this tableau is not included as an indication of the *narrative* trajectory of the film, but rather as an iconic representation of the *materiality* and *transcorporeality* of the human characters depicted in the film. The bodies we see in this shot are protectively sheathed in a work helmet, coveralls and sturdy boots. The clothing conveys 'work' and 'uniform', but it also presents bodily selves swathed in a protective external shell meant to keep the grime of their material labour off their private bodies (via the boots and coveralls), and it also protects the same from the physical dangers of falling rocks or debris (via the helmet). This work-time physical inhabitation of a kind of 'protective shell' grows out of a broader humanist fantasy that full bodily encasement and separation from the incursions of 'nature' is not only possible, but taken as a given.[4] Humanism, after all, demands that human bodies be fundamentally distinct from their natural surroundings, which constantly present the threat of unwanted penetration or incursion through that bodily membrane and external 'shell' of clothing and protective gear in which humans enclose themselves. In this tableau the protective shell has already clearly been breached, with some kind of opening into Emil's body having spilled its blood down the side of the coveralls. Something from the outside world has not only *gone into* Emil's body in this apparent wound, but Emil's bodily fluids have begun to *spill out* as well. The transit between body and surroundings is thus a two-way street: not only does the world penetrate the imagined membrane of the body, but the body expels bits of itself out into the world. In other words, the human body depicted here is a *transcorporeal* one – it is not distinct from its surroundings, but fully – externally and internally – enmeshed in them.

I take this notion of human bodies as *transcorporeal* from Stacy Alaimo, a feminist ecocritic who first developed this central idea within the sub-field of material ecocriticism. In *Bodily Natures: Science, Environment, and the Material Self*, Alaimo posits this notion of transcorporeality to counter the tendency in humanist thinking to assume that human beings are somehow distinct from nature and insulated from their environmental surroundings. Instead, Alaimo emphasises the crucial 'transit between body and environment' (Alaimo 2010: 15), noting that human beings are 'always already part of an active, often unpredictable, material world' (17).

A reading of *Winter Brothers* that takes Alaimo's ideas into account could read this tableau of Emil and his brother lying encased in a pile of wood and stone as a lingering image of the fundamental transcorporeality of human bodies. These are bodies that are clothed in protective barriers, but even these membranes are shown to be more porous than they might appear, with the opening in Emil's flesh having spilled some of his own substance into the surrounding world. Rather than presaging human death and decay, the image presents human bodies as absorbed into a material assemblage that conjoins animal (human), vegetable (wood) and mineral (rock). Not only is human indistinct from animal, but animal and vegetable are not separated (by virtue of a vitalistic life principle) from the more apparently inert mineral matter of stone. All three of these forms of matter are part of the same cluster of material objects. This reading of the tableau as a representation of the transcorporeal enmeshment of organisms in their material environments is reinforced by comparing it to Sigurður Guðmundsson's *Mountain* (1982), a photographic print housed at the National Gallery of Iceland, in which the artist captures an image of his own body encased in a strikingly similar composition of stone, wood and earth. The similarities between Guðmundsson's photograph and the shot from *Vinterbrødre* are so immediately apparent it would be implausible to argue that Pálmason is not paying homage to the earlier work. Like Guðmundsson's piece, which captures a fleeting sculptural composition that integrates a prone human form into a geomorphic assemblage of neatly arranged natural materials, Pálmason's composition depicts the intersection (and interpenetration) of the cultural and the natural.

With this image, Pálmason presents human bodies as indistinguishable from other material objects via the dualities of subject and object. We might then not only draw on the transcorporeality of Stacy Alaimo to read this image, but also the 'meshwork theory' of anthropologist Tim Ingold, who reasons that 'we should no longer speak about relations between people and things because *people are things too*' (2012: 437–38, emphasis in original). Ingold's contribution to the growing proliferation of various 'thing theories' in cultural studies in recent years emphasises not only the *fact* that living bodies are enmeshed in their material surroundings, but the *necessity* of their porousness. As Ingold puts it, the living body 'is sustained thanks only to the continual taking in of materials from its surroundings and, in turn, the discharge into them, in the process of respiration and metabolism' (2012: 438). In that regard, living bodies are functionally not unlike a gardening pot – in order to continue functioning, they must be able to both *receive* material input and to *discharge* their waste:

> Things can exist and persist only because they *leak*: that is, because of the interchange of materials across the ever-emergent surfaces by which they differentiate themselves from the surrounding medium. The bodies of organisms and other things leak continually; indeed, their lives depend on it (2012: 438).

The 'leaky' quality of bodies is not a bug, but in fact an indispensable feature. Even in Pálmason's unsettling image, in which the 'leakiness' of one of the bodies seems to signify a possibly lethal wound, we may read such a corporeal puncture as a sign of the vital porousness of living organisms: a crucial stigma (in the Christian sense) of their *thingness* in Ingold's material-ecological model of enmeshment.

In presenting us with this image in the moments before the film's title card, Pálmason inaugurates his debut film with an icon of human bodies as parts of larger material collectives: in other words, bodies fully situated as material objects, objectified in the same way in which the wood in the same image may be put to instrumental use to build a cabin or to heat up a stove. Emil and Johan's bodies are not just *surrounded* by material objects in a carefully arranged pile; in a very real sense, they are just two of the many material objects assembled on screen, not more or less valuable as objects than pieces of wood or stone. As this image makes vividly clear, *people are things, too*.

Beyond this opening icon of human materiality, the film continues to present bodies as transcorporeally enmeshed in their material surroundings in various ways. One of the most obvious of these is evident in the film's fixation on the accumulation of particulate matter on the surfaces of things. Nearly every surface in the film is covered in particulate matter of various kinds: Emil's body, the bodies of the other workers and almost all the surfaces in the mining facility are depicted as dusted or caked with chalk; the wintery landscape and architectural surfaces are decked with a fine layer of snow; rotating industrial drums are coated in calcium and rust, which Emil and his brother are tasked with scraping off at one point. Their work and their daily lives shower them with bits of material that accumulate in spite of any efforts to contain or clean.

Are these grimy, dusty, or muddy surfaces throughout the film simply tokens of uncleanliness? Do they cast a classist gaze upon the proletarian setting of the film, in the same way as, for instance, Danish-American immigrant Jacob Riis's photographs of urban squalor in the tenements of Gilded Era New York (see Riis 1890) had done years before? I argue that, rather than indicating poverty or contamination, the grimy surfaces of *Winter Brothers* contribute to the broader emphasis on the material, earth-bound enmeshment of living bodies within the film.

One of the most striking examples of grimy surfaces in *Winter Brothers* comes from the middle of the film, after Emil has been roughed up and unceremoniously tossed out of the mine by his boss and his henchmen. In the wake of the beating, Emil (and the camera) enters another kind of subterranean landscape in a sequence in which we follow Emil to what seems to be his unconscious or at the very least some imaginative space within his subjective landscape. During a single, remarkable shot, we see Emil caked in chalk from head to toe, curled up in a foetal position and shivering alongside a completely clean Anna. Both of the figures are encircled in an iris of light within an otherwise completely black landscape. Anna fulfils Emil's deepest desire by telling him 'Jeg vil have dig, Emil' (I want you, Emil). When Emil tells her that he wants her, too, Anna replies, more alarmingly: 'Jeg vil spise dig' (I want to eat you). Emil agrees and says he wants to be 'elsket' (loved) and 'kneppet' (fucked), to which Anna responds: 'Jeg elsker dig. Jeg er din' (I love you. I am yours.).

At the moment when the exchange is about to reach its culmination – Anna finally leans in to kiss Emil – the shot cuts abruptly to a close-up of Emil lying curled up on a pile of chalk-covered rocks, shivering violently and caked completely in limestone as he regains consciousness. Emil claws his way up and off the pile, awkwardly clambering onto his feet, resembling nothing so much as a kind of demi-human struggling to assume its properly bipedal gait. Walking back to his dwelling, Emil is confronted with the revelation of Johan sleeping with Anna, prompting an enraged and humiliated Emil to engage his nude, post-coital brother in (nearly mortal) hand-to-hand combat.

Figure 19.2   A foetal Emil caked in chalk. Framegrab from *Winter Brothers*.

The shots of Emil during this crucial sequence in the film fixate on the impasto quality of the caked-on splotches of chalk that cover his entire body. This thick layer of grime has the effect of presenting Emil's body as another kind of material assemblage that bears some similarities to the opening tableau described above. Emil is not merely 'human' in this scene, but in fact a material conglomerate of animal (human body, leather boots), vegetable (cotton work clothing) and mineral (calcium sludge). The textural thickness of this grimy film covering Emil reinforces the haptic qualities of the images in the sequence, allowing the viewer's eyes to 'brush over' the surfaces of skin and clothing and 'feel' them with their vision, in a way that gives some of the same impressions as manual touch. In this sense, the film's emphasis on grimy surfaces (which extends to the noticeable graininess of the 16mm film Pálmason used to shoot *Winter Brothers*) is a suitable case-study for the growing body of film theory on haptic and tactile visuality by scholars such as Laura U. Marks (2000, 2002), Jennifer Barker (2009) and, in the Danish film studies context, Bodil Marie Stavning Thomsen (2016, 2018).

Is this emphasis on grime and particulate build-up merely an aesthetic gesture on Pálmason's part? It could reasonably be argued that the grime is simply a kind of side-effect of Pálmason's transmedial art outside of filmmaking, which includes serious work in photography and various other visual art media (see Pálmason n. d.). It is a sign, one might say, of Pálmason's professional interest (as a transmedial artist) in the forms and surfaces of his various artistic media.

Rather than seeing this grimy materiality as a merely formalist gesture, however, I read it as absolutely central to the broader aesthetic concerns of the film, which stages a gradual narrative progression from the realm of idealist romantic fantasy to materialist, earth-bound disillusionment via the very human experience of unrequited love. In that sense, the film shares more with some of the canonical works of modern Nordic literature – with their persistent interest in disillusionment, resignation and gritty naturalism as correctives to flights of idealist fantasy (think Söderberg's *Doktor Glas* or Ibsen's *Hedda Gabler*) – than it does with formalist modernism in the visual arts or film.

In pointing out Pálmason's aesthetics of grimy materiality in *Winter Brothers*, I build on the work of scholars working in material ecocriticism, such as Heather Sullivan, who proposes a framework of 'dirt theory' as 'an antidote to nostalgic views rendering nature a far-away and "clean" site' (2012: 515). The implication of this re-framing of dirt in Sullivan's theory, she writes, is that 'there is no ultimate boundary between us and nature' (2012: 515). As Sullivan notes in her analysis of several examples from German literature, works that fixate on 'body-dirt connection' (2012: 520) foreground the 'fundamental relationship between humanity and the soil' (2012: 518), although generally framing earth as 'dirt' to avoid the Romantic connections to fruitfulness and nationalism in a word like 'soil'.

Are these figurations of Emil as a not-merely-human 'dirt-person' purely negative images? Do they only serve to show Emil's total abjection and humiliation? Is the dirt a token of his worthlessness, soon to be confirmed in this scene by his discovery of Anna and Johan's relationship? I argue against this assumption and instead suggest that these images do not situate Emil as 'less-than-human', but rather (through a more ecocritical and materialist lens) as a 'not-*only*-human' conglomerate of various types of earth-bound matter. The narrative trajectory of *Winter Brothers* should thus be understood not as a movement from hope to hopelessness and humiliation via sexual frustration. Instead, I suggest Pálmason's grimy materialism presents a narrative that proceeds from illusion to disillusion, from idealism to materialism, through the universal human experience of unrequited love.

Notes

1. In the Nordic film studies context, Pietari Kääpä's expansive study of contemporary Nordic ecological cinema (2014) is the most wide-ranging single work by far, and it serves as an excellent starting place for becoming familiar with fundamental issues in ecocinema. Kääpä's study shows the pervasiveness of ecological themes and aesthetics in hundreds of examples in many different film genres, examining contemporary Nordic cinema as a transnational mode of filmmaking. Hennig, Jonasson and Degerman's recent volume on Nordic ecological narratives (2018) is a helpful

anthology that examines film, literary and other examples from a variety of critical perspectives.
2. For a more exhaustive list of awards, see 'Festivaler og Priser' on the film's page from the Danish Film Institute's film database (https://www.dfi.dk/viden-om-film/filmdatabasen/film/vinterbrodre).
3. The interview given by Pálmason in connection with the film's premiere, available as a video clip on YouTube by Filmexplorer Switzerland (2018), is only one of several similar interviews that show the director using this peculiar phrasing.
4. This idea of (usually masculinised) shells of clothing and armour being typical of anti-ecological ideologies and a generalised attitude prevalent in 'carbon-heavy' masculinities is also a central premise of Stacy Alaimo's recent book *Exposed: Environmental Politics and Pleasures in Posthuman Times* (2016).

20. REGIONAL FILM FUNDS AND PRODUCTION

Pei-Sze Chow

Regional film funds are a relatively recent addition to the Danish film landscape, with the first appearing only in the late 1990s. Before this, there was the long-held notion that, as a small nation already punching above its weight in audiovisual production and talent development, there was no need to alter the status quo of concentrating the film milieu in Copenhagen. After all, key institutions such as the Danish Film Institute (DFI) were located there, as well as the strong networks and relationships between policymakers, film businesses and practitioners – a concentration that still exists today. This mirrored the Norwegian and Swedish contexts, where the first regional film funds were also only established around the turn of the new century – with the exception of Film i Väst in the western Swedish municipality of Trollhätten, which was founded earlier in 1992. The Nordic media landscape was undergoing a shift during this time, as new formulations of European, regional Nordic and local funding arrangements and policies were being discussed or established (Hansen and Waade 2017: 155).

As the new millennium came into view, new modes of thinking at the policy level about Danish cinema began to effect a change. To be precise, this was a shift from thinking about film as culture and as 'public good' within the welfare state ideology, to a reframing of film as a business and economic sector that enabled new ways of stimulating growth in the nation's peripheries. The latter has also taken place against the background of a growing sense of the economic inequality between the capital and regions, as well as inequality in terms of political and cultural representations. Film production environments in regions outside of the capital – or 'provinces', as they are also known in official discourse – were to serve as an alternative to Copenhagen and effect a measure of 'regional balancing' (Albrecht 2001). Thus, regional film funds increasingly began to play a crucial role within a growing discourse on 'diversity' in Danish film culture – in this particular case, geographical diversity – and they have become important sources of funding and support for film businesses and productions taking place outside of the capital region.[1]

This chapter contextualises the emergence of regional film funds in Denmark since the early 2000s, beginning with film-political developments in publicly funded regional screen intermediaries, before moving on to an overview of the two regional film funds in Denmark: FilmFyn (Film Funen) and Den Vestdanske Filmpulje (The West Danish Film Fund, DVF). A third entity, the short-lived and more internationally focused Copenhagen Film Fund (CFF, 2013–18), is an interesting case-study in relation to the shifting realities of financial and political support for regional funds,[2] but for reasons of brevity, it will not be discussed here. The chapter concludes with an analysis of the current trends and challenges faced by regional screen industries.

The Emergence of Regional Film Funds in Denmark: Cultural Politics and Economic Justifications

Regional film funds became a topic for serious official (state) consideration shortly after the beginning of the new millennium. In May 2001, both the Kulturministeriet (Ministry of Culture) and Økonomi- og Erhvervsministeriet (Ministry of Economic and Business Affairs) set up a joint task force to create a framework for the establishment of regional film funds. This task force comprised representatives from both ministries, Erhvervs- og Boligstyrelsen (Business and Housing Authority), Konkurrencestyrelsen (Competition Authority), VækstFonden (Danish Growth Fund), the DFI, Producentforeningen (Danish Producers' Association), FilmFyn and Vestdansk Filmmiljø (West Danish Film Milieu). Their objective was to provide legal, economic and organisational recommendations for the development of regional film funds in Denmark, based on findings from the concrete experiences of foreign film funds – primarily Film i Väst, Rotterdam Film Fund and the Media Agency for Wales – as well as the two new regional Danish initiatives on the island of Funen and in Aarhus (Denmark's second-largest city). The result was a fifty-page report, *Regionale filmfonde*, detailing the strategies and proposals for future activities and further development of regional film funds in Denmark (Taskforcen for regionale filmfonde 2001).

At that time, many in the Danish film industry looked abroad to Film i Väst as a paragon of what could be achieved in terms of developing a successful regional film milieu.[3] The 2001 report heavily referenced the practices and organisational setup of Film i Väst, stressing in particular the economic effects of locating film production activities in regional territories. In the case of Västra Götaland, the west Swedish county that owns Film i Väst, the number of full-time jobs across the territory has more than tripled while the presence and work of the film fund has facilitated a growth in the number of audiovisual media companies. This is not to mention also the positive knock-on effects on the overall regional economy in related industry sectors that benefitted from the uptick in production activity.

The report represents a key shift in policy thinking about the public value of film in Denmark: that is, film shifted from being a phenomenon possessing cultural and social value that needs to be subsidised and supported by the state, to film's instrumental value as a business area to be capitalised on in order to foster economic development, especially in areas outside the capital. That the report supports this reframing of film activity is unsurprising, given the fact that the task force was chaired by the ministry responsible for economic policy, and that this was happening as part of a broader neoliberal tendency in Danish industrial policy to address the challenges of globalisation (Lorentzen 2012: 464). Nevertheless, this development echoes broader discussions about the ways in which culture, society and the economy are increasingly intertwined in these recent decades (see Howkins 2001, Hesmondhalgh 2013).

The political and economic arguments that establishing regional film funds and film centres outside of the capital are important to the decentralisation of film activity in Denmark thus became more prominent over time, and it could be said that this momentum built on existing legislation. Section 18 of the 1997 Film Act provided the legislative grounds for supporting regional film funds, by giving municipalities the possibility to produce films or support the production of film works by private companies or via a film fund:

> §18. Municipalities or counties may undertake the production of films as set out in legislation on the tasks of municipalities and counties. Municipalities and counties may also show and distribute films and may provide assistance in the form of subsidies, loans or guarantees for loans for production and distribution of films and for operation of cinemas (Kulturministeriet 1997).

Successive Film Agreements since the publication of the report saw modest change in state support for regional film production. The agreements for 2007–10 and 2011–14 both stipulated that seven million Danish kroner per year would go towards regional film production across Denmark as a whole. It was not until the 2015–18 Film Agreement that the state subsidy for regional productions was specifically shared equally between the two regional film funds, with FilmFyn and DVF receiving seven million kroner each. This money was offered on top of the fourteen million kroner to be distributed by the DFI to regionally based productions that are not receiving support from either of the two regional film funds. This was a move which Carsten Holst, then chief of the DVF, said was 'a political endorsement that films should be made all over the country' (Jensen 2014).

The most recent 2019–23 Film Agreement represents a leap in the political attention given to the cultural and economic potentials of regional film production and was the result of concerted lobbying by representatives from the DFI, practitioners and businesses from the film industry, as well as regional municipalities. The CEO of the DFI, Claus Ladegaard, said in 2018 that diversity was one of the three key priorities for the DFI over the period of 2019–23 and that, aside from 'diversity' in terms of gender and social background, geographical diversity in Danish cinema was a specific focal point (Mitchell 2019). In this period, both film funds have each been allocated 23.7 million kroner annually, which is more than triple the amount that they had previously received from the state (Kulturministeriet 2018). Yet, according to FilmFyn's CEO, this additional money from the state comes with 'handcuffs' in that it may only be used to fund productions of 'artistic quality' and productions that further the cause of Danish cinema. More specifically, the money may only be used to develop feature films, documentaries, short films and animated films. This means that certain types of productions are excluded – for example, incoming international productions, television series, or web series. Such projects would be supported by a different pot of money to which municipalities directly contribute.

Nevertheless, for both funds, the new injection of state funds is a significant boost to their ability to not only support more productions, but also to contribute to a momentum that will generate a steady production volume to sustain the respective regional film ecosystems.

REGIONAL FILM FUNDS AND THEIR REGIOSCAPES

Regional film funds vary widely in size, organisational structure and strategy focus, but all have the core activity of co-financing films (including features, shorts and documentaries) in order to attract productions to a specific, geographically delineated region. Yet, the scope of their work extends beyond the distribution of money to projects. They play active roles in fostering the growth and sustainability of the regional film industry and, through the selection process of choosing projects to fund, are thus ultimately involved in sculpting and shaping the character of what I call the local *regioscape* – that is, the region's screen ecosystem which includes people (various types of practitioners), material objects and spaces (for instance, equipment, studios, buildings for businesses, film locations, cinemas), audiovisual representations of the region, as well as the formal and informal relationships that link these entities. Film funds construct or rent out production facilities within the region, initiate or co-finance film-educational programmes and/or create and manage the support framework for film productions in the region. Funds thus have the responsibility to develop – with the resources available – the facilities, skills, competencies and networks that would support the growth of the local film industry (Taskforcen for regionale filmfonde 2001: 6–7).

Financial support from a regional film fund can constitute up to about 10 to 15 per cent of a film's budget, on the condition that the production be wholly or partly recorded in the region using local film talent; it is not unusual for a single film production to receive financial support from more than one regional film fund. In the context of increasing cross-border co-productions in European film, as a co-producer, regional funds also play a role in facilitating transnational collaboration between producers and filmmakers in neighbouring countries (Hedling 2018a: 176), bringing about the various scales of milieu-building and affinitive transnationalism described by Mette Hjort (2010b). Beyond their work in the domestic space, both FilmFyn and DVF are active members in larger international networks, such as the North Sea Screen Partners, a network of regional film bodies that worked together from 2007 to 2013 to raise the profile of the North Sea region as a screen production hub. This Northern European-wide cooperation is supported by the European Regional Development Fund and has transformed into what is now known as Create Converge, of which Filmby Aarhus is currently a part.

The following sections introduce the two Danish regional film funds, FilmFyn and DVF, tracing their beginnings and outlining their main activities in their respective regioscapes. While there is much that the two have in common, there are areas in which they diverge significantly.

DVF: The West Danish Film Fund

Denmark's second-largest city is Aarhus, commonly known as the unofficial capital of the administrative area of Jutland. Its Sydhavnskvarteret (South Harbour district) is home to a cluster of creative enterprises that occupy former industrial buildings and warehouses. Alongside agribusiness factories that are still in operation and whose towering grain silos can be spotted from across the city, Filmby Aarhus (Film City Aarhus) sits inconspicuously in the harbour area, comprising two buildings and two former turbine halls that were previously part of an energy company. The plans for a film city in Aarhus had been in play since 1999, with much interest from the municipality and key players in the Danish film and television industry; the plans have resulted in what is called a 'digital visual media cluster' comprising companies with both national and international reach. Filmby Aarhus houses a cluster of over eighty media companies of various sizes, two film studios, VIA University College's Film &

Transmedia programme, the startup incubator space Ideas Lab and, last but not least, the Den Vestjyske Filmfond (DVF) or the West Danish Film Fund.[4]

Preceding the establishment of a regional film fund was the early presence of a small film community in Aarhus, anchored in the DFI's regional branch, called Filmhuset and located in the city centre. From this, Aarhus Municipality and the county administration – bolstered by the DFI – worked to intensify the activities of the local film community and film production through a regional film fund. Thus, Denmark's first regional film fund, then called Den Østjyske Filmfond (East Jutland Film Fund), was established in 1997, as the result of a recognised need to develop a regional film production milieu in the western part of Denmark (Jellinge 2010: 25). This regional entity was driven by a combination of economic and cultural goals, where, by supporting artistically significant film projects, a stronger production community would be fostered and the region would gain from an increase in overall employment and return on investment (ROI) across different sectors. The understanding was, and continues to be for both regional funds, that the greater the volume of film productions, the more people would be employed in not only film-related activities, but also in ancillary sectors such as catering, hotels and transportation.

Today, the fund is backed by ten member municipalities in central and north Jutland. It is organised as an association with a board comprising representatives from each of the municipalities. The board decides on the distribution of the DVF's funds while day-to-day operations are handled by a small secretariat who are employees under Aarhus Municipality's Culture Department. The key purpose of the DVF's support is to 'secure artistically interesting productions that have cultural references to the West Danish area and which also promote the development of the West Danish film and media industry' (Den Vestdanske Filmpulje 2019: §1.3). One could interpret the phrases 'cultural references' and 'promote the development' in very broad ways indeed, and such similar territorial stipulations, including those that require productions to have an 'artistic and/or technical connection' to the region have been deliberately left open. For instance, there is no specific artistic criterion which states that projects should further only local voices, nor are there minimum spend criteria specifying how much of a film's budget should be spent in the region. As Steen Risom, General Manager of the DVF, puts it, the fund's primary emphasis is on raising production capacity in the region, and projects have to meet the criteria of having a high artistic quality while at the same time being creatively or technically anchored in the region (interview, 2018).

The DVF offers two types of funds: regional film support or 'A-funds' aimed at projects that fulfil the fund's aims of developing the production environment in the west Danish regions, and state film support or 'B-funds' that go to projects that specifically fulfil the goals and requirements of the Film Agreement. Projects supported include the development and production of feature films, documentary films, short films, animation, TV series, games development and festivals. The latter three, however, are not covered by the B-funds, as the Film Agreement is focused solely on support for the film medium. A special condition in the Film Agreement also stipulates that at least 25 per cent of the financial support available must be given to films aimed at children and young adults.

The DVF has been involved in over sixty major productions since its inception, supporting feature films such as *Nymph()maniac* (Lars von Trier, 2013) and *Sorg og glæde* (*Sorrow and Joy*, Nils Malmros, 2013), as well as popular television crime drama series such as *Dicte* (2012–16) and *Norskov* (2015–17). One work of note that was supported by the DVF (alongside DFI and TV2 Østjylland) is *Ghettodrengen* (*No Man's Land*, Kasper Bisgaard, 2012), which was broadcast on TV2 and subsequently nominated for a Robert Prize for Best Documentary (Short) in 2013. The film follows the work of a youth counsellor, Fadi Kassem, who supports and guides boys at risk in Gellerupparken, Denmark's largest social housing estate and an area in Aarhus that has a high concentration of immigrants. The documentary was filmed over five years and is a reflection on issues related to the integration of ethnic minority communities into Danish society. In its frank depiction of the obstacles and dangers that young boys of immigrant background face while growing up in a country known for equality and welfare for all its citizens, *No Man's Land* forces the viewer to confront ugly truths about the place and status of ethnic minorities in Denmark.

FilmFyn

FilmFyn was established in 2003 as a public-private limited company with a yearly budget of 11.5 million kroner. It is managed by a CEO who is appointed by a board of directors – the latter comprises a mix of representatives from the municipalities and local film businesses. Its current CEO is Klaus Hansen who had formerly served as head of the Danish Producers' Association and who also previously sat on FilmFyn's board of directors. Hansen, however, had been part of FilmFyn from its very inception, being one of the 'founding fathers' who rallied the local politicians into backing the idea of creating a regional film fund in Faaborg.

The initial motivation for establishing a Funen-based film fund was primarily a business and economic move to create growth in south Funen (Vestergaard 2000). This focus continues today, as the stated purpose of FilmFyn is 'to create business growth and employment by investing in productions wholly or partly produced in the Funen area' (2019). The fund is backed by nine municipalities in Funen, whose foremost interests in contributing to the fund are in raising the self-esteem of the local population while simultaneously creating new jobs and employment possibilities in the film business for local residents. The fund's office is located in the middle of a pedestrian street in the town of Faaborg at the southwestern edge of the island of Funen. Nestled amongst shoe boutiques, eateries, a hardware store, optician's shop, bank and hair salon, the physical location of FilmFyn in the heart of Faaborg mirrors the way in which the fund is embedded within the local community. The productions supported by Film-Fyn that arrive in the town and its surroundings are greeted by locals who share 'an openness down here to get involved', as Hansen puts it (interview 2019).

Similar to the DVF, FilmFyn has two funding tracks which distribute grants to projects according to whether the money comes from the state or the region. Track 1 funding (23.7 million kroner from the state) is reserved for features and documentary film, and Track 2 funding (4.1 million kroner from municipalities) will go to television series and films by new talent.

For a time, FilmFyn was at the forefront of film tourism in Denmark (Wolfhagen 2011), successfully capitalising on the popularity of films shot in Funen, such as the very first production supported by the fund, *De grønne slagtere* (*The Green Butchers*, Anders Thomas Jensen, 2003), *Adams æbler* (*Adam's Apples*, Anders Thomas Jensen, 2005) and *Hævnen* (*In A Better World*, Susanne Bier, 2010), which won an Oscar for Best Foreign Language Film in 2011. Successful television series that have made international breakthroughs include the family drama *Arvingerne* (*The Legacy*, Pernilla August, 2014–17) and *1864* (Ole Bornedal, 2014), a big-budget historical drama based on the events surrounding the Second Schleswig War between Denmark and Prusso-Austrian forces. *1864*, in particular, became the basis for a carefully coordinated film tourism campaign which has not only brought much attention and many visitors to the island, but contributed to the regional economy in diverse ways (Østergaard and Waade 2016).

Seeing an opportunity to capitalise on Funen's reputation for idyllic landscapes while further increasing production volume – and also inspired by the success of the transnational Oresund Film Commission (renamed Film Greater Copenhagen since 2016) – Film Commission Fyn was founded in 2013 as an initiative by FilmFyn, becoming the first Danish film commission offering a plethora of services to attract international productions. Among other things, the commission provided information on locations in the region, labour and hospitality, and it served as a crucial link between international producers and local authorities and service providers. However, the commission was shut down when funding ran out at the end of 2018. This reflects a shift in priorities for the regional film fund, in that supporting Danish productions and Danish film talent should be top priority. International efforts are, for the time being, on hold.

Regional Futures

The regional film funds have a dynamic future ahead. There is at present emphatic political support for the regionalisation of Danish film, as reflected in the increased funding provided through the latest Film Agreement. Sustaining a higher production volume and visibility of the respective regional film milieus are now priorities for the regional film funds, particularly as production volume and the ability to attain a critical mass is crucial to fulfilling the cultural and economic promises of increased expertise and growth in the region. With the latest injection of funds from the state comes a particular dilemma: should regional film funds support a greater number of small productions, or focus on fewer high-profile and high-quality productions? Finding the right balance between the two options is one of the challenges that they currently face.

Related to the question of production volume is talent development and retention: the presence of a stable base of talented and skilled film professionals is, among other factors, central to the sustainability of regional film milieus. Yet, despite the presence of viable regional opportunities, Copenhagen remains a magnet for emerging talent, simply due to the concentration of expertise and opportunities in the capital built up over decades of film production. It is thus clear to the managers of both funds that a sustainable means of nurturing local talent is just as important as being able to distribute generous funds for productions. One of the ways in which regional film funds are attempting to address this is to diversify the scope of their support beyond traditional film, reflecting global trends in television drama production, virtual and augmented reality experiences, and other digital visual media. The DVF in particular is able to pursue this direction, as Filmby Aarhus and the broader West Danish region is already a growing hub for practitioners in these fields, and the participation of Filmby Aarhus and VIA Film & Transmedia in European-level initiatives like Create Converge has fostered a multiplicity of opportunities for local regional talent to be involved in international projects and cross-sectoral collaborations.

Another way is to work collectively to increase the capacity for film and audiovisual production in Denmark as a whole. Vision Denmark is an alliance of organisations across the nation – including the regional film funds – that has been campaigning for the introduction of tax incentives to make Denmark a competitive place for international productions. An analysis of how tax incentives would work in Denmark is currently underway, and a pilot phase was due to take place in 2020 (Vision Denmark 2018: 22–23). As the digital visual industry grows, calls for the introduction of tax incentives in Denmark are growing stronger (Holse 2018), since the country is one of the rare few in Europe that do not offer tax incentives for foreign productions to date (other countries include Luxembourg and Liechtenstein).

The overview of regional film funds in this chapter has only scratched the surface of the multifaceted dynamics underlying regional film funding and production. The examples of regional entities that have dissolved, such as Film Commission Fyn and the CFF, hint at an element of precarity in how the work of film funds can be affected by, *inter alia*, the flavour of the country's political priorities at a specific time. Further, a critical eye needs to be cast at the rationale that pumping yet more money into regional film production will yield sustainable economic growth over the long term, as well as the basis on which these reported economic effects of past film productions are made.[5] Furthermore, what cultural impact do such funding policies have on the actual representation of regional stories, voices and places on screen, if – as is frequently the case – productions simply parachute into a region only to shoot on location for a temporary period, or perfunctorily include a 'regional element' in the screenplay for the purposes of securing regional film funding? That one of the main criteria for receiving funding from the DVF or FilmFyn remains rather vague (or, from another perspective, rather generous) – a project simply has to demonstrate an 'artistic and/or technical connection' to the region, without quite specifying what form this connection should take – could result in films that may contribute very little towards improving the diversity of representation in Danish film. Yet, for now, the decentralisation of film culture is a trend that will not be reversed any time soon; as is clear, regional film funds are actively engaging in initiatives to cement their relevance for the Danish film and digital media landscape.

Acknowledgments

Research for this chapter was supported by project funding from the European Union's Horizon 2020 research and innovation programme under the Marie Skłodowska-Curie Grant Agreement No. 753597.

Interviews

Hansen, K. (2019) Telephone interview with Klaus Hansen, conducted by Pei-Sze Chow. 12 March.
Risom, S. (2018) Interview with Steen Risom, conducted by Pei-Sze Chow. 22 August.

Notes

1. Similar developments were mirrored in Norway and Sweden, especially in the latter which has had a head start in the regionalisation of film in a Scandinavian context. Blomgren and Blomgren (2003) suggest that the regionalisation process in the Swedish context is a result of two things: growing autonomy of regions and in film policy, and the fact that film as an activity is no longer a form of culture to be subsidised, but rather a business area to be fostered for greater growth.
2. The CFF lost its core funding from the Municipality of Copenhagen; the money that had been previously agreed upon in the budget for 2019 was to be redirected towards social welfare causes (á Rógvi 2018).

3. Film i Väst operates as a co-producer in film productions; as an equity investor, it can invest in up to a maximum of 100 per cent of the production costs allocated to the region; the full regulations for co-productions can be found on their website (Film i Väst 2017).
4. At the time of writing, a third building is being constructed at Filmby Aarhus which will house the Aarhus Film Workshop, the Super8 film collective, with more office space for film and media businesses, thus further consolidating the film milieu in the harbour area. Filmby3, as it is known, will be fully functional from 2020 onwards and will add 300 jobs and 4,400 square metres of space to the existing campus.
5. Bille et al. (2016) argue that decisions in contemporary Nordic cultural policy are often justified using economic themes (over cultural themes), where the dominant political discourse emphasises potential growth, jobs, or branding value as impact factors that weigh heavily on whether certain cultural projects should be publicly funded. This continues to be the prevailing attitude, despite much research in cultural economics showing that the analyses of high economic returns on which policymakers and institutions relied were often exaggerated, biased and based on selective data (Bille et al. 2016: 239).

21. 'FINALLY, WE'RE BEGINNING TO TELL OUR OWN STORIES': FILMMAKING IN GREENLAND

Isak Thorsen and Emile Hertling Péronard

Danish cinema began with an image of Greenland. The earliest surviving Danish film, shot by royal court photographer Peter Elfelt in 1897, has the title *Kørsel med grønlandske hunde* (*Driving with Greenlandic Dogs*). The forty-second film features the colonial administrator and aspiring actor Johan Carl Joensen on a sled pulled by a team of four huskies across a snow-covered landscape. Elfelt anticipates the practice of film editing by playing with the frame for comedic effect: Joensen and his dogs exit the frame only to implicitly move behind the camera and enter the frame on the other side, this time with the man frantically pursuing the runaway dogs. The trees on the horizon give the game away: this footage was not shot in Greenland at all, but in Copenhagen's Fælled Park. That the first film to be shot in Denmark features a fictionalised fantasy of Greenland, at that time a Danish colony (and yet a fiction that features genuine huskies and a real-life colonial bureaucrat), is emblematic of the extent to which Greenland was the object of Denmark's technocratic power, as much as it was an object of what has been termed the European borealist gaze (Briens 2016).

Greenland's breathtaking scenery and 'exotic' population attracted filmmakers from early in the history of cinema, but an indigenous Greenlandic film production began only this century – that is, in the era of self-government (*Selvstyre*). In the last decade, a range of scholarly work on the literature, visual culture and music of Greenland has emerged as part of a broader wave of Critical Arctic Studies. Exploring the imagology of the North, such work examines how the arts have shaped, and been shaped by, the geopolitics and colonial histories of the Arctic region (see, for example, Körber and Volquardsen 2014; MacKenzie and Stenport 2014a, 2014b; Körber, MacKenzie and Stenport 2017; Stenport and Lunde 2019). Arguably, the story and study of Greenlandic cinema most properly falls within this broader field of Critical Arctic Studies. To include a chapter on Greenlandic cinema within *A History of Danish Cinema* could be regarded as a re-colonisation of Greenlandic culture. However, not to acknowledge the entangled histories of Danish and Greenlandic cinema and the role played by cinema in the cultures' respective and collective self-understandings would be to ignore a key aspect of that shared history. Even in the most basic film-historical terms, the earliest Danish film, the first Danish sound film and the first Danish colour film took Greenland as their subject.

Nonetheless, we wanted to invite Greenlandic cinema to 'speak' for itself, rather than attempting to pin down its history from a Danish perspective. This chapter, then, takes a deliberately fragmented approach: the reader is invited to explore recent work in Critical Arctic Studies (referenced above and in what follows); an outline of the development of cinema in Greenland and Greenlandic cinema, with basic historical context, is offered below as a starting point for further exploration; and an interview with Emile Hertling Péronard fleshes out the contemporary scene in Greenland from the perspective of an Indigenous producer.

GREENLAND AND DENMARK: HISTORICAL AND COLONIAL RELATIONS

Although Greenland is an autonomous territory, the world's largest island forms part of the Kingdom of Denmark. Greenland's relations with mainland Scandinavia stretch back to the Viking Age, when Norsemen migrated to the island, which had long been inhabited by Inuit peoples. From 1261 onwards, Greenland came under the Norwegian crown and then, from 1380 onwards, under the Danish-Norwegian realm. A cooling climate led to the Norse settlement dying out around 1500, and it was not until the eighteenth century that contact was re-established (Sørensen 1995: 85–86). In 1721, the Norwegian missionary Hans Egede was granted permission by the Danish King Frederik IV to establish a mission at Godthåb. The settlement later became the capital of Greenland and was renamed Nuuk in 1979. In 1814 Greenland was officially declared a Danish colony in the post-Napoleonic accords that ceded Norway to a Union of Crowns with Sweden.

Greenland remained a colony until 1953, when its status changed due to a range of pressures. The island had been cut off from Denmark during the Second World War and had managed its own economic affairs as well as hosted US bases. The post-war United Nations Assemblies required reporting of 'non-governing territories'. And the Social Democratic government elected in

Denmark in 1947 wanted to re-set relations with Greenland on a more equal footing (Sørensen 1995: 97–100). In 1953, Greenland was granted the status of a constituent country of the Danish realm, as well as a county (*amt*) of Denmark. In the subsequent two decades, the overall aim was a modernisation of Greenland from a hunter-gatherer society to an urbanised and industrialised modern welfare state. Many Greenlanders, however, were left feeling that they were mere 'spectators of the construction of a new society' (Sørensen 1995: 100).

A movement towards greater independence began in the 1970s, which led to home rule in 1979. Driven by the Fourth World movement and by Denmark's entry into the EEC in 1973, the basic principle espoused by a new generation of Greenlandic politicians in the 1970s was to work towards a society which would be 'as Greenlandic as possible and as Danish as necessary' (Sørensen 1995: 101). Negotiations resulted in Home Rule in 1979, which devolved certain areas to the Greenlandic authorities, including hunting and fishing, municipal organisation and taxes; schools, culture, health and housing were devolved later and continued to be funded by the Danish state. Notably, Greenland elected to leave the EC in 1985. After a referendum in 2008, *selvstyre* (self-government) was achieved in 2009 (see Naalakkersuisut n. d.).

Greenland on Screen

While Elfelt's 1897 film was shot in Copenhagen, Danish and foreign filmmakers travelled to Greenland to make films there from as early as 1909, when the Danish ethnographer Thomas Thomsen shot films in Uummannaq. The legendary Danish polar explorer and anthropologist Knud Rasmussen was responsible for a number of early documentaries about Greenland, for example, *Den store Grønlandsfilm* (*The Great Greenland Film*, Eduard Schnedler-Sørensen, 1922) – the same year as Robert Flaherty's *Nanook of the North* did so much to 'codify how the Arctic was seen and imagined cinematographically' (MacKenzie and Stenport 2014a: 5). Rasmussen also wrote the script for the feature fiction *Palos Brudefærd* (*The Wedding of Palo*, Friedrich Dalsheim, 1934), a love story set in a pre-colonial Inuit community.

The use of Greenland as a backdrop in film drama developed in the 1930s. Like other Arctic landscapes, Greenland could serve as a 'sublime' space of desolation and drama as well as one of stunning, stark natural beauty (MacKenzie and Stenport 2014a: 3, 12). The Norwegian-Danish feature *Eskimo* (George Schnéevoigt, 1930), which by some is considered the first Danish sound film, was set in Greenland, and a German film expedition, headed by Arnold Fanck, resulted in *S. O. S. Eisberg* (*S. O. S. Iceberg*, 1933), starring Leni Riefenstahl. A recurrent theme in the Danish features set in Greenland consists of stories about civilised yet somewhat troubled Danes searching for and reflecting on themselves in the unspoilt nature of Greenland. This theme can be found in

Nordhavets Mænd (*Men of the North Sea*, Lau Lauritzen Jr, 1939), Erik Balling's Oscar-nominated *Qivitoq* (1956) and Palle Kjærulff-Schmidt's *Tukuma* (*Man in Too Much of a Hurry*, 1984).

The distinctive colour palette of Greenland's landscape – brilliant blue-white ice fields punctuated by colourful peat houses on grassy slopes – emerged on screen in a notable Danish film of 1955, *Hvor bjergene sejler* (*Where Mountains Float*), directed by Bjarne Henning-Jensen. Billed in its lavishly-illustrated programme as 'the first major Danish production in colour' ('Hvor bjergene sejler' 1955), *Where Mountains Float* was commissioned by the Danish state primarily as an educational film for children, orienting them about life in Greenland and de-mystifying hospital treatment. At forty-nine minutes in length, however, the film is more epic and ambitious than the ten- or twenty-minute shorts that dominated state-sponsored film at the time (see Thomson 2016, 2018a) and thus targeted the international film festival circuit; indeed, it was nominated for an Academy Award for Best Documentary Feature and won a Grand Prix for documentary at Venice. Through the eyes of the young boy Mikisoq, the film juxtaposes life in the cramped peat houses of rural Greenland with the gleaming hospital facilities of a larger town where the boy is taken for treatment for the tuberculosis that has killed his mother. While Mikisoq is exploring town life, his father must decide whether to move his family to the state-sponsored housing that he is offered. On one hand, then, *Where Mountains Float* is a snapshot of the process of urbanisation and modernisation in 1950s Greenland, driven by Denmark's burgeoning welfare structures and its paternalistic application of those structures to Greenland. On the other hand, the film also allows us to witness the lived experience of the Inuit men who hunt seals from kayaks; stunning sequences of ice fields from the point of view of the hunter depict the stunning beauty of the still waters and the sudden impact of a calving iceberg. *Where Mountains Float* is a snapshot of the Danish perception of the post-war wave of welfare colonialism, a snapshot that was later updated for another era; in 1983 the film was re-released with a new voice-over in Greenlandic, replacing the original Danish narration that had 'translated' Mikisoq's experience.

In the 1950s the Danish government produced films to motivate the Greenlandic population to embrace industrialisation and urbanisation, but a more critical and unorthodox cinematic approach towards the country's development and towards traditional society became apparent in the 1960s. Most notable here are the documentaries by the Danish filmmakers Jette Bang and Jørgen Roos. Roos made many documentaries in and about Greenland, including *Knud* (1966) and *Sisimiut* (1966). The Danish artist Per Kirkeby and the Greenlandic poet and politician Aqqaluk Lynge collaborated to tell the tale of the dismantling of the mining town Qullissat in the documentary *Da myndighederne sagde stop* (*And the Authorities Said Stop*, 1972). A notable literary intervention in the Danish popular imaginings of their former colony in the Home Rule period came in 1992, with novelist Peter Høeg's international best seller *Frøken Smillas fornemmelse for sne* (*Miss Smilla's Feeling for Snow*). The novel was adapted for film by Danish director Bille August as an English-language German-Danish-Swedish co-production in 1997, under the title *Smilla's Sense of Snow*, bringing both the conflicted hybridities of Dano-Greenlandic citizens and the ice-scapes of Greenland to international screens, in the guise of a rip-roaring thriller. The Danish production *Lysets hjerte* (*Heart of Light*, Jakob Grønlykke, 1998), written in collaboration with the Greenlandic writers Hans Anton Lynge and Josef Motzfeldt, had a Greenlandic cast and, above all, a Greenlandic main character, played by the popular folk music singer Rasmus Lyberth.

Towards a Greenlandic Film Industry

The movement towards a domestic film production can be divided into two waves. The first wave was initiated by the short fiction comedy *Sinilluarit* (*Goodnight*, 1999) directed by Inuk Silis Høegh, as well as the animated short film *Nanoq* (*Polar Bear*, 2000) by Kunuk Platou and the documentary *Inuk Woman City Blues* (Laila K. Hansen, 2002), about homeless Greenlandic women in Copenhagen. But attempts to stimulate and organise a Greenlandic film environment did not succeed until the premiere of Otto Rosing and Torben Bech's feature *Nuummioq* (*A Man from Nuuk*, 2009), which launched the second and current wave in Greenlandic cinema. The amateur comedy *Tikeq, Qiterleq, Mikileraq, Eqeqqoq* (*Fore Finger, Middle Finger, Ring Finger, Little Finger*, Ujarneq Fleischer, 2008), made on a tiny budget of 500 Danish kroner (around £50), can be considered the first feature-length film produced by a Greenlander. However, it was the domestic and international recognition achieved by *Nuummioq* that proved to be a watershed for Greenlandic film production, as Emile Hertling Péronard explains in the interview below.

Director Malik Kleist and producer Aká Hansen, who had both worked in television, established the film production company Tumit Production; their first feature was the highly successful comedy *Hinnarik Sinnatunilu* (*Hinnarik's Dream*, Angajo Lennert-Sandgren 2009). Tumit Production went on to produce the biggest box-office hit to date in Greenland, *Qaqqat Alanngui* (*The Shadows of the Mountains*, Malik Kleist, 2011), which sold 19,000 tickets. The film combines Greenlandic myths with traits from American and Asian horror films. A similar mix can also be found in films like *Unnuap Taarnerpaaffiani* (*In the Deep Dark of the Night*, Malik Kleist, 2014) and *Tarratta Nunaanni* (*Among Us – In the Land of Our Shadows*, Marc Fussing Rosbach, 2017). In 2012, the filmmakers' association FILM.GL. was established to promote and encourage filmmaking in Greenland, and production has remained steady with a number of short films and documentaries, as well as typically one feature film a year.

A notable production was the feature-length documentary (or rockumentary) *Sumé - Mumisitsinerup Nipaa* (*Sumé – The Sound of a Revolution*, Inuk Silis Høegh, 2014). *Sumé* reconstructs the career of the eponymous 1970s rock band, who sang in Greenlandic and became an important voice in the movement demanding independence from Denmark (see Mackenzie and Stenport 2017). Combining a soundtrack well known to the Greenlandic audience with historical footage and self-reflexive elements such as an itinerant guitar amp, *Sumé* is a portrait of a nation quite literally finding its voice. In the interview that follows, both *Nuummioq* and *Sumé* emerge as watershed moments in the development of Greenlandic cinema. This is so not only because of the kinds of stories that they tell, but also because of the transformative effects of their production and distribution histories on the fledgling film industry.

Interview with Producer Emile Hertling Péronard of Ánorâk Film

Isak Thorsen: How would you describe your involvement in Greenlandic cinema?
Emile Hertling Péronard: It was around 2008 that one of my good friends, Mikisoq H. Lynge, was working on *Nuummioq*. He tried to persuade me to travel with him to Greenland and play some kind of role in what he had started to build. I was studying at the university in Copenhagen at the time, and I remember thinking that it seemed completely daft to make films in Greenland. There wasn't enough money, and people didn't have the right training. It seemed completely unrealistic to make a feature film there. But against all odds, a film was made – and a lovely film, too. It was shot digital, but at that time everything was projected on 35 mm, and Mikisoq flew to the premiere in Nuuk safeguarding the film reels between his knees as hand baggage. He didn't want to entrust it to anybody else. The premiere in Nuuk was grand, and then of course it was a massive thing that *Nuummioq* was the first Greenlandic film ever to be screened at Sundance, in January 2010.

IT: So Nuummioq was very important?
EHP: Absolutely, in that it was the first Greenlandic feature film ever to go international. I don't think we can underestimate what it means for young talent to see that this is possible. That's true of every Greenlandic film that gets made, and this one was the first. Funnily enough, several other film projects were underway at the same time – feature films. It wasn't more than a few months after *Nuummioq*'s premiere that *Hinnarik Sinnattunilu* (*Hinnarik's Dream*, Angajo Lennert-Sandgren, 2009) was released.

IT: Can you say more about how you got involved with Greenlandic film?
EHP: How I got into working with film in Greenland was a complete coincidence. After many years in Denmark, I started to want to get back to Greenland,

where I had grown up, and I realised that this connection was something I had been missing; I actually needed Greenlandic culture, because it's a part of me too. It hit me like a bolt of lightning one night when I walked into the Rex bar in the centre of Copenhagen, and they were playing the band Sumé on the speakers. Something within me clicked into place. I started to wonder why no one had made a film about Sumé. Coincidentally, that evening I was with Karen Marie, who at that time was the girlfriend of Malik Høegh, the lead singer in Sumé. She said: 'We're bloody well going to make that film, we absolutely have to!' And she phoned Malik and asked him what he thought about Emile and [director] Inuk Silis Høegh making a film about the band, and Malik said yes during that first phone call. I hadn't even asked Inuk at that point if he was interested in the idea. After the phone call I cycled over to the Nørrebro district where Inuk lived. He saw right away that it was a great idea and said yes. *Sumé* is the first film made by Greenlanders about the history of Greenland. The underlying idea was to deal with the history of the independence movement of the 1970s, the shoulders that we stand on. I was born in 1979, the same year that Home Rule was implemented. So I wasn't there when Sumé emerged, but I grew up with the songs and sensed the aura that surrounded that time. What was so unique about our mode of telling that story as Greenlanders was that we believed in the music 100 per cent, all the way through, and we knew that the music had to be at the centre of the film. Another filmic principle was that the story had to be told by the people who were actually there at the time. In other words, not by so-called experts. I think that a Danish television producer or documentarist would have told the story differently. That's what DR [the Danish public service broadcaster] thought about the film when we pitched it: that the political history ought to weigh more heavily, and the music should have less of a role. But we didn't want to tell the political story for its own sake. It was only when that history was linked to the history of the band Sumé that it was relevant to the film. I studied film at university and had worked in film marketing, but I'd never produced a film in that sense before. It took a little more than four years from idea to finished film. It was a kind of film school course for me to find out how everything worked, especially so because we made it as a Greenlandic film. So it was a 'learning by doing' process, which was really exciting, and there wasn't a single day that I didn't enjoy working on that project. It was a very absorbing process, and when the film was finished, I realised that we'd accrued an enormous amount of knowledge. Not just about the history and about filmmaking, but also quite simply about how to produce films. Knowledge that not many people in Greenland have. So you take it step by step, every film is important, and that's how we saw it with *Sumé*. That we were making the film with one hand and creating a film industry with the other. Shortly before that, a new film industry association had been set up, FILM.GL, and that gave us the opportunity to share our knowledge with other people. Inuk and I were both members of

FILM.GL from the beginning, and around the time *Sumé* was released, I joined the board of directors so that I could help to spread that knowledge. I served on the board from 2014 to 2017 but have continued to do FILM.GL-related work ever since. When there are so few of us, and we have so little experience, at least if we stand together, we become a bit bigger.

IT: So FILM.GL dates from 2012?
EHP: FILM.GL was established in November 2012. There had been an earlier film association in the 2000s, called Assilissat, but eventually it ran out of steam.

IT: How big is the Greenlandic film industry?
EHP: I usually say that there are about fifty people in the industry. Fifty people who work independently and professionally or semi-professionally with film. So we don't count for instance people with full-time jobs at KNR [Kalaallit Nunaata Radioa, the Greenlandic public service broadcaster].

IT: And can they make a living from it?
EHP: Not from making films exclusively. The typical income will consist of a patchwork of film- and media-related jobs, for example, filmmaking, advertisements, work on photo shoots, as photographers, in the Film Workshop.

IT: What's the purpose of FILM.GL?
EHP: To begin with, we wanted a lot of different things to happen. A film industry is finally getting established in Greenland. Finally, we're starting to tell our own stories. At the start, we identified four main aims: more money for the industry; talent development in Greenland, both young talent and across the industry more generally; international work, promotion of Greenlandic film and film practitioners on the international scene, and later film festivals; and locations, that was the fourth aim.

IT: What do you mean by locations?
EHP: Developing Greenland as a film location. We held location conferences and invited film commissioners from Europe and North America to visit us, as well as people who work with locations either at production companies or film institutes, so they could tell us how you build up that sort of thing. In collaboration with Visit Greenland, we created a website where you can explore where to find particular kinds of landscapes in different parts of Greenland.

IT: What's the situation with international collaborations?
EHP: Our international activities grew out of the films getting premieres around the world, at film festivals, including some of the big festivals. I think it really

began when *Sumé* was screened at imagineNATIVE in Toronto in October 2014, and then had its European premiere at the Berlinale in 2015. When the film was selected for Berlin, I was exhausted. It had been showing in Nuuk since September, in Canada in October and in November at CPH:DOX in Denmark, and then it was selected for Berlin the next February. I was quite burnt out by having to launch the film again and again for months, and I wasn't sure we had the resources to make a big splash with it in Berlin. But then I had the idea of creating a Greenlandic showcase instead of a traditional *Sumé* premiere. We threw a big party, 'Meet the Greenlanders', after the film was screened, and we met lots of people who were interested in films from Greenland. In some cases, their interest was in Indigenous filmmaking more generally, and we discovered that there was a big network in Indigenous cinema that we had missed out on. And so we got involved in a collaboration called NATIVe, which is a regular fixture at Berlin. We've participated in NATIVe as a partner every year since 2016, and we've discovered that beyond our little film world in Greenland there are industries in other nations that are struggling with the same problems and challenges. For example, there are the Sámis in northern Scandinavia, a very small film industry and a small population, and Indigenous people, too, who find it hard to tap into the resources of the national film institutes. Equally, there are indigenous populations in Canada, Alaska, South America, New Zealand and Australia. So the world opened up to us, and we decided to put some work into international outreach via NATIVe in Berlin and then the imagineNATIVE festival in Toronto, the world's biggest festival for Indigenous screen content. One thing that this kind of work has opened our eyes to is that it really means something to tell our own stories. Who is the originator of the message behind the films, and whose gaze is represented in the films – these things make a difference. That's the story we tell every day out on the film market. Film professionals come from every country imaginable, and some of them just happen to walk past our stand and think it looks interesting and ask about it, and we explain. Sometimes people visit and say that they would like to make a film about, for example, Aborigines, and how would they do that? And it's our job to explain why it is important that, when these stories are told, they are told from the inside; that it's important to proceed respectfully when engaging with something sacred or with meaningful traditions attached to it. Marginalised voices and communities can't always just patent their histories, as more powerful groups are able to. One can call a film that is about Indigenous people an *Indigenous-themed* film, but what we are trying to promote are *Indigenous-led* films; that is, films which are created with Indigenous people as the creative driving force.

IT: What has it meant for Greenlandic cinema to participate in such a network? Is it self-respect? Have you got co-funding out of it? Is it about knowledge-sharing?

EHP: There have been various effects. First and foremost, our horizons have expanded. It opens up the field in the sense that we've discovered that there is a wider audience, a bigger group of people we can collaborate with, that we have things in common with. We feel it when we are at Indigenous film festivals showing the films; there is a special understanding that isn't so tangible when we screen them in Denmark and other places. But now some more concrete collaborations have been initiated as well. *Anori* by Pipaluk K. Jørgensen, which was the first feature Greenlandic film directed by a woman, came out in 2018. The film was part financed by the International Sámi Film Institute (ISFI) based in Norway and was the first film to get money from that source. At the moment I'm working on a film called *Twice Colonized* which is supported by Nunavut Film Development Corporation in Northern Canada. It's the first formal co-production amongst the Inuit communities across the Canada-Greenland border. So there are some possibilities, but ISFI has limited resources, as has Nunavut. But transnational activities are definitely starting to blossom, though it's still hard because it involves a lot of administration, there are not many of us to do it, and it's expensive.

IT: There are some differences too, though: there are film institutes in the Faroe Islands and in the north of Norway. What about Greenland?
EHP: Greenland doesn't have its own film institute yet. Iceland is in a totally different league compared to Greenland and the Faroes. It is striking how far ahead Iceland is, both in regard to experience and track record. It's significant that they have a population six times bigger than we do in Greenland or the Faroes; there's more of an infrastructure, and a different kind of economy. That was the case even before the Faroese Film Institute was set up. That's the one big thing we're missing in Greenland: people with full-time salaries who can work on the kind of thing that we've been working on *pro bono* for years. Obviously, there are limits to how much time we can spend on it without pay, as we have to earn our keep another way, and we're trying to cover so much. So it's hard to sustain.

IT: How does support for Greenlandic films work without a film institute?
EHP: Indeed, film funding has been one of FILM.GL's four areas of focus. In connection with the production of *Nuummioq* a separate film fund within the government was established. There were few applications at first, then more started to arrive, and the sums applied for increased. At the moment the total is around three million kroner [around £350,000] per annum, which is distributed under the rubric of the Greenlandic government's funds for film production. This is quite a small sum; by Scandinavian standards, it would be hard to make even one low-budget film for that amount, and it has to stretch

to everyone's needs for a whole year. How it works is that there are three application deadlines annually, and Greenlandic production companies can apply. There are civil servants in the Department of Culture who read and evaluate the applications, check that the criteria have been met and divide up the money. You can only speculate as to how they do it, as there are no published criteria and no specialist panel or consultants to judge the applications. The civil servants who make the decisions have no formal expertise to inform their decisions about whether they think a project is good or not, and nothing laid down as to what kind of projects they prioritise. So this is an idea we have tried to push: that there should be an expert panel to evaluate the applications. Our suggestions were influenced by how it was done on the Faroe Islands before the film institute was established, with two-person panels with no conflict of interest, as they are not in the film industry; people such as authors or dramatists with a professional capacity to assess the projects. This kind of panel could make strategic decisions about what would strengthen Greenlandic cinema in the longer term. This is how it works in Denmark, too; it's always a thankless task to be a film consultant, you always annoy someone. But the 'arm's length principle' [*armslængdeprincippet*, whereby state funding is distributed by specialist consultants] ensures that no one can claim the decisions are politically motivated.

IT: You mentioned talent development as an important goal for FILM.GL. Who finances the Film Workshop in Nuuk?
EHP: It is also financed by the Greenlandic government and Sermersooq municipality, which encompasses Nuuk, Paamiut, Qeqertarsuatsiaat and Greenland's entire east coast. I think it's important because if a kid is sitting in their bedroom or their cellar or whatever, and they get the urge to try out some kind of filmmaking beyond their phone or TikTok, they know they have somewhere to go. The film industry has organised talent development initiatives since day one, but talent recruitment has been very hard. We desperately need to build critical mass in the Greenlandic film industry; we simply need more people. People who have a perspective or a story to tell, but also people who want to learn how you record sound or handle a camera or how you light a scene. As in all small film industries, most people want to direct or maybe be a cinematographer, so for many years we had no dedicated sound engineers and hardly any producers. A lot of projects come to nothing when there are not enough people to develop film narratives. So I think that the Film Workshop is incredibly important, a real game-changer for Greenlandic cinema.

IT: Only 56,000 people live in Greenland. Why does it make sense to have your own film industry?

EHP: We have a population and a people and a country that has a rich history to relate, and a mythology. All of the Greenlandic and Inuit culture. We have a strong tradition of storytelling, so it's only natural that people would want to test out their stories in new media.

IT: When I watched *Nuummioq*, I realised that it isn't a typical Greenlandic story. What about the storytelling tradition you mention – the myths and sagas – does any of that come through in the film narratives?

EHP: Yes and no. I think that for many Greenlandic filmmakers, it's been about breaking with stereotypes about what Greenland is like. In *Nuummioq*, a central principle was to up-end the dichotomy of the happy, proud hunter in his kayak, on the one hand, and the unhappy, superannuated alcoholic on a bench in a Copenhagen square, on the other. Neither of those things gives a full picture of Greenland. The filmmakers sought the middle ground and made a film set in Nuuk, about a Nuummioq – someone from Nuuk – but telling a completely universal story. The film is about Malik, who is diagnosed with incurable cancer and has to decide what to do with the time he has remaining. If he travels to Denmark, he can get life-extending treatment, but he can also choose to stay at home and look some of the ghosts of his past in the eye. That story could have been set anywhere, and that was the whole idea. At one point, he's out paddling in his canoe. I've never seen a canoe in Greenland, except for in that film. It was a point of principle that he shouldn't be in a kayak. When it comes to the storytelling traditions, I sometimes think what we need in Greenland is a Zacharias Kunuk, who made *Atanarjuat (The Fast Runner)* in Canada in 2001. I remember that he was asked if he would one day make a film set in the present day. He replied that we already have enough images of the present, we need to apply our efforts to recreating non-existent images from the past. We haven't really seen a Greenlandic filmmaker try to do a proper period piece depicting Greenland in the old days. That could be fun. On the other hand, there are established filmmakers like Malik Kleist, who draws on the past and historical narratives in a modern context, so a mythical creature features in a horror film, for example. Or the shamanic realm Angakkoq, which appears as a shadow universe in Mark Fussing Rosbach's sci-fi *Tarratta Nunaanni (Among Us – In the Land of our Shadows*, 2017). So we have a bit of everything, one might say, and that's how it should be in a narrative world that is so complex, where there are so many stories. What I don't think we'll see is that Greenlanders get the urge to make films like the recent Danish documentary *Kampen om Grønland (The Fight for Greenland*, Kenneth Sorento, 2020). It's a wonderful film, really thought-provoking and well made. But it is obviously from a helicopter's-eye-view, whereby it tries to cover the independence debate from a number of different perspectives. It's a film that is very clearly made by an outsider trying to understand this very complex and nuanced universe that we live in. My experience is that the kind of stories that Greenlanders themselves want to tell are more about dipping into an aspect of all that, or a character, and developing a story that is more intimate from that perspective.

IT: There are only three cinemas in Greenland: in Nuuk, Sisimiut and Ilulissat. Where else do films get screened?
EHP: It's really up to the filmmakers to decide how ambitious they want to be about distribution. There are no distribution companies, but we all want our films to come out and be seen. We also want the films to be seen by the people who have paid for them through taxes. The three largest towns encompass 46 per cent of the Greenlandic population, so actually a majority of the population lives outside the three towns where there happens to be a cinema. Sometimes we just have to pick up the film, maybe a projector and screen as well, and travel around to set up screenings. We did that with *Sumé*. We hired a screen from Denmark and a really good projector and crossed our fingers that we'd be able to source PA equipment in all the little towns that we toured round. There's always some kind of performance venue, and it worked fine. You just have to get out and about and show the films in any place that's big enough, like community halls, schools, sports centres or whatever. People really want to see these films, especially Greenlandic films. It's a great, exciting, beautiful experience, but also so time-consuming, and in many cases financially risky, because it's very expensive to travel in Greenland. When we were touring around with *Sumé*, showing it in community centres, it was quite an eye-opener to see how much it meant to people to see precisely this story told in precisely this way and with these visual materials; many people saw themselves on screen – not just metaphorically but literally, as the film contains archive footage of people from that period in private homes and at events.

IT: Overall, why is it so important to develop film production in Greenland?
EHP: Well, why is culture important? Why is it important to know who you are? I think that culture is the stories we tell ourselves about ourselves; that's really what it's about. It's about understanding ourselves, who we are, and that's a story that pre-dates colonisation. Maybe it's not the same story we heard in school. That story was often about colonisation, about modernisation and Hans Egede and all of that history. This is about diving into topics that don't come down to us from above, we might say. For example, what about the wave of facial tattoos that's all the rage now? That's actually also about telling our own story. The search for something or other that indicates

who we really are. I think film can do that so beautifully, because film speaks to all the senses. It's about understanding ourselves, who we are, and about taking that knowledge with us as we go forward. In that sense, film also points us to the future.

Note

The interview was conducted on 10 March 2020 by Isak Thorsen; the transcription was translated from Danish to English by C. Claire Thomson. This version has been lightly edited for clarity and approved by Emile Hertling Péronard.

REFERENCES

Note: the Danish letters æ, ø and å are alphabetised in the same order as they would be in Danish, that is: . . . x, y, z, æ, ø, å. Vowels with other accents have been alphabetised without regard to the accent. Interviews conducted by contributors are listed at the end of the relevant chapters.

á Rógvi, M. (2018), 'Københavns Kommune trækker støtte til Copenhagen Film Fund', TV 2 Lorry, 14 September 2018, <https://www.tv2lorry.dk/artikel/koebenhavns-kommune-traekker-stoette-til-copenhagen-film-fund> (accessed 1 August 2020).

Abend, L. (2019), 'An Island for "Unwanted" Migrants Is Denmark's Latest Aggressive Anti-Immigrant Policy', *Time*, 26 January, <https://time.com/5504331/denmark-migrants-lindholm-island/> (accessed 26 January 2020).

Adetunji, J. (2009), 'Copenhagen's Little Mermaid Heads to China', *The Guardian*, 13 March, <https://www.theguardian.com/world/2009/mar/13/little-mermaid-copenhagen-china> (accessed 9 May 2019).

Affron, C. (1982), *Cinema of Sentiment*, Chicago and London: Chicago University Press.

Agger, G. (2005), *Dansk tv-drama: Arvesølv og underholdning*, Frederiksberg: Samfundslitteratur.

Agger, G. (2006), 'Television-drama', in S. Hjarvard (ed.), *Dansk tv's historie*, Frederiksberg: Samfundslitteratur, pp. 145–78.

Agger, G. (2015), 'Strategies in Danish film culture – and the Case of Susanne Bier', *Kosmorama*, 259, <https://www.kosmorama.org/en/kosmorama/artikler/strategies-danish-film-culture-and-case-susanne-bier> (accessed 2 August 2017).

Alaimo, S. (2010), *Bodily Natures: Science, Environment, and the Material Self*, Bloomington: Indiana University Press.

REFERENCES

Alaimo, S. (2016), *Exposed: Environmental Politics and Pleasures in Posthuman Times*, Minneapolis: University of Minnesota Press.

Albrecht, J. (2001), 'Ny filmby giver løft til Århus', *Information*, 16 May.

Allen, J. K. (2019), 'The Brightest Stars of Early Danish Film', *Danish Silent Film*, Danish Film Institute, <https://www.stumfilm.dk/en/stumfilm/themes/brightest-stars-early-danish-film> (accessed 2 August 2020).

Alsted, C. (1985), 'Gyngerne og karusellerne', *Sekvens 1985*, pp. 138–52

Altman, R. (1984), 'A Semantic Syntactic Approach to Genres', *Cinema* Journal, 23: 3, pp. 6–18.

Altman, R. (1987), *The American Film Musical*, Bloomington and Indianapolis: Indiana University Press.

Andersen, F. S., O. Harsløf, F. Pagh, G. Pedersen, K. Dyssel, H.V. Petersen and I. Z. Sørensen (1977), *Bogen om Morten Korch: en småborgers virksomhed*, Copenhagen: Samleren.

Anderson, B. (1983), *Imagined Communities: Reflections on the Origin and Spread of Nationalism*, London: Verso.

Anderson, B. (1991), *Imagined Communities: Reflections on the Origin and Spread of Nationalism*, revised edition, London: Verso.

Andrew, J. D. (1976), *The Major Film Theories*, Oxford: Oxford University Press.

Anonymous (1910), 'Die Kinematographen-Verhältnisse in Dänemark', *Der Kinematograph*, 196, 28 September.

Anonymous (1912), 'Dänemark und Deutschland: In der Filmkunst', *Der Kinematograph*, 280, 8 May.

Anonymous (1970), 'Standset af en telefonbombe', *Biograf-bladet* no. 11, Nov, p. 15.

Arnedal, P., in cooperation with B. Christensen (2006), *Nordisk Film, en del af Danmark i 100 år*, Copenhagen: Aschehoug Dansk/Nordisk Film.

'Asta Nielsen' (1912), *Maanedsmagasin*. 24 November.

Bach, C. (2005), 'God underholdning i vores egen historie', *Kristeligt Dagblad*, 13 July, <https://www.kristeligt-dagblad.dk/historie/god-underholdning-i-vores-egen-historie> (accessed 1 August 2020).

Badley, L. (2010), *Lars von Trier*, Urbana: University of Illinois Press.

Baggini, J. (2020), *Babette's Feast*. London: The British Film Institute.

Bainbridge, C. (2007), *The Cinema of Lars von Trier: Authenticity and Artifice*, London: Wallflower Press.

Bakker, G. (2008), *Entertainment Industrialised*, Cambridge: Cambridge University Press.

Ballesteros, I. (2015), *Immigration Cinema in the New Europe*, Bristol: Intellect.

Barker, J. M. (2009), *The Tactile Eye: Touch and the Cinematic Experience*, Berkeley: University of California Press.

Baudry, J.-L. (1986), 'Ideological Effects of the Basic Cinematic Apparatus', in P. Rosen (ed.), *Narrative, Apparatus, Ideology*, New York: Columbia University Press, pp. 286–98.

Bazin, A. (1971a), 'An Aesthetics of Reality: Cinematic Realism and the Italian School of the Liberation', in *What is cinema? Vol. II*, Berkeley: University of California Press, pp. 16–40.

Bazin, A. (1971b), 'Bicycle Thieves', in *What is cinema? Vol. II*, Berkeley: University of California Press, pp. 47–60.
Bazin, A. (1971c), 'Umberto D: A great work', in *What is cinema? Vol. II*, Berkeley: University of California Press, pp. 79–82.
Beindorf, C. (2001), *Terror des Idylls: Die kulturelle Konstruktion von Gemeinschaften in Heimatfilm und Landsbygdsfilm 1930–1960 (Die kulturelle Konstruktion von Gemeinschaften im Modernisierungsprozess)*, Baden-Baden: Nomos.
Bell, E. (2005), 'Lars von Trier: Anti-American? Me?', *The Independent*, 21 October, <https://www.independent.co.uk/arts-entertainment/films/features/lars-von-trier-anti-american-me-321010.html> (accessed 17 September 2019).
Bennett, J. (2010), *Vibrant Matter: A Political Ecology of Things*, Durham and London: Duke University Press.
Bergmann, E. (2017), *Nordic Nationalism and Right-Wing Populist Politics: Imperial Relationships and National Sentiments*. London: Palgrave Macmillan.
Bhabha, H. K. (1994), 'DissemiNation: Time, Narrative and the Margins of the Modern nation', in *The Location of Culture*, London and New York: Routledge, pp. 139–70.
Bille, T., A. Grønholm and J. Møgelgaard (2016), 'Why Are Cultural Policy Decisions Communicated in Cool Cash?', *International Journal of Cultural Policy*, 22: 2, pp. 238–55.
Billig, M. (1995), *Banal Nationalism*, London: Sage.
Birkvad, S. (2020), *Da dyden gik amok*, Odense: Syddansk Universitetsforlag.
Bjerre, J., M. Drescher and K. Tofting (2019), 'Indvandrere og efterkommere i de nordiske lande', Danmarks Statistik, <https://www.dst.dk/Site/Dst/Udgivelser/nyt/GetAnalyse.aspx?cid=32554> (accessed 26 January 2020).
Bjørklund, E. (2012), *The Most Delicate Subject: A History of Sex Education Films in Sweden*, Lund: Centre for Languages and Literature.
Björkman, S. (1997), 'An Interview About Kingdom', *Reocities.com*.
Björkman, S. (2003), *Trier on von Trier*, London: Faber and Faber.
blk. (1937), 'Novra!', *Berlingske Tidende*, 17 September.
Blomgren, A.-M. and R. Blomgren (2003), 'Film Production in Sweden – From Art Policy to Industrial Management', Unpublished paper, 7th International Conference on Arts and Cultural Management, Bocconi University, Milan, Italy <http://ernest.hec.ca/video/pedagogie/gestion_des_arts/AIMAC/2003/resources/pdf/B/B14_Blomgren.pdf> (accessed 29 June 2021).
Bondebjerg, I. (n. d.). 'Staten og filmkulturen', Danish Film Institute, <https://www.dfi.dk/viden-om-film/filmhistorie/staten-og-filmkulturen> (accessed 25 July 2020).
Bondebjerg, I. (1984), 'Kritisk humanisme og social engagement', in G. Agger et al. (eds). *Dansk litteraturhistorie 1901-45*, 7, København: Gyldendal, pp. 473–84.
Bondebjerg, I. (1997a), 'Television-mediets gennembrud', 'Monopolkulturens programflade', in K. B. Jensen (ed.), *Dansk mediehistorie, vol. 3: 1960–1995*, Copenhagen: Samleren, pp. 118–48.
Bondebjerg, I. (1997b), 'Dansk film 1972–1997. Æstetisk fornyelse og internationalisering', in I. Bondebjerg, J. Andersen and P. Schepelern (eds), *Dansk film 1972–1997*, København: Gyldendal, pp. 10–25.

REFERENCES

Bondebjerg, I. (2003), 'Dogme 95 and the New Danish Cinema', in M. Hjort and S. MacKenzie (eds), *Purity and Provocation: Dogme 95*, London: British Film Institute, pp. 70–85.

Bondebjerg, I. (2005a), *Filmen og det moderne. Filmgenrer og filmkultur i Danmark 1940–1972*, København: Gyldendal.

Bondebjerg, I. (2005b), 'The Danish Way: Danish Film Culture in a European and Global Perspective', in A. Nestingen and T. G. Elkington (eds.), *Transnational Cinema in a Global North: Nordic Cinema in Transition*, Detroit: Wayne State University Press, pp. 111–38.

Bondebjerg, I. (2012), *Virkelighedsbilleder. Den moderne danske dokumentarfilm*, Frederiksberg: Samfundslitteratur.

Bondebjerg, I. (2014a), *Engaging with Reality. Documentary and Globalization*, Chicago: Chicago University Press.

Bondebjerg, I. (2014b), 'A Social Poetics of Documentary: Grierson and the Scandinavian Documentary Tradition', in Z. Druick and D. Williams (eds), *The Grierson Effect. Tracking Documentary's International Movement*, BFI/Palgrave: London, pp. 79-93.

Bondebjerg, I. (2014c), 'Max Kestner', in M. Hjort, I. Bondebjerg, and E. Redvall (eds.), *The Danish Directors 3. Dialogues on the New Danish Documentary Cinema*, Chicago: Chicago University Press, pp. 163-81.

Bondebjerg, I. (2016), 'Regional and Global Dimensions of Danish Film Culture and Film Policy', in M. Hjort and U. Lindqvist (eds.), *A Companion to Nordic Cinema*, Malvern: John Wiley & Sons, pp. 19–40.

Bondebjerg, I. (2018), 'Verden i Danmark og dokumentar', in G. Agger, J. Christensen and L. Jacobsen (eds), *TV-analyse*, Århus: Systime, pp. 105–23.

Bondebjerg, I., J. Andersen and P. Schepelern (eds) (1997), *Dansk film 1972–1997*, København: Gyldendal.

Bondebjerg, I. and U. Bondebjerg (2017), *Dansk film og kulturel globalisering*, Frederiksberg: Samfundslitteratur.

Bondebjerg, I., E. N. Redvall, C. Astrupgaard, R. Helles, S. S. Lai and H. Søndergaard (2017), *Transnational European Television Drama: Production, Genres and Audiences*, Basingstoke: Palgrave Macmillan.

Booth, M. (2014), *The Almost Nearly Perfect People: Behind the Myth of the Scandinavian Utopia*, London: Vintage.

Bordwell, D. (1981), *The Films of Carl-Theodor Dreyer*, Berkeley, Los Angeles: University of California Press.

Bordwell, D. (1986), 'Classical Hollywood Cinema: Narrational Principles and Procedures', in P. Rosen (ed.), *Narrative, Apparatus, Ideology*, New York: Columbia University Press, pp. 17–34.

Bordwell, D. (2010), 'The Dreyer Generation', *Carl Th. Dreyer: The Man and His Work*, Danish Film Institute, <http://english.carlthdreyer.dk/AboutDreyer/Visualstyle/The-Dreyer-Generation.aspx> (accessed 28 February 2019).

Bordwell, D., K. Thompson and J. Staiger (1985), *The Classical Hollywood Cinema. Film Style and Mode of Production to 1960*, London: Routledge.

Bradshaw, P. (2003), 'Wilbur Wants to Kill Himself: Review', *The Guardian*, 5 December, <https://www.theguardian.com/film/News_Story/Critic_Review/Guardian_review/0,,1099881,00.html> (accessed 20 December 2019).

Bradshaw, P. (2011), 'Drive: Review', *The Guardian*, 22 September, <https://www.theguardian.com/film/2011/sep/22/drive-ryan-gosling-film-review> (accessed 16 September 2019).
Brandes, G. (1877), *Emigrantlitteraturen*. Anden omarbejdede Udgave, Kjøbenhavn: Gyldendalske Boghandels Forlag.
Breitenborn, U. (1994), 'Stereotype der Olsenbandenfilme und deren Rezeption in Ostdeutschland', *Text & Kontext. Zeitschrift für germanistische Literaturforschung in Skandinavien*, 17: 1, pp. 124–47.
Breuning, U. (2002), 'Danske børnefilm', in U. Breuning (ed.), *De pokkers unger*, København: Høst & Søn, pp. 9–53.
Briens, S. (2016), 'Boréalisme: Le Nord comme espace discursif', *Études germaniques* 282: 2, pp. 179–88. DOI: 10.3917/eger.282.0179
Brooks, P. (1976), *The Melodramatic Imagination: Balzac, Henry James, Melodrama, and the Mode of Excess*, New Haven: Yale University Press.
Brown, M. (2016), 'Sounding Off: Inaudible Dialogue is Rife among Dramas', Royal Television Society, May 2016 <https://rts.org.uk/article/sounding-inaudible-dialogue-rife-among-dramas> (accessed 19 February 2020).
Bruzzi, S. (2002), *New Documentary. A Critical Introduction*, London, New York: Routledge.
Budtz-Jørgensen, A. (2016). 'Danske Oscar-vindere fra 1931 og frem', *DFI nyheder*, Danish Film Institute, <https://www.dfi.dk/nyheder/danske-oscar-vindere-fra-1931-og-frem> (accessed 25 July 2020)
Budtz-Jørgensen, A. (2019), 'Biografbilletter 1976–2019', *Viden om film*, Danish Film Institute, <https://www.dfi.dk/viden-om-film/tal-og-fakta/billetsalg-i-danske-biografer-1976-2018> (accessed 30 July 2020).
Bundgaard, P. (1988), *Livet er skønt: Erindringer*, Frederiksberg: Fisker.
Burns, R. (2007), 'Towards a Cinema of Cultural Hybridity: Turkish-German Filmmakers and the Representation of Alterity', *Debatte: Journal of Contemporary Central and Eastern Europe*, 15:1, pp. 3–20.
Carroll, N. (1991), 'Notes on the Sight Gag', in A. Horton (ed.), *Comedy, Cinema, Theory*, Berkeley: University of California Press, pp. 25–42.
Carroll, N. (1996), *Theorizing the Moving Image*, Cambridge: Cambridge University Press.
Carter, O. (2018), 'Original Climax Films: Historicizing the British Hardcore Pornography Film Business', *Porn Studies*, 5: 4, pp. 411–25.
Chernilo, D. (2006), 'Social Theory's Methodological Nationalism: Myth and Reality', *European Journal of Social Theory*, 9:1, 5–22.
Christensen, C. L. (2002), 'Piger og drenge i danske børnefilm', in U. Breuning (ed.), *De pokkers unger*, København: Høst & Søn, pp. 54–75.
Christensen, C. L. (2006), 'Børne- og ungdoms-tv', in S. Hjarvard (ed.), *Dansk TV's Historie*, København: Forlaget Samfundslitteratur, pp. 65–104.
Christensen, C. L. (2008), 'Ung er ung værst: Danske ungdomsfilm efter 2000', *Tidsskriftet Ungdomsforskning* 6: 4, pp. 9–12.
Christensen, C. L. (2013), 'Engaging, Critical, Entertaining: Transforming Public Service Television for Children in Denmark', *Interactions: Studies in Communication and Culture* 4: 3, pp. 271–87.

REFERENCES

Christensen, T. C. (1997), 'Isbjørnens fald: Nordisk Films Kompagni og første verdenskrig', in H. K. Haastrup and T. K. Grodal (eds), *Sekvens 97: Filmæstetik og Billedhistorie. Filmvidenskabelig årbog 1997*, Copenhagen: Institut for Film og Medievidenskab, Københavns Universitet, pp. 229–39.

Christiansen, F. J. (2016), 'The Danish People's Party: Combining Cooperation and Radical Positions', in T. Akkerman, S. L. de Lange and M. Rooduijn (eds), *Radical Right-Wing Populist Parties in Western Europe: Into the Mainstream?* London: Routledge, pp. 94–112.

Committee for Film, 2006, 'Canon for Film', <https://kulturkanon.kum.dk/english/film/> (accessed 26 July 2020).

Cowie, E. (2011), *Recording Reality, Desiring the Real*, Minneapolis & London: University of Minnesota Press.

Dam, F. (2018), 'Phie Ambo søger svar i de højere luftlag', Women in Nordic Film, <http://www.nordicwomeninfilm.com/phie-ambo-soger-svar-i-de-hojere-luftlag/> (accessed 24 November, 2019)

Danish Film Institute (2010–21), 'Carl Th. Dreyer – The Man and His Work', <https://www.carlthdreyer.dk/en> (last accessed 3 January 2020).

Danish Film Institute (2014), *10 år med New Danish Screen* [10 Year Anniversary Publication], Copenhagen: DFI.

Danish Film Institute (2016a), *Undersøgelse af kønsfordelingen i dansk film*, Copenhagen: Det Danske Filminstitut, <https://www.dfi.dk/branche-og-stoette/viden-og-publikationer/publikationer/undersogelse-af-konsfordelingen-i-dansk> (accessed 1 August 2020).

Danish Film Institute (2016b), 'Radical Filmmaking on Low-Budget', <https://www.dfi.dk/en/english/radical-filmmaking-low-budget> (accessed 1 October 2019).

Danish Film Institute (2018a), *Køn i dansk film 2012–2017*, Copenhagen: Det Danske Filminstitut, <https://www.dfi.dk/branche-og-stoette/publikationer-og-indsatser/publikationer/kon-i-dansk-film-2012-2017> (accessed 1 August 2020).

Danish Film Institute (2018b), *Undersøgelse af etnisk mangfoldighed i dansk film*, <https://www.dfi.dk/branche-og-stoette/publikationer-og-indsatser/publikationer/undersogelse-af-etnisk-mangfoldighed-i> (accessed 12 February 2020).

Danish Film Institute (2018c), 'Filmaftale 2019–2023', Om Filminstituttet, <https://www.dfi.dk/omdfi/filmaftaler-og-okonomi/filmaftale-2019-2023> (accessed 3 August 2020).

Danish Film Institute (2019), 'Skitsen2', <https://www.dfi.dk/branche-og-stoette/stoette/skitsen2> (accessed July 24, 2020)

Danish Film Institute (2020), 'Tal og fakta', <https://www.dfi.dk/viden-om-film/tal-og-fakta> (accessed 12 February 2020).

Danish Silent Film 2019, 'About', Danish Film Institute, <https://www.stumfilm.dk/en/stumfilm/about> (accessed 27 July 2020).

Danmarks Statistik (2020), 'Statistikbanken: Befolkning og valg', <https://www.dst.dk/da/Statistik/emner/befolkning-og-valg> (accessed 1 August 2020).

Dansk Folkeparti (2020), 'Pas på Danmark', <https://danskfolkeparti.dk/pas-paa-danmark/> (accessed 26 January 2020).

Davison, A. (2013), 'Title Sequences for Contemporary Television Serials', in J. Richardson, C. Gorbman and C. Vernallis (eds), *The Oxford Handbook of New Audiovisual Aesthetics*, Oxford: Oxford University Press, pp. 146–67.

Den Vestdanske Filmpulje (2019), 'Vilkår for støtte', <https://filmpuljen.dk/wp-content/uploads/2019/05/DVF-midlertidige-støttevilkår-2019.pdf> (accessed 10 April 2020).
Dinesen, Isak [Karen Blixen] (2001) [1958], 'Babette's Feast', in *Anecdotes of Destiny*, London: Penguin Classics, pp. 21–68.
Dinnesen, N. J. and E. Kau (1983), *Filmen i Danmark*, Copenhagen: Akademisk Forlag.
Doty, A. (2000), *Flaming Classics: Queering the Film Canon*, New York: Routledge.
Douglas, M. (1991), 'Jokes', in C. Mukerji and M. Schudson (eds), *Re-Thinking Popular Culture*, Berkeley: University of California Press, pp. 291–311.
Dreyer, C. T. (1931), 'Carl Th. Dreyer udtaler sig: Hvorledes Amerikanerne optager Film', *Politiken*, 26 April, section 2, p. 8.
Dreyer, C. T. (1973a), 'New Roads for the Danish Film – H. C. Andersen (1939)', in D. Skoller (ed.), *Dreyer in Double Reflection: Carl Dreyer's Writings on Film*, New York: Dutton, pp. 79–89.
Dreyer, C.T. (1973b), 'Swedish Film (1920)', in D. Skoller (ed.), *Dreyer in Double Reflection: Carl Dreyer's Writings on Film*, New York: Dutton, pp. 21–29.
Drotner, K. (1997), 'Filmkultur i børnehøjde', in I. Bondebjerg, J. Andersen and P. Schepelern (eds), *Dansk film 1972–1997*, København: Gyldendal, pp. 134–65.
Drouzy, M. (1982), *Carl Th. Dreyer, né Nilsson*, Paris: Éditions du Cerf.
Drouzy, M. (1988), 'Une oeuvre de foi "en l'art et la vérité"', *L'Avant-Scène Cinéma*, 367–8, pp. 9–13.
Drouzy, M. (1993), 'Les Années noires de Dreyer', *Cinémathèque*, 4, pp. 68–83.
Drum, D. D. and J. Drum (2000), *My Only Great Passion: The Life and Films of Carl Th. Dreyer*, Scarecrow Filmmakers Series; no. 68; Lanham, MD: Scarecrow Press.
Dunleavy, T. (2017), *Complex Serial Drama and Multiplatform Television*, New York: Routledge.
Eberlein, F. (2001), *Das große Lexikon der Olsenbande*, Berlin: Schwarzkopf & Schwarzkopf.
Ebert, R. (2004), 'Wilbur Wants to Kill Himself', <https://www.rogerebert.com/reviews/wilbur-wants-to-kill-himself-2004> (accessed 20 December 2019).
Ebert, R. (2007), 'Things We Lost in the Fire', <https://www.rogerebert.com/reviews/things-we-lost-in-the-fire-2007> (accessed 8 August 2019).
Element Film 1987, *Epidemic*, Press Kit, p. 6.
Elkington, T. G. (2005), 'Costumes, Adolescence, and Dogma: Nordic Film and American Distribution', in A. K. Nestingen and T. G. Elkington (eds), *Transnational Cinema in a Global North: Nordic Cinema in Transition*, Detroit: Wayne State University Press, pp. 31–53.
Ellis, J. (1982), *Visible Fictions: Cinema, Television, Video*, London: Routledge.
Elster, J. (1992), 'Conventions, Creativity, Originality', in M. Hjort (ed.), *Rules and Conventions: Literature, Philosophy, Social Theory*, Baltimore: The Johns Hopkins University Press.
Elster, J. (2000), *Ulysses Unbound: Studies in Rationality, Precommitment, and Constraints*, Cambridge: Cambridge University Press.
Engberg, M. (1966), *Asta Nielsen*, Copenhagen: Det danske filmmuseum.
Engberg, M. (1977), *Dansk stumfilm – de store år I & II*, København, Rhodos.
Ehrlich, D. (2019), '"The Kindness of Strangers" Review: Great Performances Can't Save Lone Scherfig's Awkward Melodrama', *Indiewire*, 7 February, <https://www.indiewire.

REFERENCES

com/2019/02/the-kindness-of-strangers-review-berlinale-2019-1202042103/> (accessed 7 February 2019).

Ernst, J. (1964), 'Lars Peter Elfelt', *Kosmorama*, 66, pp. 156–61, <https://www.kosmorama.org/kosmorama/arkiv/66/lars-peter-elfelt> (accessed 3 August 2020).

Fiedler, L. [1969] (1977), 'Cross the Border – Close the Gap', in *A Fiedler Reader*, New York: Stein and Day, pp. 270–94.

Filmexplorer Switzerland (2018), 'Interview, Hlynur Pálmason, "Vinterbrødre" (Winter Brothers)', YouTube, August 25 <https://www.youtube.com/watch?v=FxhlODcqNb8> (accessed 29 September 2019).

FilmFyn (2019), 'Funding', FilmFyn, <http://www.filmfyn.dk/funding/> (accessed 10 April 2019).

Film i Väst (2017), 'Film i Väst as Co-Producer', Film i Väst, <https://filmivast.com/postproduction-companies/> (accessed 27 February 2020).

Florin, B. (2010), 'Victor Sjöström and the Golden Age', in M. Larsson and A. Marklund (eds), *Swedish Film: An Introduction and Reader*, Lund: Nordic Academic Press, pp. 76–85.

Florin, B. (2012), *Transition and Transformation: Victor Sjöström in Hollywood 1923–1930*, Amsterdam: Amsterdam University Press.

FLP (FilmLab Palestine) (2017), 'PFM Talks – Low-Budget Film Production', <http://pcd.flp.ps/content/pfm-talks-low-budget-film-production> (accessed 1 October 2019).

Forbes, J. (1988), 'Axel's Feast', *Sight and Sound*, 57: 2, pp. 106–7.

Freeland, C. (2010), *Portraits and Persons*, Oxford: Oxford University Press.

French, P. (2005), 'Spin Cycle: The Perils of Political Intrigue are Examined in a Powerful Danish Thriller', *The Observer*, 25 September, <https://www.theguardian.com/theobserver/2005/sep/25/features.review47> (accessed 29 July 2020).

Fridja, N. and E. S. Tan (1999), 'Sentiment in Film Viewing', in C. Plantinga and G. M. Smith (eds), *Passionate Views. Film, Cognition, and Emotion*, Baltimore: John Hopkins Press, pp. 48–64.

Fønss, O. (1930a), *Danske skuespillerinder*, Copenhagen: Nutids Forlag.

Fønss, O. (1930b), *Films-Erindringer gennem 20 aar*, Copenhagen: Nutids Forlag.

Gandrup, C. (1919), *Olaf Fønss: En monografi*, Copenhagen: Lindhardt and Ringhof.

Gentikow, B. (1994), 'Zwei deutsche Olsenbanden: Übersetzung zwischen Kulturtransfer und kultureller Hegemonie, *Text & Kontext. Zeitschrift für germanistische Literaturforschung in Skandinavien*, 19: 1, pp. 148–71.

Grau, R. (1914), *The Theatre of Science: A Volume of Progress and Achievements in the Motion Picture Art*, New York, London: Broadway Publishing Company.

Grodal, T. (2009), *Embodied Visions: Evolution, Emotion, Culture, and Film*, New York: Oxford University Press.

Grønlund, A. and E. Dybdal (2020), 'En film uden kajakker? Et lokationsstudie af grønlandsfilmen Nuummioq. Del 1: Filmen', *16:9*, 6 February <http://www.16-9.dk/2020/02/gronlandsfilmen-del1/> (accessed 1 March 2020).

Hagener, M. (2014), 'Introduction: Emergence of Film Culture', in M. Hagener (ed.), *The Emergence of Film Culture: Knowledge Production, Institution Building, and the Fate of the Avant-Garde in Europe, 1919–1945*, New York: Berghahn Books, pp. 1–18.

Hall, S. (1999), 'Encoding, Decoding', in S. During (ed.), *The Cultural Studies Reader*, 2nd edn, London and New York: Routledge, pp. 507–17.
Hallam, J. with M. Marshment (2000), *Realism and Popular Cinema*, Manchester: Manchester University Press.
Hankins, J. (2007), 'Humanism, Scholasticism, and Renaissance Philosophy', in J. Hankins (ed.), *The Cambridge Companion to Renaissance* Philosophy, Cambridge: Cambridge University Press, pp. 30–48.
Hansen, K. T. and A. M. Waade (2017), *Locating Nordic Noir: From Beck to The Bridge*, Basingstoke: Palgrave Macmillan.
Hansert, A. (2007), *Asta Nielsen und die Filmstadt Babelsberg: Das Engagement Carl Schleussners in der deutschen Filmindustrie*, Petersburg, Germany: Michael Imhof Verlag.
Hardy, F. (1947), 'Denmark Has Thriving Film Movement To-day', *Weekly Scotsman*, archived in DI, A: Vredens Dag, 145, Carl Th. Dreyer Archive, Danish Film Institute.
Harrison, E. (2017), 'Why Is It So Hard to Hear the Dialogue in Television Dramas?', *Radio Times*, 23 February, <https://www.radiotimes.com/news/tv/2017-02-23/tv-sound-problems-drama-dialogue/> (accessed 19 February 2020).
Hartvigson, N. H. (2006), 'Early Danish Musical Comedies', in I. Conrich and E. Tincknell (eds), *Film's Musical Moments*, Edinburgh: Edinburgh University Press, pp. 171–82.
Hartvigson, N. H. (2007), *1930'ernes danske filmkomedie i et lyd-, medie- og genreperspektiv*, Copenhagen: Det humanistiske fakultet, Grafisk KUA.
Hartvigson, N. H. (2013), 'Rural Intentions: Sexuality in Danish Homeland Cinema', *Journal of Scandinavian Cinema*, 3: 2, pp. 107–24.
Hartvigson, N. H. (2016), 'Queer teori og Baronessen fra Benzintanken', in J. R. Christensen and S. L. Christiansen (eds), *Mærkk – Æstetik og Kommunikation: Filmanalyse*, AAU, Aalborg: Systime, pp. 251–65.
Hartvigson, N. H. (2017a), 'Annelise Reenberg', Nordic Women in Film, <http://www.nordicwomeninfilm.com/person/annelise-reenberg/> (accessed 1 August 2020).
Hartvigson, N. H. (2017b), 'En kvindelig komiker', Nordic Women in Film, <http://www.nordicwomeninfilm.com/en-kvindelig-komiker> (accessed 1 August 2020).
Hauge, H. (2003), *Post-Danmark: Politik og æstetik hinsides det nationale*, Copenhagen: Lindhardt & Ringhof.
Hedling, E. (2015), 'The Battle of Dybbøl Revisited: The Danish Press Reception of the TV-series 1864', *Kosmorama*, 261, <https://www.kosmorama.org/kosmorama/artikler/battle-dybbol-revisited-danish-press-reception-tv-series-1864> (accessed 1 August 2020).
Hedling, O. (2007), 'Smilende gyldenbrune øjne: De politisk korrekte indvandrerreportrætters dominans i svensk film', *Kosmorama*, 240, pp. 33–49.
Hedling, O. (2018a), 'The Regional Film Fund as Co-production Crusader: The Case of Film i Väst', in J. Hammett-Jamart, P. Mitric and E. N. Redvall (eds), *European Film and Television Co-production*, Cham: Palgrave Macmillan, pp. 175–89.
Hedling, O. (2018b), 'Contemporary Scandinavian Cinema between Art and Commerce', in R. Stone, P. Cooke, S. Dennison and A. Marlow-Mann (eds), *The Routledge Companion to World Cinema*, London: Routledge, pp. 146–56.

REFERENCES

Heindry, J. (1997), *What Wild Ecstasy: The Rise and Fall of the Sexual Revolution*, New York: Simon and Schuster.

Hending, A. (1942), *Valdemar Psilander*, Copenhagen: Urania.

Hending, A. (1943), *Olaf Fønss*, Copenhagen: Urania.

Hending, A. (1958), 'Det københavnske Hollywood', *Historiske meddelelser om København*, 4th series, vol. 4, Copenhagen: C. E. C. Gad.

Hennig, R., A.-K. Jonasson and P. Degerman (2018), 'Introduction: Nordic Narratives of Nature and the Environment', in R. Hennig, A.-K. Jonasson and P. Degerman (eds), *Nordic Narratives of Nature and the Environment: Ecocritical Approaches to Northern European Literatures and Cultures*, Lanham, MD: Lexington Books, pp. 1–18.

Henningsen, P. ['P-H'] (1928), 'Pornografiens pædagogiske værdi', *Kritisk Revy*, hefte 2, juli, pp. 48–52.

Hesmondhalgh, D. (2013), *The Cultural Industries*, London: SAGE Publications.

Hirschsprung Collection (n. d.), 'The Skagen Painters', <https://www.hirschsprung.dk/en/collection/theme/samling-skagensmalerne> (accessed 31 July 2020).

Hjort, M. (2003), 'Dogme 95: A Small Nation's Response to Globalisation', in M. Hjort and S. MacKenzie (eds), *Purity and Provocation*, London: BFI, pp. 31–47.

Hjort, M. (2005), *Small Nation, Global Cinema: The New Danish Cinema*, Minneapolis: University of Minnesota Press.

Hjort, M. (2006), 'Gifts, Games and Cheek: Counter-Globalisation in a Privileged Small-Nation Context: The Case of *The Five Obstructions*', in C. C. Thomson (ed.), *Northern Constellations: New Readings in Nordic Cinema*, Norwich: Norvik Press, pp. 111–29.

Hjort, M. (2007), 'Denmark', in M. Hjort and D. Petrie (eds.), *The Cinema of Small Nations*, Edinburgh: Edinburgh University Press, pp. 23–42.

Hjort, M. (ed.) (2008), 'On the Five Obstructions' (theme issue), *Dekalog* 1, London: Wallflower.

Hjort, M. (2010a), *Lone Scherfig's* Italian for Beginners. Seattle: University of Washington Press.

Hjort, M. (2010b), 'On the Plurality of Cinematic Transnationalism', in N. Ďurovičová and K. E. Newman (eds), *World Cinemas: Transnational Perspectives*, New York and Oxon: Routledge, pp. 12–33.

Hjort, M. (2014), 'Mikala Krogh', in M. Hjort, I. Bondebjerg and E. N. Redvall (eds), *The Danish Directors 3*, Bristol & Chicago: Intellect Press, pp. 181–205.

Hjort, M. (2015), 'The Risk Environment of Filmmaking', in J. Blankenship and T. Nagl (eds), *European Visions*, Bielefeld: Transcript Verlag, pp. 49–64.

Hjort, M. (2017), 'Dogme 95 – arven', in P. Schepelern (ed.), *Lars von Trier: Det gode med det onde*, Odense: Brandts Klædefabrik, pp. 111–15.

Hjort, M. (2018), 'Gender Equity in Screen Culture: On Susanne Bier, the Celluloid Ceiling, and the Growing Appeal of TV Production', in M. Molloy, M. Nielsen and M. Shriver-Rice (eds), *ReFocus: The Films of Susanne* Bier, Edinburgh: Edinburgh University Press, pp. 134–54.

Hjort, M. (2019), 'The Ontological Transnationalism of the Filmmaker: Solidarity-Based Talent Development across Borders', *Transnational Screens*, 10: 1, pp. 53–58.

Hjort, M. and I. Bondebjerg (2001), 'Introduction: Danish Cinema: A Small Nation in a Global Culture', in M. Hjort and I. Bondebjerg (eds), *The Danish Directors: Dialogues on a Contemporary National Cinema*, Bristol: Intellect, pp. 8–22.
Hjort, M. and I. Bondebjerg (eds) (2001), *The Danish Directors: Dialogues on a Contemporary National Cinema*, Bristol: Intellect.
Hjort, M., E. Jørholt and E. N. Redvall (eds) (2010), *The Danish Directors 2: Dialogues on the New Danish Fiction Cinema*, Bristol: Intellect.
Hjort, M. and U. Lindqvist (2016), 'Introduction: Nordic Cinema: Breaking New Waves since the Dawn of Film', in M. Hjort and U. Lindqvist (eds), *A Companion to Nordic Cinema*, New York: John Wiley & Sons, Inc, pp. 1–13.
Hjort, M. and S. MacKenzie (eds) (2003), *Purity and Provocation: Dogma 95*, London: BFI Publications.
Hjort, M. and D. Petrie (eds) (2007), *The Cinema of Small Nations*, Edinburgh: Edinburgh University Press.
Hobsbawm, E. [1983] (2014), 'Introduction: Inventing Traditions' in E. Hobsbawm and P. Granger (eds), *The Invention of Tradition*, Cambridge: Cambridge University Press, pp 1–14.
Hochscherf, T. and H. Philipsen (2017), *Beyond The Bridge: Contemporary Danish Television Drama*, Basingstoke: Palgrave Macmillan.
Holse, L. S. (2018), 'No Investments From Copenhagen Film Fund in 2019', Copenhagen Film Fund, 13 November, http://cphfilmfund.com/en/no-investments-from-copenhagen-film-fund-in-2019/ (accessed 4 April 2019).
Hong, N. (2012), *Occupied: Denmark's Adaptation and Resistance to German Occupation 1940–45*, Copenhagen: Frihedsmuseets Venners Forlag.
Honig, B. and L. J. Marso (eds) (2016), *Politics, Theory, and Film: Critical Encounters with Lars von Trier*. Oxford: Oxford University Press.
Howkins, J. (2001), *The Creative Economy*, London: Allen Lane.
Hvidt, A. R. (ed.) (2007), *Hammershøi > Dreyer. Billedmagi*, Copenhagen: Ordrupgaard.
'Hvor Bjergene sejler' (1955) [film programme], 'Hvor Bjergene sejler', Statens Filmcentral særsamling, Danish Film Institute.
Høeg, P. (1996), *The History of Danish Dreams*, trans. Barbara Haveland, London: Harvill (e-book).
Ingold, T. (2012), 'Toward an Ecology of Materials', *Annual Review of Anthropology*, 41 (October), pp. 427–42, <http://dx.doi.org/10.1146/annurev-anthro-081309-145920> (accessed 1 August 2020).
'Instruktørernes valg . . .' (1963), *Kosmorama*, 63, pp. 18–21.
Iversen, E. (1997), 'Die Olsen-Bande', in H. Lange-Fuchs (ed.), *"Ich habe einen Plaan!" Die Olsen-Bande: Slapstick-Komik zwischen Klamauk und Subversion*, Lübeck: Nordische Filmtage, pp. 11–14.
Jacobsen, W., A. Kaes and H. H. Prinzler (eds) (1993), *Geschichte des deutschen Films*, Stuttgart: J. B. Metzler.
Jellinge, M. (2010), *Filmby Århus: et processtudie af projektet Filmby Århus fra idé til etablering*, Aarhus: Aarhus University.
Jensen, J. R. (2014), 'New Danish Film Agreement Signed', Screen Daily, 10 November, <https://www.screendaily.com/news/new-danish-film-agreement-signed/5079842.article> (accessed 1 August 2020).

REFERENCES

Jensen, K. B. (ed.) (2001), *Dansk mediehistorie, Vol. 2: 1880–1960*, Copenhagen: Samfundslitteratur.

Jensen, P. M., J. I. Nielsen and A. M. Waade (2016), 'When Public Service Drama Travels: The Internationalization of Danish Television Drama and the Associated Production Funding Models', *Journal of Popular Television*, 4: 1, pp. 91–108.

Jerslev, A. (2005), 'Performativity and documentary: Sami Saif's and Phie Ambo's *Family* and performativity', in R. Gade and A. Jerslev (eds), *Performative Realism*, Copenhagen: Museum Tusculanum Press, pp. 85–117.

Johnson, R. (1986–87), 'What Is Cultural Studies Anyway?', *Social Text*, 16 (Winter), pp. 38–80.

Jupskås, A. R. (2019), 'Why Did the Danish People's Party Lose More Than Fifty Percent of its Votes?', C-REX, Center for Research on Extremism, University of Oslo, <https://www.sv.uio.no/c-rex/english/news-and-events/right-now/2019/danish-election-2019.html> (accessed 28 January 2020).

Jørgensen, A. D. [1882] (1998), *40 Fortællinger af Fædrelandets Historie*, Copenhagen: Sesam.

Jørholt, E. (2001), '1940–49: Voksen, følsom og elegant', in P. Schepelern (ed.), *100 års dansk film*, Copenhagen: Rosinante.

Jørholt, E. (2008), '1940–49: Voksen, følsom og elegant', in P. Schepelern (ed.), *100 års dansk film*, København: Rosinante, pp. 121–64.

Jørholt. E. (2020), '"The Real Deal": Queering Danish National Identity', *Kosmorama*, 278, <https://www.kosmorama.org/real-deal-queering-danish-national-identity> (accessed 30 May 2021).

Kääpä, P. (2014), *Ecology and Contemporary Nordic Cinemas: From Nation-Building to Ecocosmopolitanism*, London: Bloomsbury.

Kääpä, P. and T. Gustafsson (eds) (2013), *Transnational Ecocinema: Film Culture in an Era of Ecological Transformation*, Bristol: Intellect.

Kau, E. (1989), *Dreyers filmkunst*, [Copenhagen]: Akademisk forlag.

Kelley, S. (2017), '*The Dark Tower* Reviews: What the Critics Are Saying', *Variety News*, 3 August, <https://variety.com/2017/film/news/the-dark-tower-review-roundup-idris-elba-1202514697/> (accessed 2 August 2020).

Kelly, R. (2000), *The Name of this Book is Dogme 95*, London: Faber and Faber.

Kistrup, J. (1977), 'Gensynet med gamle lystspils-film', *Politiken,* 23 September.

Kjældgaard, L. H. (2011), '"An Open System with an Objective External to Itself": The Rapprochement Between Danish Politics and Literature in the Golden Age of the Welfare State, 1950–1980', *Scandinavica* 50: 1, pp. 9–26.

Kjørup, S. (1991), 'Folkelig underholdning før fjernsynet', *Kosmorama*, 198, pp 13–17.

Kloster Bro, R. (2019a), 'Video-skitsen som grundlæggende arbejdsredskab', Research project, Copenhagen: National Film School of Denmark. [NB Kloster Bro 2019b is an interview listed in Chapter 16.]

Knegt, P. (2010), 'A Danish "Grey Gardens"? Eva Mulvad On Her "Good Life"', *IndieWire*, 16 November, <https://www.indiewire.com/2010/11/a-danish-grey-gardens-eva-mulvad-on-her-good-life-244386/> (accessed 24 November 2019).

Koerber, M. (2008), 'Some Notes on the Restoration of Dreyer's *Vampyr* (1932)', <https://www.carlthdreyer.dk/carlthdreyer/some-notes-restoration-dreyers-vampyr-1932> (accessed 4 February 2020).

Körber, L.-A. and E. Volquardsen (eds) (2014), *The Postcolonial North Atlantic: Iceland, Greenland and the Faroe Islands*, Berliner Beitrage zur Skandinavistik, Band 20. Berlin: Nordeuropa-Institut der Humboldt-Universität.

Körber, L.-A., S. MacKenzie and A. Westerståhl Stenport (eds) (2017), *Arctic Environmental Modernities: From the Age of Polar Exploration to the Anthropocene*, Switzerland: Palgrave Studies in World Environmental History. Cham: Springer for Palgrave Macmillan.

Koutsourakis, A. (2013), *Politics as Form in Lars Von Trier: A Post-Brechtian Reading*, London: Bloomsbury Academic.

Kracauer, S. (1961), *Theory of Film: The Redemption of Physical Reality*. Oxford: Oxford University Press.

Kruuse, J. (1964), *Holbergs maske*, Copenhagen: Uglebog.

Kulturministerens udvalg om dansk film i udlandet (2010), *Dansk film: En styrkeposition for den global markedsføring af Danmark*, Copenhagen: Det Danske Filminstitut, <https://www.dfi.dk/files/docs/2018-02/udvalgsrapport_2010.pdf> (accessed 30 July 2020).

Kulturministeriet (n. d.), 'Welcome to the Cultural Canon!', <https://kulturkanon.kum.dk/english/about-kulturkanon/> (accessed 25 July 2020).

Kulturministeriet (1997), The Film Act: No. 186 of 12 March 1997.

Kulturministeriet (2018), '560 mio. kr. om året til dansk film', 2 November, <https://www.regeringen.dk/nyheder/filmaftale-paa-plads/> (accessed 2 August 2020).

Kutchinsky, B. (1970), *Studies on Pornography and Sex Crimes in Denmark, a Report to the US Presidential Commission on Obscenity and Pornography*, Copenhagen: Social Science Monographs 17.

Kutchinsky, B. (1973), 'Pornografi', in A. Diderichsen and J. Israel (eds.), *Sexologi*, København: Hans Reitzels forlag, pp. 277–78.

Kvam, K., J. Risum and J.Wiingaard (1993), *Dansk teaterhistorie: Bind 2, Folkets teater*, Copenhagen: Gyldendal.

Lachmann, M. (1997), 'Vom Ereignis zum Kult', in H. Lange-Fuchs (ed.), *"Ich habe einen Plaan!" Die Olsen-Bande. Slapstick-Komik zwischen Klamauk und Subversion*, Lübeck: Nordische Filmtage, pp. 15–18.

Ladegaard, C. (2019), 'Welcome to Facts & Figures 2020', *Facts & Figures 2020*, Copenhagen: Danish Film Institute, p. 3, <https://www.dfi.dk/en/english/numbers-and-statistics/facts-figures-2020> (accessed 31 July 2020).

Lange-Fuchs, H. (ed.) (1997), *"Ich habe einen Plaan!" Die Olsen-Bande. Slapstick-Komik zwischen Klamauk und Subversion*, Lübeck: Nordische Filmtage.

Langkjær, B. (2002), 'Realism in Danish Cinema', in A. Jerslev (ed.), *Realism and 'Reality' in Film and Media: Northern Lights*, Copenhagen: Museum Tusculanum Press, pp. 15–40.

Langkjær, B. (2005), 'Reality under Critical Examination: Ole Palsbo's Feature Films', in T. Grodal (ed.), *Visual Authorship. Creativity and Intentionality in Media: Northern Lights*. Copenhagen: Museum Tusculanum Press, pp. 169–95.

Langkjær, B. (2012), *Realismen i dansk film*, Frederiksberg: Samfundslitteratur.

Langsted, A. (1918), *Asta Nielsen*, Copenhagen: Nyt Nordisk Forlag.

Larsen, L. O. (1993), 'Egons planer og Olsenbanden som komedie: Et notat om planens bidrag til Olsenbandens narrative struktur', in K. Skretting (ed.), *Kringkasting og kino*, Oslo: Norges forskningsråd, pp. 122–33.

REFERENCES

Larsen, R. E. (2006), 'Dannebrog-initiativet', <https://www.humanisme.dk/diverse/dannebrog-initiativ.php> (accessed 25 July 2020).

Larsen, S. P. (2019), 'Western Arabs: Inheriting the Cultural Divide', DFI News, 30 January, <https://www.dfi.dk/en/english/news/western-arabs-inheriting-cultural-divide> (accessed 12 February 2019).

Lauzen, M. (2017), *Women in Independent Film, 2016–2017*, Center for the Study of Women in Television & Film, San Diego State University, <https://womenintvfilm.sdsu.edu/wp-content/uploads/2017/05/2016-17_Women_in_Independent_Film_Report.pdf> (accessed 24 November 2019).

Lawson, T. (2007), 'Review: Things We Lost in the Fire', *Detroit Free Press*, 21 October, <https://www.spokesman.com/stories/2007/oct/21/people-for-del-toro-things-were-found-in-fire/ > (accessed 16 September 2019).

Lay, S. (2002), *British Social Realism: From Documentary to Brit Grit*, London: Wallflower Press.

Lefebvre, M. (2006), 'Between Setting and Landscape in the Cinema', in M. Lefebvre (ed.), *Landscape and Film*, New York: Routledge, pp 19–60.

Leigh, D. (2016), 'Nicolas Winding Refn: "I Bring the Singular, the Narcissistic, the High Art"', *The Guardian*, 1 July, <https://www.theguardian.com/film/2016/jul/01/nicolas-winding-refn-neon-demon-interview> (accessed 23 October 2018).

Leiserowitz, A. (2004), 'Before and After the Day After Tomorrow: A US Study of Climate Change Risk Perception', *Environment*, 46: 9, pp. 22–44.

Lej– (1969), 'Mild porno og dejlige naturbilleder', *Silkeborg Avis*, 25 November.

Lindberg, I. (1972/73), 'Erik Balling omkring en filmserie og en television-serie', *Kosmorama*, 115/116, pp. 240–45.

Lindberg, I. (1982), 'Et farvel til et årligt holdepunkt', *Kosmorama*, 157, pp. 32–33.

Linnet, M. (1983), *Ungdomsfilm mellem studenteroprør og BZ*, unpublished dissertation, København: Københavns Universitet.

Lorentzen, A. B. (2012), 'The Experience Turn of the Danish Periphery: The Downscaling of New Spatial Strategies', *European Urban and Regional Studies*, 20: 4: pp. 460–72.

Low, R. (1949), *The History of British Film, 1906–1914*, London: George Allen & Unwin Ltd.

Lumholdt, J. (ed.) (2003), *Lars von Trier: Interviews*. Jackson: University Press of Mississippi.

Lysne, A. (2016), 'On Becoming and Belonging: The Coming of Age Film in Nordic Cinema', in J. Lothe and B. Larsen (eds), *Perspectives on the Nordic*, Oslo: Novus Press, pp. 127–42.

MacKenzie, S. (2003), 'Manifest Destinies: Dogma 95 and the Future of the Film Manifesto', in M. Hjort and S. MacKenzie (eds), *Purity and Provocation*, London: BFI, pp. 48–57.

MacKenzie, S. and A. W. Stenport (2014a), 'Introduction: What are Arctic Cinemas?', in S. MacKenzie and A. Westerståhl Stenport (eds), *Films on Ice: Cinemas of the Arctic*, Edinburgh: Edinburgh University Press, pp. 1–28.

MacKenzie, S. and A. W. Stenport (eds) (2014b), *Films on Ice: Cinemas of the Arctic*, Edinburgh: Edinburgh University Press.

MacKenzie, S. and A. W. Stenport (2017), 'Sumé, Grønland og den sosialhistoriske rockumentaren', *Z filmtidsskrift*, 138, pp. 28–39.
Madsen, K. B. (1937), 'Potpourri over danske Lystspilsfilm', *B.T*, 17 September.
Malik, S. (1996), 'Beyond "The Cinema of Duty"? The Pleasures of Hybridity: Black British Film of the 1980s and 1990s', in A. Higson (ed.), *Dissolving Views: Key Writings on British Cinema*, London: Cassell, pp. 202–15.
Malmkjær, P. (2000), *Asta: Mennesket, myten og filmstjernen*, Copenhagen: P. Haase & Søn.
Marks, L. U. (2000), *The Skin of the Film: Intercultural Cinema, Embodiment, and the Senses*, Durham and London: Duke University Press.
Marks, L. U. (2002), *Touch: Sensuous Theory and Multisensory Media*, Minneapolis: University of Minnesota Press.
Martin, B. (2007), '"European Cinema for Europe!" The International Film Chamber, 1935–42', in D. Welch and R. Van de Winkel (eds), *Cinema and the Swastika. The International Expansion of Third Reich Cinema*, Palgrave Macmillan, pp. 25–41.
McCabe, C. (1986), 'Theory and Film: Principles of Realism and Pleasure', in P. Rosen (ed.), *Narrative, Apparatus, Ideology*. New York: Columbia University Press, pp. 179–97.
McCabe, J. and K. Akass (eds) (2007), *Quality TV: Contemporary American Television and Beyond*, London: I. B. Tauris & Co.
McCarthy, T. (2003), 'It's All About Love', *Variety*, 22 January, <https://variety.com/2003/film/reviews/it-s-all-about-love-1200543912/> (accessed 16 September 2019).
McGillis, R. (2009), *He Was Some Kind of a Man: Masculinities in the B Western*, Waterloo, Ontario: Wilfried Laurier University Press.
McNair, B. (2013), *Porn? Chic! How Pornography Changed the World and Made it a Better Place*, London: Routledge.
Mills, B. (2013), 'What Does It Mean to Call Television "Cinematic"?', in J. Jacobs and S. Peacock (eds), *Television Aesthetics and Style*, New York and London: Bloomsbury Academic, pp. 57–66.
Mitchell, W. (2019), 'Danish Film Institute Set to Back Higher-Budget Productions', Screen Daily, 11 January, <https://www.screendaily.com/danish-film-institute-set-to-back-higher-budget-productions-/5135725.article> (accessed 4 April 2019).
Mittell, J. (2015), *Complex TV: The Poetics of Contemporary Television Storytelling*, New York: New York University Press.
M. L. (1943), 'Thit Jensen-Filmen "Det Brændende Spørgsmaal" paa Paladsteatret', *Berlingske Tidende*, 26 March.
Molloy, M. (2018), 'Susanne Bier's Hollywood Experiments: *Things We Lost in the Fire* and *Serena*', in M. Molloy, M. Nielsen and M. Shriver-Rice (eds), *ReFocus: The Films of Susanne Bier*, Edinburgh: Edinburgh University Press, pp. 56–82.
Molloy, M., M. Nielsen and M. Shriver-Rice (eds) (2018), *ReFocus: The Films of Susanne Bier*, Edinburgh: Edinburgh University Press.
Monggaard, C. (2018), *Olsen Banden*, Copenhagen: Book Lab/Nordisk Film.
Monty, I. (ed.) (1998), *Asta Nielsen: Breve 1911–71*, Copenhagen: Gyldendal.

REFERENCES

Movin, L. (2006), 'Orden i Danmark: Interview with Max Kestner', *Ekko*, 35, <https://www.ekkofilm.dk/artikler/orden-i-danmark/> (accessed 2 August 2020).

Movin, L. (2013), *Alt er i billedet: Om Jørgen Leths film*, København: Gyldendal.

Mumford, G. (2018), '"Vomitive. Pathetic": Lars von Trier Film Prompts Mass Walkouts at Cannes', *The Guardian*, 15 May, <https://www.theguardian.com/film/2018/may/15/vomitive-pathetic-lars-von-trier-film-prompts-mass-walkouts-at-cannes> (accessed 8 June 2018).

Møller, B. T. (2012), 'Greenland', in J. Sundholm, I. Thorsen, L. G. Andersen, O. Hedling, G. Iversen and B. T. Møller, *Historical Dictionary of Scandinavian Film*, Lanham, Maryland: Scarecrow Press, pp. 181–82.

Musiał, K. (2002), *Roots of the Scandinavian Model: Images of Progress in the Era of Modernisation*, Baden-Baden: Nomos.

Mørch, K. (2008), *Gabriels gæstebud: Portræt af en filmmager*, Copenhagen: Gyldendal.

Mørch, S. (1996), *Den sidste Danmarkshistorie*, Copenhagen: Gyldendal.

Naalakkersuisut (n. d.), 'The Government', <https://naalakkersuisut.gl//en/Naalakkersuisut> (accessed 2 August 2020).

Naficy, H. (2001), *An Accented Cinema: Exilic and Diasporic Filmmaking*, Princeton, New Jersey: Princeton University Press.

Nannestad Jørgensen, L. (1989), 'Introduction', in M. Drouzy and L. Nannestad Jørgensen (eds), *Letters about the Jesus Hilm: 16 Years of Correspondence between Carl Th. Dreyer and Blevins Davis*, Copenhagen: Sekvens: særrække, pp. 5–22.

Neale, S. (1986), 'Melodrama and Tears', *Screen*, 27: 6, pp. 6–23.

Neale, S. (2000), *Genre and Hollywood*, London: Routledge.

Neale, S. and F. Krutnik (1990), *Popular Film and Television Comedy*, London: Routledge.

Necef, M. Ü. (2003), 'De fremmede og Det Onde: Fra kitsch til hybriditetens glæder', in A. Toftgaard and I. H. Hawkesworth (eds), *Nationale spejlinger: tendenser i ny dansk film*, Copenhagen: Museum Tusculanum, pp. 167–89.

Neergaard, E. (1950), 'The Rise, the Fall, and the Rise of Danish Film', *Hollywood Quarterly*, 4: 3, pp. 217–32.

Neergaard, E. (1960), *Historien om dansk film*, Copenhagen: Gyldendal.

Nelson, R. (2007), *State of Play: Contemporary 'High-end' TV Drama*, Manchester and New York: Manchester University Press.

Nestingen, A. K. (2008), *Crime and Fantasy in Scandinavia: Fiction, Film and Social Change*, Seattle: University of Washington Press.

Nestingen, A. K. and T. G. Elkington (eds) (2005), *Transnational Cinema in a Global North: Nordic Cinema in Transition*, Detroit: Wayne State University Press.

Neunsinger, S. (2010), 'Cross-over! Om komparationer, transferanalyser, histoire croisée och den metodologiska nationalismens problem', *Historisk tidskrift (Stockholm)*, 130: 1, pp. 3–24.

Nichols, B. (1995), *Blurred Boundaries: Questions of Meaning in Contemporary Culture*, Bloomington and Indianapolis: Indiana University Press.

Nichols, B. (2001), *Introduction to Documentary*, Bloomington: Indiana University Press.

Nielsen, A. (1966), *Den tiende muse*, Copenhagen: Gyldendal.

Nielsen, A. P. and J. B. Halling (2006), 'Seeradfærd og seerpræferencer', in S. Hjarvad (ed.), *Dansk televisions historie*, Frederiksberg: Samfundslitteratur, pp. 331–62.

REFERENCES

Nielsen, H. B. (2014), 'Velkomst/Welcome', in *10 år med New Danish Screen*, Copenhagen: Danish Film Institute.

Nielsen, J. E. (2009), *Dickens i Danmark*, Copenhagen: Museum Tusculanum Press.

Nielsen, J. I. (2016), 'The Danish Way to Do It The American Way', *Kosmorama*, 263, <https://www.kosmorama.org/en/kosmorama/artikler/danish-way-do-it-american-way> (accessed 19 February 2020).

Nielsen, M. B. O. (2011), *Den danske mandskabsfilm: En karakteristik og diskussion af begrebet mandskabsfilm*, Copenhagen: Det Humanistiske fakultet.

Nielsen, S. O. (2001), *Røde Kro teater 1892–1961 – historien om det navnkundige teater på Amager*, Copenhagen: Sundby Lokalhistoriske Arkiv.

NIFF (Neuchâtel International Fantastic Film Festival) (2019). *NIFF Extended*, <https://www.nifff.ch/wp-content/uploads/2019/05/NIFFF_ExtendedFold_A5.pdf> (accessed 1 October 2019).

Nissen, D. (1980), 'Olsen-Banden: Småborgeren og protesten mod den umenneskelige kapitalisme , in A. Troelsen (ed.), *Levende Billeder af Danmark. Analyser af danske spillefilm fra besættelsestiden til i dag*, Copenhagen: Medusa, pp. 344–68.

Nissen, D. (2001a), 'Filmens moderne gennembrud 1960–69', in P. Schepelern (ed.), *100 års dansk film*, Copenhagen: Rosinante, pp. 199–236.

Nissen, D. (2001b), 'Alternativernes år 1970–79', in P. Schepelern (ed.), *100 års dansk film*, Copenhagen: Rosinante, pp. 237–78.

Nordea Fonden (2015), 'Fokus på danskernes egne historier med ny online medie- platform', <https://nordeafonden.dk/nyheder/fokus-paa-danskernes-egne-historier-med-ny-online-medie-platform> (accessed 2 August 2020).

Nordin, L. (1984), 'Typisk dansk – genrer og typer i danske spillefilm 1972–1982', *Sekvens 1984*, pp. 145–99.

Nordin, L. (1985), 'Flere fandens mælkebøtter end roser' *Sekvens 1985*, Copenhagen: Institut for filmvidenskab, pp. 5–54.

Nordisk Film & TV Fond (2020), 'Celebrating 30 in 2020', <https://www.nordiskfilmogtvfond.com/about-us > (accessed 31 July 2020).

Nørgaard, E. (1971), *Levende billeder i Danmark,* Copenhagen: Lademann.

Nørrested, C. (1997), 'Den store happening: Thorsen-affæren', in I. Bondebjerg, J. Andersen and P. Schepelern (eds), *Dansk film 1972–1997*, København: Munksgaard: Rosinante.

Nørrested, C. (2003), 'Blandt eskimoer eventyrere og etnografer: Filmdokumentarisme om Grønland', *Kosmorama*, 232, pp. 68–98.

Olsen, O. (1941), *Filmens Eventyr og mit eget*, København. Jespersen og Pios Forlag.

Olsen, O. and T. Kaarsted (1991), *Gyldendal og Politikens Danmarkshistorie, vol. 13: Krise og Krig*, Copenhagen: Gyldendal.

Olsen, R. A. (2004), *41 fortællinger om folk i fædrelandets historie*, Copenhagen: Lindhardt & Ringhof.

Oscarson, C. (2013), '*Terje Vigen, Naturbilder* and the Natural History of Film in Sweden', *Journal of Scandinavian Cinema*, 3: 1, pp. 69–86.

oscars.org (1988), '"Babette's Feast" Wins Best Foreign Language Film', <https://www.oscars.org/videos-photos/60th-oscars-highlights> (accessed 25 July 2020)

oscars.org (1989), '"Pelle the Conqueror" Wins Best Foreign Language Film', <https://www.oscars.org/videos-photos/61st-oscars-highlights> (accessed 25 July 2020).

REFERENCES

O'Sullivan, M. (2017), 'Everything Was Torn Apart: How Director Thomas Vinterberg Had to Start His Life All Over Again', *The Washington Post*, 18 May, <https://www.washingtonpost.com/lifestyle/style/everything-was-torn-apart-how-director-thomas-vinterberg-had-to-start-his-life-all-over-again/2017/05/18/28977c80-3a57-11e7-8854-21f359183e8c_story.html> (accessed 16 September 2019).

Pálmason, H. (n.d.), 'h.pálmason, <http://www.hpalmason.com/> (accessed 28 May 2020).

Patten, D. (2016), '"The Night Manager" Ratings Score Best Ever Debut Live + 3 Rises For AMC', *Deadline*, 25 April, <https://deadline.com/2016/04/the-night-manager-ratings-live3-surge-amc-hugh-laurie-tom-hiddleston-1201743872/> (accessed 2 August 2020).

Pedersen, P. K. (2012), *Direktør Lau Lauritzen – 2. del af historien om filmmanden Lau Lauritzen Junior og ASA Film*, Copenhagen: Books on Demand.

Pedersen, P. K. and N. J. Klement (2016), *Historien om Saga Studio – John Olsen-tiden*, Copenhagen: Mellemgaard.

Perez, S. (2018), '*Bird Box* Breaks a Netflix Record with 45M+ People Watching in Its First Week', TechCrunch, 28 December, <https://techcrunch.com/2018/12/28/bird-box-breaks-a-netflix-record-with-45m-people-watching-in-its-first-week/> (accessed 28 December 2019).

Petersen, B. (2013), 'En bankman får noget fremmed', *16:9*, 11: 51, <http://www.16-9.dk/2013-06/side06_feature3.htm> (accessed 2 August 2020).

Petersen, Brian (2017), 'Kvinder i dansk films guldalder', Nordic Women in Film, <http://www.nordicwomeninfilm.com/kvinder-i-dansk-films-guldalder/> (accessed 25 July 2020).

Pham, A. (2015a), 'Zentropa Opens Doors to China with Hans Christian Andersen', Nordisk Film & TV Fond, 18 December, <http://www.nordiskfilmogtvfond.com/news/stories/zentropa-opens-doors-china-hans-christian-andersen> (accessed 25 August 2019).

Pham, A. (2015b), 'Sigrid Dyekjær: "You Can Never Start Too Early to Think Who the Audience Is"', Nordisk Film & TV Fond, <http://www.nordiskfilmogtvfond.com/news/stories/sigrid-dyekjaer-you-can-never-start-too-early-think-who-audience> (accessed 24 November 2019).

Pham, A. (2016), 'May We Live in Interesting Times', Danish Film Institute, 10 February, <https://www.dfi.dk/en/english/may-we-live-interesting-times> (accessed 10 August 2019).

Philipsen, H. (2005), *Dansk films nye bølge. Afsæt og aftryk fra Den Danske Filmskole*, Odense: University of Southern Denmark.

Pinkert, E.-U. (2010), 'Olsen-banden taler tysk – i spændingsfeltet mellem "lovlig" og "ulovlig kriminalitet" og mellem Tyskland-satire og EU-aversion: Kriminalitetsdiskursen i Olsen-banden-filmene', in J. R. Christensen and K. T. Hansen (eds), *Fingeraftryk: Studier i krimi og det kriminelle (Festskrift til Gunhild Agger)*, Aalborg: Aalborg Universitetsforlag, pp. 81–93.

Pinkert, E.-U. (2011), 'Der hässliche Deutsche als Watschenmann in den dänischen Olsen-Bande-Filmen', in F. Clara, M. R. Sanches and M. Matos (eds.), *Várias viagens: Estudos oferecidos a Alfred Opitz*, Ribeirao: Edições Húmus, pp. 221–35.

Pischiutta, B. and D. Trifu (2012), Global Non-Violent Film Festival, <https://filmfreeway.com/GlobalNonviolentFilmFestival> (accessed 16 September 2019).

Pontoppidan, C. (1968), *Eet liv – mange liv*, Copenhagen: Steen Hasselbalchs Forlag.
Preston, A. (2014), 'Fear of Flying: The Spectre that Haunts Modern Life', *The Guardian*, 28 December, <https://www.theguardian.com/world/2014/dec/28/fear-of-flying-phobia-we-cant-overcome> (accessed 2 August 2020).
Qvist, P. O. (1986), *Jorden är vår arvedel: Landsbygden i svensk spelfilm 1940–1959*, Uppsala: Filmhäftet.
Rahbek, B. (2008), 'Sådan er de jo, de arabere!', *Information*, 4 June, <https://www.information.dk/debat/2008/06/saadan-arabere> (accessed 12 February 2020).
Ranjbar, G. (2015), *The Evaluation of the Iranian Immigrants' Attitude Towards the Representation of the Immigrant Characters in Danish Films*, unpublished MA Thesis, University of Copenhagen.
Rasmussen, S. H. (2017), *Fri porno*, Aarhus: Aarhus Universitetsforlag.
Redvall, E. N. (2010), 'Teaching Screenwriting in a Time of Storytelling Blindness: The Meeting of the Auteur and the Screenwriting Tradition in Danish Film-Making', *Journal of Screenwriting*, 1, pp. 59–81.
Redvall, E. N. (2012), 'The Case of New Danish Screen', in M. Hjort (ed.), *Film and Risk*, Detroit: Wayne State University Press, pp. 209–26.
Redvall, E. N. (2013), *Writing and Producing Television Drama in Denmark: From The Kingdom to The Killing*, Basingstoke: Palgrave Macmillan.
Redvall, E. N. (2014a), 'Pernille Rose Grønkjær', in M. Hjort, I. Bondebjerg and E. N. Redvall (eds), *The Danish Directors 3*, Bristol & Chicago: Intellect Press, pp. 107–25.
Redvall, E. N. (2014b), 'Eva Mulvad', in M. Hjort, I. Bondebjerg and E. N. Redvall (eds.), *The Danish Directors 3*, Bristol & Chicago: Intellect Press, pp. 263–83.
Redvall, E. N. (2014c), 'Phie Ambo', in M. Hjort, I. Bondebjerg and E. N. Redvall (eds), *The Danish Directors 3*, Bristol & Chicago: Intellect Press, pp. 29–49.
Redvall, E. N. (2015), 'Craft, Creativity, Collaboration, and Connections: Educating Talent for Danish Television Drama Production', in M. Banks, B. Conor and V. Mayer (eds), *Production Studies, The Sequel!*, Basingstoke: Palgrave Macmillan, pp. 75–88.
Redvall, E. N. (2016), 'The Writing of Television Drama: Issues of Creative Collaboration and Authorship in Danish Writers' Rooms', in M. Hjort and U. Lindqvist (eds), *A Companion to Nordic Cinema*, Malden, MA: Wiley-Blackwell, pp. 491–509.
Redvall, E. N. (2019), 'Nordic Noir as a Calling Card: The International Careers of Danish Film and Television Talent in the 2010s', In A. W. Stenport and A. Lunde (eds), *Nordic Film Cultures and Cinemas of Elsewhere*, Edinburgh: Edinburgh University Press, pp. 190–204.
Redvall, E. N. (2020), 'Can you export a production culture? *The Team* as a European Nordic Crime Drama', In A. M. Waade, E. N. Redvall and P. M. Jensen (eds): *Danish Television Drama: Global Lessons from a Small Nation*, Basingstoke: Palgrave Macmillan pp. 125–45.
Reestorff, C. M. (2017), *Culture War: Affective Cultural Politics, Tepid Nationalism and Art Activism*. Bristol: Intellect.
Rerup, L. (1995), 'National Minorities in South Jutland/Schleswig', in S. Tägil (ed.), *Ethnicity and Nation-Building in the Nordic World*, London: Hurst and Co., pp. 247–81.
Restivo, A. (2019), *Breaking Bad and Cinematic Television*, Durham and London: Duke University Press.

REFERENCES

Riis, J. A. (1890), *How the Other Half Lives: Studies Among the Tenements of New York*, New York: Charles Scribner's Sons.

Roberts, M. (2003), 'Decoding D-Day: Multi-Channel Television at the Millennium', in M. Hjort and S. MacKenzie (eds), *Purity and Provocation: Dogma 95*, London: BFI, pp. 158–72.

Rosello, M. (1998), *Declining the Stereotype: Ethnicity and Representation in French Cultures*, Hanover, NH: University Press of New England.

Rosenbeck, B. (1987), *Kvindekøn: Den moderne kvindeligheds historie 1880–1980*, København: Gyldendal.

Rud (1972), 'Bordellet runder millionen', *Ekstra Bladet*, 3 November.

Rugg, L. H. (2005), 'Globalization and the Auteur: Ingmar Bergman Projected Internationally', in A. K. Nestingen and T. G. Elkington (eds), *Transnational Cinema in a Global North: Nordic Cinema in Transition*, Detroit: Wayne State University Press, pp. 221–41.

Rukov, M. (2002), *FESTEN og andre skandaler. Udvalgte artikler 1992–2002 ved Claus Christensen*, Copenhagen: Lindhardt og Ringhof.

Rust, S., S. Monani and S. Cubitt (eds) (2012), *Ecocinema: Theory and Practice*, AFI Film Readers, New York: Routledge.

Sandberg, M. (2006), 'Mastering the House: Performative Inhabitation in Carl Th. Dreyer's *The Parson's Widow*', in C. C. Thomson (ed.), *Northern Constellations: New Readings in Nordic Cinema*, Norwich: Norvik Press, pp. 23–42.

Sandfeld, G. (1966), *Den stumme Scene*, København: Nyt Nordisk Forlag. Arnold Busck.

Sayad, C. (2013), *Performing Authorship. Self-Inscription and Corporeality in the Cinema*, London & New York: I. B. Tauris.

Schaefer, E. (2014a), 'Introduction: Sex Seen: 1968 and Rise of "Public" Sex', in E. Schaefer (ed.), *Sex Scene: Media and the Sexual Revolution*. Durham: Duke University Press, pp. 1–23.

Schaefer, E. (2014b), 'I'll Take Sweden: The Shifting Discourse of "Sexy Nation" in Sexploitation Films', in E. Schaefer (ed.), *Sex Scene: Media and the Sexual* Revolution, Durham: Duke University Press, pp. 207–34.

Schaefer, E. (2015), 'Hardcore Education: The Case of *Sexual Freedom in Denmark*', *Journal of Scandinavian Cinema*, 5: 2, pp. 115–28.

Schatz, T. (1981), *Hollywood Genres: Formulas, Filmmaking and The Studio System*, New York: McGraw-Hill.

Schepelern, P. (2000), *Lars von Triers film: Tvang og Befrielse*, Copenhagen: Rosinante.

Schepelern, P. (2003), 'Kill Your Darlings: Lars von Trier and the Origin of Dogma 95', in M. Hjort and S. MacKenzie (eds), *Purity and Provocation: Dogma 95*, London: BFI, pp. 58–69.

Schepelern, P. (2004), 'The Making of an Auteur: Notes on the Auteur Theory and Lars von Trier', in T. K. Grodal, I. T. Laursen and B. Larsen (eds), *Visual Authorship, Northern Lights*, Copenhagen: Museum Tusculanum Press, pp. 103–28.

Schepelern, P. (2005), 'Film According to Dogma', in A. K. Nestingen and T. G. Elkington (eds), *Transnational Cinema in a Global North: Nordic Cinema in Transition*, Detroit: Wayne State University Press, pp. 73–107.

Schepelern, P. (2006a), 'The Last Tycoon – Erik Balling and the Survival of the Nordisk', in L. R. Larsen and D. Nissen (eds), *100 Years of Nordisk Film*. Copenhagen: Danish Film Institute, pp. 215–29.

Schepelern, P. (2006b), 'The American Connection: Inspiration and Ambition in the New Danish Cinema', in L. Hølbjerg and H. Søndergaard (eds), *European Film and Media Culture*, vol. 4, Copenhagen: Museum Tusculanum Press, pp. 237–50.

Schepelern, P. (2010), 'Dansk Filmhistorie 1896–2009', Danish Film Institute, <https://www.dfi.dk/viden-om-film/filmhistorie/dansk-filmhistorie-1896-2009> (accessed 23 July 2020).

Schepelern, P. (2011), 'The Element of Crime and Punishment: Kaurismäki, Trier, and the Nordic Traditions', *Journal of Scandinavian Cinema*, 1: 1, pp. 87–103.

Schepelern, P. (2013), 'After The Celebration: The Effect of Dogme on Danish Cinema', *Kosmorama*, 251 <https://www.kosmorama.org/en/kosmorama/artikler/after-celebration-effect-dogme-danish-cinema> (accessed 2 August 2020).

Schepelern, P. (2015), 'Forget about Love: Sex and Detachment in Lars von Trier's "Nymphomaniac"', *Kosmorama*, 259, <https://www.kosmorama.org/en/kosmorama/artikler/forget-about-love-sex-and-detachment-lars-von-triers-nymphomaniac> (accessed 2 August 2020).

Schepelern, P. (2018), 'Lars von Trier Through the Black Forest' [interview with Lars von Trier], Louisiana Museum, <http://channel.louisiana.dk/video/lars-von-trier-through-the-black-forest> and <https://vimeo.com/265532625> (accessed 2 August 2020).

Schröder, S. M. (2010), 'The Script Consultant', Carl Th. Dreyer – The Man and His Work, Danish Film Institute, <https://www.carlthdreyer.dk/en/carlthdreyer/about-dreyer/biography/script-consultant> (accessed 2 August 2020).

Sémolué, J. (2005), *Carl Th. Dreyer: Le mystère du vrai*, Paris: Cahiers du cinéma.

Shriver-Rice, M. (2011), 'Adapting National Identity: Ethical Border Made Suspect in the Hollywood Version of Susanne Bier's Brothers', *Film International*, 9: 2, pp. 8–19.

Shriver-Rice, M., (2015). *Inclusion in New Danish Cinema: Sexuality and Transnational Belonging*, Bristol: Intellect Books.

Shriver-Rice, M. (2018), 'Danish Privilege and Responsibility in the Work of Susanne Bier', in M. Molloy, M. Nielsen and M. Shriver-Rice (eds), *ReFocus: The Films of Susanne Bier*, Edinburgh: Edinburgh University Press, pp. 229–60.

Smaill, B. (2014), 'The Male Sojourner, the Female Director, and Popular European Cinema: The Worlds of Susanne Bier', *Camera Obscura*, 29: 1 (85), pp. 5–31.

Smith, A. D. (1983), 'Nationalism and Classical Social Theory', *British Journal of Sociology*, 34: 1, pp. 19–38.

Stanitzek, G. (2009), 'Reading the Title Sequence (Vorspann, Générique)', *Cinema Journal*, 48: 4, pp. 44–58.

Steene, B. (1992), 'Barnvoksenfilmen – en ny genre', *Z Filmtidsskrift*, 42, pp. 31–37.

Stenport, A. W. and A. Lunde (eds) (2019), *Nordic Film Cultures and Cinemas of Elsewhere*, Edinburgh: Edinburgh University Press.

Stevenson, J. (2002), *Lars von Trier*, London: British Film Institute.

Stevenson, J. (2003), *Dogme Uncut: Lars von Trier, Thomas Vinterberg, and the Gang that Took on Hollywood*, Santa Monica: Santa Monica Press.

Stevenson, J. (2010), *Scandinavian Blue: The Erotic Cinema of Sweden and Denmark in the 1960s and 1970s*, Jefferson: McFarland & Company, Inc.
Stevenson, J. (2012), 'Why', in: J. Nordstrøm (ed.), *Dansk porno*, København: Nordstrøms, pp. 292–96.
Strand, T. (2010), 'The Making of a New Cosmopolitanism', *Studies in Philosophy and Education*, 29: 2, pp. 229–42.
Straubhaar, J. (2007), *World Television: From Global to Local*, Thousand Oaks, CA: Sage Publications.
Stumfilm (2019), 'Afgrunden', Danish Film Institute, <https://www.stumfilm.dk/stumfilm/streaming/film/afgrunden> (accessed 27 July 2020).
Sullivan, H. I. (2012), 'Dirt Theory and Material Ecocriticism', *Interdisciplinary Studies in Literature and Environment*, 19: 3, pp. 515–31.
Synnott, V. (1997), 'Statistiske oplysninger om danske spillefilm 1972–1996', in I. Bondebjerg, J. Andersen and P. Schepelern (eds.), *Dansk film 1972–1997*, København: Gyldendal, pp. 403–32.
Sørensen, A. K. (1995), 'Greenland: From Colony to Home Rule', in S. Tägil (ed.), *Ethnicity and Nation Building in the Nordic* World, London: Hurst and Co., pp. 85–105.
Sørensen, J. (1980) (ed.), *Danmarksfilmen og danske billeder*, København: Gyldendal.
Sørensen, L.-M. (2014), *Dansk film under nazismen*, Copenhagen: Lindhardt & Ringhof.
Sørensen, L-M. (2018), 'More than Goebbels Bargained For: Nazi Newsreel Dissemination in Occupied Denmark and the Golden Age of Danish Documentary', in C. Chambers, M. Jönsson, R. van de Winkel (eds), *Researching Newsreels: Local, National and Transnational Case Studies*, Basingstoke: Palgrave MacMillan, pp. 143–55.
Sørensen, L.-M. (2019), *Sidste nyt fra Berlin*, Copenhagen: Lindhardt & Ringhof.
Sørensen, L-M., T. Helseth and M. Jönsson (2012), 'Nazi Newsreels in the North: The German Masterplan and its Nordic Inflictions', *Journal of Scandinavian Cinema*, 2: 3, pp. 285–98.
Sørenssen, B.; H. Salmi, E. V. Kau and J. Olsson (eds) (2012), 'World War II and Scandinavian Cinema: An Overview', *Journal of Scandinavian Cinema*, 2: 3, pp. 201–12.
Tägil, S. (ed.) (1995), *Ethnicity and Nation Building in the Nordic World*, London: Hurst and Co.
Tallents, S. (1968), 'The Birth of the British Documentary (Part III)', *Journal of the University Film Association,* 20: 3, pp. 61–66.
Taskforcen for regionale filmfonde (2001), *Regionale filmfonde*, Kulturministeriet Økonomi- og Erhervsministeriet, <https://kum.dk/publikationer/2001/regionale-filmfonde/> (accessed 2 August 2020).
'Teater og Tribune' (2011), *Politiken* (Copenhagen), 16 April.
Tellkamp, U. (2014), 'Das geheime Dossier: Eine Liebeserklärung an die Olsenbande', *Frankfurter Allgemeine Zeitung*, 22 March, p. 11.
Thestrup, K. (1976), *Mit livs gågade*, København: Det Schønbergske Forlag.
Thompson, K. (1988), *Breaking the Glass Armor: Neoformalist Film Analysis*, Princeton: Princeton University Press.
Thomsen, B. M. S. (2016), *Lars von Triers fornyelse af filmen 1984–2014: Signal, pixel, diagram*, København: Museum Tusculanums forlag.

Thomsen, B. M. S. (2018), *Lars von Trier's Renewal of Film 1984–2014: Signal, Pixel, Diagram*, Aarhus: Aarhus University Press.

Thomsen, O. (1986), *Komediens Kraft – en bog om genre*, Copenhagen: Akademisk forlag.

Thomson, C. C. (2007a), 'The Tale-End of History: Literary Form, Historiography, and the Danish (Post)-National Imagination', in R. C. M. Mole (ed.), *Discursive Constructions of Identity in European Politics*, Basingstoke: Palgrave Macmillan, pp. 45–69.

Thomson, C. C. (2007b), 'It's All About Snow: Limning the Post-Human Body in *Copuc/Solaris* (Tarkovsky, 1972) and *It's All about Love* (Vinterberg, 2003)', *New Cinemas: Journal of Contemporary Film*, 5: 1, pp. 3–21.

Thomson, C. C. (2013a), *Thomas Vinterberg's Festen (The Celebration)*, Seattle: University of Washington Press.

Thomson, C. C. (2013b), 'Lamps, Light and Enlightenment: Poul Henningsen's *Denmark* and Ole Roos' *PH Light*', *Kosmorama*, 249, <https://www.kosmorama.org/en/kosmorama/artikler/lamps-light-and-enlightenment-poul-henningsens-denmark-and-ole-roos-ph-light> (accessed 2 August 2020).

Thomson, C. C. (2015), 'History Unmade: Dreyer's Unrealised *Mary, Queen of Scots*', *Kosmorama*, 260, <https://www.kosmorama.org/en/kosmorama/en/history-unmade-dreyers-unrealised-mary-queen-scots> (accessed 28 February 2019).

Thomson, C. C. (2016), '"Education, Enlightenment, and General Propaganda": Dansk Kulturfilm and Carl Th. Dreyer's Short Films', in M. Hjort and U. Lindqvist (eds), *A Companion to Nordic Cinema*, Chichester: Wiley-Blackwell, pp. 78–97.

Thomson, C. C. (2017), 'The Archive, the Auteur and the Unfilmed Film: Reflections on Dreyer's and von Trier's *Medea*', *Journal of Scandinavian Cinema*, 7: 2, pp. 99–112.

Thomson, C. C. (2018a), *Short Films from a Small Nation: Danish Informational Cinema 1935–1965*, Edinburgh: Edinburgh University Press.

Thomson, C. C. (2018b), 'Welcome to Denmark', Danmark paa film, Filmcentralen, <https://filmcentralen.dk/museum/danmark-paa-film/tema/welcome-denmark> (accessed 3 August 2020).

Thorsen, I. (2012), 'Gabriel Axel', in J. Sundholm, I. Thorsen, L. G. Andersson, O. Hedling, G. Iversen and B. T. Møller (eds), *Historical Dictionary of Scandinavian Cinema*, Plymouth: Scarecrow Press, pp. 65–66.

Thorsen, I. (2015), 'Family-Porn: The Zodiac-Film – Popular Comedy with Hard Core Sex', *Journal of Scandinavian Cinema*, 4: 3, pp. 289–304.

Thorsen, I. (2016a), 'Incorporation of the Transgressive: Sex in the Danish Feature Films of the 1970s', *Cine-Excess. European Erotic Excess: Identity, Desire and Disgust*, 1: 2, <https://www.cine-excess.co.uk/incorporation-of-the-transgressive-sex-and-pornography-in-danish-feature-films-of-the-1970s.html> (accessed 2 August 2020).

Thorsen, I. (2016b), '"Vi maatte passe paa" – Selvcensur og selvregulering i Nordisk Films Kompagnis produktion', *Kosmorama*, 262, <https://www.kosmorama.org/kosmorama/artikler/vi-maatte-passe-paa-selvcensur-og-selvregulering-i-nordisk-films-kompagnis> (accessed 2 August 2020).

Thorsen, I. (2017a). *Nordisk Films Kompagni, 1906–1924: The Rise and Fall of the Polar Bear.* KINtop Studies in Early Cinema, vol. 5. East Barnet, UK: John Libbey Publishing Ltd.

REFERENCES

Thorsen, I. (2017b), 'Hjerteslag, syfilis, mord eller selvmord – Myterne om Valdemar Psilanders død', *Kosmorama*, 267, <https://www.kosmorama.org/kosmorama/artikler/hjerteslag-syfilis-mord-eller-selvmord> (accessed 2 August 2020).

Thorsen, I. and E. N. Redvall (2019), 'When Grand Ambitions Meet the Harsh Realities of Filmmaking: Celebrating the 100th Anniversary of Two Classic Letters by Danish Director Carl Th. Dreyer on His Artistically Ambitious Silent Film *Leaves from Satan's Book*', *Journal of Scandinavian Cinema*, 9: 2, pp. 143–56.

Trier, Lars von (1985), *Information*, 31 January 1985.

Trier, Lars von and Thomas Vinterberg 1995, 'Dogme 95', <http://www.dogme95.dk/the-vow-of-chastity/> (accessed 29 July 2020).

Troelsen, A. and M. B. Andersen (1980), *Levende billeder af Danmark: Analyser af danske spillefilm fra besættelsestiden til i dag*, Copenhagen: Medusa.

Tybjerg, C. (1996), *An Art of Silence and Light: The Development of the Danish Film Drama to 1920*, unpublished dissertation, Copenhagen: University of Copenhagen.

Tybjerg, C. (1999), 'Red Satan: Carl Theodor Dreyer and the Bolshevik Threat', in J. Fullerton and J. Olsson (eds), *Nordic Explorations: Film Before 1930*, Sydney: John Libbey, pp. 19–40.

Tybjerg, C. (2001), 'Dreyer and the National Film in Denmark', *Film History*, 13: 1, pp. 23–36.

Tybjerg, C. (2003), 'The Sense of *The Word*', in L. Højbjerg and P. Schepelern, *Film Style and Story*, Copenhagen: Museum Tusculanum, pp. 171–213.

Tybjerg, C. (2015), 'On the Periphery of the "National Film": Danish Cinematic Border Crossings, 1918–1929', *European Journal of Scandinavian Studies*, 45: 2, pp. 169–88.

Tybjerg, C. (2016), 'Searching for Art's Promised Land: Nordic Silent Cinema and the Swedish Example', in M. Hjort and U. Lindqvist (eds), *A Companion to Nordic Cinema*, Chichester: Wiley-Blackwell, pp. 271–90.

Tybjerg, C. (2019a), 'Dreyer's *Jeanne d'Arc* at the Cinéma d'Essai: Cinephiliac and Political Passions in 1950s Paris', in A. W. Stenport and A. Lunde (eds), *Nordic Film Cultures and Cinemas of Elsewhere*, Edinburgh: Edinburgh University Press, pp. 305–18.

Tybjerg, C. (2019b), 'Den stumme kunst: Da Danmark var Hollywood', stumfilm.dk, Danish Film Institute, <https://www.stumfilm.dk/stumfilm/temaer/den-stumme-kunst-da-danmark-var-hollywood> (accessed 27 July 2020).

Ulrichsen, E. (1956), 'La belle époque', in S. Kragh-Jacobsen, E. Balling and O. Sevel (eds), *50 Aar i dansk film*, Copenhagen: A/S Nordisk Films Kompagni, pp. 29–39.

Ulrichsen, E. (1960), 'Dansk spillefilm 1956–59', in E. Neergaard (ed.), *Historien om dansk film*, Copenhagen: Gyldendal, pp. 151–54.

Van de Velde, D. (2018), 'Vision and Ethics in *A Second Chance*', in M. Molloy, M. Nielsen and M. Shriver-Rice (eds), *ReFocus: The Films of Susanne Bier*, Edinburgh: Edinburgh University Press, pp. 173–86.

Vestergaard, J. (2000), 'Konkurrence mellem regionale filmfonde', *CinemaZone*, <http://cinemazone.dk/news.asp?id=101> (accessed 2 August 2020).

Villadsen, E. (1997), 'Familiehyggens årti', *Kosmorama*, 220, pp. 110–34.

Vision Denmark (2018), *Incitamentsordninger for den digitale visuelle industri*, V. Denmark.

Wamberg, H. (1917), *Valdemar Psilander*, Copenhagen: Nyt Nordisk Forlag.
Ward, S. (2013), 'Finding "Purpose" in "Subtitled Oddities": Framing BBC Four's Danish Imports as Public Service Broadcasting', *Journal of Popular Television*, 1: 2, pp. 251–57.
Werner, M. and B. Zimmermann (2006), 'Beyond Comparison: Histoire Croisée and the Challenge of Reflexivity', *History and Theory*, 45: 1, pp. 30–50.
Whipp, G. (2007), 'Film Review: "Things We Lost in the Fire": "Fire" Draws its Heat from Del Toro', *Los Angeles Daily News*, 19 October, <https://web.archive.org/web/20071022145459/http://www.la.com/movies/10652576.html> (accessed 16 September 2019).
White, H. (1973), *Meta-History: The Historical Imagination in Nineteenth-Century Europe*, Baltimore: The Johns Hopkins University Press.
Wiedemann, V. (2009), *The Art of Individual Decision Making: A Competency Development Report for Nordic Film Commissioners*, Nordisk Film and TV Fund, <https://www.dfi.dk/files/docs/2018-02/artofindividual.pdf> (accessed 30 July 2020).
Winkel, R. Van de, M. Jönsson, L.-M. Sørensen and B. Sørenssen (2012), 'German Film Distribution in Scandinavia during World War II', *Journal of Scandinavian Cinema*, 2: 3, pp. 263–80.
Widding, A. S. (1998), 'Denmark', in T. Soila, A. S. Widding and G. Iversen, *Nordic National Cinemas*, London: Routledge, pp. 7–30.
Williams, L. (1999), *Hard Core: Power, Pleasure, and the 'Frenzy of the Visible'*, Berkeley: University of California Press.
Wolfhagen, R. (2011), 'Filmturisme: På sporet af Adams Æbler', *Information*, 17 June.
Women's Media Center (2018), *The Status of Women in the US Media 2018* <http://www.womensmediacenter.com> (accessed 24 November, 2019).
Women's Media Center (2019), *The Status of Women in the US Media 2019*, <http://www.womensmediacenter.com>, (accessed 24 November, 2019).
Wyatt, J. (1994), *High Concept: Movies and Marketing in Hollywood*, Austin: University of Texas Press.
Yang, J. Q M. [楊秋凌] (2013), *Towards a Cinema of Contemplation: Roy Andersson's Aesthetics and Ethics*, thesis, University of Hong Kong, Pokfulam, Hong Kong SAR. <http://dx.doi.org/10.5353/th_b5016281> (Accessed 10 October 2016).
Yazdani, J. P. (2018a), 'Özil har valgt ikke længere...' [Facebook post 24 July 2018, 16:12], <https://www.facebook.com/philip.yazdani/posts/10217021807966984> (accessed 12 February 2020).
Yazdani, J. P. (2018b), 'Jeg var i TV2 news tidligere...' [Facebook post 26 July 2018, 17:04], <https://www.facebook.com/philip.yazdani/videos/10217037666523438/> (accessed 12 February 2020).
Yde, K. H. (2014). 'Nu skal vi fandme se fremad!' [interview with Vinca Wiedemann and Henning Camre], in *10 år med New Danish Screen: 'Rammer'/'Frameworks'*, Copenhagen: Danish Film Institute, pp. 18–28, <https://issuu.com/detfi/docs/final_nds_printfiles_rammer_indhold> (accessed 2 August 2020).
Zentropa (2009), 'Director's Confession', *Antichrist* Press Kit.

INDEX

Liderlige Lisbeth see *Birthday Party, The* (1971)
Life in Denmark (1972), 97, 99–101
Life on Hegnsgaard (1938), 106
Lifeboat (2018), 205
Lille soldat see *Little Soldier* (2008)
Lille Virgil og Orla Frø-Snapper see *Little Virgil and Orla Frog Face* (1980)
Lindholm, Tobias, 182, 183
Little Soldier (2008), 184, 185–6
Little Virgil and Orla Frog Face (1980), 133
live theatre, 31, 33, 34
Livet i Danmark (*Life in Denmark*, 1972), 97, 99–101
Livet paa Hegnsgaard see *Life on Hegnsgaard* (1938)
Lloyd, Harold, 121
local-regional films, 93–4
location shooting, 90–1
Long-and-Short films, 120
Love Addict (2011), 224–5, 226, 227
Love at First Hiccough (1999), 80
Love One Another (1922), 47
low-budget filmmaking, 208, 236
Lysets hjerte see *Heart of Light* (1998)

Madsen, Ole Christian, 171, 193, 234
magic realism, 131, 133
Malberg, Peter, 73, 107, 116
Malmros, Nils, 9, 137–8
Mam'zelle Nitouche (1963), 73
Man Divided (2017), 242
Man from Nuuk, A (2009), 267, 268, 274
Man in Too Much of a Hurry (1984), 266
Manderlay (2005), 157, 159
Manslaughter (2005), 171
Marshment, Margaret, 86
masculinity-in-crisis trilogy, 178
Master of the House (1925), 47
Matador (1978–81), 78, 80, 189
material ecocriticism, 246–7, 250
materiality, 242–3, 245, 250
Me and Charly (1978), 135, 136–7
Me and Mama Mia (1989), 134
Mechanical Love (2007), 224, 226
Med døden til følge see *Death as a Consequence* (2011)

Medea (1988), 153, 159
Meiling, Connie (later Linck), 74
Meineche, Annelise, 142
Melancholia (2011), 157–8, 159, 211
melodrama, 109–10, 155
Men of the North Sea (1939), 266
Mens vi lever see *While We Live* (2017)
Menthe – The Happy One (1979), 152, 159
'meshwork theory,' 248
Michael (1924), 47
Mig og Charly see *Me and Charly* (1978)
Mikkelsen, Brian, 2
Mikkelsen, Mads, 168–9, 171
Mill, The (1943), 106
Miller, Henry, 148
Ministry of Culture, 2010 report, 169–70
Minor Mishaps (2002), 172
Min søsters børn see *Six Kids and their Uncle* (1966–71)
Min søsters børn see *My Sister's Kids series* (2001–15)
Modern Man, A (2017), 224, 225, 227
Molloy, Missy, 180, 181
Monastery, The (2006), 224, 225, 226, 228
montage, 91, 96
Monty, Ib, 39
Moodysson, Lukas, 184
Mordet paa Fyn see *Murder on Funen, The* (1907)
Mordets Melodi see *Murder Melody* (1944)
Mosekongen see *King of the Marshes* (1951)
Motion Picture Patent Company, United States, 23
Movin, Lisbeth, 163
multiple-reel films, 22, 23–7
Mulvad, Eva, 219, 224–5, 226, 227
Murder Melody (1944), 52–3
Murder on Funen, The (1907), 140–1
My Father from Haifa (2010), 236
My Sister's Kids series (2001–15), 139
Møllen see *Mill, The* (1943)
Mørch, Søren, 6

Naar bønder elsker see *When Peasants Love* (1942)
Nanoq see *Polar Bear* (2000)

REFERENCES

Østergaard, I. A. and A. M. Waade (2016), '1864 på Fyn: FilmFyn, branding, filmturisme og location placement', in K. T. Hansen (ed.), *1864: Tv-serien, historien, kritikken*, Aalborg: Aalborg Universitetsforlag, pp. 209–29.

Østergaard, U. (2003), 'Danish National Identity: Between Multinational Heritage and Small State Nationalism', in H. Branner and M. Kelstrup (eds), *Denmark's Policy towards Europe after 1945: History, Theory and Options*, Odense: University Press of Southern Denmark, pp. 139–84

Østergaard, U. (2012), 'The Danish Path to Modernity', in J. Árnason and B. Wittrock (eds), *Nordic Paths to Modernity*, New York, Oxford: Berghahn Books, pp. 49–68.

INDEX

Page numbers in *italic* refer to illustrations. Entries are alphabetised according to the Danish alphabet, i.e. the letters æ, ø and å follow x, y, z

½ *Revolution* (2011), 236
1:1 (2006), 172, 234
17 Op. see *Sally's Bizniz* (1989)
24 Hours with Ilse (1971), 146
1864 (2014), 259

Aakeson, Kim Fupz, 172
Aakjær, Jeppe, 106, 110
Aarhus, Filmby Aarhus, 256–7, 260
Abbasi, Ali, 238
Abyss, The (1910), 6, 7, 23, 34–5, 141
Academy Awards, 161, 176, 179
Adam's Apples (2005), 234, 259
Adams æbler see *Adam's Apples* (2005)
Afgrunden see *The Abyss*, 1910
Afsporet see *Derailed*, 1942)
After the Wedding (2006), 172, 178
agency, 113, 128, 134
Ahmad, Fenar, 237
Al Medina (2015), 236
Alaimo, Stacy, 246
Alami, Milad, 237–8
Alstrup, Carl, 111, *112*
Altman, Rick, 67

Amazon Productions, 180
Ambo, Phie, 219, 224, 225, 226, 227
Among Us – In the Land of our Shadows (2017), 274
Ancient Gold, The (1951), 113
And the Authorities Said Stop (1972), 266
Andersen, Johnny, 201
Anderson, Benedict, 94
Andersson, Roy, 184
animation, 132, 267
Anori (2018), 272
Another Round (2020), 173, 183
Antichrist (2009), 157, 159
anti-naturalism, 70
Arcel, Nikolaj, 179
Arven see *Inheritance* (2003)
Arvingerne see *Legacy, The* (2014–17)
ASA (film company), 21, 57, 59, 60, 107, 108
asylum-seekers, 232
Atlantis (1913), 24, 37
audiences, and *folkekomedie*, 70, 72, 76–8
audiovisual sketches, 204, 207

INDEX

August, Bille, 131, 137–8, 161, 198, 267
auteurs, 8, 9
'Autoren' films, 24
Avaz Brothers, 238
Axel, Gabriel, 142, 161, 162–3;
  see also *Babette's Feast* (1987)

Babette's Feast (1987), 10, 161, 162–5, 169
Babettes gæstebud see *Babette's Feast* (1987)
'bad immigrant' stereotype, 235
Badehotellet see *The Seaside Hotel* (2013–)
Baggini, Julian, 163
Bahs, Henning, 119
Ballesteros, Isolina, 232
Ballet Dancer, The (1911), 36
Balletdanserinden see *Ballet Dancer, The* (1911)
Balling, Erik, 79–80, 119, 120, 121, 122, 124, 266
Bamboozled (2000), 167
Bang, Jette, 266
Barken Margrethe see *Bark Margrethe, The* (1937)
Bark Margrethe, The (1934), 67–8
Barnet see *Child, The* (1940)
Baronessen fra Benzintanken see *Baroness from the Gas Station, The* (1960)
Baroness from the Gas Station, The (1960), 110, 116
Bauder, Carl, 54, 55–6, 57, 61
Bazin, André, 89
Be Dear to Me (1957), 9
Bech, Torben, 267
Bedside films, 147–8
Bedtime Mazurka (1970), 147
Bench, The (2000), 171
Bendtsen, Henning, 153
Bennys badekar see *Benny's Bathtub* (1971)
Benny's Bathtub (1971), 132
Berlin, NATIVe, 271
Besættelse see *Possession* (1944)
Beth's Diary (2006), 227
Bicycle Thieves (1948), 88, 89–90
Bier, Susanne, 4, 9, 161, 169, 172, 178, 180–2
  Academy Awards, 176
  transnational trilogy, 183–4

Billig, Michael, 3
Birdbox (2018), 181
Birthday Party, The (1971), 145
Björk, 156
Bjørnkjær, Kristen, 97, 99
black comedies, 76
Black Dream, The (1911, also known as *The Circus Girl*), 35, 36, 80
Blade fra Satans Bog see *Leaves from Satan's Book* (1920)
Blair Witch Project, The (1999), 167
Bleeder (1999), 171
Blinkende lygter see *Flickering Lights* (2000)
Blom, August, 31
Blue Balloon, The (1971), 145
Blue Boys, The (1933), 70
Blændværk see *Delusion* (1955)
Bodnia, Kim, 171
Bondebjerg, Ib, 131, 168, 170, 171
Bonderøven see *Farmer, The* (2008–)
Bordello, The (1972), 147
Bordwell, David, 41, 45
Borgen (DR, 2010–13), 170, 196
Borgman, Daniel Joseph, 242
Bornedal, Ole, 171, 193, 198
Bornholms Stemme see *Gone with the Fish* (1999)
Boss of It All, The (2006), 157, 159
box office, 53, 240
Breaking the Waves (1996), 155, 159
Brecht, Bertolt, 157
Brewer's Daughter, The (1912), 36
Bride from Dragstrup, The (1955), 107, 113
Bride of Glomdal, The (1926), 47
British films, social realism, 84, 86
Brotherhood (2011), 184, 186
Brothers (2004), 172, 178
Bruden fra Dragstrup see *Bride from Dragstrup, The* (1955)
Brusendorff, Ove, 145
Bruzzi, Stella, 223
Brydesen, Lars, 97, 98
Bryggerens datter see *The Brewer's Daughter* (1912)
Brødre see *Brothers* (2004)
Bundfald see *Sin Alley* (1957)
Bundgaard, Poul, 119, 120, 124, 147
Burning Question, The (1943), 83, 84, 85

INDEX

burqa ban, 231
Busters verden see *Buster's World* (1984)
Buster's World (1984), 131, 133–4

Café Paradis (*Cafe Paradise*, 1950), 85–6
Cairo Garbage (2009), 226
Cairo skrald see *Cairo Garbage* (2009)
Camre, Henning, 168, 204
Candy Film, 144
Cannes festival, 61, 156, 177, 180
Caspersen, Karen, 69–70
Catch the Dream (2013), 109, 112
Celebration, The or *Dogme #1: Festen* (1998), 10, 165–6, 170, 177, 235
censorship, 12–13, 26, 55, 140–1, 148
chance event (*tilfældigheden*), 87
Chaplin, Charlie, 120
characters, homeland cinema
    and landscape, 111–12
    and sexuality, 114–17
Charles tante see *Charley's Aunt* (1959)
Charley's Aunt (1959), 73
Charlot and Charlotte (DR, 1996), 193
Charmer, The (2017), 237–8
Child, The (1940), 83
child pornography, 144
child stars, 74
Children of Divorce (1939), 84
children's films, 128–34; see also youth films
Chinaman (2005), 184
Christa see *Swedish Fly Girls* (1971)
Christensen, Benjamin, 33, 38
Christensen, Theodor, 14
Christian IV – Den sidste rejse see *Christian IV – The Last Journey* (2018)
Christian IV – The Last Journey (2018), 205, 209
cinema(s)
    and multiple-reel film, 24
    state intervention in, 4
cinematography, 91, 153
Clausen, Erik, 76, 233
climate activism, 241
Clown (TV2, 2005–18), 73
collaboration, 179
Collision (2019), 238, 240
colonialism, 11, 264

Command, The (2018), 182
Commune, The (2016), 182–3
constraint-based approach, 200
Copenhagen, 145, 162, 252
    as film motif/location, 87, 90
Copenhageners (1933), 76
Could We Maybe (1976), 135
Crazy Paradise (1962), 141
creativity under constraint, 200, 206–7
'crew' films, 74
crime genre, 52, 83, 87–8, 189–90, 196
criminal immigrant, trope of, 234
Critical Arctic Studies, 263
critical postnationalism, 3
Crumbs, The (1991), 80
Cultural Canon, 169–70
cultural integration, theme of, 67, 71
cultural materialism, 242
cultural radicalism, 143
Cultural Studies, 77, 78
culture wars, 2–3
Cutterhead, sketch, 210–14
Cutterhead (2019), 205

D-Day (1999–2000), 156
Da myndighederne sagde stop see *And the Authorities Said Stop* (1972)
Damgaard Sørensen, Mette, 203, 205, 207, 208–9
Dancer in the Dark (2000), 155, 156, 159
Dangerous Youth (1953), 74, 135
Danish Blue (1968), 142
Danish Broadcasting Corporation (DR), 203
Danish Cultural Canon (2006), 2, 3, 4–5, 7
Danish Documentary Productions, 221–2, 229
Danish Film Institute (DFI), 148, 153, 162, 175
    archives, 44, 54
    Copenhagen, 15, 252
    on diversity, 255
    on ethnic diversity, 239–40
    founded, 14, 97
    on gender distribution, 220–1
    streaming site, 94
    see also New Danish Screen (NDS)
Danish Film Museum, 168
Danish immigration policies, 231–2

305

Danish Nazi party, 52, 57, 59
Danish People's Party, 231
Danishness
  and the Cultural Canon, 4
  folkekomedie genre, 74–5
  and integration, 237
  and its Others, 125–6
Danmark A+B (1976), 97, 99
Danmark dit og mit see *Denmark Yours and Mine* (1981)
Danmarks Radio (DR), 131, 189, 191, 193
Danmarksfilm (Denmark-films), 93–104
Danmarksfilmen see *Denmark Film, The* (1926)
Danmarks sønner see *Sons of Denmark* (2019)
Dansk Astra Film, 37
Danske billeder see *Images of Denmark* (1970)
Dark Tower, The (2017), 179
Darkland (2017), 237, 240
Davidsen, Hjalmar, 31
Day of Wrath (1943), 10, 48, 163
De blaa Drenge (*The Blue Boys*, 1933), 70
De fem benspænd see *Five Obstructions, The* (2003)
De frigjorte see *Fish Out of Water* (1993)
De grønne slagtere see *Green Butchers, The* (2003)
De pokkers Unger see *Those Damned Kids* (1947)
de Renzy, Alex, 143
De røde Enge see *The Red Meadows* (1945), 61, 83
De røde heste see *Red Horses, The* (1950)
De Sica, Vittorio, 88
Dear Wendy (2005), 182
Death as a Consequence (2011), 226
Dejlige Danmark see *Delightful Denmark* (1960)
Delightful Denmark (1960), 97
Delusion (1955), 135
Den anden side see *Other Side, The* (2017)
Den gamle Mølle på Mols see *Old Mill on Mols, The* (1953)
Den hvide Slavehandel see *The White Slave Trade* (1910)
Den hvide Slavehandels sidste Offer see *In the Hands of Imposters* (1911)
Den kloge Mand see *Quack, The* (1937)
Den sorte Drøm see *Black Dream, The / The Circus Girl* (1911)
Den Vestdanske Filmpulje *see* West Danish Film Fund (DVF)
Denmark (1948), 97
Denmark, Yours and Mine (1981), 99
Denmark Film, The (1926), 95
Denmark-films, 93–104
Den perfekte muslim see *Perfect Muslim, The* (2009)
Den sidste dans see *Last Dance, The* (2005)
Depression Trilogy, 158
Der brænder en ild see *Fire Burns, A* (1962)
Der er et yndigt land see *Land of Plenty* (1983)
Der fremde Vogel see *The Strange Bird* (1911)
Der var engang en Vicevært see *Once Upon a Caretaker* (1937)
Der var engang see *Once upon a Time* (1922)
Derailed (1942), 51–2, 59, 83, 87
Det Brændende Spørgsmaal see *The Burning Question* (1943)
Det forsømte forår see *Stolen Spring* (1993)
Det gamle guld see *Ancient Gold, The* (1951)
Det gode liv see *Good Life, The* (2010)
Det kære lejetøj see *Danish Blue* (1968)
Det perfekte menneske see *Perfect Human, The* (1967)
Det store Ansvar see *The Heavy Responsibility* (1944)
Deutsche Bioscop, 35, 36
Dickens, Charles, 157
director-screenwriters, 171–2
'dirt theory,' 250
Discretion Wanted (1946), 82, 83, 88–9, 91
Diskret ophold see *Discretion Wanted* (1946)
distribution, 13, 24–5, 53–4, 56–7
Ditte, Child of Man (1946), 9, 82, 87, 89, 91, 106

Ditte, Menneskebarn see *Ditte, Child of Man* (1946)
diversity, 255
documentaries
  Denmark-films, 93–104
  gender distribution, 221
  Greenland, 265, 266
  homeland themes, 109
  sex/porn, 143
  shorts, 48, 82–3
Dogme 95 films, 5, 155–6, 161–2, 164, 165–7, 168, 169
  in the Canon for Film, 170
  collaborative efforts, 175, 176
  as medium-concept, 170
  see also Trier, Lars von
Dogme 95 Manifesto, 176, 206–7
Dogville (2003), 156–7, 159
Dorian Grays Portræt see *The Portrait of Dorian Gray* (1910)
Douglas, Mary, 185
Drabet see *Manslaughter* (2005)
Dreyer, Carl Theodor, 6, 33, 41–50, 153, 163
Drive (2011), 179
Driving with Greenlandic Dogs (1897), 22, 263
Dronningen see *Queen of Hearts* (2019)
Druk see *Another Round* (2020)
Drum, D. D. and J. Drum, 41
Du er ikke alene see *You are Not Alone* (1978)
Du skal ære din Hustru (*Master of the House*, 1925), 47
DVF *see* West Danish Film Fund (DVF)
Dyekjær, Sigrid, 219, 221, 222–3
Dødsspring fra Cirkuskuplen see *Great Circus Catastrophe, The* (1912)

Eagle, The (DR, 2004–6), 190
East Jutland Film Fund, 257
ecocritical approaches, 241, 242, 250
ecological awareness, 241, 242, 244–5
economic development, and film policy, 254
Education, An (2009), 179
EEC, 126
Efter brylluppet. see *After the Wedding* (2006)
Ege, Ole, 145

Ekstra Bladet uden for citat see *Newsroom, The: Off the Record* (2014)
Election Night (1998), 171
Element of Crime, The (1984), 152–3, 159
Elf Hill (1939), 78
Elfelt, Peter, 17–18, 22, 263
Elling, Tom, 152
Elly Petersen (1941), 83, 87, 89
Elsker dig for evigt see *Open Hearts* (2002)
Elskovsleg see *Game of Love* (1910)
Elton, Arthur, 1, 96–7
el-Toukhy, May, 238
Elverhøj see *Elf Hill* (1939)
Emma's Shadow (1988), 134
En chance til see *Second Chance, A* (2014)
En Fremmed banker på see *Stranger Knocks, A* (1959)
En frygtelig kvinde see *Horrible Woman, A* (2017)
En mand kommer hjem see *When a Man Comes Home* (2007)
En søndag på Amager see *A Sunday on Amager* (1941)
Enemies of Happiness (2006), 226
Engberg, Marguerite, 36
En Herre i Kjole og Hvidt see *Gentleman in Top Hat and Tails, A* (1942)
En kongelig affære see *Royal Affair, A* (2012)
En soap see *Soap, A* (2006)
entangled history approach, 43–5
entertainment tax (*forlystelsesafgift*), 84
environmentalism, Nordic, 241
Epidemic (1987), 153, 158, 159
Et døgn med Ilse see *24 Hours with Ilse* (1971)
Et Hjerte af Guld (*Faithful unto Death*, 1912), 36
Et par ord om Danmark see *Introduction to Denmark* (1962)
Europa (1991), 153–4, 159
Europa Trilogy, 153–4
European art films, 45
European *fin-de-siècle* culture, 157
European Regional Development Fund, 256

INDEX

Eventyrrejsen see *Fairytale Journey, The* (1960)
expressionist symbolism, 91–2

Factory Outing, The (1978), 232–3
Fairytale Journey, The (1960), 71, 76
Faithful unto Death (1912), 36
Familien på Bryggen see *Family From Bryggen, The* (2011–)
Family (2001), 224
family *folkekomedie*, 73–4, 80
Family from Bryggen, The (TV3, 2011–), 73
Far From the Madding Crowd (2015), 182
Far til fire see *Father of Four* (1950)
farce, 76
Farkas, Jenö, 101
Farlig ungdom (*Dangerous Youth*, 1953), 74
Farm, The (2017–), 109
Farmer, The (DR, 2008–), 109
Farmer Wants a Wife, The (TV2, 2012–), 109
Farvel, jeg hedder Kurt see *Goodbye, my Name is Kurt* (1969)
fate (*skæbnen*), 87
Father of Four (1950), 73–4
Father of Four films, 73–4, 75–6, 129, 139
feature films, Cultural Canon, 4
Federal Republic of Germany (FRG), 125
Federspiel, Birgitte, 163
female documentary filmmakers, 221–9
Festen see *Celebration, The* (1998)
fiction film, gender distribution, 221
Fight Against Injustice, The (1949), 83
Fight for Greenland, The (2020), 274–5
Fight for the Red Cow, The (1987), 108, 109
Fighter (2007), 233
Film Agreements, and regional funding, 254–5, 257–8
Film Commission Fyn, 259
film companies, Danish, 21, 27
Film i Väst, 253–4
Film Laws
  1930s, 13
  1964, 14, 97
  1972, 14, 79, 97, 108, 167
  1997, 15–16, 168, 254

Film Museum, 13, 15
film stars, Danish, 26–7, 30; *see also* names of individual stars
film subsidies, 130
Film Workshop, Nuuk, 273
Filmby Aarhus, 256–7, 260
Filmbyen (Film Town), 168
FilmFyn, 255, 258–9, 261
FILM.GL, 269–70, 272
Filmhuset (Film House), Copenhagen, 15
FilmLab Palestine, 201
Filmsfonden, 13
Filmsrådet, 13
Fire and Earth (1955), 114
Fire Burns, A (1962), 116
Firmaskovturen see *Factory Outing, The* (1978)
Fischer, Leck, 83
Fish Out of Water (1993), 71, 76
Five Obstructions, The (2003), 156, 159
Flickering Lights (2000), 76, 169, 171
Flintesønnerne see *Flint Sons, The* (1956)
Flint Sons, The (1956), 113, 114
Flow (2014), 237, 240
folkekomedie genre, 65–80
  and audiences, 70, 72, 76–8
  character types in, 71, 72–3
  critics and scholars on, 71, 78, 79
  film adaptations, 75, 78
  and the film institutions, 78–80
  and homeland cinema, 108, 110
  prototypes, 73–5
Forbrydelsen see *Killing, The* (DR, 2007–12)
Forbrydelsens element see *Element of Crime, The* (1984)
Forbrydelser see *In Your Hands* (2004)
forced marriage, 233, 234
Fore Finger, Middle Finger, Ring Finger, Little Finger (2008), 267
Forestillinger see *Performances* (2007)
Fotorama, 23, 32, 35
Fra den gamle købmandsgård see *From the Old Merchant's House* (1951)
Fra Haifa til Nørrebro see *My Father from Haifa* (2010)
framing, 158–9
Frank, Preben, 97
Fredløs see *Outlaw* (1935)
Freeland, Cynthia, 227–8

Fremskridtspartiet (political party), 123, 231
French, Philip, 173
French film companies, 24
French New Wave, 145
French poetic realism, 83, 87
Frische, Axel, 70
Frische, Grethe, 108
From the Old Merchant's House (1951), 113–14
Fruen på Hamre see *Lady of Hamre, The* (2000)
Frøken Nitouche see *Mam'zelle Nitouche* (1963)
Full Frontal (2002), 167
Fyrtaarnet-og-Bivognen see Long-and-Short films
Fønss, Olaf, 30, 31, 36–38, 40

Gad, Urban, 34, 35, 38
Game of Love (1910), 32
Gamle mænd i nye biler see *Old Men in New Cars* (2002)
Gandrup, Carl, 36, 40
Genboerne see *Opposite Neighbours, The* (1939)
gender distribution, 220–3
  documentaries, 221
  fiction film, 221
Genetic Me (2014), 226
genre films, 158, 169
Gentleman in Top Hat and Tails, A (1942), 53
German cinema, 39, 40, 47, 48, 105, 106
German Democratic Republic (GDR), 124
German occupation, and Danish film production, 84, 96
German Reich Film Chamber, 54, 55–6
Gezeichneten, Die see *Love One Another* (1922)
Gift see *Venom* (1966)
Girls at Arms (1975), 74, 75
Gislason, Tómas, 152
Global Non-Violent Film Festival, 185
globalisation, 102, 187, 254
Glomdalsbruden see *Bride of Glomdal, The* (1926)
Go with Peace Jamil (2008), 172, 236, 240
Goebbels, Joseph, 53, 58

Gold Heart Trilogy (Trier), 158
Gone with the Fish (1999), 110
Good Life, The (2010), 224, 225
Good Things Await (2014), 225, 226, 228–9
Goodbye, My Name Is Kurt (1969), 134
Goodnight (1999), 267
Grasten, Ragnar, 80, 109
Grau, Robert, 24
Great Circus Catastrophe, The (1912), 36
Green Butchers, The (2003), 169, 259
Greenland
  films set in, 263, 265–6
  history of, 264–5
Greenlandic cinema, 265–76
Griffith, D. W., 45
Grunwald, Morten, 119, 124
Grønkjær, Pernille Rose, 219, 222, 224, 225, 227
Guðmundsson, Sigurður, 246–7
Guest Workers (1968), 232
Gummi Tarzan see *Rubber Tarzan* (1981)
Gypsy Orchestra, The (1912), 37
Gæstearbejdere see *Guest Workers* (1968)
Gå med fred, Jamil see *Go with Peace, Jamil* (2008)

Habibti min elskede see *Habibti My Love* (2002)
Habibti My Love (2002), 233
Hagener, Malte, 44–5
Hake, Hans-Jürgen Maximilian von, 54, 57, 58–9
Halalabad Blues (2002), 233
Hallam, Julia, 86
Hammershøi, Vilhelm, 163
handheld camera, 159, 165
Hansen, Aká, 267
Hansen, Klaus, 258
haptic and tactile visuality, 249
Harpiks see *Resin* (2019)
Hauptmann, Gerhardt, 24
Hawks, Howard, 141
Häxan (Häxan: Witchcraft Through the Ages, 1922), 33
HBO Nordic, 198
Heads or Tails (1937), 69–70
Heart of Light (1998), 267
Heavy Responsibility, The (1944), 84–5

Hedling, Olof, 234
Hegelers, Inge and Steen, 146
Heiberg, Johan Ludvig, 72, 78
Hending, Arnold, 32, 34, 37, 40
Henning-Jensen, Astrid, 9, 82, 232
Henning-Jensen, Bjarne, 9, 82
Henningsen, Poul, 95–6, 103, 143
heritage films, 163, 169
Hertling Péronard, Emile, 268–76
Himmelskibet see *Trip to Mars, A* (1918)
Hinnarik's Dream (2009), 267, 268
Hinnarik Sinnatunilu see *Hinnarik's Dream* (2009)
histoire croisée, 43–5
Historien om Hjortholm see *Story of Hjortholm, The* (1950)
historiography, 5–6
Hjemmefronten – fjenden bag hækken see *Home Front, The* (2010)
Hjem til garden see *Farm, The* (2017–)
Hjort, Mette, 167, 169, 175, 185
Holger-Madsen, 6
Hollywood, 42–3, 53, 67
Hollywood-inspired films, 179–81
Home Front, The (2010), 226
homeland cinema, 105–17
　comedies, 110
　critics on, 106
　and *folkekomedie*, 108, 110
　landscape, 110–13
　sexuality, 114–17
Homunculus (German serial), 37
Horrible Woman, A (2017), 205
Hottest Show in Town, The (1974), 143–4
House on Christianshavn, The (1970–7), 79–80
House That Jack Built, The (2018), 158, 159, 177
Hovmand, Annelise, 9, 146
humanism, 88, 245–6
humour, and ethics, 185–6
Hunger (1966), 4, 10
Hunt, The (2012), 178, 182, 235
Huset på Christianshavn see *The House on Christianshavn* (1970–7)
Husmandstøsen see *Smallholder's Lass, The* (1952)
Hvidsten Gruppen see *This Life* (2012)
Hvor Bjergene sejler see *Where Mountains Float* (1955)
Hvorfor gør de det? see *Why?* (1971)
hyggefilm, 9
Hævnen see *In a Better World* (2010)
Høeg, Peter, 17
Høegh, Malik, 269
Højholt, Per, 99
Høyer, Edgar, 45

I, a Woman (1965), 142
Idioterne see *Idiots, The* (1998)
Idiots, The, or *Dogma #2: The Idiots* (1998), 2, 155, 159, 170
I jomfruens tegn see *In the Sign of the Virgin* (1973)
I Kina spiser de hunde see *In China They Eat Dogs* (1999)
Ild og jord see *Fire and Earth* (1955)
Images of Denmark (1970), 97, 98–9
imagineNATIVE, Toronto, 271
immigrants, immigration, 184, 230–40
immigration cinema, 232–40, 258
In a Better World (2010), 161, 172, 178, 180, 259
In China They Eat Dogs (1999), 76, 169, 234
In the Deep Dark of the Night (2014), 267
In the Hands of Imposters (1911), 25, 32
In the Sign of the Virgin (1973), 147
In Your Hands (2004), 170, 172
Indigenous-led films, 271–2
Ingen tid til kærtegn see *Be Dear to Me* (1957)
Ingold, Tim, 247
Inheritance (2003), 171, 172
integration, principle of, 67, 71, 74, 237
International Film Chamber, Berlin, 57–8
International Sámi Film Institute (ISFI), 272
Introduction to Denmark (1962), 97
Inuk Woman City Blues (2002), 267
Ipsen, Bodil, 9, 53, 85
Italian for Beginners (2000), 169, 170, 178
Italian neorealism, 88
It's All About Love (2003), 177, 182, 187–8
Iversen, Jon, 114

Jacobsen, Johan, 82, 141
Jagten see *Hunt, The* (2012)
Jalla! Jalla! (2000), 234
Jeg – en kvinde see *I – A Woman* (1965)
Jenny and the Soldier (1947), 82, 87, 88, 90–1, 92
Jensen, Anders Thomas, 171–2, 180, 184, 234
Jensen, Arne, 97
Jensen, Arthur, 147
Jensen, Verner, 82, 91
Jews, 54, 55, 60
Joensen, Bodil, 144
Just Like Home (2007), 178
Jørgensen, Jacob, 101
Jørgensen, Pipaluk K., 272

Kalle, Kasper, 205, 209
Kammerspielfilm, 47
Kampen mod Uretten. see *Fight Against Injustice, The* (1949)
Kampen om den røde ko see *Fight for the Red Cow, The* (1987)
Kampen om Grønland see *Fight for Greenland, The* (2020)
Karmark, Henning, 51–2, 57–8, 59–60, 61, 107
Kau, Edvin, 41
Kessler, Linse, 73
Kestner, Max, 102–3, 242
Kierkegaard, Ole Lund, 133
Killing, The (DR, 2007–12), 170, 190, 194–7
Kinamand see *Chinaman* (2005)
Kindness, of Strangers, The (2019), 183
Kinematograph, Der, 24
King of the Marshes, The (1951), 107, 113
Kingdom, The (DR, 1994–7), 148, 154, 159, 191–3
King's Game (2004), 173
Kistrup, Jens, 67
Kjærulff-Schmidt, Palle, 266
Kleist, Malik, 267, 274
Kloster Bro, Rasmus, 204, 205, 206, 210–14
Klovn see *Clown* (2005–18)
Kobitzsch, Adolf, 53
Kollektivet see *Commune, The* (2016)
Kollision see *Collision* (2019)
Konfetti (1912), 36

Kongekabale see *King's Game* (2004)
Kongens foged – sat på gaden see *Royal Bailiff: Out on the Street* (2012)
Korch, Morten, 107, 109, 116
Kragh-Jacobsen, Søren, 131, 133, 156
Krigen see *War, A* (2016)
Kristallnacht, 54
Krogh, Mikala, 219, 225, 226, 227
Kronhausen, Eberhaus and Phyllis, 143
Krummerne see *The Crumbs* (1991)
Kuhlau, Friedrich, 121
Kundskabens træ see *Tree of Knowledge* (1981)
Kutchinsky, Berl, 144
Kærlighed ved første hik see *Love at First Hiccough* (1999)
Københavnere see *Copenhageners* (1933)
Kørsel med grønlandske Hunde see *Driving with Greenlandic Dogs* (1897)

Ladri di Biciclette (Bicycle Thieves, 1948), 88, 89–90
Lady of Hamre, The (2000), 108
Lamb, John, 143
Landmand søger kærlighed see *Farmer Wants a Wife* (2012–)
Land of Opportunity, 156
Land of Plenty (1983), 108
landscape, 91, 110–13
Langsted, Adolf, 39
language, 14–15, 167
Language of Love series, 146
La' os være see *Leave Us Alone* (1975)
Larsen, Viggo, 22–3, 31
Last Dance, The (2005), 225–6, 228–9
Laterna Film, 98
Lauritzen Jr, Lau, 52, 59–60, 85
Lauritzen Sr, Lau, 31
Lawrence, Jennifer, 180
Lay, Samantha, 84
Leave Us Alone (1975), 135
Leaves from Satan's Book (1920), 33, 45–6
Lefbvre, Martin, 110–11
Legacy, The (DR, 2014–17), 196, 259
Lerdorff Rye, Preben, 163
Leth, Jørgen, 97, 99–101, 102, 156, 204
Levring, Kristian, 156
Liberty (DR, 2018), 198
Lichtenberg, Nicolai, 97

narrative structure in social realism, 88–9
National Film Board, 15, 168
National Film School of Denmark, 108, 152, 172, 200
nationalism, Danish, 3–4
nationality and national culture, 94–5
Nattevagten see *Night Watch* (1994)
nature
  and 'dirt theory,' 250
  and humanism, 245–6
Nazi Germany, 53–61
  and the Danish film industry, 55–6, 60
  as film theme, 126
  films/newsreels, 54, 57, 59, 61
  Ministry of Foreign Affairs, 56
  Propaganda Ministry, 53, 56, 57–8
Negerkys og labre larver see *Tootsiepops and Candyfloss* (1987)
Neighbours Across the Street (1939), 75
Neon Demon, The (2016), 180
Neon Heart (2018), 205
Nestingen, Andrew, 170
Netflix, 181, 198
Neuchâtel International Fantastic Film Festival (NIFF), 201
New Danish Cinema, 161, 169, 171, 172, 175–6
New Danish Screen (NDS), 168, 207, 220, 236
  Sketch initiative, 204–6
  talent development, 202–4
New Fiction Film Denmark, 168
newsreels, Nazi-German, 57, 59, 61
Newsroom, The: Off the Record (2014), 225
Nielsen, Asta, 7, 30, 31, 34–6, 39–40, 141
Nielsen, Henrik Bo, 202
NIFF Extended, 201
Night Manager, The (BBC, 2016), 181
Night Watch (1994), 171
Nissen, D., 123
No Man's Land (2012), 258
Nocturne (1981), 152
Nordhavets Mænd see *Men of the North Sea* (1939)
Nordic Film and Television Fund, 15, 167–8

Nordisk Films Kompagni, 21–9, 32, 107
  and censorship, 140–1
  and Dreyer, 45–6
  and Nazi Germany, 53, 54, 55–6, 58
  and Olsen, 31
  Psilander at, 34
  and Trier, 154
  see also Balling, Erik; Bauder, Carl
Nordvision, 189
North Sea Screen Partners, 256
Nuummioq see *Man from Nuuk, A* (2009)
Nymph()maniac (2013 and 2014), 158, 159, 258
Nystad, Henning, 97
... *Når du kigger væk* see ... *When You Look Away* (2017)

October Roses (1946), 87, 89
O'Fredericks, Alice, 9, 59, 107–8, 110
Oktober-Roser see *October Roses* (1946)
Old Men in New Cars (2002), 234
Old Mill on Mols, The (1953), 107
Olesen, Annette K., 170, 172
Olsen-banden see Olsen Gang
Olsen-banden deruda see *Olsen Gang Strikes Again, The* (1977)
Olsen-banden går i krig see *Olsen Gang Goes to War, The* (1978)
Olsen-banden i Jylland see *Olsen Gang Plays for High Stakes, The* (1971)
Olsen-banden over alle bjerge see *Olsen Gang over the Hill, The* (1981)
Olsen-banden overgiver sig aldrig see *Olsen Gang Never Surrenders, The* (1979)
Olsen-banden ser rødt see *Olsen Gang Sees Red, The* (1976)
Olsen, John, 57, 59
Olsen, Lasse Spang, 234
Olsen, Ole, 22–3, 25, 27, 28, 32, 34–5
Olsen Gang films, 72, 76, 79, 118–27
Olsen Gang Goes to War, The (1978), 121
Olsen Gang Never Surrenders, The (1979), 126
Olsen Gang over the Hill, The (1981), 126
Olsen Gang Plays for High Stakes, The (1971), 126

Olsen Gang Sees Red, The (1976), 121, 122
Olsen Gang Strikes Again, The (1977), 123
Once Upon a a Caretaker (1937), 69
Once Upon a Time (1922), 33, 46
One Day (2011), 183, 185
One Swedish Summer (1968), 145
Only God Forgives (2013), 179–80
Open Hearts (2002), 169, 178
Opposite Neighbours, The (1939), 75
Orchid Gardener, The (1977), 152, 159
Ordet see *The Word* (1955)
Other Side, The (2017), 224, 225
Otto er et næsehorn see *Otto is a Rhino* (1983)
Otto is a Rhino (1983), 133
Outlaw (1935), 53

Palladium, 21, 48, 53, 56, 107, 143, 147
Pálmason, Hlynur, 242–3, 245–7, 249–50
Palos Brudefærd see *Wedding of Palo, The* (1934)
Palsbo, Ole, 82
Parson's Widow, The, 46
Passer, Dirch, 73
Passion de Jeanne d'Arc, La (1928), 41, 47, 48
Paw (1959), 9
Pelle erobreren see *Pelle the Conqueror* (1987)
Pelle the Conqueror (1987), 108, 161, 169
Penaguiao, Joao, 101
Per Fly, 171, 193, 198
Perfect Human, The (1967), 156, 204
Perfect Muslim, The (2009), 237
Performances (DR, 2007), 198
performative documentary, 224, 227
picture pornography, 140
Piger i trøjen see *Girls at Arms* (1975)
Pizza King (1999), 234
Plat eller Krone see *Heads or Tails* (1937)
Polar Bear (2000), 267
Politiken (newspaper), 96
Pontoppidan, Clara Wieth *see* Wieth, Clara

popular theatre, and *folkekomedie*, 66, 69–70, 77
Porn Chic wave, 145
Pornografi — En musical see *Pornography — A Musical* (1971)
pornographic films, feature-length, 143, 144–5
pornographic industry, Danish, 144, 146
pornography, liberalisation of, 140, 148
Pornography – A Musical (1971), 145
Pornography in Denmark – A New Approach (1970), 143
Portrait of Dorian Gray, The (1910), 32
Possession (1944), 87–8
Prästänkan see *Parson's Widow, The* (1920)
President, The (1919), 45
privileged-world guilt, narratives of, 184
problem films, 84–6
Progress Party *see* Fremskridtspartiet (political party)
Protectors, The (DR, 2009–10), 190
Provinsen kalder – ! (*The Provinces are Calling – !*), 68
Præsidenten see *President, The* (1919)
Psilander, Valdemar, 27, 30, 35, 36
  early life and career, 31
  global fame, 34, 38, 39
  and Wieth, 32–4
psychological realism, 137
Psychomobile #1: The World Clock (1996), 156
Pusher (1996), 171, 234

Qaqqat Alanngui see *Shadows of the Mountains, The* (2011)
QEDA see *Man Divided* (2017)
Qivitoq (1956), 266
Quack, The (1937), 106, 111
Queen of Hearts (2019), 238
queerness, 116–17
Quiet Days in Clichy (1970), 148

Rami and Juliet (1988), 233
Ranjbar, Golrang, 235, 238
Rasmussen, Knud, 265
Red Horses, The (1950), 105, 107, 111, 114, *115*
Red Meadows, The (1945), 61, 83
Reenberg, Annelise, 9, 107

Reestorff, Camilla Møhring, 2–3, 4
Regia Kunstfilms, 32
regional DVDs, *The History of the Danes*, 94
regional film funds, 252–61
Reichhardt, Paul, 107, 116
Renoir, Jean, 88
Resin (2019), 242
Resistance, Danish, 60, 61
Rifbjerg, Klaus, 97, 98–9, 104
Riget (*The Kingdom*, DR, 1994) see *Kingdom, The* (DR, 1994–7)
Riis, Jacob, 248
Riot Club, The (2014), 183
Risom, Steen, 257
robinsonades, 135
Rodox, 144
Roos, Jørgen, 266
Rosbach, Mark Fussing, 274
Rosing, Otto, 267
Royal Affair, A (2012), 179, 240
Royal Bailiff: Out on the Street (2012), 226
Rubber Tarzan (1981), 131, 133
Rukov, Mogens, 171, 172
Russian audiences, 26

Saga (film company), 21, 79, 107, 110
Salim, Dar, 237
Salim, Ulaa, 205, 238–9
Sally's Bizniz (1989), 134, 233
Sandberg, A. W., 31, 147
Sandfeld, Gunnar, 24
Sayad, Cecilia, 224
Schaefer, Eric, 141
Schatz, Thomas, 67
Scherfig, Hans, 128
Scherfig, Lone, 169, 172, 176, 178–9, 183, 185, 193, 206
Schwarz, Günther, 55, 56–7
Schyberg, Frederik, 78
Schønberg, Ib, 69–70, 76
screenwriting, 172
screwball comedies, 52
Seaside Hotel, The, TV2, (2013–), 109, 198
Second Chance, A (2014), 181
Secret Sex Lives of Romeo and Juliet, The (1969), 145
sentimentalism, 88

Serena (2014), 179, 180–1
Sex 69 (sex trade fair), 143–4
sex cirkusse see *Hottest Show in Town, The* (1974)
sex comedies, 141, 147–8
Sex en gros see *Sex Galore* (1971)
Sex Galore (1971), 146–7
sexuality
  homeland cinema, 114–17
  in Trier's work, 159
  youth films, 135
Shadows of the Mountains, The (2011), 267
Shargawi, Omar, 172, 236, 237
Shelley (2016), 238, 240
silent cinema, 6–8, 21, 120–1
Sin Alley (1957), 84
Sinan's Wedding (1997), 234
Sinilluarit see *Goodnight* (1999)
Six Kids and Their Uncle (1966), 74
Sjöström, Victor, 43, 46
Sketch films see New Danish Screen
Skilsmissens Børn see *Children of Divorce* (1939)
Skot-Hansen, Mogens, 48
Skyggen af Emma see *Emma's Shadow* (1988)
Smallholder's Lass, The (1952), 114
Smilla's Sense of Snow (1997), 267
Smith, Anthony D., 43
Smugglers, The (1924), 120
Soap, A (2006), 172
social justice themes, 184–5
'social problem' films, 74
social realism, 81–92, 131
Soldaten og Jenny see *Jenny and the Soldier* (1947)
Som havets nøgne vind see *One Swedish Summer* (1968)
Sommer i Tyrol see *White Horse Inn* (1964)
songs, homeland cinema, 106, 107
Sonja fra Saxogade see *Sonja from Saxo Street* (1968)
Sonja from Saxo Street (1968), 134
Sons of Denmark (2019), 205, 238–9
Sorg og glæde see *Sorrow and Joy* (2013)
Sorrow and Joy (2013), 258
sound comedies, 1930s, 66–71, 79
Sparrows under the Eaves (1944), 83, 87, 89, 91

INDEX

Sprogøe, Ove, 119, 124
Spurve under Taget see *Sparrows under the Eaves* (1944)
state censorship, 12–13
state subsidies to film production, 130, 167
Statens Filmcentral (SFC), 97, 98
Steene, Birgitta, 134
Stegger, Karl, 147
Steinhof, Hans, 54
Stille dage i Clichy see *Quiet Days in Clichy* (1970)
Stolen Spring (1993), 128
Story of Hjortholm, The (1950), 110
Strand, Torill, 187
Strange Bird, The (1911), 36
Stranger Knocks, A (1959), 141, 142
stumfilm.dk, 15
style, 90, 91
Submarino (2010), 182
Sucksdorff, Arne, 242
Sullivan, Heather, 250
Sult see *Hunger* (1966)
Sumé – The Sound of a Revolution (2014), 268, 269, 271, 275
Sundance film festival, 268
Sunday on Amager, A (1941), 78
Super 16 (film school), 236, 237
Super Carla (1968), 134
Swedish cinema, 43, 46, 234
Swedish Fly Girls (1971), 146
Søltoft, Ole, 147
Sørensen og Rasmussen (Sørensen and Rasmussen, 1940), 78

Tafdrup, Christian, 202
Ta', hvad du vil ha' see *Take Whatever You Want* (1947)
Take Pelle with You (1952), 114
Take Whatever You Want (1947), 82, 87
talent development, 201, 202–4, 205–6, 270, 273
Ta' Pelle med see *Take Pelle with You* (1952)
Tarkovsky, Andrei, 157
Tarok see *Catch the Dream* (2013)
Tarratta Nunaanni see *Among Us – In the Land of Our Shadows* (2017)

Tarzan Mama Mia see *Me and Mama Mia* (1989)
tax incentives, 260
Taxa (DR, 1997–9), 193
Teatrenes Films-Kontor, 54, 56, 57
television
  crime drama series, 258
  and *folkekomedie*, 71, 78, 79
  homeland series, 109
  serial dramas, 170
Temptations of a Great City (1911), 33
Tharnæs, Charles, 83
Theander brothers, 144
theatres, and *folkekomedie*, 78–9
Their Finest (2016), 183
Things We Lost in the Fire (2007), 178, 180
This Life (2012), 109
Thompson, Kristin, 89–90
Thomsen, Knud Leif, 142
Thomsen, Thomas, 265
Thorsen, Jens Jørgen, 148
Those Damned Kids (1947), 82, 89
Three Years After (1948), 82
Tid til forandring see *What's Wrong with This Picture?* (2004)
Tikeq, Qiterleq, Mikileraq, Eqeqqoq see *Fore Finger, Middle Finger, Ring Finger, Little Finger* (2008)
Too Old to Die Young (2019), 180
Tootsiepops and Candyfloss (1987), 134
transcorporeality, 245–7
Tree of Knowledge, The (1981), 131, 137, 138
Tre År Efter see *Three Years After* (1948)
Trier, Lars von, 14–15, 139, 167
  as auteur, 8, 151–2, 177
  on the Cultural Canon, 2
  'Europa trilogy,' 191
  launch of Dogme 95, 161, 173
  and Zentropa, 168
  see also *Kingdom, The* (DR, 1994–7)
Trip to Mars, A (1918), 6
Tro, håb og kærlighed see *Twist and Shout* (1984)
Tukuma see *Man in Too Much of a Hurry* (1984)
Tumit Production, 267

INDEX

Två människor see *Two People* (1945)
Twist and Shout (1984), 131, 138
Two People (1945), 49

Uden en trævl see *Without a Stitch* (1968)
Ufa, 28, 56, 58, 59, 60
Umberto D (1952), 88, 89
Underverden see *Darkland* (2017)
Unge piger forsvinder i København see *Young Girls Disappear in Copenhagen* (1951)
Unit One (DR, 2000–4), 190
Universum Film Aktiengesellschaft (Ufa) *see* Ufa
Unnuap Taarnerpaaffiani see *In the Deep Dark of the Night* (2014)
Usynligt hjerte see *Neon Heart* (2018)

Valgaften see *Election Night* (1998)
Valhalla (2019), 237
Valhalla Rising (2009), 179
variety shows, 22
Ved Fængslets Port see *Temptations of a Great City* (1911)
Velkommen til Danmark see *Welcome to Denmark* (1951)
Venice Film Festival (1942), 52
Venom (1966), 142
Verden i Danmark see *The World in Denmark* (2007)
Vest, Niels, 146
Vestergaard, Jørgen, 97, 99
victim, immigrant as, 235
Vilde pornolyster see *Blue Balloon, The* (1971)
Vil du se min smukke navle? see *Wanna See My Beautiful Navel?* (1978)
Vinterberg, Thomas, 155, 156, 162, 169, 176, 177–8, 182–3; see also *Celebration, The* (1998); *It's All About Love* (2003);); *Submarino* (2010); *Hunt, The* (2012); *Commune, The* (2016); *Another Round* (2020)
Vinterbrødre see *Winter Brothers* (2017)
Vinterbørn see *Winter-Born* (1978)
Violer er blå see *Violets are Blue* (1975)
Violets are Blue (1975), 146

Vision Denmark, 260
voice-overs, 86, 157
Vredens Dag see *Day of Wrath* (1943)
Vørsel, Niels, 154

Wamberg, Helge, 38
Wanna See My Beautiful Navel? (1978), 135–6
War, A (2016), 184
Wedding of Palo, The (1934), 265
Week-end (*Weekend*, 1935), 74
Weel, Arne, 75
Weel, Liva, 70
Welcome to Denmark (1951), 97
Welles, Orson, 141
Werner, Michael, 43
West Danish Film Fund (DVF), 255, 257–8, 261
Western Arabs (2019), 236–7
What's Wrong with This Picture? (2004), 76
When a Man Comes Home (2007), 182
When Peasants Love (1942), 108, 110
…When You Look Away (2017), 225, 226, 227
Where Mountains Float (1955), 266
While We Live (2017), 238, 240
White Horse Inn (1964), 73
White Slave Trade, The (1910), 23, 32
Why? (1971), 143
Wiedemann, Vinca, 204
Wieselmann, Illona, 51, 52
Wieth, Clara, 30, 31, 32–4, 38
Wilbur Wants to Kill Himself (2002), 178
Wiltrup, Aage, 82
Winding Refn, Nicolas, 171, 179–80, 234
Winter Brothers (2018), 242–50
Winter-Born (1978), 232, 233
Without a Stitch (1968), 142, 145
women filmmakers, 9–10
Word, The (1955), 48–9, 163
World in Denmark, The (2007), 102–3
Wyatt, Justin, 170

Yazdani, Jens Philip, 230–1
Year of Hope, A (2017), 223, 226
You are Not Alone (1978), 135
Young Girls Disappear in Copenhagen, 74, 86

317

youth films, 134–9
youth revolution, 130

Zappa (1983), 131, 138
Zentropa (film company), 2, 154, 168, 177
Zigeunerorkesteret see *The Gypsy Orchestra* (1912)

Zimmermann, Bénédicte, 43
Zodiac films, 147–8

Ørnbak, Henning, 97
Ørnen see *Eagle, The* (2004-6)
Ørsted, Claus, 97, 98

Århus *see* Aarhus

EU representative:
Easy Access System Europe
Mustamäe tee 50, 10621 Tallinn, Estonia
Gpsr.requests@easproject.com

www.ingramcontent.com/pod-product-compliance
Lightning Source LLC
Chambersburg PA
CBHW050334230426
43663CB00010B/1850